IT'S WHO YOU KNOW!

IT'S WHO YOU KNOW!

How to Make the Right
Business Connections—
and Make Them Pay Off

Bret Saxon & Elliot Goldman

BERKLEY BOOKS, NEW YORK

IB

A Berkley Book
Published by The Berkley Publishing Group
A division of Penguin Putnam Inc.
375 Hudson Street
New York, New York 10014

This book is an original publication of The Berkley Publishing Group.

PRINTING HISTORY
Berkley trade paperback edition / August 2001

Visit our website at
www.penguinputnam.com

Library of Congress Cataloging-in-Publication Data

Saxon, Bret.
It's who you know! : how to make the right business connections—and make them pay
off / Bret Saxon & Elliot Goldman.
    p. cm.
Includes bibliographical references and index.
ISBN 0-425-17984-2
1. Business networks. I. Title: It is who you know. II. Goldman, Elliot, 1972- III. Title.

HD69.S8 S29 2001
650.1'3—dc21

2001035980

PRINTED IN THE UNITED STATES OF AMERICA

10 9 8 7 6 5 4 3 2 1

CONTENTS

ACKNOWLEDGMENTS

A special and sincere thank-you to Jason Snyder, who worked his heart out doing research for this book, and Jenny Specht, who was Mr. Goldman's valuable assistant during this endeavor.

We would like to thank the following people, places, and things that gave us inspiration and support. (There are a lot of you, but what would you expect from a couple of networkers?): Rose and Bob "767" Baird; Kit Sawyer; The Shirtless One; Slippery Chicken; Does the orange beef come in any other color?; shiitake mushrooms; Ted Turner's girlfriend; Wayne "Put Down Your Spears" Brink; Joe Bayer; Gary Martha; Marilyn Carron; Valerie "The Hammer" Case; Greg Renker; the Davids; Joe Canipari; Leonardo "And I Am Not Talking DiCaprio" Hornstein; Lori, Alecia, and Michelle; Fred; The Girls at Innovative; Sean and Vanessa Alpert; Trevor "Tweva" Alpert; True Bregandi Quality; The Balloon Brothers; Dr. Tatum; Tom and Amanda Stallings; Phil Purevich; Ann Levine; "Teddy Ball Game" Cruz; Heidi; Mike Berry; Dave Carney; Earl Greenburg, Joel Margulies, Duncan, Jim, Meg, Jane, David, Kim, Joan, and the gang at TMP; Rich and Amy Wilkes; Brittney; Kelsey Jo; Amy; Ian Shapolsky; Dave "Ruby Slippers" Elkouby; Steve "Go Mets" Etinger and his bacon-loving dog Max; Greg "Mr. Breitling" Horangic; Jasmine and Bahman; my Roswell buddy Colet; Lawrence "Mr. JIC" Johnson; Frank and Ana; Mark "Thanks for the Norm Tapes" Stroman; Kristin Bauer; Matty Bolero; Linn "Dog's Best Friend" Boyke; Hugo Boss; Gary Dell'Abate; Houston "Mr. Producer" Curtis; Fred at Eros; Marc "Put the Bags Down" Held; Dom Irrera; P. F. Changs; Norm Macdonald; Don Knotts; Scott "I Loved WROC" Mertz; Frank "She Wanted Me" McNeil; Steve SeaSucker; David "Never Give

Up" Ortiz; Bob Pouliot; Gary "Fahget About It" Tabb; Larry "Tied the Big One" Rosen; Hillary "Frombe" Schupf; Phill "Mr. White House" Swagel; Claudia Schiffer (Thanks for the tip; the shrimp were great); Dan Saxon; Howard Stern; Doug Goodstein; Lenny "Nice Goatee" Stein; Ed Tabb; Matt Swagel; GeorgeAnn Woodward; Paul Dinas; Stuart Burton; Norena Barbella; Emily Bestler; Chris Doherty; anyone named Swagel; Bruce Cutler, Esq.; George W. Bush; Linda Goldstein, Esq.; Stephen Breimer, Esq.; Christine "C. Z." Zika; Britney Spears; Barney; Lynda and Harry; Myron and Alice; Scott; Jill; Derek Jeter; Ms. Wu; Mr. Fernandez; Mr. Quijada; Breitling and Kenjo; Jerry "Mr. Broadway" Taft; William Janiec; Chuck "Mr. Spago" Craig; Brian "Chief of Stuff" Reich; Craig Koller; Adam "The Hardest Working Man in Publishing" Abraham; Lance Bass; Jerome at John Barrett; my friends at Shah Abbas; Amanda and the gang at Café Pranzo; Stephen "Good Eye for Talent" Alpert; Robert, Jody, and Sarah Redfeather; the wonderful Pitt family; Kevin and Bean; the midget rodeo; the National Hot Dog, Sausage, and Meat Institute; Leroy Neiman; Senator Edward M. Kennedy; John McCerrick; Laurie Raiber; Rus Sarnoff; Mr. and Mrs. McDwyer; Gordo; Johnny Mac's Girlfriend's Foot; Senator Dacshel's Eco-Terrorist; lamp shade puppy on Fifth; Hot and Crusty Bagel; New York hot dog vendors; the unknown 109th Justice; white suede dining room chairs; Kendal Alling Schreyach; The Amazing Kreskin; Kara and John McDwyer; Aunt Gerry; Barry and Susan Gross; Michael and Rachel Goldman; Jeremy Goldman; Why the Hall Not; Vice President Dan Quayle; Les Novitsky; Cliff Shannon; Robert Blagman; Jim O'Neill; Jack, Patsy, Kerry, and John O'Neill; Jim Harrison; Karl Rove; David Beckwith; Dan Poland; Sara Weddington; Dennis Miller; the late Ray Nitschke; Pat Choate; Cindy Jordan; Jeffrey Cokin; Ron Burton; Jay Batley; Shelby Weiss; Erin Weidner, Lisa Jansen; Melissa Culomb; Peter Pfeifle; Leah, Able, Donnell, and Hanna; Dr. Etier and Donna; John and Renee Eiband; Myron Flemming; Larry Fuente; Gumby; Sherbear and Aaron Handler; Sally Horton; Vin DiBona; Lisa Jung; Tammi and Kipp Kennedy; Chris and Karen Robinson; Jeff Giordano; Madeline Simmons; Jake Jelich; Danielle Meany; Erin Newberry Huson; Becca Nelson; Louisa; Rhonda Pape; Jennifer Packer; John Reed; Dr. Joe and Janie Shatten; Jeffrey Wright; Alan Sanford; U.S. Senator Kay Bailey Hutchinson; Will "It Add Up" Griffin; Mr. Whoozit; Oliver Peeples; Machiavelli; Enzo Ferrari; Tom Dwyer; Pat Murphy; Huck Newberry; Ft. Worth Tips Club; The Spirtas Brothers; Bruce Johnson; John Sluzar; Confab Jim; Rachel Laffer; Ned Staton; Mark "Mr. Sandbag" Seban; The Honorable Casper Weinberger; the Dalai Lama; Niva and Evelyn; Joe and Mary Smith; the inventor of Lucite; the inventor of the Name Game; the genius who signed the bear; Marty and Ruth Horning; the Ohlaugs; Monika; Mike Ackerman; Scott Carstons; Cousin Jeff, the Ferrari inspector; the Apetzs; Jeremy Goldman; John and Renee Danielson; Rich Rinaolo; Peter Theil; Adam Ross; Gumbo, M., Bipper, N. G., M. M., A. C., J. D., C. R.,

B. R., J. E., A. J. and the rest of the team; Don and Marge Galluch; Blanche and Val Pikkell.

Elliot gives a special thanks to his beautiful daughter Grace Elizabeth and wife Heather Ann. In addition to his family, Bret would like to specially thank Earl Greenburg and Joel Margulies. A special thanks to Elvis.

Every effort has been made to create this book in the most accessible, logical way. The goal is to help you become successful through networking. One of the decisions made was to write this book in the third person. Please rest assured that Bret and Elliot wrote every exciting word.

First Things First

History Behind the Book

Networking. Successful people do it; unsuccessful people don't. It's that simple. If you're good at it, you can own the world. If you're not, you will miss out on many valuable opportunities. The power of knowing the right people, having the right connections, and being a player is tremendous. When you network effectively, all the pieces fall into place—your career takes off, your investments are all the right ones, your connections get you the best seats at any event—you can have anything you want, and life is good.

Those at the top will attest to the power of networking. In a candid moment, most of them will actually credit their success to networking. We have all heard "It's not what you know but who you know." And networking is the tool you need to increase your "who you know." This book is unique in that it not only gives you the how and why of networking, but the who, what, where, and when.

In the following chapters you will delve into the specifics of all the *W*s. In sections on how to network, you will look at style, techniques, and planning. In descriptions of why to network, you will hear anecdotes from the authors showing concrete examples of why you would network to get ahead in your endeavors. This book will also help you identify who you should network with, where to network for maximum results, and when the best networking times and opportunities take place. All angles are covered to give you the most comprehensive look at how to be successful through networking.

Once you recognize the power of networking, the next step is to practice and master the skills involved. In the first part of this book, networking basics are laid out in detail. The section continues with specialized and advanced techniques. But this book goes well beyond "how to." *It's Who You Know* recognizes that even with the skills in place, the hardest part is still ahead: finding the power elite. You can network with the local members of the PTA and help your spouse's chances of being elected treasurer, but if you want to move into the true power circles, what do you do next? How do you know *where* to network? How do you know *who* to network with? That is where the power of this book comes in. Here you'll get an in-depth look at the organizations and individuals holding the power, whether it is political, financial, corporate, or entertainment. This book clearly describes the events and opportunities available for anyone to network with the power elite.

It's Who You Know offers a previously untapped collection of networking resources. There are hundreds of prime networking events held every year, along with thousands of networking opportunities. Here are a few examples of almost unknown opportunities:

- Once a year, over a hundred of the top CEOs in the country gather for the CEO of the Year awards. No matter what field you are interested in, you can meet the power players who run the industry.

- There is a small church in Sumpter County, Georgia, where former President Jimmy Carter teaches Sunday school. If you are interested in networking your way into government, a former president isn't a bad place to start.

- Dallas hosts the Cultural Arts Awards each year, and the top news broadcasters attend. If you are looking to network your way into that industry, this is one way to meet with Dan Rather, Sam Donaldson, and their peers.

The authors, Bret Saxon and Elliot Goldman, have spent years building contacts and discovering the events that are priceless for networkers. Those years of experience are contained in this book, which will tell you who will be where. If you are interested in a particular industry, this book will lay out the key events and pinpoint the key players. If you are interested in meeting particular individuals, this book will tell you all you need to know to find and network with them, from the events they attend to the charities they support.

Picture yourself discussing politics with world leaders at an invitation-only event at the United Nations. Or pitch your latest business idea to Donald Trump at a fundraiser held in the ballroom of a four-star hotel in New York. Whatever your interests, this book will guide you to the right people at the right time. This book will show you when and where to find anyone.

It comes down to a simple premise based on the two ways to go through life, and a quick example will illustrate the point:

Scenario 1: You stand in line at the ticket counter, and after half an hour of waiting, you buy overpriced tickets to the Indy 500. You then sit for two hours in traffic to get to the race. Heading to your seat in the last row of turn two, you get trounced as you fight the huge crowds. Once in your seat, you have trouble even seeing because of the odiferous six foot eleven guy sitting in front of you. After the race, you again fight the crowd all the way to the parking lot where you find your car has been keyed. You have another two hours to think about it as you fight the traffic out of the Motor Speedway, until finally you arrive home exhausted.

Scenario 2: You use this book to find the someone involved with the Indy 500 parade and network with him over drinks at the IFEA Trade Conference. You then get complimentary all-access medallions and pit passes to the race as a VIP celebrity escort. You are escorted to the race by the police and are given trackside parking. You spend the prerace time in the pits and watch the start of the race from the owner of the Motor Speedway's suite. Later that night, refreshed from your relaxing day at the track, you join Mario Andretti and Tim Allen for drinks.

The difference between Scenario 1 and 2 is simply networking. Obviously, Scenario 2 sounds much better, but it might seem impossible. The fact is, however, Scenario 2 is the actual situation that our authors were in recently. They aren't professional race car drivers, and neither of their fathers are VIPs. They have no special contacts. They simply used networking and the techniques in this book to position themselves for this VIP treatment. And so can you.

To get a picture of how networking works, one needs to look no further than how the two authors of this book met. They come from differing backgrounds. Bret Saxon has become successful in the entertainment field, while Elliot Goldman has attained prominent stature in government and business. Both of them were quick to recognize not only the power of networking but also the importance it played in their successes. Additionally, it was through specific networking techniques in this book that the two met and began collaborating on projects.

In early January 1997, Elliot Goldman became very interested in the numerous entertainment-based award shows on television. He had the idea that it would be fun to take his wife out to Los Angeles and walk with her up the red carpet, past all the paparazzi, into a major awards show.

As a T-shirt salesman from Fort Worth, Texas, conventional wisdom would hold that Elliot had an uphill battle. However, Elliot understood networking, and brimming with confidence, he set his goal to attend the Emmy Awards in September of 1997.

Not long after beginning his trek toward the Emmys, Elliot was watching *Dateline NBC*, which was running a story about a young Los Angeles resident who attended every major Hollywood event. The young man was Bret Saxon, the coauthor of this book. Bret was on *Dateline* describing how he was able to attend the Oscars, movie premiers, Superbowls, and every major event in between, all through networking. Elliot started making calls and within a week was in touch with Bret.

Elliot recognized that Bret could be his ticket to not just the Emmy Awards but the entire entertainment event schedule. Using a highly effective networking technique that will be discussed at length later in the book to ingratiate yourself to a VIP, Elliot invited Bret to Washington, D.C., to attend the annual dinner at the Supreme Court of the United States. Elliot had built a relationship through networking that gave him access to these prized Washington tickets. It is difficult to meet even one Supreme Court justice, as they are not beholden to the voters. They have their job for life. It is actually easier to meet the president, as he gets out and attends political events. The opportunity to meet all of the justices is extremely rare. There are only three events in a given year that will bring out all of the justices: a Joint Session of Congress for the State of the Union Address by the president; the Alfalfa Club dinner, which is covered in some detail later in this book; and the annual dinner held at the Supreme Court. The dinner only holds 180 people, so it is a very tough ticket.

During the phone call inviting Bret to Washington, Elliot learned that Bret happened to be in law school at the time. He hit the jackpot. Bret jumped at the chance to mingle and dine with Clarence Thomas and his peers.

By having Bret out to Washington and providing him with tickets, Elliot had just accomplished the most important thing in networking: making yourself valuable to others. Bret and Elliot met for the first time in Washington, and the two had dinner with Chief Justice Rehnquist and the entire Supreme Court of the United States. At the end of the dinner, Bret invited Elliot and his wife out to Hollywood for the Emmy Awards. Success. Elliot made himself valuable to the person with whom he wanted to network and then was able to achieve his goal.

When Elliot arrived in Los Angeles, Bret treated him to an experience that he had not even imagined. Elliot and his wife spent a couple of days with Bret eating at great celebrity-filled restaurants, touring the movie studios, and attending Hollywood parties. Elliot met many celebrities and was having the time of his life, and the big event was still to come.

When Bret led Elliot and his wife down the red carpet at the Emmy Awards, Elliot quickly reflected on the fact that only six months earlier he had been watching celebrities walk down the red carpet on television and had set out to attend the Emmys. Looking at the red carpet under his feet and the hundreds of photographers lined up on either side, he smiled. Mission accomplished. Elliot's introspection ended quickly when he realized that directly in front of him was Helen Hunt. Bret introduced Elliot and his wife to Helen, and Elliot was able to enjoy a short conversation. As they said their "It was nice to meet you"s, Elliot turned around and literally bumped into Tony Bennett. He quickly apologized, and Tony, suave and gracious as always, told Elliot it was no problem. Elliot spoke with Tony for a few minutes before they all turned to continue into the building. Once inside, Bret introduced Elliot to the entire cast of *Seinfeld*. This was all completely new for Elliot, and he did not know what to expect, but he found the celebrities to be down-to-earth, gracious, and fun to talk to. For the next half hour, Elliot met and schmoozed with a who's who of Hollywood.

When the Emmy show was about to begin, everyone took their seats inside, and the lobby doors closed. Bret explained to Elliot that at the Emmy Awards, during commercial breaks, many celebrities go out to the lobby to socialize or get a drink. If a person does not make it back in before the commercial break, they have to wait until the next commercial break to get back to their seats. Elliot was truly enjoying meeting all of the celebrities, so Bret suggested they stay in the lobby. This proved to be the best seat in the house. In addition to the people socializing in the lobby, award winners came from the backstage press area to the lobby to talk with friends, take a break, or go back to their seats. After each Emmy winner got their award, they were rushed backstage for a press conference. After the press conference, they had to go to the lobby before returning to their seats. The lobby was the place to be. During every break, Elliot was able to meet new and interesting people. At some point during the evening, Bret took Elliot over to meet Jay Leno. Bret knew Jay loved cars and was very fond of Ferraris, so Bret used the proven networking technique of beginning a conversation with a topic that is interesting to the target. Bret's opening line to Jay was about Ferrari models. He said, "Elliot and I were having a debate. I love the Mondial, and he loves the 328. Which car do you prefer, Jay?" Jay's interest in cars made a conversation about the best Ferrari fun. He shot back, "I prefer the Ferrari GTO, personally." The conversation built from there, and Bret and Elliot were able to create a relationship with Jay Leno.

The whole evening progressed the same way, conversation after conversation, celebrity after celebrity. When the evening was over, there was the usual mad rush to the limousines. With the Emmys accommodating many, many VIPs, everyone had to stand in line for their ride. This provided another twenty minutes for Elliot and Bret to socialize and network. It was during this time that the two ran into Dennis Miller. And though Elliot is a huge fan of Dennis Miller, he had heard that Dennis was not the most approachable person in Hollywood. However, knowing Dennis's style and his impressive vocabulary, Bret and Elliot figured a good opening line might be to try and stump him with a seldom-used word. Bret approached him and said, "My friend and I were debating what the word *eleemosynary* meant. Any help, Dennis?" They stumped Dennis. Dennis was interested to find out that the word meant *charitable*. The three talked for a while and then took a picture together. Bret thought it would be fun to include the two Emmys Dennis won that night in the picture, so he asked for another shot. Dennis surprised the two when he simply handed the Emmys to Bret and Elliot and said, "Have fun." Dennis turned to Elliot's wife and said, "Just make sure I get those back from those two." Elliot realized he was again standing on the red carpet, surrounded by celebrities, holding an actual Emmy Award statuette. Bret rounded out Elliot's Hollywood experience that evening by taking him and his wife out for dinner to a sushi restaurant that Robert DeNiro had suggested to Bret a few months earlier.

The evening proved to Elliot, once again, that through networking you can accomplish anything. Elliot had set a goal: to attend the Emmy Awards. He had attained his goal, and he could credit the success to networking. He set out to meet Bret, the person he determined was *who you need to know,* created a quick relationship by making himself valuable to Bret, and achieved the desired results.

Meeting Bret and enjoying the pomp of Hollywood wasn't the only goal Elliot identified and realized. Elliot has also built a very successful apparel business. The building blocks of his success are honesty and relationships. Bret has leveraged his entertainment industry acumen and his networking skill into becoming president of Impact Entertainment Consulting Group based in Los Angeles, California. His firm creates nontraditional publicity and marketing deals between high-profile individuals and corporate clients. Bret also credits networking with his successes.

Key Issues in Networking

It is imperative to keep in mind the fundamental keys to networking, the networking building blocks. Once these keys are identified and you focus your networking activities toward these keys, success is imminent. It is important to spend some time now identifying the keys, exploring their value, and describing specific action items to accomplish the goals. The building blocks can be categorized into three areas: What do I want? How do I get there? How do I make myself valuable? If you can answer these three questions, you are well on your way to creating a workable plan that will facilitate your networking to the top.

WHAT DO I WANT?

While this phrase seems trite, the fact is that if you cannot answer it, you are lost, and your networking will be doomed to aimless schmoozing. Understand your goals and crystallize them into a specific plan. Write down on paper what you want. The act of writing and identifying exactly what you are after gives you focus. The more succinctly you define your goals/needs/wants, the more successful you will be at attaining them. Goals such as "I want to be rich" are much harder to specifically define and accomplish than more specific goals such as "I want a job in the tele-communications industry in Manhattan" or "I want to meet Troy Aikman" or "I want to attend the Kentucky Derby." The more nebulous you are, the less focus you will have to network properly. Can opportunity change what you want? Certainly. But once your goals change, remember to write them down again. Your goals will prob-ably fluctuate as you network and become more and more successful. Remember that the people you meet as you work toward your original goals can also help you toward your new goals.

When Elliot was just moving to Washington, D.C., to work in the White House, he set a number of networking goals, one of which was to have access to provide tours of the Pentagon, which he knew was an unbelievable experience. As he was moving into his apartment, he introduced himself to everyone he could find. One of his neighbors, Erin, told Elliot that she had a small desk job at the Pentagon. A few weeks later, Elliot invited Erin to lunch at the White House, and he developed a true win-win relationship with her. A few months after that, Elliot called Erin and asked if she could set up a tour of the Pentagon for some family that was coming in to visit with Elliot. Erin was very apologetic, but much to Elliot's surprise, she was not able to set up the tour. While Elliot was able to set up the tour through a different contact, he used smart networking skills and maintained his relationship with Erin. Not only did she make great chicken noodle soup, which is very important, consid-ering Elliot's lack of culinary skill, but she also ended up working for the House Armed Services Committee and became a great resource for Elliot whenever a VIP would appear before the committee to testify. No contact is a wasted one.

Networkers are constantly thriving for more, and when you identify new goals, make sure you know specifically what you want. A good example of these concepts occurred a number of years ago, when Bret was interested in meeting Arnold Schwar-zenegger. Arnold was coming off a huge hit with *Terminator 2*, and Bret was inter-ested in speaking with him about the process of working with *Terminator 2* director James Cameron. Bret identified a clear goal: to meet Schwarzenegger and discuss the *Terminator 2* set. The next step was research. Bret identified events Arnold was likely to attend. After a few phone calls, Bret decided that the upcoming Golden Globe Awards was the perfect place to achieve his goal because the Golden Globes is an award show that brings out the biggest names in Hollywood—movies, TV, and music are all represented. The event is set up as a large party. The attendees are relaxed and spend a good amount of the evening socializing. By meeting Arnold at the Golden Globes, Bret would be able to spend some time speaking with him in a social situation. With this information in hand, Bret was able to then narrow his networking goal to meeting Schwarzenegger at the Golden Globe Awards.

The first step was to create a plan to get into the Golden Globe Awards. Bret called Dick Clark Productions, which produces the show. He offered to provide free flowers for many of the celebrity holding areas, as well as the food area. Dick Clark Productions agreed with Bret's pitch that flowers would look nice and help dress up the look of the holding areas, making the celebrities feel more comfortable. Bret asked for four all-access passes in return for what amounted to about $5,000 in free flowers. Bret's next call was to a local florist. Bret pointed out to the florist that not only would pictures of his flowers decorating the celebrity-filled Golden Globe Awards look good hanging on his wall, but so would his status in the local community as florist to the stars when he showed his friends and customers pictures of himself standing with Tom Cruise and Sharon Stone! After a quick discussion, the florist recognized his good fortune in being able to provide flowers to the Golden Globe Awards, and he agreed to provide the flowers free of charge. Bret gave the florist two of the passes and used two himself.

During the awards ceremony that night, Bret went to the bar in the back of the ballroom. As he waited for the bartender to pour his soft drink, Arnold Schwarzenegger walked up. Bret used some networking small talk to engage Arnold. Fifteen minutes later, the two parted, but not before Bret had met his goal of meeting Schwarzenegger and discussing the making of *Terminator 2*. Bret also developed a very powerful contact; it never fails to impress when Bret attends an event with a friend, and Arnold Schwarzenegger walks in and makes a point to say hi to Bret.

HOW DO I GET THERE?

Once you have clearly identified your goals, you must design a tangible networking plan. The actual planning and an explanation of how planning to network is varied in differing institution types is covered later in this book. However, in each networking scenario, you must create a road map. Success depends on the methods employed, and a clear understanding of how each step in the process builds on itself and leads to the goal is crucial. You must train yourself to create road maps that are multidirectional; that is, they contain several avenues to success. In each of the sections that follow, you will be taught how to specifically network within various situations: government, business, sports, etc. The key is to realize that no matter what industry you are networking in, you don't want to place all your eggs in one basket. Additionally, you must include in your road map the exploration of unconventional avenues. Organization is a key to a successful road map. You must sit down and plan actual specifics. You must track your progress, including making sure you save all of the contacts from dead ends. Even though dead ends seem useless, there is no such thing as a useless contact. It may prove valuable at a later time.

In the next section on networking techniques, you will be instructed on the concept of *meet and bond* as opposed to just *meet*. This book, if used superficially, will get you into a position to meet with power players from every industry and situation in life. But this book can be much more. Follow the advice in each of the sections, and you will learn to bond as well as meet. The bonding is a key to obtaining your networking goals.

HOW DO I MAKE MYSELF VALUABLE?

It is imperative to remember that when you are networking and you meet someone, your target is always asking themselves, *What can this person do for me?* By anticipating this never-spoken query, you can turn the question into an advantage for yourself by answering it in ways that make you seem valuable. You can subtly work into the conversation answers to that question that range from people you know who are important to the target, or the fact that you have money or connections to institutions with money, or perceived media exposure you can generate for the target, to as simple a concept as mutual friends. Networkers must make sure they are efficient at subtly proving they bring something to the table. The best people do it without trying to blatantly shout out, "I'm valuable." It is much more effective for others to come to their own conclusion that you are valuable. This book will demonstrate techniques that can help you create perceived value.

As a quick example, Bret had the opportunity to speak with Sylvester Stallone at a media event for Planet Hollywood. Bret noticed that everyone who went up to talk to Stallone was a reporter asking a question about a possible *Rambo* sequel, as there was a rumor going around at the time. When Bret approached, he started a conversation with Stallone about Ferrari automobiles, knowing that Stallone was a big admirer of the Ferrari marque. The approach worked, as Stallone was interested in the conversation—the first conversation he had been interested in all evening. Bret made himself valuable by offering Stallone an opportunity to discuss something besides the rumors revolving around the *Rambo* sequel. Never underestimate the value of good conversation. Stallone was clearly happy to be engaging in a conversation in which he had an interest. Bret made himself valuable by providing an entertainment of sorts, good conversation.

There are many ways to make yourself valuable, and being able to create interesting conversations is but one of them. As this book continues, you will learn many techniques in making yourself valuable as you network through to your goals.

Introduction to the Institutions Concept

This book spends a great deal of time demonstrating the power of institutions and demonstrating that their power is the best networking opportunity available. This section looks at this in depth by exploring the infrastructure of the institutions, the motivations, and the opportunities. Institutional networking is almost always event- or donation-driven, and this section will teach the reader to master the art of attending the events, especially without making large donations. Each industry section will look at the VIPs at institutions, VIP treatment opportunities for networkers with the right techniques, and a clear description of the institution's understanding of its role as a social conduit. At this stage, it is important to get a broad understanding of institutions, how to leverage their infrastructure and motivations, and how to make the opportunities afforded by institutions valuable for networking.

WHAT DO INSTITUTIONS WANT?

The simplest answer to that question is *money*. Whether for-profit or nonprofit, the institution needs money to survive. The trick is to capitalize on that concept without having to actually give the institution any of your own money. By offering other value, institutions can see how the networker can lead to money. The value can be implied through many techniques, including connections to powerful people, friends who sit on a board of directors, or relatives who donated in the past. But even if you don't have connections to large donors, you can still create value for the institution and make yourself valuable.

Not long ago, Elliot was interested in meeting Dallas Cowboy legend Troy Aikman. Elliot knew that Troy, along with many other football dignitaries, would be attending the Davey O'Brian Awards, which were to be held in Elliot's hometown in Texas. The Davey O'Brian Awards celebrate the best quarterbacks in football. Elliot's first step was to visit the Davey O'Brian offices. He simply walked into the offices and told the receptionist about his interest in Davey O'Brian. After visiting with some of the office employees, creating relationships, he was given a tour of the Davey O'Brian tribute area. He noticed that they had put together an impressive collection of Davey O'Brian memorabilia: uniforms worn during a game, signed footballs, etc. Noticeably missing, however, was a Davey O'Brian football card. After leaving the offices, Elliot headed out to a football card dealer and bought two O'Brian football cards for under twenty dollars. The next day, Elliot called the chairman of the Davey

O'Brian Foundation and offered to donate the football cards to help round out the O'Brian tribute area. The O'Brian organization was so thankful, they offered Elliot two VIP passes to the upcoming awards banquet. Elliot attended the event with his wife, and they were able to meet and talk with Troy Aikman, achieving Elliot's networking goal. Elliot has kept in touch with the Davey O'Brian organization and has attended many other functions as a result of his ability to make himself valuable. He had created a true win-win relationship. The key to the story is that the Davey O'Brian institution was invaluable in creating an opportunity for Elliot to achieve his networking objective. Institutions are invaluable for networking. Elliot was able to identify a need that the institution had, even though they might not have even realized the need. He was able to fulfill that need and make himself valuable.

When dealing with institutions, you must be ready to investigate what the institutions want. By being ready for the *What can you do for me?* question, the networker can generate invitations to events put on by the institutions, and network successfully.

HOW TO USE INSTITUTIONS

Institutions are quite simply the most effective way to network. The institutional events allow the networker to push a personal or business agenda in a social environment, which is much more conducive to obtaining the networking goals. Institutions give both the networker and the target an automatic common bond. Whatever the event, both are attendees interested in the same area. As an example, a few years ago, Bret was asked by a small film company to arrange for high-end men's suits for the wardrobe in an upcoming limited-release feature film. Bret could have called Hugo Boss or Armani and tried to make an appointment with a promotions person, but instead he decided to create a networking plan. He first made some calls and found out a number of charity events that were sponsored by Hugo Boss. He then did some research and found out who the Boss executives were in the United States and which ones were likely to attend the Hugo Boss–sponsored charity events. Bret went to a Los Angeles–based event sponsored by Boss, found one of the executives, and started up a conversation. An immediate bond was created as both Bret and the Boss executive were out in a social setting. It wasn't long before Bret described the upcoming film and the opportunity for Boss to donate clothing that would be worn as wardrobe for the film. If Bret took the traditional approach, he might have waited weeks for an appointment with some low-level promotions person, who hears pitches all day. The odds of Boss donating clothing to a small film would be slim. Instead, Bret used networking techniques to seek out a Boss executive in a social situation and was able to get the deal done.

In the Boss situation, Bret used two institutions to achieve a networking goal. The first was a corporate institution, Hugo Boss. The other was the charity that Boss was sponsoring. By understanding how institutions work and how to use them for networking purposes, Bret was able to create a win-win situation. Bret won by getting the wardrobe deal; Hugo Boss won by being able to create publicity for their clothing in a feature film.

Institutions are the key to successful networking. Each of the upcoming industry sections will look at how institutions work in an industry and how to navigate within them. It is important at this point, however, to understand the incredible power and opportunity afforded by institutions.

How to Use the Book

With an understanding of the goal concept of networking and the key areas to concentrate on—What do I want? How do I get there? How do I make myself valuable?—it is time to delve into the heart of this book. Read through the next section on techniques. These techniques are your tool kit for networking. You need to know how to deal with people, navigate within institutions, and go after your goals. Once you have these concepts in mind, the next step is actually using this book for a practical application. No more theory! This book actually works, and it is time to use it to the fullest. Following the section on techniques will be descriptions and examples of each type of institution: corporations, charities, trade shows, government, and general institutions. Included in each section will be a description of how to use the information in each category, and the value of the information. Each industry section will include case studies, which lay out a specific goal, then utilize the institution entries to identify and create the networking road map. These detailed case studies will include every step and detail that was used to obtain the networking goal. These case studies will demonstrate how to use this book to its fullest. The techniques sections give you the structure to develop a plan and the knowledge to implement the plan. The industry sections of the book give you the specifics about individual institutions you utilize to achieve your networking goals quickly.

An understanding of the integral value of institutions to the process of networking is fundamental to success. That understanding and the information about them in this book will help you achieve any networking goal you can imagine, no matter what the goal, no matter what the level, no matter what the social segment.

CHAPTER TWO

Networking Techniques and Implementation

It's Not What You Know

We have all heard it before: It is not what you know, it is *who* you know. Not only is the expression a cliché, it is downright boring. However, it is important to understand that the truth of the statement cannot be questioned. It may be a cliché, but if you are going to be successful at networking, no matter how many times you remind yourself of the saying, it will not be enough. Networking is not just important to success, it is everything. No matter what the industry, there are always many smart, good-looking people out there trying to achieve the same goals. Networking is what sets you apart. Networking is how to make up for any perceived shortcomings. To be successful, you must learn networking skills, refine techniques, and work carefully at implementation.

As has been already discussed, you can achieve a successful networking goal by implementing a three-step plan.

1. First, answer the 5 *W*s:
   - Who do I network with?
   - What is my networking goal?
   - Where do I go to network?
   - When is the best time to network?
   - How can I make this networking plan happen?

2. The next step is to do the research to identify the players, understand the opportunities, and develop the road map.

3. The final step is to answer the question: How do I make myself valuable?

With the three main steps in mind, along with an understanding of the importance of institutions, it is time to look at specific techniques and implementation.

Dispelling the Myth That Not Everyone Can Network

When someone thinks of the stereotypical classic networker, the picture generated is usually a very outgoing, gregarious, people person. The truth of the matter, however, is that great networkers come in all shapes and sizes and have many different personality types. The only thing they have in common is a firm understanding that people make the world go round. When networking, people will meet and deal with all types, from plumbers to corporate CEOs, from artists to accountants to attorneys. It isn't just the outgoing, life-of-the-party personality that appeals to all of these different people. Networkers, specifically very effective networkers, appeal to a wide range of people and are able to identify their own personality type and use it to their advantage. Some networkers will be introverts and some will be extroverts, some smart and some not the brightest, some will be good looking while others will be more average. For every personality type and physical makeup, there is a networking style that will work.

An illustration of the concept that you can be successful even if you don't fit the traditional mold involves a friend of Elliot's who is a major player at an investment bank. The classic investment banker is a bold, brash, cocky, swanky, outgoing person who takes control of a room to do the deal. Yet Elliot's friend, Mike Swagel, has become the most successful banker at his firm despite the fact that he is a shy, quiet guy, an extreme introvert. Mike is extremely bright and has a reputation for using good judgment. On a recent visit, Elliot made a point to ask Mike what he thought made him successful. He said, "I stand out by not standing out. Everyone in the room knows everything about everyone in the room. Their strengths and weaknesses are discussed. I'm not a loud, best-friend type of personality. Clients come to me because there is a comfort zone. I don't throw out a huge sales pitch. I just lay out the facts. It seems to work for me." Mike has done a good job of identifying his own strengths and weaknesses. He is successful because he knows how to work with clients: no high-energy schmoozing but simple, effective, and clear strategy and implementation. That doesn't mean that Mike doesn't go out and try to land business. Just the opposite. He knows how to network within his personality type. He didn't become someone he's not, and he is more successful for it.

The outgoing librarian, the humble sports athlete, the religious television producer, they all exist, and they can all be successful at networking without changing who they are. Everyone has the potential to be a great networker. So get over the fear of networking because you aren't typically the life of the party. Read on and learn the networking techniques that follow. Then fine-tune them for your own personality. They will work for anyone.

It's Time to Meet People

The most important thing you can achieve when meeting people is to convey that you are honest. If you begin your networking career by putting on a false front or promising people things you cannot or will not deliver, you are doomed to failure in the long run. You must not only be honest, use good judgment, and be trustworthy, but you must let the people you meet understand these things about you. These three elements are critical to meeting people and bonding with them. These are fundamental bedrock principles: honesty, good judgment, and trustworthiness. Be true to your word. Without these merits, a networker is dead in the water.

First, be honest. People do not want to form long-term, lasting relationships with a person who is a BSer. You can be funny and you can tease. There is nothing wrong with what is known in Washington as spin, putting the best face on a situation. However, an out-and-out lie is a sin. People do not want to do business with liars, and people do not want to build friendships with liars.

Second, it is important to show people that you use good judgment. Powerful people in corporate America get paid huge salaries to basically sit around all day long and make judgment calls. The better judgment they use, the higher they can rise on the corporate ladder. Their days are filled with questions such as which projects to use company resources for, who to network with, which projects need their attention, and who to hire and fire. Their job is to make these judgment calls quickly and effectively. All great networkers need to instill a belief in others that they use good judgment. Elliot once asked Supreme Court Justice Antonin Scalia what makes a great leader. He answered that success in any field is for a person to use good judgment. This couldn't be more true for networkers.

The third imperative is to instill the feeling in people that you are trustworthy. This obviously takes time. A reference that says your word is as good as gold is hugely valuable. If you are trustworthy, the news will get out. You will build a reputation. If you are just starting out, this process will take time. The key is to be true to your word.

As an example, in Washington, your word is your bond. If a member of Congress tells someone they will vote for a bill, they do it. If they don't, their credibility is lost, usually forever. In Washington and many other places, that price is too high to pay. Proving that you are trustworthy may be difficult, but it is well worth the effort.

Along these lines, it is also important to be dependable. Show up on time. Do not break appointments. Dependability goes to the issue of trustworthiness. It is important to be dependable.

Fundamentals of Networking and Answering the Five *Ws*

As was mentioned earlier, to become a successful networker, you have to implement the three-step plan, and success will be yours. First you have to answer the five *Ws*. Second, you have to do the research necessary to accomplish you goal. Third, you have to be able to answer the question, "How do I make myself valuable?" We'll take a look at each of these steps one at a time.

First you must ask yourself the five *Ws*: who, what, where, when, and how.

WHO SHOULD I NETWORK WITH?

It is very important to ask the question: Who do I network with to accomplish my goals? Many people make a mistake when targeting a potential contact. You can aim too high as well as aim too low. You can target someone who actually can't help your networking goal, or you can spend too much time reaching a difficult person when a much easier path is available. You might contact a controversial figure in a highly political environment, or you might forget to use a strategic intermediary. Think carefully when identifying your networking target. Don't be afraid to switch to a new target along the way if your original target begins to show signs of being a mistake.

Take, for example, Bill Johnson. Bill was trying to sell a line of golf club covers to a national specialty chain store. To sell his product, he tried to contact the president of a multibillion-dollar company in order to make a sale. He figured the top-down approach was his best bet. He spent about a month trying to get the president on the phone. Once he did, he was simply referred to someone farther down the corporate ladder. More time passed, and he ended up missing the selling season. If he had started with the merchandise manager, he would have gotten the job done. Bill misjudged his target.

Be aware of your goals, and try to identify the most accessible person who has the power to make a decision. While in Bill's case the president could make the purchasing decision, the merchandise manager could also make the decision and is certainly more accessible. Additionally, the merchandise manager is also more comfortable with the decision as it falls within his bailiwick.

WHAT DO YOU WANT?

All successful networkers know what they want. The key is to identify specific goals. Saying "I want to be rich" is a very broad goal, making it difficult to create a concrete networking plan. You can spend all your time running in all directions and never get anywhere. "I want to be rich" is not a good answer to the question. "I want to be rich by becoming a computer magnate" is better. At least there is some specific direction and focus. A much better goal would be "I want to become rich by getting a well-paying job at a major software manufacturer such as Microsoft or Oracle or IBM." Now you have a more detailed view of what you truly want. You have clearly defined the goal. You have chosen a field you would enjoy working in, and you have even created a list of companies that have corporate environments that are suited to your personality.

Once you have focused on specific goals, you will not waste time. You will be able to use more of your limited and precious time to accomplish your specific goal. Once you identify this specific goal, write it down. It might sound silly or even trite, but write it down. When you see it in writing, it helps to crystallize it in your mind, and it becomes a powerful tool in your success.

WHERE DO I GO TO ACCOMPLISH MY GOAL?

The next question you have to ask is, where do you go to accomplish you goal? If your goal is to find a job at a software manufacturer, it would be tough to obtain the goal in Montana. A job-hunting trip to Silicon Valley or Seattle would be a good place to start. A trip to the National Consumer Electronics Show or Comdex would be another place to go. (In later sections, you'll see how these trade shows can be hugely valuable networking opportunities, offering strong options for answering the *where* question.) Another option is to develop a relationship with one of the target companies' major customers, like Dell. Begin by making a list of all the places you can go or need to go to accomplish your networking goal. Look for all of the connections your target might have. Which trade shows would IBM attend? Who are Oracle's major customers? Which charities does Microsoft support, and when are those events? If you wanted to meet Bill Gates for a job, for investment in a business idea, or to discuss some issue with him, you would ask these questions.

Two years ago, Bret wanted to meet Mr. Gates to get a firsthand view of Gates's opinions of the Microsoft monopoly case. As Bret was in the middle of an antitrust class in law school, he figured there was no better place for a look at the inside than one of the biggest antitrust cases in history. Bret began to research Microsoft connections and possible places to meet Gates. The question of *where* was critical.

Simply asking for an appointment is nearly pointless. Bret decided his best bet was to meet Gates while he was out making an appearance. Bret made a list of speeches Gates was set to make, conferences and conventions that Microsoft was attending, and charities that Gates supported. It was clear that the *where* question was going to be a critical link to achieving Bret's networking goal. When Bret found out that Gates was set to make a joint appearance with Steven Spielberg to announce a Microsoft alliance with Spielberg's movie studio DreamWorks SKG, he knew he had found a great answer to *where*. Since the appearance was in Los Angeles, and Bret had connections built through networking with Los Angeles media and with people at DreamWorks, this opportunity was perfect. After a few calls, Bret secured a place at the press conference. He arrived very early and got the lay of the land. Continuing with his networking research, Bret spoke with dozens of people. He found out that Gates was arriving forty minutes before the conference and was scheduled to meet various DreamWorks executives in a small room just off the stage. Bret sought out a DreamWorks executive who had taken Bret up on his offer for all-access passes to the GRAMMY Awards and asked the executive for a pass for the small room. Once inside, Bret waited patiently for Gates to arrive. When Mr. Gates came into the room about forty-five minutes before the event, he was accompanied by six people, which consisted of assistants and security personnel. In the room with Bret were a number of DreamWorks executives who all introduced themselves and mentioned something about it being an honor to meet Gates. When a lull in the introductions occurred, Bret walked up to Mr. Gates and introduced himself. He then explained his interest in discussing the antitrust case and how he ended up in the position to talk to Gates. Gates was very gracious, seeming to enjoy the opportunity to be professorial to law-student Bret, and he gave Bret a number of insights into antitrust law.

It is important to note that it is possible to attempt to network with someone, and the conversation turns negative. With the pressure and importance of the antitrust lawsuit, it was possible that Gates would have been annoyed at the questions. These situations will eventually crop up in a networker's travels. The key is to maintain composure, and don't fight the situation. Try to change the subject after a very quick apology. Long apologies only serve to prolong the negative subject matter. If your attempt at a change of subject also draws negativity, move on. You will live to network another day.

Luckily for Bret, Gates was in a good mood, and the conversation went very well. The toughest part about networking with a very hard-to-reach target is *where*. If you can identify a place that will offer the opportunity to meet your target and speak with him for a few minutes, you are well on your way.

WHEN IS THE RIGHT TIME TO NETWORK?

Another thing to think about when networking is timing. A great networking plan can easily be derailed by bad timing. A number of years ago, Elliot set out to meet Michael Jordan and spend some time visiting with him. Elliot put all of the components in place. He answered the five Ws, did his research, and even accomplished the third step, making himself valuable to Jordan. His plan worked perfectly, and he ended up face-to-face with Michael at the Rose Elders Golf Tournament in Washington, D.C. However, his timing was bad. Jordan's father had died a few weeks earlier, and he was understandably not in a make-new-friends mood. Elliot quickly sensed that he should pass on the opportunity and regroup later. The key is to be able to identify when the timing is not working out and pull back. There will always be another time, another way.

In addition to being able to recognize when timing is not working out, there are a number of timing issues that you can plan for. Be cognizant of the setting of your potential networking. For instance, if you want to network with A-list movie actors, it is easier to get a conversation going at the Golden Globe Awards, where the celebrities are having a fun time and there isn't much pressure, as opposed to the Academy Awards, where careers are on the line and celebrities are very tense and not very approachable. The same thought should go into everyday networking settings. Approaching networking targets while they are eating or in the middle of a heated argument is obviously bad, though approaching targets while they are standing bored in the corner of a room at a party is optimal. In the real world, however, the lines won't be as clear. Try to empathize with your target. Would you want to be approached in the same situation? Take in all the variables. What is the event? What is the occasion? What is the mood of the event? All of these variables are important in understanding the mood and approachability of the target.

Another timing issue that is important involves the life of the networker. When networking, you must decide if it is the right time in your life to dedicate to building a relationship with someone. If you are busy at work, or you just had a baby, or you are not getting any sleep and are constantly tired, or you just bought a new house, you might want to ask yourself if this is the best time to try to develop a relationship with someone. Every situation will be different. If you just brought a new baby into the family and have been getting no sleep, it still might be a good time to network if a pediatrician just moved in next door. If it is a civic leader who you think might ask you to sit on a community board, the contact might be better delayed.

HOW DO I ACHIEVE MY GOAL?

The next question focuses on *how.* You have to figure out how to achieve your goal, but more than that, you have to figure out how to achieve your goal in the most efficient way possible. The key is to outline your plan of attack. You will have all the techniques you need once you are finished reading this book. Additionally, the industry sections of this book will explain how to network within specific circles. But you must make sure that you create an outline of your plan. As you go through the research phase, the outline will more than likely change, and that's not bad. You are always looking for the most efficient way to effect your goals. For instance, if you want to meet the Pope, spending your life going to the seminary and studying to be a priest is one way to do it. It's not very efficient, however. Another more practical way might be to get involved with Catholic charities or volunteer working for the Cardinal of Chicago. You have to come up with an initial plan of attack, work through your research, and modify your plan as you go along.

WHY AM I DOING THIS?

There is one last thing to keep in mind about the fundamentals. When you are networking to accomplish a goal, you must constantly ask yourself, *Why am I doing this?* Sometimes you are not honest with yourself. You might join a board because of the contacts you can make but care nothing about the organization. Doing something like this is a huge mistake. People who join a nonprofit board exclusively to make contacts are in for a rough road. It does not take long for members of the organization to recognize that you have ulterior motives. Instead of the networking opportunities you expect, you are the negative gossip of the organization. You must constantly ask yourself, *Why am I doing this?*

The Research

Once you identify your networking goals, answer the key questions, and define a clear plan, you will move into the research phase. Your research will vary from industry to industry, but it is imperative in this phase of your networking campaign to be organized, thorough, and creative. The quality of the research you do could determine success or failure. This area is not to be overlooked or skimped on.

So far, we have seen some examples of research. In the *where* section, Bret researched Microsoft, checking for charities they support, trade shows they attend, and keynote speeches that Bill Gates had scheduled. He also kept his eyes and ears open for other events until he stumbled across the DreamWorks press conference. Be thorough, and always keep an open mind.

You can find valuable information everywhere. If you are interested in networking with people from a certain company, call their investor relations department and ask for the annual report. You can check on the Internet for everything from *NSYNC tour dates to charity events put on by United Way. Make phone calls and ask lots of questions. The more questions you ask, the more information you will glean.

In each industry section, we will go through case studies that will include the research done. Get a feel for the process. Try it out in your own networking goals. You will see what works for you, what sources are valuable, and you will begin to create a research system that is effective.

RESEARCH TECHNIQUES

It is important to keep in mind that when you are doing research for a networking goal, there are many resources available. While there are hundreds of research possibilities, we will look at the most effective resources, including conventional media, the Internet, unconventional sources, telephone interviews, and direct discussions with people. The importance of the research while networking cannot be emphasized enough. Research can make a difficult project easy and open up opportunities that wouldn't otherwise be available.

CONVENTIONAL MEDIA

When doing research on a potential networking target, one of the first places to turn to is books and newspapers. Autobiographies and biographies, business books, and industry insider guides are a great place for research. The key things to look for: personal information about your networking target (like where they are from, where they have lived in the past, where they currently reside), what hobbies they enjoy, which school they attended, and other interests that might give the networker a path to success. This type of information is extremely valuable when networking with the target. These topics provide conversation starters and areas of mutual interest. The other things to look for are institutions that the person is affiliated with. This will help you find the person you are looking to meet. For example, if you find when reading a biography about Charles Schwab that he is an active alumnus of Stanford Business School, Stanford is a good place to focus your Schwab networking efforts.

Newspapers are great resources as well. They provide two distinct benefits. First, they offer current information on individuals; and second, they cover institutional events that recently occurred. You will find that there are a tremendous number of institutions and events that you did not know about in your town that can provide great networking opportunities.

When Elliot was scanning through the local Fort Worth, Texas, newspaper, the *Fort Worth Telegram*, he noticed a small story about a youth foundation dinner hosted by Bobby Bragen. Bobby was a Fort Worth resident who had managed the Atlanta Braves baseball franchise during the twilight of home run king Hank Aaron's career. Bobby had arranged for Aaron to come to Fort Worth for the dinner. Elliot placed some calls and secured invitations to the dinner. The evening turned out terrific. In addition to getting to meet Hank Aaron, Elliot found the Bobby Bragen Youth Foundation to be terrific hosts who planned a very memorable dinner. The main point is that this was a small event that would surely have gone unnoticed without the research Elliot does through the newspapers every day.

Most newspaper coverage is printed after an event, basically recounting the who, what, and where of an event. You can leverage this information by creating an event file. In your event file you should collect newspaper clippings of every event you read about through the year and mark them on a calendar. Once you have a year's worth of clippings, you have a great networking event calendar for the following year. You will know when to call the sponsoring institutions to get the details about their upcoming events.

Magazines are also highly effective, as they tend to provide both timely information and in-depth coverage. As you read about events in magazines, save the clippings in your event file. The magazines are usually better at describing who attended the event. As a result, you can begin to build a database of events and people known to attend. When a networking project comes up, you can search through your event file and find which events your target attended. If you are thorough in keeping up with magazines and newspapers, you will create an invaluable networking database.

THE NEW FRONTIER: THE INTERNET

The Internet has emerged as one of the key tools for doing research and gathering information. You can find information on almost any subject by using a search engine on the Internet. The most popular search engines are *www.excite.com, www.yahoo.com, www.infoseek.com*, and *www.altavista.com*. When you go to one of these search engines, you can enter the subject of your search. For instance, if you are researching Jim Carrey, you could enter his name in one of the search engines. The result would be a long list of Internet sites that focus on Jim Carrey. You can then scan through those sites and collect information, helping you in your research tasks. One key thing to remember is to make sure to check when the web site was last updated. It is important to know your information is current. Sometimes information does not get updated for years. When looking for updated, current sites, it helps to identify who has a financial interest in providing the information you are looking for. If you are looking for the date of the Billboard Music Awards and are having a hard time finding the information, the Internet will be a great resource. Begin by identifying who would have a financial interest in providing information on the Billboard Awards. Two ideas come immediately to mind: the Billboard organization, which wants to publicize the event, and ticket brokers, who want to sell access to the event. You would then go to one of the search engines and search on ticket broker or on Billboard. Either way, you will get the information you seek. Just keep your eye on the money. Those who have a financial interest in the topic will keep you up to date.

As a general source of information, *Access* magazine is packed with great, off-the-beaten-path web sites and descriptions of how they are useful. The magazine really does its research and will help you find many unconventional places on the Internet to do research.

The Internet is also a great place to get the most updated information regarding the corporate board of directors and executives of companies. Major corporations post press releases about big executive moves on their web site.

UNCONVENTIONAL PLACES TO DO RESEARCH

During your research phase, you should consider unconventional sources of information, which can be invaluable to completing your goal quickly. In many cases, the unconventional places yield the best information. Some of the most effective are alumni newsletters, trade publications, company annual reports, trade show guide books, and public records.

One of the institutions that most people support is their alma mater. People usually feel a sense of loyalty to their college and will either attend alumni events or offer financial assistance to the university. To coordinate alumni opportunities, most universities publish an alumni newsletter. These newsletters generally contain two things: events and happenings at the university, which are useful pieces of networking information; and fluff pieces on successful alumni. The piece almost certainly contains information about how the college was a key factor in the person's success. By publishing these alumni spotlights, the university helps you identify the people you want to network with. Of course, the college will focus on the most successful and most visible of their alumni, making the alumni newsletter a gold mine.

Trade publications are another excellent source of information. Not only will they help you stay on top of the news in an industry, they can turn you into an expert. You can pick up industry jargon, buzzwords, and be on the cutting edge of what is working today. In a casual conversation with a VIP you can work into a conversation specific industry news that you picked up in the trade publication. If the VIP has not read the trade yet, you appear to be seriously in the loop. Even if he knows the information, you will appear well informed.

Another good source for research can be found in corporate annual reports. The information contained in these reports includes the company's direction, the names of key players, their positions, and the members of the board of directors. As you begin to do research for a networking goal, you may find that the easiest way to network into a company like Intel is through another company's corporate board. The annual reports will give you complete listings of the board directors, helping you find the company and board director connections between firms. Also included in the annual reports is corporate structure information. By looking at several past annual reports—many of which are available on the Internet—you can identify key employees who are moving up the corporate ladder, as well as those employees whose careers have stalled or are on the way down.

The most important piece of information you can glean from the annual reports is a list of the institutions that the company supports. Usually located in the section on corporate giving, this list will point out networking opportunities. If you want to meet some of the top players at Kodak, and the annual report shows that Kodak is a big supporter of the charity Amnesty International, the Amnesty events are good opportunities to meet the Kodak executives.

Another effective resource is the guide books handed out at trade shows. Even if you keep up with trade publications, these guide books offer a snapshot, or source book, on an entire industry. Every major company is listed, along with the address of the company and key personnel. In addition, you can identify the major companies of the professional trade organizations. If you want to network into a specific industry, read up on the trades, and then attend the big trade show. When you get the guide book, you will now have all the information you could possibly need to identify the industry's players.

Accessing public records is another way to obtain information. More and more information about people is available on-line, and as a result, accessing public records is becoming easier and easier. You can find out about upcoming court dates, driver's license data, addresses and phone numbers, and real estate ownership. The sites that provide this information change as quickly as the Internet itself. If you want to obtain public records, search for exactly what you want using the search engines described earlier. For instance, if you want to find the owner of a car for a license plate you jotted down, search on License Plate Public Records. You will find the information you need.

Telephone interviews are another way to do research. Government public information departments, corporate communications departments, and phone communications with members of the press are all available to the networker. Don't ever be afraid to pick up the phone to call around and make inquiries. Elliot once called local NBC sports reporter Scott Murray in Dallas and asked him which events were the best for sports. Scott quickly rattled off a list of local events, which included three Elliot had never heard of. These events turned out to be everything Scott described, and Elliot ended up meeting quite a few top-name sports personalities.

One other research opportunity is through the veterans of an industry. Often in business, politics, and entertainment there is a feeling that once you're past your prime, you are out. The newly defeated congressman can't get a phone call returned; a 1980s sitcom star is no longer invited to the big Hollywood events. While it is true that those past their prime no longer have the same power and access they used to have, you have to be careful to recognize their true value. They know how to play the game. The rules might have changed a little, but not that much. These people are extremely valuable. James Noble isn't as visible in the entertainment industry anymore, but at one point, he was on top of the world, playing the governor in the hugely successful sitcom *Benson*. He doesn't have the same clout today, but while on *Benson*, he worked with Jerry Seinfeld, and he still has a relationship with him. If you want to meet with Seinfeld, Noble is a great resource. Another great example is Richard Nixon. At one time he was an industry veteran; he lost a race for president, and then lost the race for governor of California. He was out of power. He then went on to run for and win the job as president of the United States. How close do you think he was to the people who stuck with him through the two losses? Industry veterans are very important.

Another thing about industry old-timers is that they are usually accessible. They are even flattered that you are seeking their advice. Those who had a taste of being in the public eye usually find it hard to lose the recognition. When you seek them out, you stroke the part of them that longs to be the center of attention. A friend of Elliot's in Washington, D.C., once called over to former Secretary of State Clark Clifford's office. At one time Clifford was one of the most powerful men in the world. In addition to his political position, he was known as one of the world's great net-workers. He knew everyone. Elliot's friend called Clifford's office to ask for a photo for a friend. He also asked if he could pick it up. When he arrived, Clifford was there and invited him in for what turned out to be an hour-long discussion. It was the experience of a lifetime. The interesting thing about contacting industry veterans is that the *What can you do for me* question is answered. You can perpetuate their legacy.

The first time Elliot attempted to contact an industry veteran, he wrote to former Secretary of Defense and current publisher of *Forbes*, Casper Weinberger. Elliot wanted to interview Mr. Weinberger for a college paper he was writing. Weinberger invited Elliot up to his law firm, Rogers and Wells, in Washington, D.C. They sat down for an hour and discussed world leadership. Weinberger's insight was timely, his contacts were strong, and he was a gracious person. Industry veterans are invaluable.

How Do I Make Myself Valuable?

You are in the middle of a networking project. You have answered the five Ws (step one). You have also done the research (step two). Now we come to the most critical thing of all, answering the question, How can I make myself valuable to the person I want to network with? (step three).

People perceive value in many ways, but they are usually asking themselves, What can this person do for me? If you anticipate that question, you can figure out how to make yourself valuable. All the research and planning in the world will come up short if you cannot answer this important question.

When trying to make yourself valuable to an individual, there are many obvious answers, such as donating money to a cause they support, saving them money in a business deal, delivering a product faster or of higher quality, sharing some extraordinary talent you have, volunteering to do things for them, giving them gifts, or even swapping for something they want.

Swapping is one of the most effective ways to become valuable to a person you want to network with. As a hypothetical example, the public relations director of the New York Yankees gives season tickets to the public relations director of the New York Jets. The major hotels in Las Vegas all give each other great seats at their shows, so that the favor is returned. Elliot uses this technique when he needs to travel to a big event in Los Angeles, New York, or Washington, D.C. He will give his extra ticket to a member of an airline's senior management. In return for a ticket to the event, the American executive usually graciously offers to fly Elliot to his destination for free. It is a true win-win situation. Bret also uses this technique. Bret has built a circle of important Hollywood events, such as the Oscars, Golden Globes, Emmys, GRAMMYs, and dozens of others. He passes around tickets for the Oscars to people of influence at the GRAMMYs. When the GRAMMYs roll around, the thankful recipients of Oscar tickets give GRAMMY passes to Bret, who then gives some to people at the Golden Globes. The cycle continues. Everyone is happy, and Bret is the conduit to all the special event passes.

As you become more inventive in creating value for yourself, you can achieve your goal through ways that are not as apparent. One of the more effective techniques includes being a friend of a friend. By being a friend of a friend, you are already valuable to them. They know that by building a good relationship with you they will strengthen an already important relationship. Additionally, if you are a friend of someone they respect, you are valuable to your target simply because you are valuable to their friend. This goes to the point that as you network, it is important to build many relationships. Don't just focus on the immediate task at hand and throw away opportunities to build relationships with the people you meet along the way. These people can turn out to be valuable during your next networking project, or these people can end up being a friend of someone in the path of your next networking project. Build your contact base. There are no dead ends or wasted contacts.

The power that accompanies being a friend of a friend is very strong. A few years back, Elliot attended the Lenox Lewis–Ray Mercer boxing match in Madison Square Garden. As it was the first high-profile fight in New York in a number of years, there was a very large celebrity and VIP turnout. Elliot had a connection that got him a pass to an exclusive VIP room at the Garden, Suite 200. Suite 200 is a large lounge that is often set up as the VIP area for big events. Elliot arrived at the event early and was surprised to find someone had beat him to the VIP room: acclaimed artist Leroy Neiman. Mr. Neiman was sitting with his assistant at an otherwise empty table set for ten. Elliot walked over to Mr. Neiman and introduced himself and was able to get a conversation going. After a few minutes, Mr. Neiman invited Elliot to sit down. As people began arriving, the celebrities would come over to the table and say hi. Each time, Mr. Neiman introduced Elliot. Within an hour, the table was full. Christopher Walken, Danny Aiello, Tom Brokaw, and two New York City nightclub owners were seated with Elliot and Mr. Neiman. Everyone included Elliot in their conversation as Elliot was immediately valuable; he was a member of the celebrity table. He was a friend of Mr. Neiman, even if the friendship had begun only minutes earlier.

Another very effective technique is knowing people who are important to your networking target. If you have a friend who is the retail business analyst at Goldman Sachs and the person you are trying to network with is the president of Home Depot, you become very important because your friend's opinion of the president and his leadership skills has an impact on the marketplace and his stock price. As stock price is a reflection of his job performance, he will find you valuable because of your relationship. As another example, if you were interested in meeting the head of a cable company and had a friend at the FCC in charge of broadband communications, you are instantly valuable to the cable executive. The casual mention of your friend at the FCC makes you a VIP and valuable contact.

Another great way to make yourself valuable is to be known for knowing everyone. You are powerful because you know people, and people who know people are valuable by nature of their skill. This is a power of networkers. As you become good at your craft and become known for your connections and networking skills, you become valuable.

A more altruistic way to achieve value is to be caring. People want to be around people who care and are considerate. People who remember your birthday or send you a note when your child is born are people you want to be around. This isn't an area where you should fake your feelings. If you try to become valuable by pretending to care about others, it will come through quickly. It is, however, necessary to include this item here. You can work on truly being more conscientious and caring about other people. Those qualities will also shine through.

Finally, people can make themselves valuable by using the classic People Promoter Technique or, as the authors refer to it, PPT. The PPT is simply telling others how wonderful your friends are. An interesting quirk in society is that if people talk about their accomplishments, it is often seen as bragging. Yet, if others tell of your accomplishments, they are simply paying you a compliment. "He graduated at the top of his class at Harvard and is a genius," is a compliment. "I graduated at the top of my class at Harvard" is seen as boastful and obnoxious. As a result, people want to be—whether consciously or not—around friends who naturally boast about them. This makes the boasters valuable. The bottom line is, if you talk up your friends and associates, you are likely to create value in their eyes. There is an added benefit to this technique. When you extol the virtues of your friends and associates, it appears to those around you that you associate yourself with successful people. There is a cliché that success breeds success. It is a self-fulfilling prophecy. If you become valuable to successful people, you create opportunities for your own success to grow. People in every field have ways of saying it, but it is always true. One night, the authors were visiting with professional golfer Tom Kite. He mentioned that golf legend Harvey Penick had told him to hand out with good putters. No matter what industry you are in, success breeds success.

One evening, Elliot attended a dinner with his friend Ted Cruz. Ted is a classic People Promoter, as is Elliot. One by one, everyone at the table took a turn introducing themselves. When it came to Ted's turn, he merely said, "Ted Cruz, dinner participant." Elliot shot up, "Ted is just being humble. Let me tell you about Ted. He is a Princeton graduate, was at the top of his class at Harvard Law School, was editor of the *Harvard Law Review*, clerked for Supreme Court Chief Justice Rehnquist, and then went on to work for a powerful Washington, D.C., law firm. He recently took a job as George W. Bush's domestic policy advisor for the presidential campaign. And, if this is not enough, *Newsweek* chose him as one of the twenty most important young Hispanics in the United States." Elliot gave quite a different description than "dinner participant." This is a good example of how the PPT works. If Ted had given this laundry list of accolades, he would have been viewed as bragging. But with Elliot giving the introduction, Ted can still be humble, yet the entire table was made aware of Ted's incredible accomplishments.

The idea here is that you can find a way to make yourself valuable, whether you give a great introduction, or you donate money, or you provide a refreshing conversation to a bored celebrity. Earlier, we saw how Elliot gave away a football card to become valuable, and we described how Bret was able to become valuable to media-weary Sylvester Stallone by simply talking about a subject Stallone was interested in. There are many ways to make yourself valuable to people, and most do not involve cash. Never forget that "What can I do for you?" is the critical question to ask in networking. While every situation is different, there is always an angle.

What Types of People Are Important to Networkers?

Years of experience have taught Bret and Elliot that there are four distinct types of people with whom networking is particularly valuable. These four types offer opportunities to build a strong, mutually beneficial relationship. There are certainly other types with whom networking can be effective, but when you meet one of the four core types, you will want to pay special attention because they are extremely valuable.

PEOPLE AT INSTITUTIONS

The first type of person you are going to try to key in on is someone who works for an institution. People at the Baseball Hall of Fame, the Republican National Committee, Microsoft, the White House, or the Academy of Television Arts and Sciences are just a few examples of fantastic contacts. If they are top-level executives at the institution, you have the opportunity to create a great contact. However, even if they are lower-level employees, they are still extremely valuable. A friend of Elliot's, Christine Buffet, was an assistant in the West Wing of the White House, running errands and making copies. The fact was, however, that she was a better person to know than a cabinet secretary. She was involved in everything, knew everyone in the West Wing, people loved her, and she was accessible. If Elliot had friends or associates that he wanted to give the opportunity for a quick trip in to the Oval Office for a brief grin and grip with the president, it was no problem. Christine had perfect access and was certainly more accessible than a cabinet secretary. The point is that no matter what job a person has in an organization, they understand it from an insider's perspective and can help you in ways you wouldn't know without the insider's view.

ANCHORS

The next type of person that is key for networking purposes is an anchor. Anchors are people who are going to remain in their industry, location, or field for a long time. One truth about institutions is that the personnel within it constantly changes. Every four to eight years you have a complete turnover of White House staff. At the Halls of Fame you have rapid turnover in entry-level positions. It is the nature of low-paying, power-oriented jobs. It is very valuable to network and bond with someone who is going to remain in an industry. So, as an example, a key person to network with would be someone who first works at the White House, then moves on to the Federal Communications Commission (FCC), then, when their administration leaves office, they go to work for a think tank. Like most, this person changes jobs. His value is that he is staying put in the center of Washington, D.C. His industry is politics and government, and you know that in twenty years you can look him up and he will still be working in Washington. He is an anchor. The extra value that anchors provide is that once you have an anchor as a contact, it is a contact that is available for many years. There are various anchor types.

Anchors in a Geographical Area or Town

Location anchors are truly fantastic resources. "I have lived in Trenton all my life." At first glance, a statement like that might seem mundane. You don't live there, and you have no plans to move there. But this individual is a geographical anchor. He knows the town, how it works, and how it operates. During some networking project, you might be doing research and find out that Norman Schwarzkopf, whom you are trying to meet with to ask him to consult for your upstart company, grew up in Trenton, New Jersey. The anchor will likely know the family or know that Schwarzkopf attends the annual festival held in the town or some other piece of local information that can help you achieve your goal. Additionally, people who are geographic anchors are generally civic leaders and very well connected. It is commonly accepted that if you ever need anything done in Munster, Indiana, you should call Ruth Johnson. She is a geographic anchor, and she knows everyone in Munster. In addition to their local value, geographical anchors often become exponentially more valuable, as they tend to network heavily with other geographical anchors in other towns, which offers you more connections. As you meet geographic anchors in your networking travels, spend some time. They are excellent networking targets.

Anchors in an Industry

Anchors in an industry are becoming harder to find. The average American changes jobs and careers more than seven times in his or her adult working life. However, anchors in an industry are so valuable, it is worth discussing them. An industry anchor might have followed a career path that began twenty-five years ago at a Baby Bell, moved on to MCI, and is now at AT&T. He has seen a lot of changes. One thing you can count on is that he is an excellent telecommunications contact. He has been in the field for twenty-five years, watched massive changes, and seen many of the mistakes and pitfalls of the industry. His experience is a huge asset, and his contacts are invaluable. He is an individual that you don't want to miss the opportunity to network with. This personality type did not remain in an industry for twenty-five years by burning bridges. His value is clear if you want to achieve a networking objective in his industry.

Anchors in a Field

Anchors in a field are very similar to anchors in an industry except they relate to academia and science. Microbiologists, established university professors, and rocket scientists are all examples. Not only can these anchors be valuable when you are networking in their particular discipline, but they can be valuable in many other networking situations. If you are trying to create value for yourself with an executive at an Internet company specializing in streaming video, you can truly impress him by introducing the executive to a field anchor who works with NASA creating video feeds from Mars. Corporations, charities, and governments interact with academia all the time. You can help put people together and create value by introducing your networking targets to a field anchor.

THE SUPER NETWORKER

So far, we have seen two of the four key types of networking targets: people at institutions and anchors. The next type of key target is the super networker. People who are very good at networking are themselves fantastic contacts and a prime networking resource. They intimately understand the game and are usually more than willing to help a fellow networker, especially one who comes into the relationship understanding that he should be prepared to answer the question, "What can you do for me?" Networkers are key social conduits. There was a recent article published in *New Yorker* magazine about a woman named Lois Weisburg. The article was appropriately entitled, "Does This Woman Run the World?" The article spent much time discussing the amazing contacts Ms. Weisburg has and the people she has brought together. It also described how many of the contacts a person will make in life are through a single person who brings more and more people into the fold. It discusses networkers' social importance, power, and the joy they derive from bringing people together. One of the "powerhouse networkers" that the article described was a gentleman named Harry Reasoner. Not long after the article was published, Elliot ran into Mr. Reasoner at a major Washington event. Networkers get around. They can help you achieve your goals.

Another powerhouse networker is a political consultant named Dave Carney, from New Hampshire. Dave is regarded as the top Republican consultant in New Hampshire, which is a key Republican state. As a result, Dave is valuable to any candidate running for a national office. In 1994, U.S. Senator Kay Bailey Hutchison was running for the Senate for the first time. Elliot was working for Mrs. Hutchison's campaign and remembers the day Dave walked into the campaign headquarters for the first time. He was introduced to the office and then shown to his desk. He proceeded to pull out of his boxes six of the largest Rolodexes ever created. He had arrived.

It didn't take Elliot long to recognize that Dave would be one of the key people to bond with on the campaign. Elliot had no specific agenda at the time, he just identified Dave as a power networker who would be invaluable in the future. Elliot and Dave became friendly during the campaign. After Senator Hutchison was elected, Elliot moved on to work on Capitol Hill, and Dave went to work at the Republican National Senatorial Committee.

Not long after Dave and Elliot took their new jobs, the Senatorial Committee held a function that had Mikhail Gorbachev in for a dinner. Dave arranged for Elliot to get a coveted volunteer job at the dinner. Elliot was thrilled. He is always very interested in opportunities to meet with people who are historically significant. Elliot knew that he wouldn't have the opportunity to have a lengthy sit-down with Gorbachev at the dinner, as Gorbachev didn't speak English. Elliot figured that a laugh, a photograph with Gorby, and a good story to tell his kids about the man who worked with Ronald Reagan to end the Cold War would be enough.

Being the good networker that he is, Elliot began his research. He called his grandmother, who spoke Russian, and asked her how to say, "Will you take a picture with me?" The dinner went very smoothly, and Elliot spent the evening socializing with people who paid between $1,000 and $100,000 to have dinner with Gorbachev. Toward the end of the evening, Elliot decided to approach the Russian leader, and he walked up to a group that included Gorbachev, his daughter, his interpreter, Secretary of State James Baker and his wife, and security personnel. Elliot waited while Gorbachev said good-bye to Mrs. and Mr. Baker. Gorbachev then turned toward Elliot. Elliot smiled and said, *"Ya be hochetel mate photogaphe es va me."* Gorbachev smiled broadly, quite impressed that Elliot went to the trouble to deliver a feeble attempt at the Russian language. He put his arm around Elliot and said something to his interpreter, who told Elliot, "He will take one, but hurry." A friend of Elliot's quickly snapped the photo while an amused James Baker stared on. Gorby then waved to the rest of the group and walked out of the room. Elliot was the only one to be photographed with Gorbachev that night, and certainly one of the few to entertain him with broken Russian.

Dave had come through for Elliot, and Elliot is proud to say that he is on a Dave Carney Rolodex card.

CROSS-INDUSTRY NETWORKING EXPERTS

Generally when you run into a well-connected individual, he or she is connected within a specific community, whether that community is geographic or within a discipline. The connected networker will know everyone in the semiconductor industry, for instance, or they will know everyone on Capitol Hill. It is rare to find someone who has developed contacts throughout multiple industries. The most powerful Capitol Hill staffer cannot get access to Hollywood awards shows, and a major corporate executive cannot get in to see a politician without a check in hand. But cross-industry networkers can do it all. They are extremely valuable to people because some types of contacts can only be made through this type of networker. It is clear that Bill Gates can get in to see the president, but can a junior executive at Micron Technologies? The answer is yes, if he has friends in government by being a cross-industry networker or if he knows one.

Communication Techniques

We have looked at identifying who to network with and where to do the research. We will now look at specific formal and informal communication techniques. The techniques you use when you communicate, either orally or through writing, will telegraph your importance. If you come across in a conversation as very shy and reserved, it is likely that you will have a much tougher time communicating that you can be valuable.

It is important to start with oral communication. As a networker, you will encounter important situations in networking both on the telephone and face-to-face. On the telephone, there are two main areas to master: confidence, and name-dropping.

TELEPHONES

Many times when you are networking, you will not have the opportunity to have a face-to-face meeting. As a result, you will often need to communicate via telephone. There are certain techniques that are highly effective on the phone. The most important thing is to convey genuine enthusiasm and confidence. You absolutely must sound completely sure of yourself on the phone. If you have difficulty with names, you should write them down. If it makes you feel more comfortable, you can prepare a script or an outline of key points, so nothing is missed. But spend some time practicing so when you're on the phone you don't sound like you are reading from a page. Relax. Be calm. Once you have a firm grip on the subjects you want to cover and the likely conversation path, make the call. Be confident. As you continue to develop your networking skills, confidence will build, and you will get better and better. Don't get discouraged if some of the first telephone conversations are a little rough. You will become an expert both on the phone and with confidence.

Whenever you can, it is imperative that you practice name-dropping. Do it all the time. It is critical that people know people. The argument that, "I am not impressed that Bill Gates referred you" is ridiculous. You must use every name you can in the conversation. Bret was able to get his first television pitch meeting after dropping Michael Eisner's name. Bret had developed a sitcom idea and wanted to get in to the major networks to pitch it. He identified Disney as a likely fit for his project and did the research necessary to find which events the Disney executives might attend. Bret identified the Golden Globe Awards as a likely opportunity. At the awards, Bret found Disney chief Michael Eisner and started up a conversation with him. After developing a quick rapport with Mr. Eisner, Bret offered up the fact that he had a sitcom idea he would love to pitch at Disney. Eisner told Bret to call Mike Valentine, the head of the television development at Disney. The next morning, Bret called Valentine's office and explained his request for a pitch meeting. Bret was quick to point out that Eisner had referred Bret to Valentine. With the Eisner referral, Bret was quickly set up with a pitch meeting. The key is that without being able to drop Eisner's name, Bret wouldn't have been able to get the meeting during that call. You have to do your research and figure out how to leverage your knowledge and contacts when making the phone calls.

You never want to lie about your contacts or referrals, but you can work the system a little bit. For example, if you were trying to get an appointment with a buyer of routers at a major telecom company, it might be valuable to call the buyer's boss, simply to ask him who the right person is to call to sell into the chain. When the boss identifies the buyer, you can then call the buyer and tell him that his boss told you to call. This isn't a lie. You created a referral.

FACE-TO-FACE

In-person networking techniques are equally valuable. You must be able to make a great first impression. The two most important aspects of face-to-face communications are the handshake and eye contact. Do not underestimate the power of a good handshake and direct eye contact. People at the top find these to be critical. Look people in the eye and give them a firm shake. Don't crush their hand, as this produces a negative response as well. Additionally, many women in corporate America hate the "Roll Over Sissy Shake." Treat women as equals. Shake their hand properly.

As for eye contact, you have probably heard many times that eye contact is important. But the need for strong eye contact cannot be stressed enough. If you are constantly looking around and scanning the room while you speak with someone, they will get the feeling that you would most likely rather be somewhere else or with someone else. Also, if you repeatedly look down or have trouble making direct eye contact, the person you are speaking to will get the feeling that you are nervous or shy. You don't want these traits associated with you during your networking encounters. You want to project confidence. Maintain very strong eye contact. It makes the person you are talking to feel like you are giving them your undivided attention. You will appear stronger, more confident, and more valuable.

INTERMEDIARIES

Another important networking technique is networking through intermediaries. As a general rule, it is best to network directly, but there are times when networking is best done through intermediaries. The obvious downside is that you can lose control of your carefully sculpted message. However, depending on your subject, you can be more effective through intermediaries.

At one time, Elliot was working to visit with Supreme Court Justice David Souter. The most direct approach would have been to arrange the meeting through Souter's office. However, while working on Capitol Hill, Elliot had worked with Sally Horton. Sally was the daughter of a New Hampshire State Supreme Court justice. Sally's dad took Justice Souter's seat in New Hampshire when Souter became a United States Supreme Court justice. With Sally's help, and the meeting was set up very quickly. The intermediary had such a direct connection to the goal that it was much more effective to work through the intermediary than try to network directly.

WRITTEN COMMUNICATIONS

While verbal communication is paramount to success, there are many effective tools in networking that involve written communication. In some industries or social circles, written communication is critical; in others it is not as important. One of the fields that relies heavily on written communication is government. In government, written communication is the way business gets done. Writing is so important in government business because it is critical that a historical record of communication be kept because actions, or lack thereof, are open to public scrutiny. Conversely, in Hollywood, everything is done on the phone. About the only thing reduced to writing is a contract. In most business circles, communication is a mix of both written and verbal. While there are the classic handshake deals, many other interactions are put down in writing.

One thing is certain: When using written communication, it is vital to come across professionally. The writing structure should be clear, and more importantly, concise. There is no reason to be long-winded. The recipient doesn't want to plow through pages of text offering nothing more than a display of your vocabulary. The recipient wants you to get right to the point. When Elliot worked on Capitol Hill, one of his jobs included going through the incoming mail. He would get letters that were three pages long, and it wasn't until the end of the second page that the sender would get around to asking for a meeting. The sender would spend so much time in the early part of the letter discussing policy that the letter would be sent up for a stock response letter on the policy topic discussed. The scheduling team would not even see the letter. Often, the original sender would reply to the stock policy letter with an angry reply. This cycle wastes time and energy. It is much more important to simply get to the point. On Capitol Hill, a major VIP literally gets 10,000 letters per week, not to mention E-mail. If you hope to get your request heard, ask it quickly and directly.

You should try to get to a scheduling request in the first three lines of a letter whenever contacting a VIP. The VIP probably gets thousands of requests a week and generally has departments that handle nothing but this type of written communication. At any given time in the White House, there are roughly seven full-time employees just handling scheduling requests for the vice president.

Highly effective people have developed brevity in writing down to a science. The mayor of Chicago, Richard Daly, rarely writes more than two sentences in any written note, and the full two sentences are considered verbose for him. Important people are generally very busy. Be respectful of their time.

The type of paper you use to write letters is also important. Cranes brand stationery is the gold standard across the line in both government and business. Cranes is one of the oldest stationers in the United States and still makes the paper that U.S. currency is printed on. Cranes has a very distinct watermark and feel. There are specific sizes for formal writing, informal writing, and type of correspondence. A Cranes paper dealer can help you pick out the proper size. The color of the paper should be ecru white, and it should have a kidd finish.

If you looked at the stationery used by former Secretary of State James Baker, it would say "James Baker, Houston, Texas." Baseball legend Babe Ruth's stationery header said "Babe Ruth, New York, New York." VIPs have corresponded with this type of stationery for over 100 years. The return address on the back of the envelope is also very simple: just the return address, no name. You would be well suited to use this style. When a scheduling office receives a request on this type of stationery, it automatically stands out as a request that should get special attention. This is a strong first move to obtaining important appointments and requests.

There are, of course, alternatives to the very pricey Cranes stationery. Bethesda Engravers is a government-specific type of stationery. It is rather pricey but worth it. After these two brands, the cost drops significantly. The key to making stationery less expensive is to not have the stationery engraved but simply thermographed. Or buy the paper blank and just run it through a laser printer. As a last resort, if all you have access to is résumé paper, chose cream instead of white. This is something that VIP communications sorters look for.

While on the topic of VIP communications, Elliot, having spent time in the White House, often has people ask him whether the letter they received from the president was really written or signed by him. There are two types of letters that come from the president of the United States. One is handwritten, and these are easy to identify as written by the president. The other is typed on a special piece of azure green stationery. The azure green stationery is exclusive to the president of the United States and has a very distinct hue to it. The other thing to look for on a letter from the president is whether the date on the top of the letter looks like it was added at a later time. The date on a presidential signed letter is added after the letter has been typed or printed out. This is because the president might not sign a letter written for him until several days or weeks after it is drafted. The letter is never dated until the president signs it. As a result, if the date seems to be added later, it is likely that it was actually signed by the president.

We have discussed letter type, paper type, and structure. Now lets look at content. Content should be guided as much as possible by remembering that the reader will ask, "What can this person do for me?" You must write letters and other communications by remembering the theme of making yourself valuable.

In written communication, name-dropping is critical. You are, in many cases, trying to open doors. Do not be shy. Hold nothing back and drop as many names as possible. Even a brief encounter with a person in an industry can be enough to drop that person's name when you are trying to network with someone else in the same industry. Remember back when Bret called Disney and reminded the scheduler that Michael Eisner told him to call. The same can be true in written form. As an example, recently Bret was at a trade conference, and he sat in on a session where E-commerce experts were discussing new trends on the Internet. After the session, Bret went up to the panelists and introduced himself. One of the people on the panel was an E-commerce executive for Microsoft. Two weeks later, Bret was working on a project for someone who needed to get a meeting with the head of E-commerce at Amazon. Bret helped craft a letter that began, "I was recently at the E-commerce conference in Beverly Hills, and I had a chance to spend some time with Mr. Smith of Microsoft . . ." The name drop will alert the target at Amazon that you travel in important circles. The meeting was very quickly set up. Drop names as often as possible.

Another topic on scheduling appointments through written communications deals with the saying that "Timing is everything." This is especially true with VIPs. In the case of the president of the United States, scheduling requests should be sent out a minimum of three months in advance. Many VIPs have their schedule set that far out. You must plan ahead. Also be aware of the industry's busy seasons. It is obviously more difficult to get an appointment with a CPA during tax season, or an appointment with a politician during the final days of a big campaign. Keep in mind the industry of your networking target, understand their schedule ups and downs, and use that information to your advantage.

INFORMAL COMMUNICATION TECHNIQUES

In addition to the more formal techniques we have just discussed, there are also informal communication techniques that are valuable to include in your arsenal. It is important to try to master as many of these techniques as possible, because when you are out networking, you will be able to use them over and over to great advantage. The first thing to consider is your body posture. People have a way of carrying themselves that commands respect. Don't slouch. Strong, straight posture telegraphs a feeling of success. If you have bad posture, be conscious of it and work to correct it.

It may seem obvious, but you want to be sure to be exact in your manners.

During meals, use good table manners. If you are not familiar with which fork to use, as a general rule, use the utensils from the outside first. Don't say to the person next to you, "I never know which fork to use." It is better to delay for a second and watch the others at the table than mention that you aren't sure.

Dressing properly is important as well. What is trendy and fashionable in Los Angeles and New York can be very inappropriate in Washington, D.C., and vice versa. In Washington and in government in general, the dress is extremely conservative. There are very few double-breasted suits in D.C. A dark suit, a dark tie, a white shirt, and black shoes and belt are the normal, accepted uniform. For Republicans, the shoes are wingtips, and for Democrats, cap toes are typical. When dressed in this outfit, you can just about walk in everywhere. It is absolutely amazing how far your clothes can take you. The time Bret and Elliot went to tour the Capitol of the United States, they dressed in this exact style. Just by their attire, it was clear they weren't tourists. They walked right through the halls of the Capitol and directly onto the floor of the House of Representatives. They looked around and left. No one stopped them, and no one questioned them. Because of their attire, everyone assumed they were staff and belonged. This is a fantastic way to tour. They went on to walk into all the ticketed events at the Smithsonian during the height of the summer tour season. No one wears a suit and tie unless they work there. Clothing is critical. Whatever circle you plan to network in, do some research into clothing types and fit in.

The next item to work on is your energy level. Your mental attitude is the most important informal communication skill you can sharpen. The simple truth is that people love to associate with positive people. High-energy, positive people are genuinely a pleasure to be around. In some ways, refining this skill can in and of itself make a person valuable. When talking about energy level, you don't want to come across as being nervous or hyperactive. Just be highly positive. If you are discussing a plan or a business concept, don't be the one who simply explains why you think the idea won't work. Offer solutions and encouragement. If you are successful in developing this positive personality, people will want to do business with you. You will be the type of person who generates comments like, "I do business with him because he is always thinking of ways to help." People do not want to work or be around someone who is perpetually negative.

An Introduction to the Upcoming Sections: The Power of Institutions

With few exceptions, people meet almost all of their contacts through institutions. An institution is an established group or organization that holds societal or cultural significance or importance. Corporations, nonprofit foundations, trade shows, service clubs, conferences, and media outlets all fit the definition.

Institutions are where people network. If a friend makes it possible for you to attend the Academy Awards and you network with Steven Spielberg, you have two people to thank: your friend and The Academy of Motion Picture Arts and Sciences, the institution that created and produced the awards show. If a person sitting next to you at an American Cancer Society wine auction becomes a customer, you cannot discount the role the institution played in your good fortune.

A few years back, Bret and Elliot attended a dinner at the United States Supreme Court. Elliot was sitting at a table that included the guest of a high-level legal professional. The guest happened to run a cruise line that specialized in sponsored cruises for fans of professional sports teams. As Elliot is in the apparel business, he was able to become a supplier of custom shirts for the cruise line. The fact that both Elliot and the guest were at this very influential event gave Elliot instant credibility. The Supreme Court, as an institution, created common ground for both of them, as well as the credibility. They have continued to enjoy a wonderful working relationship, and Elliot has institutional networking to thank.

It is clear that institutions play a key role in networking success, but the question is how to leverage the institution to get the most networking potential out of it. The simple answer is to make yourself valuable to the institution. You must find a way to show that you can and will contribute to the institution's success. Whether through money donations, media exposure, or contacts, you must become valuable to the institution. In business, creating revenue and profits is the sole purpose. For charitable organizations, money is their lifeblood. You will have to find a way to demonstrate how you are going to contribute to the institution's survival, either directly or indirectly. You do not always have to contribute cash. You can be instrumental in getting the institution media coverage. Media coverage for the charity creates exposure, which in turn creates awareness, and that ultimately contributes to the institution's survival.

Now you know what institutions are and that they play a key role in your networking success. We have also discussed the need to make yourself valuable to the institution so that you can leverage the networking opportunities that they provide. By understanding how they work, you can maximize their potential effectiveness. This book has broken the institutions into five distinct types: trade shows, corporations, charities, general institutions, and government. The following sections look at each institution type and describe how to network through them. Each section will be followed by a listing of some of the most important institutions in each institutional type. These listings will provide valuable networking data that will give you a running start at any networking research project.

CHAPTER THREE

Corporations

When it comes to networking, there isn't a bigger gold mine than corporations. Corporations are power because they control the flow of money, and this gives them direct or indirect control over everything from television programming to the success and failure of products. Corporations have one purpose in life: to create stockholder wealth. This is the fundamental purpose guiding all of their decisions. They are not set up to become a good corporate citizen or to do charity work. These things are by-products of the companies' desire to have a positive corporate image. If it did not ultimately mean more revenue to its stockholders, they would not do it.

Corporations today are so important in the networking fold because of their control over the flow of big money. They vote with their dollars, and their vote counts. Professional athletes would not get paid huge salaries without TV exposure. TV exposure would not be available if corporate advertisers weren't pumping money into the system. If the beer manufacturers, soft drink manufacturers, and automakers decided that professional athletes were no longer a good way to sell their products or that there was another less expensive or more effective way to reach their target market, you would quickly see the end of the $25,000,000-a-year pro athlete salary. Corporations have a tremendous amount of pull. When the latest NFL contract was negotiated with the networks, meetings took place with the major corporations who advertised before any of the networks signed the billion-dollar deal.

If your networking target is someone in corporate America, it is clear that the company they work for is your first step. But you can use corporations as a fantastic back door to meeting people in other industries as well. Jell-O is a good route in to meet Bill Cosby. General Mills is a strong entrée to Lance Armstrong because of his Wheaties affiliation. Sara Lee, which owns the Hanes underwear brand is a great networking doorway to Michael Jordan, and the list goes on.

Another key thing to know about corporations is that they are political animals by nature. No one wants to rock the boat. It takes more than talent to end up at the top of the ladder in corporate America. The executives who are great at playing the game of politics rise to the top. It is very true that many corporate CEOs would make great traditional politicians. Corporate America functions like Washington, D.C., in small microcosms.

Another important item to remember about business institutions is that in addition to the marketplace there is a large outside force that has control over their revenue stream: the government. By being able to influence regulatory agencies or being well connected in government, you have a strong foothold to get into business. For example, if you just finished a two-year fellowship at the Federal Communications Commission (FCC) and want a job with Infinity Broadcasting, you have a good chance of getting it because you can be very valuable to them.

One of the things you must be careful about when trying to become valuable to a corporation is the thought that if you buy stock, even in a tremendous amount, you become instantly valuable. Buying in to the company is only useful in getting a foothold. The truth is that unless you run an institution with literally hundreds of millions or even billions of dollars, it is difficult to obtain significant pull. It is not uncommon for an investing institution to own billions of dollars' worth of a company's stock. So, even if you bought in with $500,000 dollars of your own money, you don't instantly create a power position within the company. There is an area on the Yahoo! web site that shows you who are the large shareholders of a corporation. For example, if you go to Yahoo! and click on Stock Quotes, you will be taken to the stock area. Enter the stock symbol of the company you are interested in, for instance, enter KO for Coca-Cola. The next screen will show you the current stock quote for Coke. If you click on Detailed, then Insider, and then Roster, a listing of the major stockholders appears. You will notice that Warren Buffet, the famed investor, owns 200,000,000 shares of Coca-Cola. That means that Mr. Buffet owns about eleven and a half *billion* dollars of Coca-Cola stock. So, if you purchased 10,000 shares of Coca-Cola, it would cost you over $500,000, and you would still be a small fish in a very large pond.

When networking in to a corporation, like all other networking situations, first be very clear about your goal. If you are looking for a job, or want to meet one of the executives, or you want to sell a product or service to the company, you will follow different paths, so preparation is important. Once you have clearly identified your goal, you need to develop a plan for success.

CONNECTING THROUGH CUSTOMERS

There are a number of very strong ways into a corporation. The first is through the company's customers. If you have a connection with a large sporting goods retail chain, you can use that relationship to get to Nike. Likewise, if you have a friend who is an executive at a major supermarket chain, you can ask for an introduction to a food corporation like Nabisco. Even if you don't have contacts, by identifying the corporations' big customers, you can use the knowledge in your conversations as you work your way into the company. Your understanding of their business and their customers will create perceived value, and even better, any understanding of their customers will be perceived valuable because you can actually help the corporation with a better understanding of their sales targets.

Another way in is through business schools. The large corporations tend to control the town in which they are headquartered. They will use the local business school as a human resources pipeline. Getting in with the business school will help you work yourself into the company. Additionally, the top-level executives will give lectures and speeches at the business schools, opening up opportunities for you to meet these key corporate players. Call the business schools and get a list of the upcoming special events and the guest speakers. Many companies have special relationships with business schools, such as Dell and the University of Texas or Citibank and Columbia. If you are trying to make a contact at Citibank, a quick conversation with a dean at Columbia can give you insight into your task, as well as possible introductions. The big five business schools, Wharton School of Business at the University of Pennsylvania, Stanford Business School, Kellogg at Northwestern University, Columbia, and Harvard are a direct path into most corporations. These schools are so well respected that any connection with them will help you network into almost any company.

COMPANY TOWNS

You can also frequent the typical lunch venues in company towns. In Bartlesville, Oklahoma, Phillips Petroleum is omnipresent. You can stop by almost any lunching spot and run into company players. Start up a conversation, and off you go with a direct networking path. The same is true in many company towns. If you ask around, you can usually find the best spots. There is a Japanese restaurant directly across from the Honda headquarters in Torrance, California, that hosts top-tier Honda executives on any given day. In Beverly Hills, California, the entertainment industry deal makers eat at The Grille. The key is to identify the company you are interested in, find their base of operation, and see if you can find their out-of-office lunch spot. It is a terrific way to create a casual networking opportunity.

CHARITIES

Another networking opportunity is through charities. When a corporation spends a large sum of money to support a charity, it is typical for the top executives to attend events put on by the charity. If you want to meet and network with the executives, you can find them at the charity event. To create this opportunity, first call the public relations department at the corporation. Ask for a list of charities that the company supports (many are listed for you in the entries that follow). As you scan the list, look for the ones that your target company seems to have the biggest involvement in. Then call that charity and ask about the events they hold. Attend the bigger events, and you are sure to run into the executives you are looking for. There is an added bonus in that when you meet the executive at the charity event, you immediately have common ground to discuss: the charity. This helps you begin the conversation, as well as giving you instant credibility. You are no longer someone walking off the street trying to get five minutes with a busy executive. You are a guest at a charity event who has a common bond with the executive.

SHAREHOLDERS' MEETINGS

The next networking opportunity is at shareholders' meetings. Every year, each corporation must hold a shareholders' meeting. This gives the public unique access to the very top of the corporation's power team. Most shareholders don't travel to the meeting, but if you do, you can spend some time with decision makers. If you want to discuss a television program with the head of CBS Television, this would be your chance. If you wanted to ask the vice president of marketing at IBM who to talk to in order to package your new software program with new IBM computers, you have the opportunity. The heads of the corporation are all there. Step up and begin networking. It is a rare chance to know exactly when and where the top executives will be.

TRADE SHOWS

Another terrific place to network with corporations is at trade shows. Trade shows are covered in the next section, but it is important to note that at trade shows you can not only find contacts at the major corporations, but you can find the corporations themselves in one place. If you are trying to network into the apparel industry, you can network at Guess in Los Angeles, Ralph Lauren in New York, and Hugo Boss in Chicago. Or you can find all three of them, plus hundreds more, when the apparel industry gets together at the MAGIC trade show held twice a year in Las Vegas.

If you plan on networking directly into the corporation, a good place to start is the corporate communications department. This department is set up specifically to answer questions and get the company's message out. You can find them to be a wealth of information.

A Case Study

The best way to understand how to network through and with corporations is to see an actual example. This case study will demonstrate how the techniques in this book work together to achieve a networking goal.

Not long ago, Elliot ran into a situation that wasn't a huge opportunity or major crisis, but it was an annoyance and was causing a problem for his business. He had sent a package overnight via UPS to a potential customer. The customer was under a tight deadline and needed to see the samples Elliot had rushed to him. When Elliot called the customer the next morning, the package had not arrived. Elliot immediately got on the phone and called UPS, offering up his tracking number. He was told that the last time the box had been seen was on the loading dock on the way out of Texas. The package seemed lost. Elliot pleaded with the UPS tracking people, explaining the severity of the situation. If the package didn't arrive that day, the deal was lost. The UPS representative seemed empathetic yet unmoved to action. He said all he could do was put the missing package in the computer and wait for the system to take its course. This wasn't good enough for Elliot or for his business deal. He spent the next three hours on the phone with various supervisors and supervisors of supervisors, but to no avail. The package would turn up eventually, they were sure, but they couldn't immediately send someone to sort through thousands of packages to find Elliot's.

Elliot decided it was time to put networking into action. At the beginning of this book, the basic road map to successful networking is laid out. Elliot followed the key steps:

Step 1: What do I want? Elliot clearly identified his goal. He needed to get the package to the recipient that very day. He wrote down the goal on paper to help him focus and to help remind himself that he wasn't after apologies or revenge on the trackers who wouldn't help him. He wanted the package delivered that day. Nothing else would matter to the business deal.

Step 2: How do I get there? Elliot next developed a plan. He had to answer the five *W*s: Who do I network with? What do I want from the network? Where do I go to network? When is the best time to network? How do I best network?

Three of the questions were easily answered. Elliot had already identified *what* he wanted from the networking plan. He wanted the package delivered immediately. He knew that *where* he must go to network had to be directly to the company, as there was no time for a more complicated networking plan. *When* was the best time to network was obvious: right now. If Elliot waited or took a path that might take time, the goal would not be met. The final two questions were the critical ones in this situation. He had to identify *who* to network with, and *how* to network. In deciding who to network with, Elliot began by researching UPS. This is the UPS listing in this book:

UPS

CONTACT:
United Parcel Service, Inc.
55 Glenlake Parkway NE
Atlanta, GA 30328

TELEPHONE: (404) 828-6000

WEB: *www.ups.com*

BUSINESS FOCUS: The delivery of documents and packages

COMPANY BACKGROUND: UPS is the world's largest express carrier and package delivery company, delivering more than 12 million packages each day to more than 200 countries. UPS is a supporter of The Great American Book Drive, founded by Chicago Bear Jim Flanigan.

NETWORKING SPECIFICS: UPS likes to sponsor golf tournaments. A trip to your local PGA tour stop will yield strong results.

SHAREHOLDERS' MEETING DATE: May, in Wilmington, Delaware

VIPs AFFILIATED WITH THE COMPANY: James P. Kelly—Chairman of the Board and CEO ▪ Charles L. Schaffer—Senior Vice President and COO ▪ Robert J. Clanin—Senior Vice President, Treasurer, and CFO ▪ Kenneth W. Lacy—Senior Vice President and CIO ▪ Lea N. Soupata—Senior Vice President, Human Resources ▪ William H. Brown III (Partner, Schnader Harrison Segal & Lewis LLP)—Board Member ▪ Ann Livermore (Vice President, Hewlett-Packard)—Board Member ▪ Gary E. MacDougal (Former Chairman of the Board and CEO, Mark Controls Corporation)—Board Member ▪ Kent C. Nelson (Former Chairman of the Board and CEO, UPS)—Board Member ▪ Victor A. Pelson (Senior Advisor, Warburg Dillon Read, LLC)—Board Member ▪ John W. Rogers (Former Chairman of the Board and CEO, UPS)—Board Member ▪ Robert M. Teeter (President, Coldwater Corporation)—Board Member

CHARITIES SUPPORTED: Welfare to Work ▪ School to Work ▪ Orphan Foundation of America ▪ The Great American Book Drive ▪ Big Brothers Big Sisters of America ▪ Junior Achievement ▪ 100 Black Men of America ▪ Points of Light Foundation ▪ United Way of America ▪ Habitat for Humanity ▪ YWCA ▪ YMCA ▪

Police Athletic League ▪ Boys and Girls Clubs of America ▪ Boy Scouts ▪ Special Olympics ▪ Goodwill ▪ American Cancer Society ▪ NAACP ▪ Spelman College ▪ Morehouse College ▪ Clark Atlanta University ▪ National Council of La Raza ▪ National Urban League ▪ Organization of Chinese Americans ▪ U.S. Hispanic Chamber of Commerce ▪ America's Promise—The Alliance for Youth ▪ Partnership for a Drug-Free America

As you can see, the listing provides many valuable pieces of information. It begins with the company name and contact information, giving you telephone numbers and addresses for interaction with the company. The next three fields offer a look at UPS's business, their background, and some possible networking paths. The listing also includes information about the shareholders' meeting. The next section lists the VIPs associated with the company, the board members and executives. Finally, a list of charities is supplied to help with networking activities. For Elliot's task at hand, timing wouldn't allow him to network through a charity or try to attend a shareholders' meeting. He needed immediate action. Elliot decided that he needed to view the situation by the actions that needed to be performed. Someone had to physically go and find his package. He had tried to speak with the tracking office and hadn't had any luck. He needed to network with someone who could then call down to the package processing area and get people moving, fast. He decided that he needed to network with someone with serious pull in the corporate headquarters. If an executive calls from corporate headquarters and tells a local package processing office to find a specific package, you can be sure they will—and quickly. Elliot decided that his networking entry point would be through investor relations. On the UPS listing, Elliot saw that Robert Clanin was senior vice president, treasurer, and CFO. As chief financial officer, Mr. Clanin would have serious clout in the investor relations office. The plan was to obtain a reference from Mr. Clanin to the investor relations office and get the investor office to call the local package processing plant.

Elliot's first call was to Mr. Clanin's office. After getting Mr. Clanin's assistant on the phone, Elliot mentioned that he was interested in speaking with someone at the investor relations office and wanted a referral. The assistant was happy to give Elliot the name of the head of the office, Mr. Fessier. Elliot's next call was to Mr. Fessier, and when he got Mr. Fessier's assistant on the phone, he explained that he was referred by Mr. Clanin's office. It took only minutes for Mr. Clanin's name to get Elliot to Mr. Fessier. Elliot explained his situation and mentioned that as a potential investor in UPS, he was very concerned about the situation. He asked Mr. Fessier to intercede and help find the package. After assurances by the investor relations office that the situation would be corrected, Elliot hung up the phone and waited for UPS to call with an update. An hour later, Elliot received the call that the package had been found and would be delivered within the next two hours to the customer. At the end of the day, the customer got the package, Elliot got the business deal he was looking for, and networking paid off again.

Corporate Resources

What follows are the entries for some of the most important corporate institutions in the world. Each piece of information contained in the listing can help with your networking goals. The information can help you understand the business or locate the key players. The charity listing will help you identify where the corporation donates its money and where its key executives are likely to show up. When you are faced with a networking project, study the listings. They will be invaluable to your research.

Aetna

CONTACT:
Aetna
151 Farmington Avenue
Hartford, CT 06156

TELEPHONE: (806) 273-0123

WEB: *www.aetna.com*

BUSINESS FOCUS: Health and financial services benefits

COMPANY BACKGROUND: Aetna is composed of Aetna U.S. Healthcare, Aetna Financial Services, and Aetna International. Aetna U.S. Healthcare offers health products and insurance, Aetna Financial Services markets retirement, financial planning, and investment products, and Aetna International offers Aetna's services to more than fifteen countries worldwide.

NETWORKING SPECIFICS: All the conventional routes are strong, especially shareholders and charities.

SHAREHOLDERS' MEETING DATE: The last Friday in April at headquarters in Hartford, Connecticut

VIPs AFFILIATED WITH THE COMPANY: William H. Donaldson—Chairman, President, and CEO ▪ Thomas J. McInerney—President, Financial Services ▪ Alan J. Weber—Vice Chairman, Strategy and Finance ▪ Elease E. Wright—Senior Vice President, Corporate Human Resources ▪ Betsy Z. Cohen (Chairman, Jefferson Bank Division of Hudson United Bancorp)—Board Member ▪ Barbara Hackman Franklin (President and CEO, Barbara Franklin Enterprises; Former U.S. Secretary of Commerce)—Board Member ▪ Jeffrey E. Garten (Dean, Yale School of Management)—Board Member ▪ Jerome S. Goodman (Retired Chairman, Travel One)—Board Member ▪ Earl G. Graves (Chairman and CEO, Earl G. Graves, Ltd.)—Board Member ▪ Gerald Greenwald (Retired Chairman and CEO, UAL Corporation)—Board Member ▪ Ellen M. Hancock (President and CEO, Exodus Communications, Inc.)—Board Member ▪ Michael H. Jordan (Retired Chairman and CEO, CBS Corporation)—Board Member ▪ Jack D. Kuehler (Retired Vice Chairman, International Business Machines Corporation)—Board Member ▪ Judith Rodin (President, University of Pennsylvania)—Board Member

CHARITIES SUPPORTED: University of Connecticut ▪ America's Promise—The Alliance for Youth ▪ American Heart Association ▪ Big Brothers Big Sisters of America ▪ Habitat for Humanity ▪ Salvation Army ▪ YMCA ▪ American Red Cross ▪ 100 Black Men of America ▪ National Colorectal Research Alliance ▪ Carnegie Hall ▪ The Metropolitan Museum of Art ▪ United Way ▪ Meals On Wheels

Allen & Co.

CONTACT:
Allen & Co.
711 Fifth Avenue, 9th Floor
New York, NY 10022

TELEPHONE: (212) 832-8000

BUSINESS FOCUS: Venture capital, money management, underwriting

COMPANY BACKGROUND: Allen & Co. is a privately owned banking firm with 200 employees. The company's main focus is on the media and entertainment industry, while working only in venture capital, underwriting, private placements, and money management.

EVENTS: Annual Sun Valley Conference (Held in the summer in Sun Valley, Idaho, this retreat is attended by top leaders in the business industry.)

VIP STAFF: Herbert Allen, Jr.—CEO ▪ Don Keough—Chairman

PAST VIPs ATTENDING THE RETREAT: Michael Eisner (CEO of Walt Disney) ▪ Bill Gates (CEO of Microsoft) ▪ Nobuyuki Idei (CEO of Sony) ▪ Mel Karmazin (CEO of CBS) ▪ Geraldine Laybourne (CEO of Oxygen Media) ▪ John Malone (CEO of Liberty Media) ▪ Thomas Middelhoff (CEO of Bertelsmann's) ▪ Sumner Redstone (CEO of Viacom) ▪ Bob Wright (CEO of NBC) ▪ Jeffrey Katzenberg (DreamWorks SKG) ▪ Michael Ovitz (Artist Management Group) ▪ Warren Buffett ▪ Bob Johnson (Black Entertainment Television) ▪ Rupert Murdoch ▪ Barry Diller ▪ Andy Grove (CEO of Intel Corp.) ▪ Tom Brokaw

CLIENTS: Creative Artists Agency ▪ Walt Disney ▪ Viacom ▪ King World ▪ MediaOne

CHARITY SUPPORTED: The Metropolitan Museum of Art

Allstate

CONTACT:
The Allstate Corporation
2775 Sanders Road
Northbrook, IL 60062-6127

TELEPHONE: (847) 402-5000

WEB: www.allstate.com

BUSINESS FOCUS: Insurance

COMPANY BACKGROUND: Allstate offers life, home, special property, liability, and auto insurance through over 14,000 insurance agents. Allstate has tremendous market share. They cover one out of every eight automobiles and houses in America.

SHAREHOLDERS' MEETING DATE: May, in Chicago, Illinois

VIPs AFFILIATED WITH THE COMPANY: Edward M. Liddy—Chairman, President, and CEO ▪ Robert S. Apatoff—Senior Vice President and CMO ▪ John L. Carl—Senior Vice President and CFO ▪ Joan M. Crockett—Senior Vice President, Human Resources ▪ Frank W. Pollard—Senior Vice President and CIO ▪ Casey J. Sylla—Senior Vice President and CIO ▪ F. Duane Ackerman (Chairman, President, and CEO, BellSouth Corporation)—Board Member ▪ Ronald T. LeMay (President and COO, Sprint Corporation)—Board Member ▪ Warren L. Batts (Retired Chairman and CEO, Tupperware Corporation)—Board Member ▪ H. John Riley, Jr. (Chairman, President, and CEO, Cooper Industries Inc.)—Board Member ▪ James M. Denny (Managing Director, William Blair Capital Partners, LLC)—Board Member ▪ Edward A. Brennan (Retired Chairman, President, and CEO, Sears Roebuck and Co.)—Board Member ▪ Joshua I. Smith (Chairman and CEO, The MAXIMA Corporation)—Board Member ▪ Michael A. Miles (Special Limited Partner, Forstmann, Little & Co.)—Board Member ▪ Judith A. Sprieser (Executive Vice President, Sara Lee Corporation)—Board Member ▪ James G. Andress (CEO, Warner Chilcott PLC)—Board Member ▪ W. James Farrell (Chairman and CEO, Illinois Tool Works Inc.)—Board Member ▪ Mary Alice Taylor (Chairman and CEO, HomeGrocer.com)—Board Member

CHARITIES SUPPORTED: National Civic League ▪ Boys and Girls Club ▪ NAACP ▪ Safe Home America ▪ National Fallen Firefighters Association ▪ American Red Cross ▪ America's Promise—The Alliance for Youth ▪ Easter Seals ▪ MADD ▪ YWCA ▪ Make-A-Wish Foundation

American Express

CONTACT:
American Express Company
World Financial Center
200 Vesey Street
New York, NY 10285

TELEPHONE: (212) 640-2000

WEB: *www.americanexpress.com*

BUSINESS FOCUS: Provides travel, financial, and network services

COMPANY BACKGROUND: American Express was founded in 1850. It provides its customers global travel, financial, and network services. It is also involved in offering its customers financial planning, brokerage services, mutual funds, insurance, and other investment products.

NETWORKING SPECIFICS: In addition to the countless charities and shareholders' meetings, American Express works with Tiger Woods. Their affiliation with professional golf is another way in. Check your local PGA tour stop and see if they are a sponsor.

SHAREHOLDERS' MEETING DATE: April, in New York, New York

VIPs AFFILIATED WITH THE COMPANY: Harvey Golub—Chairman and CEO ▪ Kenneth I. Chenault—President and COO ▪ Ursula F. Fairbairn—Executive Vice President, Human Resources and Quality ▪ Allan Z. Loren—Executive Vice President and CIO ▪ Gary Crittenden—Vice Chairman and CFO ▪ Daniel F. Akerson (Chairman and CEO, Nextlink Communications, Inc.)—Board Member ▪ Anne L. Armstrong (Former U.S. Ambassador; Regent, Texas A&M University System)—Board Member ▪ Edwin L. Artzt (Former Chairman and CEO, The Procter & Gamble Company)—Board Member ▪ William G. Bowen (President, The Andrew W. Mellon Foundation)—Board Member ▪ Robert L. Crandall (Former Chairman and CEO, AMR Corporation and American Airlines)—Board Member ▪ Beverly Sills Greenough (Chairman, Lincoln Center for the Performing Arts)—Board Member ▪ F. Ross Johnson (Chairman and CEO, RJM Group)—Board Member ▪ Vernon E. Jordan, Jr. (Senior Managing Director, Lazard Freres & Co.)—Board Member ▪ Jan Leschly

(Chief Executive, SmithKline Beecham PLC)—Board Member ▪ Drew Lewis (Former Chairman and CEO, Union Pacific Corporation)—Board Member ▪ Richard A. McGinn (Chairman, CEO, and President, Lucent Technologies, Inc.)—Board Member ▪ Frank P. Popoff (Chairman of the Board, The Dow Chemical Company)—Board Member ▪ Hon. Gerald R. Ford (Former President of the United States of America)—Advisor to the Board ▪ Robert L. Genillard (International Investor)—Advisor to the Board ▪ Henry A. Kissinger (Chairman, Kissinger Associates, Inc.; Former Secretary of State of the United States of America)—Advisor to the Board ▪ Tiger Woods—Spokesperson ▪ Jerry Seinfeld—Spokesperson ▪ King Abdullah II (King of Jordan)—Speaker at Global Summit on Peace Through Tourism (Sponsored by American Express)

CHARITIES SUPPORTED: United Way ▪ American Red Cross ▪ Big Brothers Big Sisters of America ▪ Habitat for Humanity ▪ March of Dimes ▪ Meals On Wheels ▪ Junior Achievement ▪ National Urban League ▪ Alzheimer's Disease and Related Disorders Association ▪ American Cancer Society ▪ American Heart Association ▪ Arthur Ashe Institute ▪ Boy Scouts of America ▪ Boys and Girls Clubs of America ▪ Easter Seals ▪ Girls Scouts of America ▪ Goodwill ▪ John F. Kennedy Center for the Performing Arts ▪ Lincoln Center for the Performing Arts ▪ Salvation Army ▪ Soloman R. Guggenheim Foundation ▪ Susan G. Komen Breast Cancer Foundation ▪ United Negro College Fund ▪ YMCA ▪ YWCA ▪ World Wildlife Fund ▪ The Metropolitan Museum of Art ▪ America's Promise—The Alliance for Youth ▪ Muscular Dystrophy Association ▪ Save the Children ▪ Project A.L.S.

American Home Products

CONTACT:

American Home Products Corporation
Five Giralda Farms
Madison, NJ 07940

TELEPHONE: (973) 660-5000

WEB: *www.ahp.com*

BUSINESS FOCUS: Pharmaceuticals, consumer health care, agricultural products

COMPANY BACKGROUND: American Home Products is one of the largest pharmaceutical research companies in the world. Its subsidiaries include Wyeth-Ayerst, Whitehall-Robins, Cyanamid, Fort Dodge Animal Health, and it is a majority owner of Immunex. Some of Whitehalls-Robin's products include Advil, Robitussin, Centrum, and Chap Stick.

NETWORKING SPECIFICS: In addition to the conventional routes in, any connections at top medical schools where AHP supports research would be a strong way in.

SHAREHOLDERS' MEETING DATE: April in Morristown, New Jersey.

VIPs AFFILIATED WITH THE COMPANY: John R. Stafford—Chairman, CEO, and President ▪ Kenneth J. Martin—Senior Vice President and CFO ▪ Bruce Fadem—Vice president and CIO ▪ René R. Lewin—Vice President, Human Resources ▪ Clifford L. Alexander, Jr. (President, Alexander & Associates, Inc.)—Board Member ▪ Frank A. Bennack, Jr. (President and CEO, The Hearst Corporation)—Board Member ▪ John D. Feerick (Dean, Fordham University School of Law)—Board Member ▪ John P. Mascotte (President and CEO, Blue Cross and Blue Shield of Kansas City, Inc.)—Board Member ▪ Ivan G. Seidenberg (Chairman and CEO, Bell Atlantic Corporation)—Board Member ▪ John R. Torell III (Chairman, Torell Management, Inc.)—Board Member

CHARITIES SUPPORTED: National Hemophilia Foundation ▪ Make-A-Wish Foundation ▪ Mary J. Linnen Primary Pulmonary Hypertension Foundation ▪ The Metropolitan Museum of Art ▪ Project HOPE

American Telephone and Telegraph (AT&T)

CONTACT:
AT&T
32 Sixth Avenue
New York, NY 10013

TELEPHONE: (212) 387-5400

WEB: *www.att.com*

BUSINESS FOCUS: Telecommunications

COMPANY BACKGROUND: AT&T is one of the three powerhouses in the telecommunications business. It is the most widely held stock in the United States. They have 90 million customers and over 125,000 employees.

NETWORKING SPECIFICS: The conventional methods of charities and corporate shareholders' events are strong.

SHAREHOLDERS' MEETING DATE: May

VIPs AFFILIATED WITH THE COMPANY: C. Michael Armstrong—Chairman and CEO ▪ Dan Somers—CFO ▪ Jon D. Zeglas—President ▪ Richard Martin—Chairman and Trustee, ATT Foundation ▪ Kenneth T. Derr (Chairman and CEO, Chevron)—Board Member ▪ George Fisher (Chairman and CEO, Eastman Kodak)—Board Member ▪ Donald Fites (Chairman and CEO, Caterpillar)—Board Member ▪ Ralph Larson (Chairman and CEO, Johnson and Johnson)—Board Member

CHARITIES SUPPORTED: Muscular Dystrophy Association ▪ Houston Opera ▪ Seattle Opera ▪ United Way ▪ American Red Cross ▪ Girl Scouts ▪ Ronald McDonald House ▪ Center for Marine Conservation ▪ Harvard University ▪ Duke University ▪ Johns Hopkins University ▪ Public Broadcasting System ▪ American's Promise—The Alliance for Youth ▪ National AIDS Fund ▪ Toys for Tots ▪ United Negro College Fund

AMR

CONTACT:
AMR Corporation
4333 Amon Carter Boulevard
Fort Worth, TX 76155

TELEPHONE: (817) 963-1234

WEB: *www.amrcorp.com*

BUSINESS FOCUS: Air travel

COMPANY BACKGROUND: AMR is the holdings company that owns American and American Eagle Airlines, as well as AMR Investments, which manages American Advantage Funds and AMR Trading Group. They are the nation's second largest air carrier.

NETWORKING SPECIFICS: AMR is extremely involved with the community. Charity events, especially in the Dallas–Fort Worth Metroplex, are the strongest way in.

SHAREHOLDERS' MEETING DATE: Held annually in May in the Dallas–Fort Worth Area

VIPs AFFILIATED WITH THE COMPANY: Donald Carty—Chairman, President, and CEO, AMR and American Airlines ▪ Robert Baker—Vice Chairman ▪ Tom W. Horton—Senior Vice President and CFO ▪ Thomas J.

Kiernan—Senior Vice President, Human Resources, American Airlines ▪ Peter M. Bowler—President, American Eagle ▪ Robert W. Reding—Senior Vice President and COO, American Eagle ▪ David L. Boren (President, the University of Oklahoma)—Board Member ▪ Edward A. Brennan (Retired Chairman, President, and CEO, Sears, Roebuck and Co.)—Board Member ▪ Armondo M. Codina (Chairman and CEO, Codina Group, Inc.)—Board Member ▪ Earl G. Graves (Chairman and CEO, Earl G. Graves Limited; Publisher and CEO, *Black Enterprise* magazine; General Partner, Black Enterprise/Greenwich Street Corporate Growth Partners, LP)—Board Member ▪ Dee J. Kelly (Partner, Kelly, Hart & Hallman, P.C.)—Board Member ▪ Ann D. McLaughlin (Chairman, The Aspen Institute)—Board Member ▪ Charles H. Pistor, Jr. (Retired Vice Chair, Southern Methodist University)—Board Member ▪ Philip J. Purcell (Chairman and CEO, Morgan Stanley Dean Witter & Co.)—Board Member ▪ Joe M. Rodgers (Chairman, The JMR Group)—Board Member ▪ Judith Rodin (President, University of Pennsylvania)—Board Member

CHARITIES SUPPORTED: The Art Institute of Chicago ▪ The Nature Conservancy ▪ National Parks Association ▪ Habitat for Humanity ▪ Lions Club ▪ YMCA ▪ YWCA ▪ Girls Scouts of America ▪ Boy Scouts of America ▪ United Negro College Fund ▪ University of Oklahoma ▪ United Way ▪ American Red Cross ▪ National AIDS Fund ▪ Cystic Fibrosis Foundation ▪ Susan G. Komen Foundation ▪ Muscular Dystrophy Association ▪ March of Dimes ▪ Meals On Wheels ▪ Special Olympics ▪ Humane Society ▪ UNICEF ▪ American Diabetes Association ▪ Juvenile Diabetes Foundation ▪ Make-A-Wish Foundation ▪ Starlight Children's Foundation ▪ Project A.L.S.

ORGANIZATION SPONSORED: Celebrity Golfers Association

Anheuser-Busch

CONTACT:
Anheuser-Busch Companies, Inc.
One Busch Place
St. Louis, MO 63118-1852

TELEPHONE: (314) 577-2000

WEB: *www.anheuser-busch.com*

BUSINESS FOCUS: Beer, adventure park entertainment, and packaging

COMPANY BACKGROUND: Anheuser-Busch Companies, Inc., is a parent corporation that is made up of numerous companies. These companies include Anheuser-Busch, Inc., which brews such beers as Budweiser, Bud Light, Michelob, Tequiza, Ziegen Bock, Red Hook, O'Douls, and Busch; Anheuser-Busch International, Inc., which operates Anheuser-Busch's global interests; Busch Media Group, Inc., which handles the advertising aspect of Anheuser-Busch; Busch Creative Services Corporation, which handles marketing, sales promotions, displays, and exhibits for Anheuser-Busch and other companies such as Ford Motor Company, Deere & Company, Primerica Financial Services, and Emerson Electric; and Busch Entertainment Corporation, which runs four Sea World sites and two Busch Gardens.

NETWORKING SPECIFICS: Anheuser-Busch sponsors numerous sporting events. We have been to several prizefights and hobnobbed with top brass. Everything from NASCAR to baseball is sponsored by Anheuser-Busch, and the bigger the event, the farther up the food chain you are liable to go.

SHAREHOLDERS' MEETING DATE: April

VIPs AFFILIATED WITH THE COMPANY: August A. Busch III—President and Chairman ▪ John E. Jacob—Executive Vice President and CCO ▪ Patrick T. Stokes—Vice President and Group Executive ▪ W. Randolph Baker—Vice President and CFO ▪ Vernon R. Loucks, Jr. (Chairman, InLight, Inc.)—Board Member ▪ William Porter Payne (Chairman, Orchestrate.com)—Board Member ▪ Joyce M. Roché (Former President and COO,

Carson, Inc.)—Board Member ▪ Douglas A. Warner III (President and Chairman, J. P. Morgan & Co., Inc.)—Board Member ▪ Bernard A. Edison (Former President, Edison Brothers Stores, Inc.)—Board Member ▪ Edward E. Whitacre, Jr. (Chairman and CEO, SBC Communications, Inc.)—Board Member ▪ James B. Orthwein (Partner, Precise Capital, L.P.)—Board Member ▪ Charles F. Knight (Chairman and CEO, Emerson Electric Company)—Board Member ▪ Andrew C. Taylor (President and CEO), Enterprise Rent-A-Car Company)—Board Member

CHARITIES SUPPORTED: Muscular Dystrophy Association ▪ Susan G. Komen Race for the Cure ▪ American Red Cross ▪ Salvation Army ▪ Hispanic Scholarship Fund ▪ Points of Light Foundation ▪ March of Dimes ▪ American Cancer Society ▪ Boys and Girls Clubs of America ▪ Children's Miracle Network ▪ Easter Seals ▪ Girl Scouts ▪ Junior Achievement ▪ Optimist International ▪ YWCA ▪ Big Brothers Big Sisters ▪ Boy Scouts ▪ NAACP ▪ Nature Conservancy ▪ YMCA ▪ Cornell University ▪ Juvenile Diabetes Foundation

ORGANIZATIONS SPONSORED: NASCAR ▪ Major League Baseball ▪ NBA/WNBA ▪ PGA/LPGA ▪ Major League Soccer

AOL Time Warner

CONTACT:
AOL Time Warner
22000 AOL Way
Dulles, VA 20166

TELEPHONE: (703) 265-1000

WEB: *www.aoltimewarner.com*

BUSINESS FOCUS: Media

COMPANY BACKGROUND: AOL Time Warner is the world's leading media enterprise. It is broken up into six businesses: interactive services (America Online), cable networks (Turner Entertainment's basic cable networks, Home Box Office, CNN News Group, and more), publishing (*Time* magazine and Time Warner Trade Publishing), music (Warner Music Group), filmed entertainment (Warner Bros. and New Line Cinema), and cable systems (Time Warner Cable).

NETWORKING SPECIFICS: Shareholders and charities are strong ways in.

SHAREHOLDERS' MEETING DATE: Not yet on the web site

VIPs AFFILIATED WITH THE COMPANY: Stephen M. Case—Chairman ▪ Gerald M. Levin—CEO ▪ R. E. "Ted" Turner—Vice Chairman and Senior Advisor ▪ Kenneth J. Novack—Vice Chairman ▪ Richard D. Parsons—Co-Chief Operating Officer ▪ Robert W. Pittman—Co-Chief Operating Officer ▪ J. Michael Kelly—Executive Vice President and CFO ▪ William J. Raduchel—Executive Vice President and CTO ▪ Paul T. Cappuccio—Executive Vice President, General Counsel and Secretary ▪ Ambassador Carla A. Hills (Chairman and CEO, Hills & Company, and former United States Trade Representative)—Board Member ▪ Daniel F. Akerson (Chairman and CEO, XO Communications Inc.)—Board Member ▪ Reuben Mark (Chairman and CEO, Colgate-Palmolive Company)—Board Member ▪ James L. Barksdale (Partner, The Barksdale Group)—Board Member ▪ Michael A. Miles (Former Chairman and CEO, Philip Morris Companies Inc.)—Board Member ▪ Stephen F. Bollenbach (President and CEO, Hilton Hotels Corporation)—Board Member ▪ Franklin D. Raines (Chairman and CEO, Fannie Mae)—Board Member ▪ Frank J. Caufield (Partner, Kleiner Perkins Caufield & Byers)—Board Member ▪ Francis T. Vincent, Jr. (Chairman, Vincent Enterprises)—Board Member ▪ Miles R. Gilburne (Partner, CGLS Fund)—Board Member

CHARITIES SUPPORTED: AARP ▪ American Red Cross ▪ America's Promise ▪ Guggenheim Museum ▪ Literacy Volunteers of America ▪ Metropolitan Museum of Art ▪ Museum of Modern Art ▪ National Urban League ▪ New York City Ballet ▪ New York City Opera ▪ New York Philharmonic ▪ Partnership for a Drug-Free America ▪ Peace Corps ▪ RainbowPUSH Coalition ▪ Rhythm & Blues Foundation ▪ Rock & Roll Hall of Fame Museum ▪ Smithsonian Institution ▪ Special Olympics ▪ STARBRIGHT Foundation ▪ Toys for Tots ▪ United Way

Apple Computers

CONTACT:
Apple Computer, Inc.
1 Infinite Loop
Cupertino, CA 95014

TELEPHONE: (408) 996-1010

WEB: *www.apple.com*

BUSINESS FOCUS: Computers

COMPANY BACKGROUND: Apple Computers is one of the oldest computer companies in America, and their founder, Steve Jobs, is one of the industry's pioneers. After hard times in the past, they are growing once again due mainly to the success of their iMac computers. Their customer base is the most loyal in the industry. Apple has close to 10,000 employees around the world.

NETWORKING SPECIFICS: Apple's Mac Users Conference is the best place to meet the corporate elite. It is held in July, with the location on a rotating basis. Apple also participates in a tremendous number of trade shows. This is another great way in.

SHAREHOLDERS' MEETING: April

VIPs AFFILIATED WITH THE COMPANY: Steven P. Jobs—CEO and Director ▪ Fred D. Anderson—Executive Vice President and CFO ▪ Edgar S. Woolard—Director ▪ Jerome B. York—Director ▪ Millard "Mickey" Drexler (President and CEO, Gap, Inc.)—Board Member ▪ Ed Woolard (Chairman and Former CEO, E. I. DuPont de Nemours and Co.)—Board Member ▪ Jerry York (Vice Chairman, Tracinda; Former CFO, IBM Corporation and Chrysler Corporation)—Board Member ▪ Larry Ellison (Chairman and CEO, Oracle Corporation)—Board Member ▪ Gareth Chang (Executive Chairman, STAR TV)—Board Member ▪ Bill Campbell (Chairman and former CEO, Intuit Corporation)—Board Member

Archer Daniels Midland Company

CONTACT:
ADM
4666 Faries Parkway
Decatur, IL 62525

TELEPHONE: (217) 424-5200

WEB: *www.admworld.com*

BUSINESS FOCUS: Agriculture

COMPANY BACKGROUND: Archer Daniels Midland Company is one of the largest agricultural businesses in the world. It focuses on many different aspects of the food production, storage, and transportation market: corn processing, ethanol, protein specialties, food additives, bioproducts, feed, grain, milling, cocoa, and oilseed processing. Globally ADM employs more than 23,000 people and it owns 274 processing plants. The interesting thing about ADM is that they are one of the most politically powerful corporations in the world. They figured out a long time ago that if you paid for commercials during political shows, thus encouraging the networks to air them, no matter what the ratings were, you would ingratiate yourself with politicians. They have had a lot of sway inside the beltway for many years. "ADM: Supermarket to the world."

NETWORKING SPECIFICS: Any connections in government, especially at the Department of Agriculture, make you valuable and are a great way in.

SHAREHOLDERS' MEETING DATE: October

VIPs AFFILIATED WITH THE COMPANY: G. Allen Andreas—Chairman and CEO ▪ John McNamara—President ▪ Doug Schmalz—Vice President and CFO ▪ Dwayne O. Andreas—Chairman Emeritus ▪ Maureen K. Asura—Corporate Vice President, Human Resources ▪ John R. Block—Board Member ▪ Richard R. Burt—Board Member ▪ Mollie Hale Carter—Board Member ▪ Gaylord O. Coan—Board Member ▪ F. Ross Johnson—Board Member ▪ M. Brian Mulroney—Board Member ▪ Robert S. Strauss—Board Member ▪ John K. Vanier—Board Member ▪ O. Glenn Webb—Board Member ▪ Andrew Young—Board Member ▪ David J. Mimran (CEO, Groupe Mimran)—Board Member

CHARITY SUPPORTED: American Heart Association

Arthur Andersen

CONTACT:
Arthur Andersen United States
33 West Monroe Street
Chicago, IL 60603

TELEPHONE: (312) 580-0033

WEB: *www.arthurandersen.com*

BUSINESS FOCUS: Taxes and finance

COMPANY BACKGROUND: Arthur Andersen employs almost 30,000 individuals and is one of the big five professional services organizations. Arthur Andersen is split into two main divisions: market offerings and industries. Market offerings is split into the following sectors: assurance, business consulting, corporate finance, E-business, human capital, legal services, outsourcing, risk consulting, and tax services. The industries division is split into the following segments: energy and utilities, financial services, government services, healthcare, products, real estate and hospitality, technology, media, and communications.

NETWORKING SPECIFICS: Networking into Arthur Andersen is most effective when you are focused on the division of Arthur Andersen that interests you. Arthur Andersen sponsors many local events in major metropolitan areas, and this is a great way in. Top local brass is accessible at many PGA tour stops as well. Because of their voracious need for personnel, top business schools are strong.

VIPs AFFILIATED WITH THE COMPANY: Jim Wadia—Worldwide Managing Partner ▪ Richard Boulton—Managing Partner, Strategy and Planning ▪ Steve Samek—Area Managing Partner, United States ▪ Michael Bennett—Managing Partner, Assurance and Business Advisory ▪ Alberto Terol—Managing Partner, Tax, Legal, and Business Advisory ▪ Chuck Ketteman—Managing Partner, Business Consulting ▪ Martin Thorp—Managing Partner, Global Corporate Finance ▪ Jim Edwards—Managing Partner, Global 1000, Industry, and North America ▪ Eric Dean—Managing Partner, Chief Information Officer ▪ Matt Gonring—

Managing Partner, Communications and Integrated Marketing • Peter Pesce—Managing Partner, Human Resources and Partner Matters • Clem Eibl—Managing Partner, Chief Financial Officer • Bob Kutsenda—Managing Partner, Global Risk Management • Dan Beckel—Managing Partner, General Counsel

SPONSORING ACTIVITY: The CFO Excellence Awards

CHARITY SUPPORTED: Habitat for Humanity

Bank of America

CONTACT:
Bank of America
100 N. Tryon Street
Charlotte, NC 28255

TELEPHONE: (704) 386-5000

WEB: *www.bankofamerica.com*

BUSINESS FOCUS: Banking

COMPANY BACKGROUND: Bank of America is the largest bank in the U.S. and also operates banks in more than thirty-five other countries. It was created by the merger of the former NationsBank with the Bank of America Corporation. Bank of America financed the Golden Gate Bridge, lent Walt Disney money to open Disneyland, and provides its banking services to McDonald's, Apple Computer, Mobil, Ford, Anheuser-Busch, and many other major companies.

NETWORKING SPECIFICS: The charitable event route is a great way in. Bank of America and Adidas are working together to donate athletic equipment and apparel to Boys and Girls Clubs of America. In the past, Bank of America has also been a supporter of the U.S. Olympic Games.

SHAREHOLDERS' MEETING DATE: April, in Charlotte, North Carolina

VIPs AFFILIATED WITH THE COMPANY: Hugh L. McColl, Jr.—Chairman and CEO • Kenneth D. Lewis—President and COO • James H. Hance, Jr.—Vice Chairman and CFO • W. W. Johnson—Chairman of the Executive Committee • Meredith R. Spangler—Trustee and Board Member • Walter E. Massey (President, Morehouse College)—Board Member • Richard M. Rosenberg (Retired Chairman and CEO, Former BankAmerica Corporation)—Board Member • O. Temple Sloan, Jr. (Chairman and CEO, General Parts Inc.)—Board Member • Ronald Townsend (Communications Consultant)—Board Member • Solomon D. Trujillo (Chairman, President, and CEO, US West)—Board Member • Jackie M. Ward (President and CEO, Computer Generation Incorporated)—Board Member • Virgil R. Williams (Chairman and CEO, Williams Group International Inc.)—Board Member • Shirley Young (Vice President, General Motors Corporation)—Board Member • Charles W. Coker (Chairman, Sonoco Products Company)—Board Member • Timm F. Crull (Retired Chairman and CEO, Nestlé USA, Inc.)—Board Member • Alan T. Dickson (Chairman, Ruddick Corporation)—Board Member • Kathleen Feldstein (President, Economic Studies Inc.)—Board Member • Paul Fulton (Chairman and CEO, Bassett Furniture Industries Inc.)—Board Member • Donald E. Guinn (Chairman Emeritus, Pacific Telesis Group)—Board Member • C. Ray Holman (Chairman and CEO, Mallinckrodt Inc.)—Board Member • Karch Kiraly (Olympic Gold Medalist)—Participant in Bank of America's Boys and Girls Club Project

CHARITIES SUPPORTED: Junior Achievement • Communities in Schools • United Negro College Fund • Native American College Fund • National Hispanic Scholarship Fund • Los Angeles Educational Partnership • United Way • Odyssey of the Mind • Boys and Girls Clubs of America • Easter Seals • Goodwill Industries

■ National AIDS Fund ■ Partnership for a Drug-Free America ■ World Wildlife Fund ■ American Foundation for AIDS Research ■ Project A.L.S.

Barnes & Noble

CONTACT:
Barnes & Noble
122 Fifth Avenue
New York, NY 10011

TELEPHONE: (212) 633-3300

WEB: *www.barnesandnoble.com*

BUSINESS FOCUS: Books and electronic games

COMPANY BACKGROUND: Barnes & Noble, Inc., operates close to 1,000 Barnes & Noble and B. Dalton bookstores and is one of the most powerful booksellers on the web. Barnes and Noble also owns many college bookstores. It owns and operates such electronic gaming stores as Funco, Inc., and Babbages, Inc., making it the largest electronic game retailer in the world.

NETWORKING SPECIFICS: Major trade shows in the book and software industry are a sure bet.

SHAREHOLDERS' MEETING DATE: June

VIPs AFFILIATED WITH THE COMPANY: Leonard Riggio—Chairman and CEO ■ Marie J. Toulantis—Executive Vice President and CFO ■ Thomas A. Tolworthy—President ■ J. Alan Kahn—COO ■ Joseph Giamelli—CIO ■ Mary Ellen Keating—Senior Vice President, Corporate Communication and Public Affairs ■ David K. Cully—President of Distribution ■ Mitchell S. Klipper—President of Development ■ Irene R. Miller (Former Vice Chairman and CFO, Barnes & Noble, Inc.)—Board Member ■ William Dillard II (President and COO, Dillard Department Stores, Inc.)—Board Member ■ Margaret T. Monaco (CAO, KECALP, Inc., a subsidiary of Merrill Lynch & Co., Inc.)—Board Member

CHARITIES SUPPORTED: First Book ■ America's Promise—The Alliance for Youth

BellSouth

CONTACT:
BellSouth Corporation
1155 Peachtree Street NE
Atlanta, GA 30309-3610

TELEPHONE: (404) 249-2000

WEB: *www.bellsouth.com*

BUSINESS FOCUS: Communications, including Internet access, local, long-distance, and wireless telephone service, cable and digital television, and directory advertising in its White and Yellow Pages

COMPANY BACKGROUND: BellSouth Telecommunications provides telephone service to customers in the southeastern U.S., and other services nationally and internationally.

NETWORKING SPECIFICS: The BellSouth Senior Classic on the Senior PGA tour is a best bet.

SHAREHOLDERS' MEETING DATE: April, in Atlanta, Georgia

VIPs AFFILIATED WITH THE COMPANY: F. Duane Ackerman—Chairman and CEO ▪ Fran Dramis—Chief Information and E-commerce Officer ▪ Jere A. Drummond—Vice Chairman ▪ Ronald M. Dykes—CFO ▪ Gary D. Forsee—Chief Staff Officer ▪ Richard Sibbernsen—Vice President, Human Resources ▪ Bill Smith—Executive Vice President, Network Planning and CTO ▪ Phyllis Burke Davis (Retired Senior Vice President, Avon Products, Inc.)—Board Member ▪ Reuben V. Anderson (Partner, Phelps Dunbar)—Board Member ▪ Leo F. Mullin (President and CEO, Delta Air Lines, Inc.)—Board Member ▪ James H. Blanchard (Chairman of the Board and CEO, Synovus Financial Corp.)—Board Member ▪ William S. Stavropoulos (President and CEO, The Dow Chemical Company)—Board Member ▪ C. Dixon Spangler, Jr. (Chairman of the Board, C.D. Spangler Construction Co.)—Board Member ▪ Kathleen F. Feldstein (President, Economic Studies, Inc.)—Board Member ▪ J. Tylee Wilson (Retired Chairman of the Board and CEO, RJR Nabisco, Inc.)—Board Member ▪ Armando M. Codina (Chairman of the Board and CEO, Codina Group Inc.)—Board Member ▪ J. Hyatt Brown (Chairman, President, and CEO, Poe & Brown Inc.)—Board Member ▪ Robin B. Smith (Chairman and CEO, Publishers Clearing House)—Board Member ▪ John G. Medlin, Jr. (Chairman of the Board, Wachovia Corporation)—Board Member

CHARITIES SUPPORTED: Habitat for Humanity ▪ Big Brothers Big Sisters ▪ American Red Cross ▪ Vanderbilt Children's Hospital ▪ Junior Achievement ▪ Girl Scouts of America ▪ Boy Scouts of America ▪ Rotary Foundation ▪ SUCCESS by 6 ▪ BellSouth Foundation ▪ American Foundation for the Blind ▪ Partnership for a Drug-Free America

ORGANIZATION SPONSORED: NASCAR

Boeing

CONTACT:
The Boeing Company
PO Box 3707, M/C 10-06
Seattle, WA 98124-2207

TELEPHONE: (206) 655-1131

WEB: *www.boeing.com*

BUSINESS FOCUS: Aerospace transportation

COMPANY BACKGROUND: Boeing is by far the largest aerospace company in the world, focusing on the production of commercial jetliners, military aircraft, and equipment for NASA, and it has been a leader in the commercial flight industry for over forty years. There are four units into which Boeing is divided: Commercial Airplanes, Space and Communications, Military Aircraft and Missiles, and Shared Services. Boeing employs upwards of 190,000 people globally.

NETWORKING SPECIFICS: Any government or military connections would be a strong way in, since Boeing is so hugely dependent on government contracts. Charitable entities that Boeing supports are a strong way in as well.

SHAREHOLDERS' MEETING DATE: Held in May in Seattle, Washington

VIPs AFFILIATED WITH THE COMPANY: Philip M. Condit—Chairman and CEO ▪ Harry C. Stonecipher—President and COO ▪ Michael M. Sears—Senior Vice President and CFO ▪ John D. Warner—Senior Vice President and CAO ▪ James B. Dagnon—Senior Vice President, People ▪ John H. Biggs (Chairman, President, and CEO, the Teachers Insurance and Annuity Association)—Board Member ▪ John E. Bryson (Chairman and CEO, Edison International Committees)—Board Member ▪ Paul E. Gray (President Emeritus, Massachusetts Institute of Technology)—Board Member ▪ Lewis E. Platt (Former Chairman and CEO, Hewlett-Packard Company)—Board Member

Bristol-Myers Squibb

CONTACT:

Bristol-Myers Squibb Company
345 Park Avenue
New York, NY 10154-0037

TELEPHONE: (212) 546-4000

WEB: *www.bms.com*

BUSINESS FOCUS: Produces and distributes pharmaceuticals, consumer medicines, nutritionals, medical devices, and beauty care products

COMPANY BACKGROUND: Bristol-Myers Squibb makes the popular brands Clairol, Excedrin, Bufferin, Enfamil, Matrix, and Aussie Hair Care. In addition, Bristol-Myers Squibb makes many other medicines to fight everything from headaches and minor infections to AIDS and cancer. Bristol-Myers Squibb's Pharmaceutical Research Institute researches and develops new drugs.

NETWORKING SPECIFICS: Bristol-Myers Squibb is extremely involved in developing medicines for and supporting the fight against cancer, AIDS, and cardiovascular disease. One way to network into Bristol-Myers Squibb is through the health charities they donate to, including the American Cancer Society and the Pediatric AIDS Foundation. Medical schools are another way in.

SHAREHOLDERS' MEETING DATE: May

VIPs AFFILIATED WITH THE COMPANY: Charles A. Heimbold, Jr.—Chairman and CEO ▪ Kenneth E. Weg—Vice Chairman ▪ Peter R. Dolan—President ▪ Peter S. Ringrose, Ph.D.—Chief Scientific Officer and President, Pharmaceutical Research Institute ▪ Charles G. Tharp—Senior Vice President, Human Resources ▪ Michael F. Mee—Executive Vice President and CFO ▪ Robert E. Allen (Retired Chairman and CEO, AT&T Corporation)—Board Member ▪ Lewis B. Campbell (Chairman and CEO, Textron Inc.)—Board Member ▪ Vance D. Coffman (Chairman and CEO, Lockheed Martin Corporation)—Board Member ▪ Ellen V. Futter (President, American Museum of Natural History)—Board Member ▪ Louis V. Gerstner, Jr. (Chairman and CEO, IBM Corporation)—Board Member ▪ Laurie H. Glimcher, M.D. (Professor of Medicine and Immunology, Harvard Medical School and Harvard School of Public Health)—Board Member ▪ Leif Johansson (President and CEO, AB Volvo)—Board Member ▪ James D. Robinson III (Chairman and CEO, RRE Investors)—Board Member ▪ Louis W. Sullivan, M.D. (President, Morehouse School of Medicine)—Board Member ▪ Lance Armstrong (1999 Tour de France Winner)—Featured in Bristol-Myers Squibb Advertisements

CHARITIES SUPPORTED: Habitat for Humanity ▪ YMCA ▪ National Urban League ▪ Nature Conservancy ▪ American Red Cross ▪ Boys and Girls Clubs of America ▪ Girl Scout Council ▪ Make-A-Wish Foundation ▪ Partnership for a Drug-Free America ▪ Ronald McDonald House ▪ Salvation Army ▪ United Way ▪ American Museum of Natural History ▪ Carnegie Hall ▪ Guggenheim Museum ▪ Museum of Modern Art ▪ Lincoln Center for the Performing Arts ▪ Kennedy Center for the Performing Arts ▪ American Indian College Fund ▪ National Merit Scholarships ▪ United Negro College Fund ▪ American Cancer Society ▪ American Diabetes Association ▪ Breast Cancer Research Foundation, Inc. ▪ Cystic Fibrosis Foundation ▪ Operation Smile ▪ Elizabeth Glaser Pediatric AIDS Foundation ▪ Project HOPE ▪ World Wildlife Fund ▪ The Metropolitan Museum of Art ▪ Breast Cancer Fund ▪ Susan G. Komen Foundation

Chevron Corporation

CONTACT:
Chevron Corporation
575 Market Street
San Francisco, CA 94105

TELEPHONE: (415) 894-7700

WEB: *www.chevron.com*

BUSINESS FOCUS: Petroleum

COMPANY BACKGROUND: Chevron explores, produces, refines, markets, and transports petroleum, with operations in more than ninety countries. In the U.S., Chevron is the third-largest producer of natural gas. Chevron's chemical manufacturing and sales operate in a joint venture with Phillips. In addition, Chevron shares strong ties with both Stanford University and the University of California at Berkeley.

NETWORKING SPECIFICS: Chevron is involved in many local charities around San Francisco. Becoming involved with these charities, such as the AIDS Walk, would be a great way in. Also any connections at UC Berkeley or Stanford would be strong.

SHAREHOLDERS' MEETING DATE: April, in San Ramon, California

VIPs AFFILIATED WITH THE COMPANY: David J. O'Reilly—Chairman of the Board and CEO ▪ Richard H. Matzke—Vice Chairman ▪ John Watson—CFO ▪ Gregory Matiuk—Vice President, Human Resources and Quality ▪ Samuel H. Armacost (Managing Director, Weiss, Peck, & Greer LLC)—Board Member ▪ Sam Ginn (Chairman of the Board and CEO, VodaFone AirTouch PLC)—Board Member ▪ Carla A. Hills (Chairman and CEO, Hills & Company International Consultants)—Board Member ▪ J. Bennett Johnston (CEO, Johnston & Associates)—Board Member ▪ Charles M. Piggott (Chairman Emeritus and Director, PACCAR Inc.)—Board Member ▪ Condoleezza Rice (Provost and Vice President, Stanford University)—Board Member ▪ Frank A. Shrontz (Former President and CEO, The Boeing Company)—Board Member ▪ Chang-Lin Tien (Former Chancellor, University of California, Berkeley)—Board Member ▪ John A. Young (Vice Chairman of the Board, Novell Inc.)—Board Member

CHARITIES SUPPORTED: United Way ▪ Susan G. Komen Race for the Cure ▪ AIDS Walk ▪ Yosemite National Park ▪ National Science Foundation ▪ World Wildlife Fund ▪ Special Olympics ▪ American Red Cross ▪ Junior Achievement ▪ 4-H Foundation ▪ Boy Scouts of America ▪ Boys and Girls Clubs ▪ Court Appointed Special Advocates ▪ Girl Scouts of America ▪ Toys for Tots ▪ YMCA ▪ Nature Conservancy ▪ George Bush Presidential Library Foundation ▪ Kennedy Center for the Performing Arts ▪ United Negro College Fund ▪ American Heart Association ▪ Make-A-Wish Foundation ▪ National AIDS Fund ▪ Christmas in April ▪ University of California at Berkeley ▪ Stanford University ▪ The Metropolitan Museum of Art ▪ Partnership for a Drug-Free America ▪ Project HOPE

Cisco Systems, Inc.

CONTACT:
Cisco Systems, Inc.
170 West Tasman Drive
San Jose, CA 95134

TELEPHONE: (408) 526-7208
(800) 553-NETS

WEB: *www.cisco.com*

BUSINESS FOCUS: Internet technology

COMPANY BACKGROUND: Cisco is a great company, and they have the market cap and P/E to prove it. Cisco Systems is the largest Internet networking company in the world. It employs over 20,000 people across fifty-five countries. Cisco is used not only by companies around the globe but also by universities, government agencies, and utilities.

NETWORKING SPECIFICS: Cisco participates in many high-tech trade shows and is active in the community. The charities route is one of the best ways in the door.

SHAREHOLDERS' MEETING DATE: November in Santa Clara, California

VIPs AFFILIATED WITH THE COMPANY: John T. Chambers—President and CEO ▪ John P. Morgridge—Chairman ▪ Larry R. Carter—Senior Vice President and CFO ▪ Judith Estrin—Senior Vice President and CTO ▪ Mary A. Cirillo (CEO, Global Institutional Services; Divisional Board Member, Global Technology and Services Deutsche Bank)—Board Member ▪ James C. Morgan (Chairman and CEO, Applied Materials, Inc.)—Board Member ▪ Carol A. Bartz (Chairman and CEO, Autodesk, Inc.)—Board Member ▪ Robert L. Puette (President and CEO, Centigram Communications Corp.)—Board Member ▪ Arun Sarin (CEO, USA/Asia Pacific Region of Vodafone AirTouch, Plc)—Board Member ▪ Masayoshi Son (President and CEO, SOFTBANK Corp.)—Board Member ▪ Steven M. West (President and CEO, Entera, Inc.)—Board Member ▪ Bret Saxon—Shareholder and Options Holder ▪ Elliot Goldman—Shareholder and Options Holder

CHARITIES SUPPORTED: Food Bank in Raleigh, North Carolina ▪ Project Bread in Chelmsford, Massachusetts ▪ Second Harvest in San Jose, California ▪ Habitat for Humanity International ▪ International Red Cross ▪ YMCA ▪ YWCA ▪ Goodwill ▪ Ronald McDonald House ▪ Girl Scouts ▪ Big Brothers Big Sisters of America ▪ Boys and Girls Clubs of America ▪ Junior Achievement ▪ Salvation Army ▪ Meals On Wheels ▪ America's Promise–The Alliance for Youth

Citigroup

CONTACT:
Citigroup Inc.
153 East 53rd Street
New York, NY 10043

TELEPHONE: (212) 559-1000

WEB: *www.citigroup.com*

BUSINESS FOCUS: A diversified holdings company whose businesses offer an array of financial services

COMPANY BACKGROUND: Citigroup was formed from a merger between Travelers Group and Citicorp. Its subsidiaries include Citibank, Travelers Property and Casualty Corp., Travelers Life and Annuity, Saloman Smith Barney, Primerica Financial Services, CitiFinancial, Global Corporate and Investment Banking, and SSB Citi Asset Management Group. It provides financial services to corporate and individual customers in more than 100 countries.

NETWORKING SPECIFICS: Shareholders and charities are strong routes in.

SHAREHOLDERS' MEETING DATE: April, in New York, New York

VIPs AFFILIATED WITH THE COMPANY: Sanford I. Weill—Chairman and CEO ▪ Robert E. Rubin—Director, Member of the Office of the Chairman; and Chairman, Executive Committee ▪ Todd Thomson—CFO ▪ William R. Rhodes—Vice Chairman and Senior International Officer ▪ C. Michael Armstrong (Chairman and CEO, AT&T Corp.)—Board Member ▪ Alain J. P. Belda (President and CEO, Alcoa Inc.)—Board Member ▪ Kenneth J. Bialkin (Partner, Skadden, Arps, Slate, Meagher & Flom LLP)—Board Member ▪ Kenneth T. Derr (Retired Chairman of the Board, Chevron Corporation)—Board Member ▪ John M. Deutch (Institute Professor, Massachusetts Institute of Technology)—Board Member ▪ Ann Dibble Jordan (Consultant)—Board Member ▪ Reuben Mark (Chairman and CEO, Colgate-Palmolive Company)—Board Member ▪ Michael T. Masin (President and Vice Chairman, Verizon Communications)—Board Member ▪ Dudley C. Mecum (Managing Director, Capricorn Holdings, LLC)—Board Member ▪ Richard D. Parsons (President, Time Warner Inc.)—Board Member ▪ Andrall E. Pearson (Chairman and CEO, Tricon Global Restaurants, Inc.)—Board Member ▪ Franklin A. Thomas (Former President, The Ford Foundation)—Board Member ▪ Edgar S. Woolard, Jr. (Former Chairman and CEO, E. I. du Pont de Nemours and Company)—Board Member ▪ Arthur Zankel (General Partner, Zankel Capital Advisors, LLC)—Board Member ▪ Hon. Gerald R. Ford (Former President, United States)—Honorary Director

CHARITIES SUPPORTED: Habitat for Humanity ▪ Christmas in April ▪ Junior Achievement ▪ YWCA ▪ YMCA ▪ Girl Scout Council ▪ Boy Scouts of America ▪ I Have a Dream Foundation ▪ Police Athletic League ▪ Boys and Girls Clubs of America ▪ Library of Congress ▪ United Way ▪ Museum of Modern Art ▪ Solomon R. Guggenheim Foundation ▪ Lincoln Center for the Performing Arts ▪ John F. Kennedy Center for the Performing Arts ▪ American Red Cross ▪ Massachusetts Institute of Technology ▪ Nature Conservancy ▪ World Wildlife Fund ▪ Salvation Army ▪ The Metropolitan Museum of Art ▪ The Smithsonian Institution ▪ America's Promise—The Alliance for Youth ▪ The Hunger Project ▪ MADD ▪ Partnership for a Drug-Free America ▪ Save the Children ▪ Project A.L.S.

Coca-Cola

CONTACT:
Coca-Cola
1 Coca Cola Plaza
Atlanta, GA 30313

TELEPHONE: (404) 676-2121

WEB: *www.cocacola.com*

BUSINESS FOCUS: Beverage sales

COMPANY BACKGROUND: Coca-Cola is a member of the Dow 30, a group of large, blue-chip companies listed on the New York Stock Exchange that are selected to reflect the health of the U.S. economy. They are one of the most admired companies in America. Their goal is to sell every person in the world a beverage every day, every time they drink (modest goal). Coca-Cola is also the most well-recognized brand in the world.

NETWORKING SPECIFICS: In addition to the charity/shareholders stand-by methods, Coke is heavily involved in the sponsorship of sports. At the major events around the United States it is not unusual to find some of Coke's top brass. Coke is also heavily involved in the Atlanta community and civic activities. The opportunities to network in Atlanta are unlimited.

SHAREHOLDERS' MEETING DATE: April

VIPs AFFILIATED WITH THE COMPANY: M. Douglas Ivester—Chairman and CEO ▪ William Casey—Senior Vice President ▪ Timmothy Haas—Senior Vice President ▪ James Chestnut—CFO ▪ Gary Fayard—Contoller ▪ Herb Allen (Investment Banker)—Board Member ▪ Ron Allen (Former Chairman and CEO, Delta Air Lines)—Board Member ▪ Cathleen Black (President, Hearst Magazine)—Board Member ▪ Warren Buffett (World's Greatest Investor)—Board Member ▪ Donald McHenry (Georgetown University)—Board Member

- Sam Nunn (Former U.S. Senator)—Board Member ▪ James Williams (Chairman and CEO, Sun Trust Bank)—Board Member

CHARITIES SUPPORTED: United Way ▪ American Red Cross ▪ Boy Scouts of America ▪ The Metropolitan Museum of Art ▪ America's Promise—The Alliance for Youth ▪ Boys and Girls Clubs of America ▪ Ronald McDonald House ▪ World Wildlife Fund ▪ Juvenile Diabetes Foundation

ORGANIZATION SPONSORED: NASCAR

Colgate-Palmolive Company

CONTACT:
Colgate-Palmolive Company
300 Park Avenue
New York, NY 10022-7499

TELEPHONE: (212) 310-2000

WEB: *www.colgate.com*

BUSINESS FOCUS: Consumer products

COMPANY BACKGROUND: Colgate-Palmolive makes a wide variety of household products. Its primary division is Oral Care, and its Colgate brand toothpaste is the number one brand worldwide. Colgate-Palmolive also makes Softsoap, Mennen, and Palmolive personal care products; Ajax cleaner; Fab laundry detergent; and Hills Prescription Diet and Science Diet pet foods.

NETWORKING SPECIFICS: The traditional routes in work well.

SHAREHOLDERS' MEETING DATE: May, in New York City

VIPs AFFILIATED WITH THE COMPANY: Reuben Mark—Chairman of the Board and CEO ▪ William S. Shanahan—President ▪ Lois D. Juliber—COO ▪ Javier G. Teruel—Chief Growth Officer ▪ Stephen C. Patrick—CFO ▪ John T. Reid—CTO ▪ Jack Haber-Chief Web Officer ▪ Robert J. Joy—VP, Global Human Resources ▪ Jill K. Conway (Visiting Scholar, Program in Science, Technology, and Society, Massachusetts Institute of Technology)—Board Member ▪ Ronald E. Ferguson (Chairman and CEO, General Re Corporation)—Board Member ▪ Ellen M. Hancock (President and CEO, Exodus Communications, Inc.)—Board Member ▪ David W. Johnson (Chairman Emeritus, Campbell Soup Company)—Board Member ▪ John P. Kendall (Officer, Faneuil Hall Associates)—Board Member ▪ Richard J. Kogan (Chairman and CEO, Schering-Plough)—Board Member ▪ Howard B. Wentz, Jr. (Chairman, Tambrands, Inc.)—Board Member

CHARITIES SUPPORTED: The Metropolitan Museum of Art ▪ America's Promise—The Alliance for Youth ▪ Boy Scouts of America ▪ Girl Scouts of the U.S.A. ▪ Boys and Girls Clubs of America ▪ Girls Incorporated ▪ Camp Fire Boys and Girls ▪ National 4-H Council ▪ Partnership for a Drug-Free America ▪ Starlight Children's Foundation

EVENT SPONSORED: Colgate Women's Games

Compaq Computer

CONTACT:
Compaq Computer Corporation
20555 State Highway 249
Houston, TX 77070-2698

TELEPHONE: (281) 370-0670

BUSINESS FOCUS: Computers, computer accessories, and computer services

COMPANY BACKGROUND: Compaq is one of the largest computing systems suppliers in the world, selling products in over 200 countries. It is currently involved in a three-way agreement with Radio Shack and Microsoft to make Internet access easier for its customers. Also, Compaq is joining with CMGI, Novell, and Sun to form CMGion, a company that will work to further develop and enhance the Internet.

NETWORKING SPECIFICS: Trade shows and their sponsorship of Formula 1 Racing are ways in.

SHAREHOLDERS' MEETING DATE: April in Houston, Texas

VIPs AFFILIATED WITH THE COMPANY: Michael D. Capellas—President and CEO ▪ Benjamin N. Rosen—Chairman of the Board ▪ Jesse J. Greene, Jr.—CFO ▪ Yvonne R. Jackson—Senior Vice President, Human Resources, Organization and Environment ▪ Robert V. Napier—Senior Vice President, Information Management, and CIO ▪ Lawrence T. Babbio, Jr. (President and COO, Bell Atlantic Corporation)—Board Member ▪ George H. Heilmeier (Chairman Emeritus, Telcordia Technologies)—Board Member ▪ Peter N. Larson (Chairman and Chief Executive, Brunswick Corporation)—Board Member ▪ Kenneth L. Lay (Chairman of the Board and CEO, Enron Corp.)—Board Member ▪ Thomas J. Perkins (General Partner, Kleiner Perkins Caufield and Byers)—Board Member ▪ Dr. Judith L. Craven (Former President, United Way of the Texas Gulf Coast)—Board Member ▪ Kenneth Roman (Former Chairman and CEO, The Ogilvy Group)—Board Member ▪ Frank P. Doyle (Former Executive Vice President, General Electric Company)—Board Member ▪ Lucille S. Salhany (Copresident and CEO, Life FX, Inc.)—Board Member ▪ Robert Ted Enloe III (Managing General Partner, Balquita Partners Ltd.)—Board Member ▪ George Bush—Compaq Computer User

CHARITIES SUPPORTED: Boys and Girls Club of America ▪ Bush Presidential Library ▪ Texas A&M's Bush School of Government and Public Service ▪ City Year ▪ National Center for Missing and Exploited Children ▪ Teaching with Technology Grant Program ▪ TECH CORPS ▪ University of Texas–Houston Health Science Center ▪ End Hunger Network ▪ American Red Cross ▪ I CAN Foundation ▪ Second Harvest Food Bank ▪ The Art Institute of Chicago ▪ American Diabetes Association ▪ Starlight Children's Foundation

Adolph Coors Company

CONTACT:
Coors Brewing Company
PO Box 4030
Golden, CO 80401-0030

TELEPHONE: (303) 279-6565

WEB: www.coors.com

BUSINESS FOCUS: Brewing alcoholic beverages

COMPANY BACKGROUND: Adolph Coors Company is a holding company whose main business is the Coors Brewing Company, the U.S.'s third largest brewer. The Coors company made the first aluminum beverage can and is still the largest manufacturer of aluminum cans in the U.S. Coors products, such as Coors, Zima, Keystone, Blue Moon, and Killian's, are available throughout the U.S. and in more than thirty other countries.

NETWORKING SPECIFICS: Coors is a huge sponsor of major sporting events. Colorado Rockies playoff games are a great place to meet top execs. In addition, use the charities route.

SHAREHOLDERS' MEETING DATE: May, in Golden, Colorado

VIPs AFFILIATED WITH THE COMPANY: William K. Coors—Chairman of the Board ▪ Joseph Coors—Vice Chairman ▪ Peter H. Coors—Vice President, Adolph Coors; Vice Chairman and CEO, Coors Brewing ▪ W. Leo Kiely III—Vice President, Adolph Coors; President and COO, Coors Brewing ▪ Timothy V. Wolf—Senior Vice President and CFO ▪ Luis G. Nogales (President, Nogales Partners)—Board Member ▪ Pamela H. Patsley (Executive Vice President, First Data Corporation)—Board Member ▪ Wayne R. Sanders (Chairman and CEO, Kimberly-Clark Corporation)—Board Member ▪ Dr. Albert C. Yates (President, Colorado State University)—Board Member

CHARITIES SUPPORTED: National 4-H Council ▪ United Way ▪ Boys and Girls Clubs ▪ United Negro College Fund ▪ Alcohol, Drunk Driving and You ▪ American Council on Alcoholism ▪ An Apple A Day ▪ BACCHUS and GAMMA Peer Education Network ▪ Buckle Up America ▪ Courtrooms to Classrooms ▪ Grow Girl! ▪ Inter-Association Task Force ▪ Mile High Council on Alcoholism and Drug Abuse ▪ National Association of Service and Conservation Corps ▪ National Coalition Against Domestic Violence ▪ National Collegiate Alcohol Awareness Week ▪ National Commission Against Drunk Driving ▪ National Safe Boating Council ▪ Network of Employers for Traffic Safety ▪ Points of Light Foundation ▪ Youth Service America

ORGANIZATION SPONSORED: Indy Racing League

Cutter & Buck, Inc.

CONTACT:
Cutter & Buck, Inc.
2701 First Avenue, Suite 500
Seattle, WA 98121

TELEPHONE: (206) 622-4191

WEB: *www.cutterbuck.com*

BUSINESS FOCUS: Sports apparel

COMPANY BACKGROUND: Cutter & Buck manufacturers and sells the finest quality golf apparel. This quality is unmatched in the business. The company has merchandising booths at the following tournaments: the U.S. Open, the PGA Championship, the British Open, the Ryder Cup, and the President's Cup.

NETWORKING SPECIFICS: Cutter & Buck is one of the main players in the golf apparel industry. Any PGA tour stop will yield contacts.

VIPs AFFILIATED WITH THE COMPANY: Harvey Jones—Chairman and CEO ▪ Martin Marks—President, COO, Treasurer, and Secretary ▪ Stephen Lowber—Vice President and CFO ▪ Philip Davis—Vice President of Operations

EVENTS INVOLVED IN: Every major gold event, including the U.S. Open, the PGA Championship, and the British Open

DaimlerChrysler

CONTACT:
DaimlerChrysler
1000 Chrysler Drive
Auburn Hills, MI 48326-2766

TELEPHONE: (248) 576-5741

BUSINESS FOCUS: Automotive products and services

COMPANY BACKGROUND: DaimlerChrysler produces such automobile lines as Mercedes-Benz, Dodge, Chrysler, and Jeep.

NETWORKING SPECIFICS: We recommended the North American International Auto Show.

SHAREHOLDERS' MEETING DATE: April

VIPs AFFILIATED WITH THE COMPANY: Robert J. Eaton—Chairman ▪ Thomas C. Gale—Executive Vice President ▪ Gunther Fleig—Human Resources Division ▪ G. Richard Thoman (President and CEO, Xerox Corporation)—Board Member ▪ Robert E. Allen (Former Chairman and CEO, AT&T Corporation)—Board Member ▪ Peter A. Magowan (President and Managing General Partner, the San Francisco Giants)—Board Member ▪ Stephen P. Yokich (President of U.A.W., International Union of United Automobile, Aerospace, and Agricultural Implement Workers of America)—Board Member

CHARITIES SUPPORTED: STEP 21 ▪ Stop Red Light Running Campaign ▪ America's Promise–The Alliance for Youth ▪ MADD ▪ Partnership for a Drug-Free America ▪ World Wildlife Fund ▪ United Negro College Fund

Dell Computer

CONTACT:
Dell Computer Corporation
One Dell Way
Round Rock, TX 78682

TELEPHONE: (512) 338-4400

WEB: *www.dell.com*

BUSINESS FOCUS: Computers

COMPANY BACKGROUND: Dell is the world's leader in the direct computer systems industry. Dell is made up of a workforce of approximately 35,800 employees in thirty-four countries around the world.

NETWORKING SPECIFICS: The University of Texas is the best way into Dell. Michael Dell went to the University of Texas and is a great supporter of its business school. Dell relies heavily on the university for human resources.

SHAREHOLDERS' MEETING DATE: July in Austin, Texas

VIPs AFFILIATED WITH THE COMPANY: Michael S. Dell—CEO and Chairman ▪ Kevin B. Rollins—Vice Chairman ▪ James T. Vanderslice—Vice Chairman ▪ Paul D. McKinnon—Senior Vice President of Human Relations ▪ Randall D. Mott—Senior Vice President and CIO ▪ James M. Schneider—Senior Vice President and CFO ▪ Donald J. Carty (President, Chairman, and CEO, AMR Corporation and American Airlines, Inc.)—Board Member ▪ Paul O. Hirschbiel (President, Eden Capital)—Board Member ▪ Michael H. Jordan (Former Chairman and CEO, CBS Corporation)—Board Member ▪ Claudine B. Malone (President, Financial & Management Consulting, Inc.)—Board Member ▪ Alex J. Mandl (Chairman and CEO, Teligent, Inc.)—Board Member ▪ Michael A. Miles (Former Chairman and CEO, Philip Morris Companies, Inc.)—Board Member ▪ Mary Alice Taylor (Corporate Executive Vice President, Global Operations and Technology for Citigroup, Inc.)—Board Member

CHARITIES SUPPORTED: United Way ▪ Juvenile Diabetes Foundation ▪ March of Dimes WalkAmerica ▪ Junior Achievement ▪ Habitat for Humanity ▪ American Cancer Society ▪ Special Olympics ▪ Big Brothers Big Sisters of America ▪ Earth Share ▪ Austin Museum of Art ▪ The Metropolitan Museum of Art

Deloitte & Touche

CONTACT:
Deloitte & Touche
1633 Broadway
New York, NY 10019-6754

TELEPHONE: (212) 489-1600 (National Office)
(800) 378-8969 (Human Resources)

WEB: *www.us.deloitte.com*

BUSINESS FOCUS: Accounting and consulting

COMPANY BACKGROUND: Deloitte & Touche is one of the big five accounting firms in the U.S. It employs over 30,000 people in over 100 cities across America. *Fortune* magazine has recognized Deloitte & Touche as one of the "100 Best Companies to Work for in America" for the past three years.

NETWORKING SPECIFICS: With the CEO as Chairman of the United Way, it is clear that United Way is a strong way in to Deloitte & Touche.

SHAREHOLDERS' MEETING DATE: December

VIPs AFFILIATED WITH THE COMPANY: J. Michael Cook—Chairman and CEO, Deloitte & Touche; Chairman, United Way ▪ Edward A. Kangas—Head of Deloitte Touche Tohmatsu ▪ James E. Copeland, Jr.—Managing Partner

CORPORATE CLIENTS: The Blackstone Group ▪ Microsoft ▪ General Motors ▪ Nissan Motors USA ▪ Allstate ▪ Hearst Corporation ▪ Kaiser Permanente ▪ Metropolitan Life ▪ Columbia University ▪ Princeton University ▪ Dillard Department Stores ▪ Lowe's ▪ Nieman Marcus ▪ Sears ▪ Charles Schwab ▪ Merrill Lynch ▪ Honeywell ▪ DaimlerChrysler ▪ Boeing ▪ Merrill Lynch Capital Partners ▪ Dow Chemical ▪ New York Times ▪ Farmers Insurance Group ▪ Bridgestone/Firestone ▪ Pennsylvania State University ▪ Albertson's ▪ The Gap ▪ Mitsubishi ▪ Nordstrom ▪ Timberland ▪ Dean Witter, Discover & Co. ▪ UPS

CHARITIES SUPPORTED: The United Way ▪ The Art Institute of Chicago ▪ American Heart Association ▪ Juvenile Diabetes Foundation

Eastman Kodak Company

CONTACT:
Eastman Kodak Company
343 State Street
Rochester, NY 14650

TELEPHONE: (716) 724-4000

WEB: *www.kodak.com*

BUSINESS FOCUS: Imaging products

COMPANY BACKGROUND: The Eastman Kodak Company is broken into four main subdivisions: the Consumer Imaging subdivision focuses on amateur photography; the Kodak Professional subdivision focuses on meeting the needs of professional photofinishers, photographers, commercial printers, and publishers; the Health Imaging subdivision focuses on supplying the health care industry with imaging products; the other Imaging subdivision focuses on serving customers in motion picture and television, business, and government. Kodak is a major player in the motion picture industry. Kodak employs approximately 80,650 employees, and its goods are sold in 150 countries around the world.

NETWORKING SPECIFICS: The routes of charities and corporate events held in Rochester are strong.

SHAREHODLERS' MEETING DATE: May in Rochester, New York

VIPs AFFILIATED WITH THE COMPANY: George Fisher—Chairman and CEO ▪ Daniel Carp—President and COO ▪ Robert Brust—Executive Vice President and CFO ▪ Carl Kohrt—Executive Vice President and CTO ▪ Michael P. Morley—Senior Vice President and Director, Human Resources ▪ John J. Chiazza—Vice President and CIO ▪ Carl E. Gustin, Jr.—Senior Vice President and CMO ▪ Charles P. Goslee—Vice President and CQO ▪ Richard S. Morabito—Vice President and CPO ▪ Richard S. Braddock (Chairman and CEO, Priceline.com)—Board Member ▪ Alice F. Emerson (Senior Advisor, Andrew W. Mellon Foundation)—Board Member ▪ Paul E. Gray (President Emeritus and Professor, Massachusetts Institute of Technology)—Board Member ▪ Durk I. Jager (Chairman, President, and CEO, The Procter & Gamble Company)—Board Member ▪ Debra L. Lee (President and COO, BET Holdings, Inc.)—Board Member ▪ Paul H. O'Neill (Chairman, Aluminum Company of America)—Board Member ▪ John J. Phelan, Jr. (Retired Chairman and CEO, New York Stock Exchange, Inc.)—Board Member ▪ Laura D'Andrea Tyson (Dean, Walter A. Haas School of Business, University of California, Berkeley)—Board Member ▪ Richard A. Zimmerman (Retired Chairman & CEO, Hershey Foods Corporation)—Board Member

CHARITIES SUPPORTED: American Health Foundation ▪ Center for Environmental Information ▪ Global Environment Management Initiative ▪ National Safety Council ▪ The Nature Conservancy ▪ World Resources Institute ▪ Habitat for Humanity ▪ United Way ▪ YMCA ▪ Black Business Association ▪ Urban League ▪ Special Olympics ▪ Children's Miracle Network ▪ Partnership for a Drug-Free America ▪ World Wildlife Fund ▪ Starlight Children's Foundation

EVENT SPONSORED: Spirits Awards

E. I. du Pont de Nemours

CONTACT:
E. I. du Pont de Nemours and Company
1007 Market Street
Wilmington, DE 19898

TELEPHONE: (302) 774-1000

WEB: *www.dupont.com*

BUSINESS FOCUS: Chemical, material, and biological sciences

COMPANY BACKGROUND: DuPont researches and develops consumer and industrial products in areas of health care, nutrition, food, apparel, home, construction, electronics, and transportation. Some of its brands include Teflon, Lycra, Mylar, and Stainmaster. DuPont operates in more than sixty countries worldwide.

NETWORKING SPECIFICS: Try traditional routes of shareholders and charities. NASCAR is another good place to start.

SHAREHOLDERS' MEETING DATE: April, in Wilmington, Delaware

VIPs AFFILIATED WITH THE COMPANY: Charles O. Holliday, Jr.—Chairman and CEO ▪ Richard R. Goodmanson—Executive Vice President and COO ▪ Joseph A. Miller, Jr.—Senior Vice President and Chief Science and Technology Officer ▪ Stacey J. Mobley—Senior Vice President, CAO, and General Counsel ▪ Gary M.

Pfeiffer—Senior Vice President and CFO ▪ Robert Ridout—Vice President, Information Systems, and CIO ▪ John D. Broyles—Senior Vice President, Corporate Human Resources ▪ Alain J. P. Belda (President and CEO, Alcoa Inc.)—Board Member ▪ Curtis J. Crawford (President and CEO, ZiLOG, Inc.)—Board Member ▪ Louisa C. Duemling (Member of the Board of Governors, Nature Conservancy; ▪ Member, Board of Trustees, Chesapeake Bay Foundation)—Board Member ▪ Edward B. du Pont (Former Chairman, Atlantic Aviation Corporation)—Board Member ▪ Deborah C. Hopkins (CFO and Executive Vice President, Lucent Technologies)—Board Member ▪ Lois D. Juliber (COO, Colgate-Palmolive Company)—Board Member ▪ Göran Lindahl (President and CEO, ABB Ltd.)—Board Member ▪ Masahisa Naitoh (Vice Chairman, ITOCHU Corporation)—Board Member ▪ William K. Reilly (President and CEO, Aqua International Partners, L.P.; Former Administrator, United States Environmental Protection Agency; Former President, World Wildlife Fund and The Conservation Foundation)—Board Member ▪ H. Rodney Sharp III (President of the Board of Trustees, Longwood Foundation, Inc.)—Board Member ▪ Charles M. Vest (President, Massachusetts Institute of Technology)—Board Member ▪ Sanford I. Weill (Chairman and CEO, Citigroup Inc.)—Board Member

CHARITIES SUPPORTED: Elton John AIDS Foundation ▪ Breast Cancer Care ▪ Boys and Girls Clubs ▪ Kids in Distressed Situations ▪ United Way ▪ National AIDS Fund ▪ National Law Enforcement Officers Memorial Fund ▪ World Wildlife Fund ▪ American Foundation for AIDS Research

EVENTS SPONSORED: World Team Tennis ▪ NASCAR Racing ▪ DuPont World Amateur Golf Championship ▪ U.S. Olympic Luge Team

Enron

CONTACT:
Enron Corp.
1400 Smith Street
Houston, TX 77002

TELEPHONE: (713) 853-6161

WEB: *www.enron.com*

BUSINESS FOCUS: Markets natural gas, electricity, and broadband communications

COMPANY BACKGROUND: Enron is the largest marketer of electricity and natural gas in the world, providing energy in North and South America, Europe, and Australia, and they are working on expanding their operations in other locations. The company has recently branched into the communications business with its Intelligence network, providing Internet service across North America. Also, Enron, along with AOL and AT&T, has formed The New Power Company, a provider of energy and other services to homes and small businesses in deregulated markets.

NETWORKING SPECIFICS: Enron is extremely involved in the Houston community and has strong affiliations with the Baker Institute, where they sponsor the Enron prize. This is the best place to meet with top brass. They are also crazy about the Houston Astros.

SHAREHOLDERS' MEETING DATE: May, in Houston, Texas

VIPs AFFILIATED WITH THE COMPANY: Kenneth L. Lay—Chairman and CEO ▪ Jeffrey K. Skilling—President and COO ▪ Robert A. Belfer (Chairman, Belco Oil & Gas Corp.)—Board Member ▪ Norman P. Blake, Jr. (CEO and Secretary General, United States Olympic Committee; Former Chairman, President, and CEO, Promus Hotel Corporation)—Board Member ▪ Ronnie C. Chan (Chairman, Hang Lung Development Company Limited)—Board Member ▪ John H. Duncan (Former Chairman of the Executive Committee, Gulf &

Western Industries, Inc.)—Board Member ▪ Joe H. Foy (Retired Senior Partner, Bracewell & Patterson, and Former President and COO, Houston Natural Gas Corp.)—Board Member ▪ Wendy L. Gramm (Former Chairman, U.S. Commodity Futures Trading Commission)—Board Member ▪ Ken L. Harrison (Former Chairman and CEO, Portland General Electric Company)—Board Member ▪ Robert K. Jaedicke (Professor Emeritus of Accounting and Former Dean, Graduate School of Business, Stanford University)—Board Member ▪ Charles A. Lemaistre (President Emeritus, University of Texas M.D. Anderson Cancer Center)—Board Member ▪ Rebecca Mark-Jusbasche (Chairman and CEO, Azurix Corp.)—Board Member ▪ John Mendelsohn (President, University of Texas M.D. Anderson Cancer Center)—Board Member ▪ Jerome J. Meyer (Chairman, Tektronix, Inc.)—Board Member ▪ Paulo V. Ferraz Pereira (President and CEO, Meriodinal Financial Group; Former President and CEO, State Bank of Rio de Janerio, Brazil)—Board Member ▪ Frank Savage (Chairman, Alliance Capital Management International)—Board Member ▪ John A. Urquhart (Senior Advisor to the Chairman, Enron Corp.; President, John A. Urquhart Associates; and Former Senior Vice President, Industrial and Power Systems, General Electric Company)—Board Member ▪ John Wakeham (Former U.K. Secretary of State for Energy and Leader of the Houses of Lords and Commons)—Board Member ▪ Herbert S. Winokur, Jr. (Chairman and CEO, Capricorn Holdings, Inc.; Former Senior Executive Vice President, Penn Central Corporation)—Board Member ▪ Yasser Arafat ▪ Nelson Mandela

CHARITIES SUPPORTED: Boys and Girls Clubs ▪ United Way ▪ National Multiple Sclerosis Society ▪ Juvenile Diabetes Foundation ▪ Ronald McDonald House ▪ The Baker Institute ▪ The Metropolitan Museum of Art ▪ America's Promise–The Alliance for Youth

Ernst & Young LLP

CONTACT:
Ernst & Young LLP
784 Seventh Avenue
New York, NY 10019

TELEPHONE: (212) 773-3000

WEB: *www.ey.com*

BUSINESS FOCUS: Tax and finance

COMPANY BACKGROUND: Ernst & Young is one of the big five accounting firms in the world. Ernst & Young audits 114 of the *Fortune 500* largest corporations. They also deal with such clients as the NBA, the NHL, and Major League Baseball.

NETWORKING SPECIFICS: Charities routes or their sponsored activities are strong.

VIPs AFFILIATED WITH THE COMPANY: Bill Kimsey—CEO, Ernst & Young International ▪ Phil Laskawy—Chairman and CEO, Ernst & Young LLP; Chairman, Ernst & Young International ▪ David A. Reed—Senior Vice Chair, Global/Major Accounts, Industries, Sales, and Marketing; Vice Chair, Global Accounts, Industries, Sales, and Marketing, Ernst & Young International ▪ Stephanie M. Shern—Global and U.S. Director, Retail and Consumer Products Markets ▪ Loren Roberts—Ernst & Young–Sponsored Golfer ▪ Kirk Triplett—Ernst & Young–Sponsored Golfer ▪ Donna Andrews—Ernst & Young–Sponsored Golfer

SPONSORING ACTIVITIES: Forbes CEO Forum ▪ United States Ski and Snowboard Association World Cup ▪ Ryder Cup ▪ PGA Championships ▪ The Masters

CHARITIES SUPPORTED: PBS ▪ I Have a Dream Foundation ▪ Broadway Cares/Equity Fights AIDS ▪ The Metropolitan Museum of Art ▪ Juvenile Diabetes Foundation

Exxon Mobil Corporation

CONTACT:
Exxon Mobil Corporation
5959 Las Colinas Boulevard
Irving, TX 75039-2298

TELEPHONE: (972) 444-1107

WEB: *www.exxon.com*

BUSINESS FOCUS: Petroleum

COMPANY BACKGROUND: The merger between Exxon and Mobil is enabling the company to achieve its objective of becoming the world's leader in premium petroleum and petrochemicals. Exxon Mobil focuses its operations on service stations, oil refining, and chemicals.

NETWORKING SPECIFICS: The standard charities and shareholders' meeting are the strongest ways in. In addition, colleges with strong petroleum engineering departments are supported by Exxon.

SHAREHOLDERS' MEETING DATE: Late April

VIP STAFF: Lee R. Raymond—President, Chairman, and CEO ▪ Robert Wilhelm—Senior Vice President ▪ T. J. Hearn—Vice President, Human Resources ▪ Rene Dahan—Senior Vice President ▪ William T. Esrey (Chairman and CEO, Sprint Corporation)—Board Member ▪ Donald V. Fites (Former Chairman and CEO, Caterpillar, Inc.)—Board Member ▪ Charles A. Heimbold, Jr. (Chairman and CEO, Bristol-Myers Squibb Company)—Board Member ▪ William R. Howell (Chairman Emeritus, JC Penney Company, Inc.)—Board Member ▪ Reatha Clark King (President and Executive Director, General Mills Foundation)—Board Member ▪ Philip E. Lippincott (Chairman, Campbell Soup Company)—Board Member ▪ J. Richard Munro (Former Chairman and CEO, Time, Inc.)—Board Member ▪ Walter V. Shipley (Retired Chairman, The Chase-Manhattan Bank and The Chase-Manhattan Corporation)—Board Member ▪ Michael Baskin (Stanford University)—Board Member

VIP SUPPORTING THE CORPORATION: Rusty Wallace

CHARITIES SUPPORTED: Save the Tiger Fund ▪ United Negro College Fund ▪ University of California, Berkeley ▪ Massachusetts Institute of Technology ▪ Brown University ▪ Mobil Pegasus Prize for Literature ▪ Masterpiece Theatre ▪ The Metropolitan Museum of Art ▪ Habitat for Humanity ▪ Partnership for a Drug-Free America ▪ World Wildlife Fund ▪ YWCA ▪ International Exotic Feline Sanctuary

Federated Department Stores

CONTACT:
Federated Department Stores
West Seventh Street
Cincinnati, OH 45202

TELEPHONE: (513) 579-7000

WEB: *www.federated-fds.com*

BUSINESS FOCUS: Retail

COMPANY BACKGROUND: With the help of its subsidiaries, FDS is one of the big names in full-line department store operations. FDS operates upwards of 400 stores in thirty-three states. These stores include

Bloomingdale's, Macy's, Goldsmith's, Lazarus, Rich's, Burdines, Stern's, Fingerhut, and Bon Marché. FDS employs 118,800 individuals to keep its operations running smoothly.

NETWORKING SPECIFICS: The standard routes in are strong.

SHAREHOLDERS' MEETING DATE: May

VIPs AFFILIATED WITH THE COMPANY: James Zimmerman—Chairman and CEO ▪ Terry Lundgren—President and CMO ▪ Karen Hoguet—Senior Vice President and CFO ▪ Thomas Cody—Executive Vice President, Legal and Human Resources ▪ Meyer Feldberg (Dean of Columbia Business School, Columbia University)—Board Member ▪ Sara Levinson (President, NFL Properties, Inc.)—Board Member ▪ Joseph A. Pichler (Chairman and CEO, The Kroger Company)—Board Member ▪ Craig E. Weatherup (Chairman and CEO, The Pepsi Bottling Group, Inc.)—Board Member ▪ Marna C. Whittington (COO, Morgan Stanley Dean Witter)—Board Member ▪ Joseph Neubauer (Chairman and CEO, ARAMARK Corporation)—Board Member ▪ Karl M. von der Heyden (Vice Chairman, PepsiCo, Inc.)—Board Member

CHARITIES SUPPORTED: Habitat for Humanity ▪ United Way ▪ Breast Health Institute ▪ Susan G. Komen Foundation ▪ YWCA ▪ Elizabeth Glaser Pediatric AIDS Foundation ▪ NAACP ▪ United Negro College Fund ▪ Oprah Winfrey's Angel Network ▪ Toys for Tots ▪ American Heart Association ▪ The Metropolitan Museum of Art ▪ America's Promise—The Alliance for Youth ▪ America's Second Harvest ▪ Breast Cancer Fund

Ferrari

CONTACT:
Ferrari North America, Inc.
250 Sylvan Avenue
Englewood Cliffs, NJ 07632

TELEPHONE: (201) 816-2600

WEB: *www.ferrari.com*

BUSINESS FOCUS: Automobiles

COMPANY BACKGROUND: Ferrari North America was formed to import and distribute Ferrari cars in North America.

NETWORKING SPECIFICS: Try attending some of the events that Ferrari sponsors; they're the best way in.

EVENTS: Ferrari of North America Challenge Rallies. Contact a local Ferrari dealership for dates, locations, and times.

VIPs AFFILIATED WITH THE COMPANY: Gian Luigi Longinotti Buitoni—President and CEO ▪ Tom Heffernan—CFO ▪ Elke Rubin—Human Resources Administrator

CHARITY SUPPORTED: Museum of Modern Art

EVENTS SPONSORED: Ferrari Challenge Rally ▪ FIA Formula 1 ▪ American Le Mans Series ▪ Concours d'Elegance ▪ Historic Challenge

First Union Corporation

CONTACT:

First Union Corporation

One First Union Center

301 South College Street, Suite 4000

Charlotte, NC 28288

TELEPHONE: (704) 374-4880

WEB: *www.firstunion.com*

BUSINESS FOCUS: Banking

COMPANY BACKGROUND: First Union Corporation is the sixth largest banking company in America. First Union serves over sixteen million customers with upward of 2,300 locations across the nation.

NETWORKING SPECIFICS: First Union sponsors many professional sports teams. Any affiliation will be your strongest way in.

SHAREHOLDERS' MEETING DATE: April in Charlotte, North Carolina

VIPs AFFILIATED WITH THE COMPANY: Edward E. Crutchfield—Chairman and CEO ▪ G. Kennedy Thompson—President ▪ Robert T. Atwood—Executive Vice President and CFO ▪ Edward E. Barr (Chairman, Sun Chemical Corporation)—Board Member ▪ Erskine B. Bowles (General Partner, Forstmann, Little and Co.)—Board Member ▪ Robert F. Brown (Chairman and CEO, B&C Associates, Inc.)—Board Member ▪ A. Dano Davis (Chairman, Winn-Dixie Stores, Inc.)—Board Member ▪ Norwood H. Davis, Jr. (Chairman, Trigon Healthcare, Inc.)—Board Member ▪ R. Stuart Dickson (Chairman, Ruddick Corporation)—Board Member ▪ B. F. Dolan (Investor)—Board Member ▪ Arthur M. Goldberg (Park Place Entertainment Corporation)—Board Member ▪ James E. S. Hynes (Chairman, Hynes, Inc.)—Board Member ▪ Ernest E. Jones (President and CEO, Philadelphia Workforce Development Corporation)—Board Member ▪ Herbert Lotman (Chairman and CEO, Keystone Foods Holding Company, Inc.)—Board Member ▪ Joseph Neubauer (Chairman and CEO, ARAMARK Corporation)—Board Member ▪ Ruth G. Shaw (Executive Vice President and CAO, Duke Energy Corporation)—Board Member

SPONSORING ACTIVITIES: Atlanta Braves ▪ Charlotte Hornets ▪ Jacksonville Jaguars ▪ Miami Dolphins ▪ Philadelphia 76ers ▪ Philadelphia Flyers ▪ Philadelphia Phantoms ▪ Tampa Bay Devil Rays

CHARITIES SUPPORTED: United Way ▪ March of Dimes ▪ American Red Cross ▪ Habitat for Humanity

Ford Motor

CONTACT:

Ford Motor Company

The American Road

Dearborn, MI 48121-1899

TELEPHONE: (800) 392-3673

WEB: *www.ford.com*

BUSINESS FOCUS: Motor vehicles and parts

COMPANY BACKGROUND: The Ford Motor Company is the parent company of Ford, Lincoln, Volvo, Mazda, Mercury, Jaguar, and Aston-Martin.

NETWORKING SPECIFICS: The North American International Auto Show is a great place to start.

SHAREHOLDERS' MEETING DATE: May

VIPs AFFILIATED WITH THE COMPANY: Jacques A. Nasser—President/CEO ▪ William Clay Ford, Jr.—Chairman ▪ James A. Yost—CIO ▪ Henry D. G. Wallace—CFO ▪ David L. Murphy—Vice President, Human Resources ▪ Irvine O. Hockaday, Jr. (President and CEO, Hallmark Cards, Inc.)—Board Member ▪ William Clay Ford (Owner and President, Detroit Lions)—Board Member ▪ Ellen R. Marram (President and CEO, Efdex, Inc.)—Board Member ▪ Carl E. Reichardt (Former Chairman and CEO, Wells Fargo & Company)—Board Member ▪ Robert E. Rubin (Director and Chairman of Executive Committee, Citigroup, Inc.)—Board Member ▪ Jorma J. Ollila (Chairman and CEO, Nokia Corp.)—Board Member ▪ John L. Thornton (Chairman and Co-COO, The Goldman Sachs Group, Inc.)—Board Member ▪ Dale Jarrett—Ford Race Car Driver ▪ Rusty Wallace—Ford Race Car Driver ▪ Mark Martin—Ford Race Car Driver

CHARITIES SUPPORTED: United Way ▪ Children's Television Workshop ▪ Digital Entertainment Network ▪ Auto-xchange ▪ Time.com ▪ Detroit Music Hall ▪ Detroit Opera House ▪ Detroit Stadium ▪ Cleveland Science Center ▪ Chicago Center for the Performing Arts ▪ New York Center for the Performing Arts ▪ Zoo Atlanta ▪ Susan G. Komen Foundation ▪ The Art Institute of Chicago ▪ National AIDS Fund ▪ Partnership for a Drug-Free America

Four Seasons Hotels and Resorts

CONTACT:
Four Seasons Hotels and Resorts
1165 Leslie Street
Toronto, Ontario
Canada M3C 2K8

TELEPHONE: (416) 449-1750 (Canada)
(800) 819-5053 (U.S.)

WEB: *www.fourseasons.com*

BUSINESS FOCUS: Hospitality

COMPANY BACKGROUND: The Four Seasons Hotels and Resorts are top-of-the-line vacation or business sites that focus on premium elegance and customer service. Four Seasons is successful both internationally and in the U.S. *Fortune* magazine voted Four Seasons into the list of the 100 best companies to work for in America.

NETWORKING SPECIFICS: Trade shows are your best bet.

SHAREHOLDERS' MEETING DATE: Late May in Toronto, Ontario, Canada

VIPs AFFILIATED WITH THE COMPANY: Isadore Sharp—Chairman and CEO ▪ H. Roger Garland—Vice Chairman ▪ Wolf H. Hengst—President and COO ▪ Douglas L. Ludwig—Executive Vice President and CFO ▪ Kathleen Taylor—President and CCO ▪ John W. Young—Executive Vice President, Human Resources ▪ Deborah Brown—Vice President, Human Resources (North America) ▪ Edmond M. Creed (Retired Executive)—Board Member ▪ Frederick Eisen (President and CEO, The Eisen Corporation)—Board Member ▪ H. Roger Garland—Board Member ▪ Charles S. Henry (President, Hotel Capital Advisors, Inc.)—Board Member ▪ Murray B. Koffler (Parter, The Koffler Group)—Board Member ▪ J. Robert S. Prichard (President, University of Toronto)—Board Member ▪ Lionel H. Schipper (President, Schipper Enterprises, Inc.)—Board Member ▪ Anthony Sharp (Entrepreneur)—Board Member

Gateway, Inc.

CONTACT:
Gateway, Inc.
4545 Towne Centre Court
PO Box 2000
San Diego, CA 92121

TELEPHONE: (858) 799-3401

WEB: *www.gateway.com*

BUSINESS FOCUS: Computers

BACKGROUND INFORMATION: Gateway, Inc., focuses mainly on the selling of personal computers, components, and related products. Gateway was one of the first computer manufacturing companies that gave the consumer the option to custom-build their own PC. The Gateway workforce is 21,000 people strong. Their distinctive cow box, when placed strategically in a college dorm room, is both functional and decorative.

NETWORKING SPECIFICS: Trade shows are your best bet.

SHAREHOLDERS' MEETING DATE: Held in May in Sioux City, Iowa

VIPs AFFILIATED WITH THE COMPANY: Ted Waitt—Chairman ▪ David Robino—Vice Chairman ▪ Jeff Weitzen—President, CEO, and Director ▪ John Todd—Senior Vice President and CFO ▪ R. Todd Bradley—Executive Vice President, Global Operations ▪ Peter Ashkin—CTO ▪ James Pollard—Senior Vice President and CIO ▪ John Renfro—Senior Vice President, Human Resources ▪ Charles Carey (Chairman and CEO, Fox Television Division of Fox, Inc.)—Board Member ▪ Richard Snyder (President, Avalon Investments)—Board Member ▪ James McCann (President, 1-800-FLOWERS.com, Inc.)—Board Member

CHARITY SUPPORTED: Public Broadcasting Service

General Electric

CONTACT:
General Electric Company
3135 Easton Turnpike
Fairfield, CT 06431

TELEPHONE: (203) 373-2211

WEB: *www.ge.com*

BUSINESS FOCUS: Industrial and communications

COMPANY BACKGROUND: GE manufactures major appliances, lighting products, motors, electrical equipment, locomotives, power generating products, nuclear energy products, aircraft engines, and plastics. GE also owns NBC. GE is one of the best run companies in the United States.

NETWORKING SPECIFICS: With the diversity of business in GE, it is imperative to focus your efforts. Attend the American Power Conference and hope to get a job on an NBC daytime soap.

SHAREHOLDERS' MEETING DATE: April

VIPs AFFILIATED WITH THE COMPANY: Jack F. Welch—Chairman /CEO ▪ Keith Sherin—Senior Vice President, Finance and CFO ▪ William Conaty—Senior Vice President, Human Resources ▪ Ann M. Fudge

(Executive Vice President, Kraft Foods, Inc.)—Board Member ▪ Scott G. McNealy (Chairman/CEO, Sun Microsystems, Inc.)—Board Member ▪ Andrea Jung (Chairman /CEO, Avon Products, Inc.)—Board Member ▪ Sam Nunn (Former Senator, Georgia)—Board Member ▪ Roger S. Penske (Chairman, Penske Corporation)—Board Member ▪ Douglass A. Warner III (Chairman/CEO/President, J. P. Morgan & Co., Inc.)—Board Member

CHARITIES SUPPORTED: United Way ▪ Elfun Organization ▪ Thomas Edison Invention Factory ▪ America's Promise—The Alliance for Youth ▪ Partnership for a Drug-Free America

ORGANIZATION SPONSORED: Celebrity Golfers Association

General Mills

CONTACT:
General Mills, Inc.
Number One General Mills Blvd.
PO Box 1113
Minneapolis, MN 55440

TELEPHONE: (612) 764-2311

WEB: *www.generalmills.com*

BUSINESS FOCUS: Consumer foods

COMPANY BACKGROUND: General Mills makes a variety of recognizable name-brand food items: Trix, Cheerios, Wheaties, Total, and Lucky Charms cereals; Betty Crocker products; Gold Medal flour; Bisquick baking mix; Fruit Roll-Ups; and Yoplait yogurt are a few of their products. Their Wheaties cereal boxes have featured many popular athletes. General Mills recently acquired Pillsbury, makers of products such as Häagen-Dazs ice cream and Green Giant vegetables.

NETWORKING SPECIFICS: Try charities routes. General Mills donates to many major charities, and they are sources of connections to its management.

SHAREHOLDERS' MEETING DATE: September, in Minneapolis, Minnesota

VIPs AFFILIATED WITH THE COMPANY: Stephen W. Sanger—Chairman of the Board and CEO ▪ Raymond G. Viault—Vice Chairman ▪ Stephen R. Demeritt—Vice Chairman ▪ James A. Lawrence—Executive Vice President and CFO ▪ Michael A. Peel—Senior Vice President, Human Resources ▪ Livio D. DeSimone (Chairman of the Board and CEO, 3M Company)—Board Member ▪ William T. Esrey (Chairman of the Board and CEO, Sprint Corporation)—Board Member ▪ Raymond V. Gilmartin (Chairman of the Board, President, and CEO, Merck & Co., Inc.)—Board Member ▪ Judith Richards Hope (Senior Counsel, Paul, Hastings, Janofsky & Walker, LLP)—Board Member ▪ Robert L. Johnson (Chairman and CEO, BET Holdings, Inc.)—Board Member ▪ Heidi Lee (Senior Vice President and CFO, Citigroup, Inc.)—Board Member ▪ Michael D. Rose (Retired Chairman of the Board, Promus Hotel Corporation)—Board Member ▪ A. Michael Spence (Dean, Graduate School of Business, Stanford University)—Board Member ▪ Dorothy A. Terrell (Senior Vice President, Natural Microsystems Corporation)—Board Member ▪ C. Angus Wurtele (Retired Chairman of the Board, The Valspar Corporation)—Board Member

CHARITIES SUPPORTED: America's Promise—The Alliance for Youth ▪ American Cancer Society ▪ American Heart Association ▪ Breast Cancer Research Foundation ▪ American Red Cross ▪ Boys and Girls Clubs ▪ Easter Seals ▪ Special Olympics ▪ Juvenile Diabetes Foundation ▪ March of Dimes ▪ National Kidney Foundation ▪ Meals On Wheels ▪ Salvation Army ▪ Second Harvest ▪ NAACP ▪ United Way ▪ John F. Kennedy Center for the Performing Arts ▪ Junior Achievement ▪ Columbia University ▪ Literacy Volunteers of America

- Princeton University
- National Merit Scholarship Corporation
- United Negro College Fund
- Girl Scouts
- Boy Scouts of America
- Big Brothers Big Sisters
- YMCA
- Habitat for Humanity
- Goodwill
- YWCA
- Susan G. Komen Foundation

SPONSORED ACTIVITIES: LPGA ▪ Richard Petty and Petty Enterprises

General Motors

CONTACT:

General Motors
1000 Renaissance Center
Detroit, MI 48234

TELEPHONE: (313) 556-5000

WEB: *www.gm.com*

BUSINESS FOCUS: Motor vehicles and parts

COMPANY BACKGROUND: General Motors is the largest industrial company in the world. They employ over 650,000 and approximately one out of every 200 workers in the United States. Their brands include Chevrolet, Buick, Cadillac, Oldsmobile, Pontiac, Saturn, and GMC. Their CEO, John Smith, is one of the most influential in the world.

NETWORKING SPECIFICS: The North American International Auto Show as well as the charity routes are best.

SHAREHOLDERS' MEETING DATE: June in Detroit, Michigan

VIPs AFFILIATED WITH THE COMPANY: John F. Smith, Jr.—Chairman and CEO ▪ Richard G. Wagoner, Jr.—President and COO ▪ Harry J. Pearce—Vice Chairman ▪ John H. Bryan (Chairman and CEO, Sara Lee Corporation)—Board Member ▪ George M. C. Fisher (Chairman, Eastman Kodak Company)—Board Member ▪ Nobuyuki Idei (President and CEO, Sony Corporation)—Board Member ▪ Karen Katen (President, Pfizer, Inc.)—Board Member ▪ J. Willard Marriott, Jr. (Chairman and CEO, Marriott International, Inc.)—Board Member ▪ John G. Smale (Former Chairman and CEO, Procter & Gamble)—Board Member ▪ Dennis Weatherstone (Former Chairman and CEO, J. P. Morgan & Company, Inc.)—Board Member ▪ Louis Sullivan (Morehouse College)—Board Member ▪ Eckhard Pfeiffer (President and CEO, Compaq Computer)—Board Member

VIPs SUPPORTING THE CORPORATION: Dale Earnhardt, Jr. ▪ Terry Labonte ▪ Jeff Gordon ▪ John Andretti ▪ Bobby Labonte

CHARITIES SUPPORTED: Memorial Sloan-Kettering Cancer Society ▪ Race for the Cure ▪ Alzheimer's Association ▪ American Cancer Society ▪ American Heart Association ▪ Arthritis Foundation ▪ Beaumont Foundation ▪ Leukemia Society of America ▪ The Nature Conservancy ▪ America's Promise—The Alliance for Youth ▪ Habitat for Humanity ▪ Partnership for a Drug-Free America ▪ Make-A-Wish Foundation ▪ Susan G. Komen Foundation

ORGANIZATIONS SPONSORED: Indy Racing League ▪ NASCAR

Goldman, Sachs & Co.

CONTACT:
Goldman, Sachs & Co.
85 Broad Street
New York, NY 10004

TELEPHONE: (212) 902-1000

WEB: *www.gs.com*

BUSINESS FOCUS: Investment banking and securities

COMPANY BACKGROUND: Goldman Sachs is one of the leading investment banking and securities firms in the world. Corporations, governments, financial institutions, and wealthy individuals are all customers of Goldman Sachs. The firm has forty-one offices in twenty-three countries spanning the globe.

NETWORKING SPECIFICS: Goldman Sachs is a major recruiter from the top MBA programs (Wharton, Kellogg, Stanford, etc.). Top business schools are the best way in.

SHAREHOLDERS' MEETING DATE: November

VIPs AFFILIATED WITH THE COMPANY: Henry Paulson, Jr.—Chairman and CEO ▪ Robert Hurst—Vice Chairman ▪ John Thain—Copresident, Co-COO, and Director ▪ John Thornton—Copresident, Co-COO, and Director ▪ David Viniar—Executive Vice President and CFO ▪ Sir John Browne (Group Chief Executive, BP Amoco)—Board Member ▪ John H. Bryan (Chairman and CEO, Sara Lee Corporation)—Board Member ▪ James A. Johnson (Chairman and CEO, Johnson Capital Partners)—Board Member ▪ Dr. Ruth J. Simmons (President, Smith College)—Board Member ▪ John C. Whitehead—Chairman, Goldman Sachs Foundation Board of Directors ▪ Stephanie Bell-Rose—President, Goldman Sachs Foundation

CHARITIES SUPPORTED: Center for Talented Youth at John Hopkins University ▪ National Foundation for Teaching Entrepreneurship ▪ Prep for Prep ▪ A Better Chance, Inc. ▪ Bank Street College of Education ▪ Columbia University ▪ University of North Carolina at Chapel Hill ▪ The Metropolitan Museum of Art ▪ Museum of Modern Art ▪ Project A.L.S.

Harry Winston's

CONTACT:
Harry Winston's New York Salon
718 Fifth Avenue
New York, NY 10019

TELEPHONE: (212) 245-2000

WEB: *www.harry-winston.com*

BUSINESS FOCUS: Manufacturing and retail of fine jewelry

COMPANY BACKGROUND: The House of Harry Winston was founded by Harry Winston, the "King of Diamonds." Its exclusive retail salons are located in New York, Geneva, Beverly Hills, Paris, Tokyo, and Osaka. Harry Winston's maintains an elite clientele that includes royalty, celebrities, and industry leaders. Harry Winston's also has in the past lent jewels to exhibitions at the Louvre and the Metropolitan Museum of New York and has donated many jewels (including the Hope diamond) to the Harry Winston Gallery at the Smithsonian museum. The company loans out jewels to celebrities for award shows. Past borrowers have included Julianne Moore, Gloria Stuart, Tyra Banks, Selma Hayek, Faith Hill, Faye Dunaway, Helen Hunt, Annette Bening, Natasha Richardson, Fran Drescher, Burt Bacharach, Heather Locklear, Whoopi Goldberg, Susan Sarandon, Jodie Foster, Angelica Huston, Winona Ryder, Uma Thurman, Kelly Preston,

Nicole Kidman, Katherine Hepburn, Sophia Loren, Elizabeth Taylor, Princess Grace Kelly, Ginger Rogers, Michelle Pfeiffer, Geena Davis, Gwyneth Paltrow, Goldie Hawn, Mira Sorvino, Angela Bassett, Halle Berry, Kate Capshaw, Liza Minelli, Holly Hunter, Rosie O'Donnell, Sarah Jessica Parker, and Madonna.

NETWORKING SPECIFICS: Hollywood connections are a great way in.

VIP AFFILIATED WITH THE COMPANY: Ronald Winston—President, Chairman, and CEO

CHARITY SUPPORTED: The Smithsonian

The Hearst Corporation

CONTACT:
The Hearst Corporation
959 Eighth Avenue
New York, NY 10019

TELEPHONE: (212) 649-2000

WEB: *www.hearstcorp.com*

BUSINESS FOCUS: Media

BACKGROUND INFORMATION: The Hearst Corporation is split up into seven main divisions: Hearst Magazines, Hearst Newspapers, Hearst Entertainment and Syndication, Hearst Business Media, Hearst Broadcasting, Hearst Real Estate, and Hearst Interactive Media. Hearst's magazine division puts out publications that are most recognizable to the public. These magazines include *Cosmopolitan, Esquire, Harper's BAZAAR, Good Housekeeping, Marie Claire, Popular Mechanics, Redbook,* and *Town & Country.* The newspaper division is responsible for such publications as the *Houston Chronicle* and the *San Francisco Examiner.* Hearst also owns 20 percent of ESPN, ESPNews, ESPN 2, and The Classic Sports Network. A&E was formed through a joint venture between ABC, NBC, and Hearst, and Hearst and ABC founded the Lifetime channel.

NETWORKING SPECIFICS: Any connection with NBC or ABC would be a great way to get into Hearst.

VIPs AFFILIATED WITH THE COMPANY: Frank A. Bennack, Jr.—President and CEO ▪ George R. Hearst, Jr.—Chairman ▪ Victor F. Ganzi—Executive Vice President and COO ▪ Cathleen P. Black—President of Hearst Magazines ▪ George B. Irish—President of Hearst Newspapers ▪ Raymond E. Joslin—President of Hearst Entertainment and Syndication ▪ Richard P. Malloch—President of Hearst Business Media ▪ Alfred C. Sikes—President of Hearst Interactive Media

CHARITY SUPPORTED: YWCA

Hershey Foods Corporation

CONTACT:
Hershey Foods Corporation
100 Crystal A Drive
Hershey, PA 17033-0810

TELEPHONE: (800) 468-1714

WEB: *www.hersheys.com*

BUSINESS FOCUS: Candy manufacturing

COMPANY BACKGROUND: Hershey is the producer of many of today's most-loved candies. These include Jolly Ranchers, Reese's, Twizzlers, York Peppermint Patties, Oh Henry!, Mounds, Almond Joy, Kit Kat, Milk Duds, Payday, Whoppers, Heath, and the long list of Hershey's pure chocolates.

NETWORKING SPECIFICS: Hershey, Pennsylvania, is a true company town. Networking with the local community will lead straight into HERSHCO.

SHAREHOLDERS' MEETING DATE: April

VIPs AFFILIATED WITH THE COMPANY: Kenneth L. Wolfe—Chairman and CEO ▪ Michael F. Pasquale—Executive Vice President and COO ▪ Allan Z. Loren (Executive Vice President and CIO, American Express Company)—Board Member

PROMOTIONAL ACTIVITIES: Universal Studios ▪ NASCAR ▪ Pro Rodeo ▪ Major League Baseball ▪ NCAA Final Four ▪ NFL ▪ U.S. Figure Skating ▪ USA Gymnastics

CHARITIES SUPPORTED: United Way ▪ Children's Miracle Network ▪ Partnership for a Drug-Free America

Hewlett-Packard

CONTACT:

Hewlett-Packard
3000 Hanover Street
Palo Alto, CA 94304

TELEPHONE: (650) 857-1501

WEB: *www.hp.com*

BUSINESS FOCUS: Computer technology

COMPANY BACKGROUND: Hewlett-Packard has been recognized as one of the best companies in America by *Fortune* magazine and one of the best companies in the world by *BusinessWeek*. Hewlett-Packard employs a workforce of over 83,000 individuals. Their CEO, Carly Fiorina, is one of the most powerful women in the world.

NETWORKING SPECIFICS: High-tech trade fairs and top business schools are strong ways in.

SHAREHOLDERS' MEETING DATE: Late February in Cupertino, California

VIPs AFFILIATED WITH THE COMPANY: Carly Fiorina—CEO and President ▪ Richard A. Hackborn—Chairman ▪ William R. Hewlett—Emeritus Director and Cofounder ▪ Robert P. Wayman—Executive Vice President and CFO ▪ Lewis A. Platt—(Former Chairman, President, and CEO, Hewlett-Packard)—Board Member ▪ Philip M. Condit (Chairman and CEO, The Boeing Company)—Board Member ▪ Patricia C. Dunn (Chairman and Co-CEO, Barclays Global Investors)—Board Member ▪ Walter B. Hewlett (Chairman, Vermont Telephone Company)—Board Member ▪ David M. Lawrence (Chairman and CEO, Kaiser Foundation Health Plan, Inc.)—Board Member

SPONSORING ACTIVITIES: British Open ▪ Jaguar Racing ▪ San Francisco 49ers ▪ HP Laserjet Women's Challenge (Biking Event) ▪ America's Cup ▪ Webby Awards ▪ Celebrity Golfers Association

CHARITIES SUPPORTED: America's Second Harvest ▪ Big Brothers Big Sisters of America ▪ Goodwill Industries

Home Depot

CONTACT:
The Home Depot, Inc.
2455 Paces Ferry Road NW
Atlanta, GA 30339-4024

TELEPHONE: (770) 433-8211

WEB: *www.homedepot.com*

BUSINESS FOCUS: Home improvement retail

COMPANY BACKGROUND: Home Depot is the world's largest home improvement retailer. Home Depot also owns Expo Design Centers, Villager's Hardware stores, National Blinds and Wallpaper, Inc., The Home Depot Maintenance Warehouse catalog, Georgia Lighting, and Apex Supply Company, Inc.

NETWORKING SPECIFICS: The Senior PGA tour stop sponsored by Home Depot is a great place to start.

SHAREHOLDERS' MEETING DATE: May, in Atlanta, Georgia

VIPs AFFILIATED WITH THE COMPANY: Bernard Marcus—Chairman of the Board ▪ Arthur M. Blank—President and CEO ▪ Mark R. Baker—Executive Vice President and COO ▪ Dennis J. Carey—Executive Vice President and CFO ▪ Ronald M. Brill—Executive Vice President and CAO ▪ Stephen R. Messana—Senior Vice President, Human Resources ▪ Kenneth G. Langone (Chairman of the Board, CEO, and President, Invemed Associates, Inc.)—Lead Director ▪ Frank Borman (Retired Chairman of the Board and CEO, Eastern Airlines Inc.; Chairman of the Board, DBT Online Inc.)—Board Member ▪ John L. Clendenin (Retired Chairman, President, and CEO, BellSouth Corporation)—Board Member ▪ Berry R. Cox (Chairman, Berry R. Cox, Inc.)—Board Member ▪ William S. Davila (President Emeritus, Vons Companies Inc.)—Board Member ▪ Milledge A. Hart III (Chairman, DocuCorp International, Inc.; Chairman of the Board, Hart Group, Inc.)—Board Member ▪ Bonnie G. Hill (Vice President, The Times Mirror Company; President and CEO, The Times Mirror Foundation)—Board Member

CHARITIES SUPPORTED: Certified Forest Products Council ▪ World Wildlife Fund ▪ World Resources Institute ▪ Forest Stewardship Council ▪ Habitat for Humanity ▪ Christmas in April ▪ Big Brothers Big Sisters ▪ Boy Scouts of America ▪ Boys and Girls Clubs of America ▪ DARE ▪ United Way ▪ YMCA ▪ YouthBuild ▪ Duke University School of the Environment ▪ American Red Cross ▪ Homes for the Holidays ▪ America's Promise—The Alliance for Youth

Intel

CONTACT:
Intel Corporation
2200 Mission College Blvd.
PO Box 58119
Santa Clara, CA 95052-8119

TELEPHONE: (408) 765-8080

WEB: *www.intel.com*

BUSINESS FOCUS: Computer and communications technology

COMPANY BACKGROUND: Intel Corporation makes semiconductor chips and provides chips, boards, systems, and software to the computer and communications industries. Intel sells its products to manufacturers, distributors, and computer users.

NETWORKING SPECIFICS: Engineering and business programs at top universities, especially Stanford, are strong. Other ways in include the standard charities and shareholder routes.

SHAREHOLDERS' MEETING DATE: May, in Santa Clara, California

VIPs AFFILIATED WITH THE COMPANY: Gordon E. Moore—Chairman Emeritus of the Board ▪ Andrew S. Grove—Chairman of the Board (This guy is a megastar) ▪ Craig R. Barrett—President and CEO ▪ Andy D. Bryant—Senior Vice President, Chief Financial and Enterprise Services Officer ▪ Patricia Murray—Vice President and Director, Human Resources ▪ John P. Browne (Group Chief Executive, BP Amoco p.l.c.)—Board Member ▪ Winston H. Chen (Chairman, Paramitas Foundation)—Board Member ▪ D. James Guzy (Chairman, Arbor Company)—Board Member ▪ David S. Pottruck (President and Co-CEO, The Charles Schwab Corporation)—Board Member ▪ Jane E. Shaw (Chairman and CEO, AeroGen, Inc.)—Board Member ▪ David B. Yoffie (Max and Doris Starr Professor of International Business ▪ Administration, Harvard Business School)—Board Member ▪ Charles E. Young (Chancellor Emeritus, University of California at Los Angeles; Interim President, University of Florida)—Board Member

CHARITIES SUPPORTED: American Red Cross ▪ United Way ▪ Junior Achievement ▪ Special Olympics ▪ Adopt-A-Family ▪ Boys and Girls Club ▪ Habitat for Humanity ▪ Salvation Army ▪ Big Brothers Big Sisters ▪ Christmas in April ▪ America's Promise—The Alliance for Youth ▪ World Wildlife Fund

EVENT SPONSORED: Webby Awards

International Business Machines

CONTACT:
IBM Corporation
New Orchard Road
Armonk, NY 10504

TELEPHONE: (914) 499-1900

WEB: *www.ibm.com*

BUSINESS FOCUS: Computers and technology

COMPANY BACKGROUND: IBM is the Rock of Gibraltar in the business world. Big Blue is involved in the fields of computer systems, software, networking systems, storage devices, and microelectronics, but they are moving out of the PC business and focusing on larger hardware and their software divisions.

NETWORKING SPECIFICS: The connection routes of trade shows, business schools, charities, and shareholders' meetings are all good ways in.

SHAREHOLDERS' MEETING DATE: Late April

VIPs AFFILIATED WITH THE COMPANY: Louis V. Gerstner, Jr.—Chairman/CEO ▪ Thomas Bouchard—Senior Vice President, Human Resources ▪ Laurence Ricciardi—CFO ▪ Cathleen Black (President, Hearst Magazine)—Board Member ▪ Nannerl O. Keohane (President, Duke University)—Board Member ▪ John B. Slaughter (President Emeritus, Occidental College)—Board Member ▪ Kenneth I. Chenault (President and COO, American Express Company)—Board Member ▪ Minoru Makihara (Chairman, Mitsubishi Corporation)—Board Member ▪ Alex Trotman (Retired Chairman and CEO, Ford Motor Company)—Board Member ▪ Lucio A. Noto (Vice Chairman, Exxon Mobil Corporation)—Board Member ▪ Charles M. Vest (President, Massachusetts Institute of Technology)—Board Member ▪ Charles Knight (Chairman and CEO, Emerson Electric)—Board Member

CHARITIES SUPPORTED: United Way ▪ American Red Cross ▪ American Cancer Society ▪ The Metropolitan Museum of Art ▪ America's Promise—The Alliance for Youth ▪ Big Brothers Big Sisters of America

International Paper

CONTACT:
International Paper
Two Manhattanville Road
Purchase, NY 10577-2196

TELEPHONE: (914) 397-1500

WEB: *www.internationalpaper.com*

BUSINESS FOCUS: Making paper and forest products

COMPANY BACKGROUND: International Paper is the world's largest paper and forest products company, operating in over forty countries. It is involved in printing paper, manufacturing packaging, and building materials. International Paper is also the largest private landowner in the world, owning almost 10 million acres worldwide. International Paper recently merged with both Union Camp and Champion.

NETWORKING SPECIFICS: The conventional routes of charities and shareholders' events are strong.

SHAREHOLDERS' MEETING DATE: May, in Purchase, New York

VIPs AFFILIATED WITH THE COMPANY: John T. Dillon—Chairman and CEO ▪ David W. Oskin—Executive Vice President ▪ C. Wesley Smith—Executive Vice President ▪ Jerome N. Carter—Senior Vice President, Human Resources ▪ John V. Faraci—Senior Vice President, Finance and CFO ▪ Peter I. Bijur (Chairman and CEO, Texaco, Inc.)—Board Member ▪ Robert J. Eaton (Chairman of the Board of Management, DaimlerChrysler AG)—Board Member ▪ Samir G. Gibara (Chairman and CEO, The Goodyear Tire & Rubber Company)—Board Member ▪ James A. Henderson (Former Chairman and CEO, Union Carbide Corporation)—Board Member ▪ John R. Kennedy (Former President and CEO, Federal Paper Board Company, Inc.)—Board Member ▪ Robert D. Kennedy (Former Chairman and CEO, Union Carbide Corporation)—Board Member ▪ W. Craig McClelland (Former Chairman and CEO, Union Camp Corporation)—Board Member ▪ Donald F. McHenry (Distinguished Professor of Diplomacy, Georgetown University)—Board Member ▪ Patrick F. Noonan (Chairman and CEO, The Conservation Fund)—Board Member ▪ Jane C. Pfeiffer (Management Consultant)—Board Member ▪ Jeremiah J. Sheehan (Chairman and CEO, Reynolds Metal Company)—Board Member ▪ Charles R. Shoemate (Chairman, President, and CEO, Bestfoods)—Board Member

CHARITIES SUPPORTED: United Way ▪ 4-H ▪ Sierra Club ▪ The Nature Conservancy ▪ National Audubon Society ▪ Auburn University ▪ Involved in wildlife preservation charities

Johnson & Johnson

CONTACT:
Johnson & Johnson
One Johnson & Johnson Plaza
New Brunswick, NJ 08933

TELEPHONE: (732) 524-0400

WEB: *www.jnj.com*

BUSINESS FOCUS: Manufacturer of health care products

COMPANY BACKGROUND: Johnson & Johnson is made up of more than 190 companies, including Band-Aid, Tylenol, and Neutrogena, which manufacture health care products that are sold in more than 175 countries.

NETWORKING SPECIFICS: Johnson & Johnson is a very complex operation. When networking in, one must be focused. Specific divisions function differently. The conventional routes in are strong.

SHAREHOLDERS' MEETING DATE: April, in New Brunswick, New Jersey

VIPs AFFILIATED WITH THE COMPANY: Ralph S. Larsen—Chairman and CEO ▪ Robert N. Wilson—Vice Chairman of the Board ▪ JoAnn Heffernan Heisen—Vice President, CIO ▪ James G. Cullen (President and COO, Bell Atlantic Corporation)—Board Member ▪ Gerard N. Burrow, M.D. (Special Advisor to the President of Yale University for Health Affairs)—Board Member ▪ Joan G. Cooney (Chairman of the Executive Committee, Children's Television Workshop)—Board Member ▪ M. Judah Folkman, M.D. (Senior Associate in Surgery, Children's Hospital; Professor, Harvard Medical School)—Board Member ▪ Ann D. Jordan (Former Director of the Social Services Department, Chicago Lying-in Hospital)—Board Member ▪ Leo F. Mullin (President and CEO, Delta Air Lines)—Board Member ▪ Paul J. Rizzo (Retired Vice Chairman, IBM Corporation)—Board Member ▪ Henry B. Schacht (Former Chairman and CEO, Lucent Technologies)—Board Member ▪ Maxine F. Singer, Ph.D. (President, Carnegie Institute of Washington)—Board Member ▪ John W. Snow (Chairman, President, and CEO, CSX Corporation)—Board Member ▪ Arnold G. Langbo (Chairman and CEO, Kellogg Company)—Board Member ▪ John S. Mayo, Ph.D. (President Emeritus, AT&T Bell Laboratories)—Board Member ▪ Toni Morrison ▪ Ray Romano ▪ Randy Newman ▪ Christopher Reeve ▪ Valerie Harper ▪ Joy Behar

CHARITIES SUPPORTED: Wolong Nature Reserve in China ▪ Diri Amba Orphanage ▪ Compeer, Inc. ▪ Juvenile Diabetes Walk ▪ Ovarian Cancer Research Fund ▪ Red Cross/Red Crescent ▪ Susan G. Komen Breast Cancer Foundation ▪ America's Blood Centers Foundation ▪ Family Friendly Programming Forum ▪ New York University (through the Family Friendly Programming Forum) ▪ University of Southern California (through the Family Friendly Programming Forum) ▪ The Metropolitan Museum of Art ▪ Partnership for a Drug-Free America ▪ Save the Children ▪ World Wildlife Fund

J.P. Morgan & Co.

CONTACT:

J.P. Morgan & Co. Incorporated
60 Wall Street
New York, NY 10260-0060

TELEPHONE: (212) 483-2323

WEB: *www.jpmorgan.com*

BUSINESS FOCUS: Finance

COMPANY BACKGROUND: J.P. Morgan & Co. is more than 150 years old, and advises, manages assets, raises capital, and makes markets for its clients in over thirty countries. Its client list includes Exxon, AT&T, and the government of France.

NETWORKING SPECIFICS: Top business schools are fantastic routes in.

SHAREHOLDERS' MEETING DATE: April, in New York

VIPs AFFILIATED WITH THE COMPANY: Douglas A. Warner III—Chairman of the Board, CEO ▪ Peter D. Hancock—CFO ▪ Thomas B. Ketchum—CAO ▪ Walter A. Gubert—Vice Chairman of the Board ▪ Roberto G. Mendoza—Vice Chairman of the Board ▪ Michael E. Patterson—Vice Chairman of the Board ▪ John F. Bradley—Human Resources ▪ Nancy Baird Harwood—Human Resources ▪ Ellen V. Futter (President, American Museum of Natural History)—Board Member ▪ Lee R. Raymond (Chairman of the Board and CEO, Exxon Mobil Corporation)—Board Member ▪ Paul A. Allaire (Chairman of the Board, Xerox Corporation)—Board Member ▪ Riley P. Bechtel (Chairman and CEO, Bechtel Group, Inc.)—Board Member ▪ Lawrence A. Bossidy (Chairman of the Board, Honeywell International, Inc.)—Board Member ▪ Martin Feldstein (President and CEO, National Bureau of Economic Research, Inc.)—Board Member ▪ Hanna H. Gray (President Emeritus and Harry Pratt Judson Distinguished Service Professor of History, University of Chicago)—Board Member ▪ James R. Houghton (President Emeritus of the Board, Corning Incorporated)— Board Member ▪ James L. Ketelsen (Retired Chairman of the Board and CEO, Tenneco, Inc.)—Board Member ▪ John A. Krol (Retired Chairman of the Board, E. I. du Pont de Nemours and Company)—Board Member ▪ Richard D. Simmons (Retired President, The Washington Post Company and International Herald Tribune)—Board Member ▪ Kurt F. Viermetz (Retired Vice Chairman of the Board)—Board Member ▪ Lloyd D. Ward (Chairman of the Board and CEO, Maytag Corporation)—Board Member ▪ Douglas C. Yearley (Chairman of the Board, Phelps Dodge Corporation)—Board Member

CHARITIES SUPPORTED: United Way ▪ National Society for the Prevention of Cruelty to Children ▪ CHASE Children's Hospice Service ▪ Habitat for Humanity ▪ Alvin Ailey American Dance Theater ▪ Lincoln Center for the Performing Arts ▪ National Dance Institute ▪ New York Shakespeare Festival ▪ American Museum of Natural History ▪ The Metropolitan Museum of Art ▪ Museum of Modern Art ▪ Columbia University Graduate School of Business ▪ Carnegie Hall Foundation ▪ Junior Achievement ▪ New York Public Library ▪ YMCA ▪ United Negro College Fund ▪ American Indian College Fund ▪ Hispanic Scholarship Fund ▪ Environmental Defense Fund ▪ World Wildlife Fund ▪ Arthur Ashe Institute for Urban Health ▪ Planned Parenthood of New York City ▪ Big Brothers Big Sisters ▪ American Red Cross ▪ The Louvre ▪ Art Institute of Chicago

Kellogg's

CONTACT:
Kellogg Company
One Kellogg Square
Battle Creek, MI 49016-3599

TELEPHONE: (616) 961-2000

WEB: *www.kelloggs.com*

BUSINESS FOCUS: Produces cereal and convenience foods

COMPANY BACKGROUND: Kellogg's is the world's leading producer of ready-to-eat cereal, and makes the brands Rice Krispies, Apple Jacks, Froot Loops, Frosted Flakes, Special K, and others. They also produce other foods such as Eggo Waffles and Pop-Tarts, and have a line of natural foods and meat alternatives under the names Morningstar Farms, Worthington, Natural Touch, and Loma Linda.

NETWORKING SPECIFICS: The conventional business routes of charities and business schools are strong.

SHAREHOLDERS' MEETING DATE: April, Battle Creek, Michigan

VIPs AFFILIATED WITH THE COMPANY: Carlos M. Gutierrez—President and CEO ▪ Thomas J. Webb—Executive Vice President and CFO ▪ James W. Larson—Vice President, Human Resources ▪ John D. Cook— President of Kellogg North America ▪ Carly S. Fiorina (President and CEO, Hewlett-Packard Company)— Board Member ▪ William D. Perez (President and CEO, S. C. Johnson & Son, Inc.)—Board Member ▪ Benjamin S. Carson, M.D. (Professor and Director of Pediatric Neurology, The Johns Hopkins Medical Institutions)—Board Member ▪ Claudio X. Gonzalez (Chairman of the Board and CEO, Kimberly-Clark de Mexico)—Board Member ▪ Gordon Gund (Chairman of the Board and CEO, Gund Investment Corporation)—Board Member ▪ Dorothy A. Johnson (President, Ahlburg Company)—Board Member ▪ Ann McLaughlin (Chairman, The Aspen Institute)—Board Member ▪ J. Richard Munro (Retired Chairman and CEO, Time Warner Inc.)—Board Member ▪ William C. Richardson (President and CEO, W. K. Kellogg Foundation)—Board Member ▪ John L. Zabriskie (Chairman, NEN Life Science Products, Inc.)—Board Member ▪ Tony the Tiger ▪ Snap, Crackle, and Pop ▪ Emme ▪ Cindy Crawford ▪ Gabrielle Reece ▪ Kristi Yamaguchi ▪ Dan Jansen ▪ Bonnie Blair ▪ Terry Labonte ▪ Jeff Gordon

CHARITIES SUPPORTED: Adopt-a-Highway ▪ Battle Creek Area Math and Science Center ▪ American Forests ▪ National Merit Scholarship Program ▪ Michigan State University ▪ U.S. Olympic Committee ▪ America's Promise—The Alliance for Youth ▪ America's Second Harvest ▪ Big Brothers Big Sisters of America ▪ Sierra Club ▪ National Urban League ▪ Starlight Children's Foundation ▪ Susan G. Komen Foundation

Kimberly-Clark

CONTACT:
Kimberly-Clark Corporation
351 Phelps Drive
Irving, TX 75038

TELEPHONE: (972) 281-1200

WEB: *www.kimberly-clark.com*

BUSINESS FOCUS: Manufactures consumer products

COMPANY BACKGROUND: Kimberly-Clark Corporation sells its products under the brand names Kleenex, Huggies, Pull-Ups, Depends, Kotex, and Scott in over 150 countries.

NETWORKING SPECIFICS: The conventional shareholders' and charity routes are good ways in.

SHAREHOLDERS' MEETING DATE: April, in Dallas, Texas

VIPs AFFILIATED WITH THE COMPANY: Wayne R. Sanders—Chairman and CEO ▪ Thomas J. Falk—President and COO ▪ John W. Donehower—Senior Vice President and CFO ▪ Kathi P. Seifert—Executive Vice President ▪ Claudio X. Gonzalez (Chairman of the Board and Managing Director, Kimberly-Clark de Mexico)—Board Member ▪ John F. Bergstrom (Chairman and CEO, Bergstrom Corporation)—Board Member ▪ Pastora San Juan Cafferty (Professor, School of Social Service Administration, University of Chicago)—Board Member ▪ Paul J. Collins (Vice Chairman, Citigroup Inc.)—Board Member ▪ Robert W. Decherd (Chairman of the Board, President, and CEO, Belo Corp.)—Board Member ▪ William O. Fifield (Partner, Sidley and Austin)—Board Member ▪ Louis E. Levy (Retired Partner and Vice Chairman, KPMG Peat Marwick)—Board Member ▪ Frank A. McPherson (Retired Chairman of the Board and CEO, Kerr-McGee Corporation)—Board Member ▪ Linda Johnson Rice (President and COO, Johnson Publishing Company, Inc.)—Board Member ▪ Wolfgang R. Schmitt (Chairman of the Board, Value America, Inc.)—Board Member ▪ Randall L. Tobias (Chairman Emeritus, Eli Lilly and Company)—Board Member ▪ June Allyson (Spokesperson, Depends)

CHARITIES SUPPORTED: Nature Conservancy ▪ Boys and Girls Club ▪ Girl Scouts ▪ Boy Scouts ▪ Junior Achievement ▪ YWCA ▪ YMCA ▪ American Urogynecologic Society ▪ June Allyson Foundation ▪ America's Promise—The Alliance for Youth ▪ Partnership for a Drug-Free America

Kmart

CONTACT:
Kmart Corporation Resource Center
3100 West Big Beaver Road
Troy, MI 48084-3163

TELEPHONE: (248) 643-1000

BUSINESS FOCUS: Discount retail stores

COMPANY BACKGROUND: Kmart owns and operates over 2,100 Kmart, Big Kmart, and Super Kmart stores throughout the United States, Guam, Puerto Rico, and the U.S. Virgin Islands.

NETWORKING SPECIFICS: The Kmart Kids Race Against Drugs, as well as the March of Dimes, are two of the charities to focus on. Look to the shareholders for networking possibilities as well.

SHAREHOLDERS' MEETING DATE: May in Detroit, Michigan

VIPs AFFILIATED WITH THE COMPANY: Charles C. Conaway—Chairman of the Board and CEO ▪ Joseph A. Osbourn—Senior Vice President and CIO ▪ Martin E. Welch III—Senior Vice President and CFO ▪ Warren F. Cooper—Executive Vice President, Human Resources and Administration ▪ Stephen F. Bollenbach (President and CEO, Hilton Hotels Corporation)—Board Member ▪ Robin B. Smith (Chairman and CEO, Publishers Clearing House)—Board Member ▪ James B. Adamson (Chairman, President, and CEO, Advantica Restaurant Group)—Board Member ▪ Lilyan H. Affinito (Former Vice Chairman of the Board, Maxxam Group Inc.)—Board Member ▪ Joseph A. Califano, Jr. (Chairman and President, The National Center on Addiction and Substance Abuse at Columbia University)—Board Member ▪ Richard G. Cline (Chairman, Hawthorne Investors Inc; Chairman, Hussmann International Inc.)—Board Member ▪ Willie D. Davis (President, All Pro Broadcasting, Inc.)—Board Member ▪ Joseph P. Flannery (Chairman of the Board, President, and CEO, Uniroyal Holding, Inc.)—Board Member ▪ Robert D. Kennedy (Former Chairman of the Board and CEO, Union Carbide Corporation)—Board Member ▪ J. Richard Munro (Former Cochairman of the Board and Co-CEO, Time Warner Inc.)—Board Member ▪ Thomas Stallkamp (Vice Chairman and CEO, MSX International)—Board Member ▪ James O. Welch, Jr. (Former Vice Chairman, RJR Nabisco Inc.; Chairman, Nabisco Brands, Inc.)—Board Member ▪ Rosie O'Donnell ▪ Kathy Ireland ▪ Penny Marshall ▪ Martha Stewart ▪ CeCe Winans ▪ Pepe Locuaz ▪ Giselle Blondet ▪ Andrea Lagunes ▪ Jaclyn Smith

CHARITIES SUPPORTED: March of Dimes ▪ Walk America ▪ Give Kids the World ▪ American Red Cross ▪ United Way ▪ Salvation Army ▪ America's Promise—The Alliance for Youth ▪ MADD

ORGANIZATION SPONSORED: NASCAR

KPMG LLP

CONTACT:
KPMG LLP
345 Park Avenue
New York, NY 10154

TELEPHONE: (212) 758-9700

WEB: *www.kpmg.com*

BUSINESS FOCUS: Taxes and finance

COMPANY BACKGROUND: KPMG is one of the big five professional service organizations. KPMG is split into financial services, consulting services, tax services, assurance services, banking and finance, insurance, real estate, regulatory services, consulting, consumer markets, industrial markets, health care/public sector. KPMG has almost 100,000 employees working out of over 820 cities in 159 countries around the world.

NETWORKING SPECIFICS: Since KPMG is split into many branches, networking will be most beneficial if it is focused. Great ways into KPMG are through any connections that you may have with any of their clients.

Another way in is to attend any of the conferences that KPMG sponsors. These methods of networking should open many doors inside KPMG.

VIPs AFFILIATED WITH THE COMPANY: Stephen G. Butler—Chairman ▪ Paul C. Reilly—CEO

CLIENTS: Banc One ▪ BellSouth ▪ BMW ▪ CBS ▪ Chase Manhattan ▪ Cisco Systems ▪ Citicorp ▪ Cornell University ▪ Del Monte Foods ▪ Duke University ▪ EDS ▪ Emerson Electric ▪ Fannie Mae ▪ Federal Express ▪ Federated Department Stores ▪ General Electric ▪ General Mills ▪ Gillette ▪ Hasbro ▪ Hewlett-Packard ▪ The Home Depot ▪ Honda Motor ▪ Hyatt Hotels ▪ IBM ▪ JC Penney ▪ J.P. Morgan ▪ Johns Hopkins University ▪ Mellon Bank ▪ Microsoft ▪ Motorola ▪ NASA ▪ National Geographic ▪ NBC ▪ Nestlé ▪ Paramount ▪ PepsiCo ▪ Pfizer ▪ Polaroid ▪ PolyGram ▪ Prudential ▪ Revlon ▪ Rubbermaid ▪ Samsonite ▪ Siemens ▪ Smithsonian Institution ▪ Sony ▪ Southwestern Bell ▪ US Airways Group ▪ U.S. Department of Housing and Urban Development ▪ U.S. Senate ▪ U.S. Navy ▪ Vanderbilt University ▪ Venator Group ▪ Visa International ▪ Washington, D.C ▪ Wells Fargo ▪ WorldCom ▪ Xerox

SPONSORING ACTIVITIES: Annual Newspaper Publisher Convention ▪ Technical and Business Expo ▪ International Banking Meeting

CHARITIES SUPPORTED: The Metropolitan Museum of Art ▪ America's Promise—The Alliance for Youth

Lehman Brothers Holdings

CONTACT:
Lehman Brothers Holdings Inc.
3 World Financial Center
New York, NY 10285

TELEPHONE: (212) 526-7000

WEB: *www.lehman.com*

BUSINESS FOCUS: Global investment banking

COMPANY BACKGROUND: Lehman Brothers Holdings is a former American Express company that became independent in 1994. Lehman Brothers is involved in banking, raising capital, corporate finances, securities trading, and commodities. Some businesses that Lehman Brothers has represented include Pepsi Bottling, Wal-Mart Stores, Enron, US West, MCI Communications, Time Warner Telecom, Coca-Cola Enterprises, and Revlon Consumer Products.

NETWORKING SPECIFICS: Lehman Brothers deals with many other businesses that it represents financially. Contacts with one of the businesses that Lehman Brothers represents would be one way to network into the company.

SHAREHOLDERS' MEETING DATE: December

VIPs AFFILIATED WITH THE COMPANY: Richard S. Fuld, Jr.—Chairman and CEO ▪ David Goldfarb—CFO ▪ Joseph M. Gregory—CAO ▪ Kevin McGilloway—CIO ▪ Mark Rufeh—COO ▪ Thomas A. Russo—Chief Legal Officer ▪ Michael L. Ainslie (Former President and CEO, Sotheby's Holdings)—Board Member ▪ John F. Akers (Retired Chairman, International Business Machines Corporation)—Board Member ▪ Roger S. Berlind (Theatrical Producer, Berlind Productions)—Board Member ▪ Thomas H. Cruikshank (Retired Chairman and CEO, Halliburton Company)—Board Member ▪ Henry Kaufman (President, Henry Kaufman & Company, Inc.)—Board Member ▪ Hideichiro Kobayashi (General Manager for the Americas, Nippon Life)—Board Member ▪ John D. Macomber (Principal, JDM Investment Group)—Board Member ▪ Dina Merrill (Vice Chairman, RKO Pictures, Inc.; Actress)—Board Member

Lockheed Martin

CONTACT:
Lockheed Martin Corporation
6801 Rockledge Drive
Bethesda, MD 20817

TELEPHONE: (301) 897-6000

WEB: *www.lockheedmartin.com*

BUSINESS FOCUS: Aerospace technology

COMPANY BACKGROUND: Lockheed designs and manufactures technology systems, services, and products for government and commercial customers. Lockheed Martin has created Space Day to educate schoolchildren about space exploration and to advance science, math, and technology education. Senator and astronaut John Glenn is a supporter of Space Day and has participated in some of its activities.

NETWORKING SPECIFICS: Lockheed Martin works closely with the U.S. military to develop ships, submarines, planes, missiles, and other defense products for them. Contacts within the U.S. military would be a good way to network into Lockheed Martin. Shareholders and charities are strong ways as well.

SHAREHOLDERS' MEETING DATE: April

VIPs AFFILIATED WITH THE COMPANY: Vance D. Coffman—Chairman and CEO ▪ Louis Hughes—President and COO ▪ Robert Stevens—Executive VP, Finance, CEO ▪ Norman R. Augustine—Chairman of the Executive Committee ▪ Marcus C. Bennett (Retired Executive Vice President)—Board Member ▪ Lynne V. Cheney (Senior Fellow, Public Policy Research)—American Enterprise Institute ▪ Houston I. Flournoy (Retired Special Assistant to the President, Governmental Affairs, University of Southern California)—Board Member ▪ James F. Gibbons (Professor, Electrical Engineering, Stanford University)—Board Member ▪ Edward E. Hood, Jr. (Retired Vice Chairman, General Electric Company)—Board Member ▪ Caleb B. Hurtt (Retired President and COO, Martin Marietta Corporation)—Board Member ▪ Gwendolyn S. King (Retired Senior Vice President, Corporate and Public Affairs, PECO Energy Company)—Board Member ▪ Eugene F. Murphy (Retired Vice Chairman and Executive Officer, General Electric Company)—Board Member ▪ Frank Savage (Chairman, Alliance Capital Management International)—Board Member ▪ Carlisle A. H. Trost (Retired Chief, Naval Operations)—Board Member ▪ James R. Ukropina (Partner, O'Melveny & Myers)—Board Member ▪ Douglas C. Yearley (Chairman of the Board, Phelps Dodge Corporation)—Board Member ▪ John Glenn

CHARITIES SUPPORTED: Girl Scouts of America ▪ 4-H Clubs ▪ National Science Foundation ▪ Texas Christian University ▪ United Way ▪ PBS ▪ American Red Cross ▪ American Cancer Society ▪ Multiple Sclerosis Association of America ▪ John F. Kenedy Center for the Performing Arts ▪ UNICEF ▪ Project HOPE ▪ United Negro College Fund

Loews

CONTACT:
Loews Corporation
667 Madison Avenue
New York, NY 10021-8087

TELEPHONE: (212) 521-2000

WEB: *www.loews.com*

BUSINESS FOCUS: Loews is a holdings company

COMPANY BACKGROUND: Loews is a diversified financial holdings company. Its subsidiaries include Loews Hotels, CNA Financial Corporation (insurance), Lorillard, Inc. (tobacco), Diamond Offshore Drilling, and Bulova Corporation (watches and clocks).

NETWORKING SPECIFICS: One of Loews subsidiaries, Loews Hotels, holds a benefit with the Parker Brothers, Loews Monopoly Power Breakfasts. This event is a chance to meet celebrities, athletes, and community leaders who are there to play a game of Monopoly to benefit charity, and it's a great place to network with the company.

SHAREHOLDERS' MEETING DATE: May, in New York City

VIPs AFFILIATED WITH THE COMPANY: Laurence A. Tisch—Cochairman of the Board ▪ Preston R. Tisch—Cochairman of the Board ▪ James S. Tisch—Office of the President, President, and CEO ▪ Andrew H. Tisch—Office of the President and Chairman of the Executive Committee ▪ Jonathan M. Tisch—Office of the President and President and CEO, Loews Hotels ▪ Peter W. Keegan—Senior Vice President and CFO ▪ Arthur L. Rebell—Senior Vice President and Chief Investment Officer ▪ Alan Momeyer—Vice President, Human Resources ▪ Charles B. Benenson (Officer and Director, Benenson Realty Company)—Board Member ▪ John Brademas (President Emeritus, New York University)—Board Member ▪ Dennis H. Chookaszian (Chairman of the Executive Committee, CNA Financial Corporation) ▪ Paul J. Fribourg (Chairman of the Board of Directors and CEO, ContiGroup Companies, Inc.)—Board Member ▪ Bernard Myerson (Chairman Emeritus, Sony Theatre Management Corporation)—Board Member ▪ Edward J. Noha (Chairman of the Board, CNA Financial Corporation)—Board Member ▪ Gloria R. Scott (President, Bennett College)—Board Member ▪ Fred Wilpon (Chairman of the Board, Sterling Equities, Inc.)—Board Member

CHARITIES SUPPORTED: National Association of Police Athletic Leagues ▪ Elizabeth Glaser Pediatric AIDS Foundation ▪ Project Cradle ▪ Second Harvest Food Bank ▪ Food for Families ▪ Head Start

Lucent Technologies

CONTACT:
Lucent Technologies
600 Mountain Avenue
Murray Hill, NJ 07974

TELEPHONE: (908) 582-8500

WEB: *www.lucent.com*

BUSINESS FOCUS: Communications networks, product development, and research (through Bell Labs)

COMPANY BACKGROUND: Lucent Technologies is involved in creating and developing information systems technology. Its products are used by many major companies, such as ABC and Sprint. Lucent works to improve Internet connectivity and create new infrastructures to support future Internet applications.

NETWORKING SPECIFICS: Business schools, engineering schools, trade shows, shareholders' meetings, and charities are all strong routes in.

SHAREHOLDERS' MEETING DATE: February

VIPs AFFILIATED WITH THE COMPANY: Richard A. McGinn—Chairman and CEO ▪ Robert C. Holder—Executive Vice President and Chief of Staff Operations ▪ Deborah C. Hopkins—Executive Vice President and CFO ▪ Curtis R. Artis—Senior Vice President, Human Resources ▪ Paul A. Allaire (CEO and Chairman of the Board, Xerox)—Board Member ▪ Carla A. Hills (Chairman and CEO, Hills & Company)—Board Member ▪

Drew Lewis (Retired Chairman and CEO, Union Pacific Corp.)—Board Member ▪ Paul H. O'Neill (Chairman and CEO, Alcoa, Inc.)—Board Member ▪ Donald S. Perkins (Retired Chairman and CEO, Jewel Companies, Inc.)—Board Member ▪ Henry B. Schacht (Director and Senior Advisor, E.M. Warburg, Pincus & Co., LLC)—Board Member ▪ Franklin A. Thomas (Consultant, TFF Study Group)—Board Member ▪ John A. Young (Vice Chairman, Novell, Inc.)—Board Member

EVENT SUPPORTED: Phoenix Open

CHARITIES SUPPORTED: Various Vietnam Charities ▪ Adopt a School ▪ Lucent Global Science Scholars ▪ Project GRAD ▪ International Youth Foundation ▪ Lucent Universal Preschool Initiative ▪ Blind Foundation for India ▪ United Way ▪ Big Brothers Big Sisters of America ▪ Stanford University School of Engineering ▪ Habitat for Humanity ▪ Ronald McDonald House ▪ American Indian Science and Engineering Society ▪ Girls, Inc. ▪ National Action Council for Minorities in Engineering ▪ The Art Institute of Chicago ▪ The Metropolitan Museum of Art ▪ The Smithsonian Institution ▪ World Wildlife Fund

MBNA

CONTACT:
MBNA America Bank NA
1100 North King Street
Wilmington, DE 19884

TELEPHONE: (800) 441-7048

WEB: *www.mbna.com*

BUSINESS FOCUS: Credit cards

COMPANY BACKGROUND: MBNA is the largest independent credit card issuer in the world. MBNA manages loans totaling $73 billion. The MBNA workforce consists of 23,000 employees. For the past three years, *Fortune* magazine has ranked MBNA within the top ten companies to work for in America. MBNA is the official credit card for the NFL, NASCAR, PGA, NHL, and Major League Baseball. The main subsidiary of MBNA Corporation is MBNA America; the subsidiaries under MBNA America are Insurance Services, Marketing Systems, Consumer Services, and Hallmark Information Services.

NETWORKING SPECIFICS: MBNA uses many institutions to sell credit cards: everything from your local college alumni association to the NFL. Any of the institutions can be used as a reverse contact back to MBNA.

SHAREHOLDERS' MEETING DATE: April

VIPs AFFILIATED WITH THE COMPANY: Charlie Cawley—President ▪ John R. Cochran III—CMO ▪ Bruce L. Hammonds—COO ▪ M. Scot Kaufman—CFO ▪ Alfred Lerner—CEO and Chairman ▪ Michelle D. Shepherd—Vice Chairwoman ▪ Richard K. Struthers—Senior Vice Chairman ▪ Lance L. Weaver—Senior Vice Chairman ▪ William L. Jews (CEO of CareFirst Blue Cross Blue Shield)—Board Member

ORGANIZATIONS ENDORSING MBNA: GO Network ▪ Marine Corps Association ▪ Auburn University ▪ Georgetown University Alumni Association ▪ American Management Association ▪ American Automobile Association ▪ Montreal Canadiens ▪ National Football League ▪ National Education Association ▪ L. L. Bean ▪ SunTrust ▪ Sierra Club ▪ NASCAR ▪ Penn State University ▪ Toronto Raptors ▪ Northwestern University ▪ Baltimore Orioles ▪ Carnegie Hall ▪ Pittsburgh Pirates ▪ New York Yankees ▪ Gateway, Inc. ▪ Ameritrade ▪ Comerica

CHARITIES SUPPORTED: Many college alumni associations ▪ Garth Brooks Touch 'em All Foundation ▪ America's Promise—The Alliance for Youth

ORGANIZATION SPONSORED: NASCAR

McDonald's

CONTACT:
McDonald's Corporation
McDonald's Plaza
One McDonald's Drive
Oak Brook, IL 60523

TELEPHONE: (630) 623-3000

WEB: *www.mcdonalds.com*

BUSINESS FOCUS: Fast-food restaurants

COMPANY BACKGROUND: McDonald's is the largest food service retailer in the world, with restaurants in more than 115 countries. It operates McDonald's, Aroma Café, Chipotle Mexican Grill, Donatos Pizza, and Boston Market restaurants.

NETWORKING SPECIFICS: McDonald's is very committed to its Ronald McDonald House projects. This is a strong way in. The Olympics is another.

SHAREHOLDERS' MEETING DATE: May, in Rosemont, Illinois

VIPs AFFILIATED WITH THE COMPANY: Michael Conley—Executive Vice President, CFO ▪ Jack Greenburg—Chairman and CEO ▪ James Cantalupo—Vice Chairman and President ▪ Marlena Peleo-Lazar—Vice President, CCO ▪ Michael Quinlan—Chairman of the Executive Committee ▪ Fred Turner—Senior Chairman ▪ June Martino—Honorary Director ▪ Jeanne Jackson (CEO, Wal-Mart.com)—Board Member ▪ Walter Massey (President, Morehouse College)—Board Member ▪ Hall Adams, Jr. (Retired CEO, Leo Burnett & Co., Inc.)—Board Member ▪ Gordon Gray (Chairman, Rio Algom Limited)—Board Member ▪ Enrique Hernandez, Jr. (Chairman and CEO, Inter-Con Security Systems Inc.)—Board Member ▪ Donald Keough (Chairman, Allen & Company Incorporated)—Board Member ▪ Donald Lubin (Partner, Sonnenschein Nath & Rosenthal)—Board Member ▪ Andrew McKenna (Chairman and CEO, Schwarz Paper Company)—Board Member ▪ Terry Savage (Financial Journalist, Author, and President of Terry Savage Productions, Ltd.)—Board Member ▪ Roger Stone (Retired President and CEO, Smurfit-Stone Container Corporation)—Board Member ▪ Robert Thurston (Business Consultant)—Board Member ▪ Blair Vedder, Jr. (Retired COO, Needham Harper Worldwide, Inc.)—Board Member ▪ Tipper Gore ▪ U.S. Surgeon General David Satcher ▪ Jade Smalls (Miss Illinois 1999) ▪ Sammy Sosa ▪ Grant Hill ▪ Jason Alexander ▪ Michael Jordan ▪ Larry Bird

SPONSORING ACTIVITIES: NASCAR Winston Cup Racing Teams ▪ NASCAR Busch Racing Teams ▪ NBA ▪ Olympic Games ▪ McDonald's All-American High School Basketball Game ▪ McDonald's LPGA Championship

CORPORATE ALLIANCE: Disney

CHARITIES SUPPORTED: Ronald McDonald House ▪ Environmental Defense Fund ▪ UNESCO ▪ Interplast ▪ Operation Smile ▪ American Foundation for Suicide Prevention ▪ Y-ME National Breast Cancer Foundation ▪ American Diabetes Association

MCI WorldCom

CONTACT:
MCI WorldCom
500 Clinton Center Drive
Clinton, MS 39056

TELEPHONE: (601) 460-5600
(800) 844-1009

WEB: *www.wcom.com*

BUSINESS FOCUS: Telecommunications

COMPANY BACKGROUND: MCI WorldCom focuses on the future of communications through global networking and digital technology. WorldCom has recently been strengthened by mergers with MCI, CAI Wireless, Wireless One, and SkyTel. WorldCom consists of a workforce of 71,000 employees in over sixty-five countries.

NETWORKING SPECIFICS: Clinton, Mississippi, is a small town. Integration into the local Clinton/Jackson community should lead you anywhere you want to go into MCI WorldCom.

SHAREHOLDERS' MEETING DATE: June in Clinton, Mississippi

VIPs AFFILIATED WITH THE COMPANY: Bert C. Roberts, Jr.—Chairman ▪ Bernard J. Ebbers—President and CEO ▪ John W. Sidgmore—Vice Chairman ▪ Scott D. Sullivan—CFO and Secretary ▪ Clifford L. Alexander, Jr. (President, Alexander & Associates, Inc.; Chairman and CEO, Dunn & Bradstreet Corporation)—Board Member ▪ Judith Areen (Dean, Law Center, Georgetown University)—Board Member ▪ Max E. Bobbitt (Director, Cereus Technology Partners, Inc.)—Board Member ▪ Francesco Galesi (Chairman, Galesi Group)—Board Member ▪ Stiles A. Kellett, Jr. (Chairman, Kellett Investment Corporation)—Board Member ▪ John A. Porter (Chairman, TelTek, Inc.)—Board Member ▪ Lawrence C. Tucker (General Partner, Brown Brothers Harriman & Co.)—Board Member ▪ Juan Villalonga (Chairman and CEO, Telefonica de Espana, S.A.)—Board Member

CHARITIES SUPPORTED: National Council on Economic Education ▪ National Geographic Society ▪ National Endowment for the Humanities ▪ Council of the Great City Schools ▪ National Council of Teachers of Mathematics ▪ American Association for the Advancement of Science ▪ The Kennedy Center ▪ America's Promise—The Alliance for Youth ▪ Junior Achievement ▪ Susan G. Komen Foundation

ORGANIZATION SPONSORED: Indy Racing League

Merck

CONTACT:
Merck & Co., Inc.
One Merck Drive
PO Box 100
Whitehouse Station, NJ 08889-0100

TELEPHONE: (908) 423-1000

WEB: *www.merck.com*

BUSINESS FOCUS: Researches, manufactures, and markets health products and services

COMPANY BACKGROUND: As well as producing health products such as medicines and vaccines, Merck publishes *The Merck Index*, an encyclopedia of chemicals, drugs, and biologicals; *The Merck Manual*, a medical text; *The Merck Veterinary Manual*, a veterinary text; and *The Merck Manual of Geriatrics*, a geriatrics text. Merck's research is done through the Merck Research Laboratories, including the Merck Gene Index and the Merck Genome Research Institute.

NETWORKING SPECIFICS: Medical schools and charities are strong routes in.

SHAREHOLDERS' MEETING DATE: April, in North Branch, New Jersey

VIPs AFFILIATED WITH THE COMPANY: Raymond V. Gilmartin—Chairman, President, and CEO ▪ Judy C. Lewent—Senior Vice President and CFO ▪ Wendy L. Yarno—Senior Vice President, Human Resources ▪ Edward M. Scolnick, M.D.—Executive Vice President, Science and Technology; President, Merck Research Laboratories; Board Member ▪ H. Brewster Atwater, Jr. (Retired Chairman and CEO of General Mills, Inc.)—Board Member ▪ Lawrence A. Bossidy (Chairman of Honeywell International Inc.)—Board Member ▪ William G. Bowen, Ph.D. (President of The Andrew W. Mellon Foundation)—Board Member ▪ Johnnetta B. Cole, Ph.D. (Presidential Distinguished Professor, Emory University)—Board Member ▪ Lloyd C. Elam, M.D. (Professor of Psychiatry, Meharry Medical College)—Board Member ▪ Carleton S. Fiorina (President, CEO, and a Director, Hewlett-Packard Company)—Board Member ▪ William B. Harrison, Jr. (Chairman and CEO, The Chase Manhattan Corporation and The Chase Manhattan Bank)—Board Member ▪ William N. Kelley, M.D. (Professor of Medicine, Biochemistry, and Biophysics, University of Pennsylvania School of Medicine)—Board Member ▪ Anne M. Tatlock (President, CEO, and a Director, Fiduciary Trust Company International)—Board Member ▪ Samuel O. Thier, M.D. (President, CEO, and a Director, Partners Health Care System, Inc.)—Board Member ▪ Dennis Weatherstone (Retired Chairman, J.P. Morgan & Co. Incorporated and Morgan Guaranty Trust Company of New York)—Board Member

CHARITIES SUPPORTED: Ministries of Health ▪ World Health Organization ▪ The World Bank ▪ UNICEF ▪ United Nations Development Program ▪ Project HOPE ▪ Harvard AIDS Institute ▪ New Jersey Performing Arts Institute ▪ University of Cape Town, South Africa ▪ United Negro College Fund ▪ National AIDS Fund ▪ Partnership for a Drug-Free America

Metropolitan Life Insurance

CONTACT:
Metropolitan Life Insurance Company
One Madison Avenue
New York, NY 10010

TELEPHONE: (212) 578-2211

WEB: *www.metlife.com*

BUSINESS FOCUS: Insurance and financial services

COMPANY BACKGROUND: Metropolitan Life Insurance Company is America's largest life insurer, covering one out of every eleven U.S. households. In January 2000, its policyholders voted for the company to become a stock company, called MetLife, Inc.

NETWORKING SPECIFICS: Charities are strong ways in.

VIPs AFFILIATED WITH THE COMPANY: Robert H. Benmosche—Chairman of the Board and CEO ▪ Gerald Clark—Vice Chairman of the Board and Chief Investment Officer ▪ Stewart G. Nagler—Vice Chairman of the Board and CFO ▪ William J. Toppeta—President, Client Services and CAO ▪ Curtis H. Barnette (Chairman and CEO, Bethlehem Steel Corporation)—Board Member ▪ Joan Ganz Cooney (Chairman, Executive

Committee, Children's Television Workshop)—Board Member ▪ Burton A. Dole, Jr. (Retired Chairman, President, and CEO, Puritan Bennett)—Board Member ▪ James R. Houghton (Chairman of the Board, Emeritus, Corning Incorporated)—Board Member ▪ Harry P. Kamen (Retired Chairman of the Board and CEO, Metropolitan Insurance Company)—Board Member ▪ Helene L. Kaplan (Of Counsel, Skadden, Arps, Slate, Meagher, & Flom)—Board Member ▪ Charles M. Leighton (Retired Chairman and CEO, CML Group, Inc.)—Board Member ▪ Allen E. Murray (Retired Chairman of the Board and CEO, Mobil Corporation)—Board Member ▪ John J. Phelan, Jr. (Retired Chairman and CEO, New York Stock Exchange, Inc.)—Board Member ▪ Hugh B. Price (President and CEO, National Urban League, Inc.)—Board Member ▪ Ruth J. Simmons (President, Smith College)—Board Member ▪ William C. Steere, Jr. (Chairman of the Board and CEO, Pfizer Inc.)—Board Member ▪ Snoopy—MetLife's Mascot

CHARITIES SUPPORTED: United Way ▪ Partnership for a Drug-Free America ▪ National AIDS Fund ▪ Alzheimer's Association ▪ National Center for Health Education ▪ PBS ▪ Lincoln Center ▪ The Smithsonian Institution ▪ American Ballet Theatre ▪ Boys and Girls Clubs of America ▪ National 4-H Council ▪ National Urban League ▪ Habitat for Humanity ▪ National Equity Fund ▪ The Metropolitan Museum of Art

Microsoft Corporation

CONTACT:
Microsoft Corporation
One Microsoft Way
Redmond, WA 98052-6399

TELEPHONE: (425) 882-8080

WEB: *www.microsoft.com*

BUSINESS FOCUS: Computer software

COMPANY BACKGROUND: Microsoft Corporation is the world's leading manufacturer of software as well as personal and business computing. Microsoft employs around 70,000 individuals throughout America and across the globe. Their chair, Bill Gates, is one of the great pioneers of the Information Age. The Bill and Melinda Gates Foundation has over twenty billion dollars. They are slowly becoming the largest charitable donors in the world.

NETWORKING SPECIFICS: Trade shows and business schools are the best way in.

SHAREHOLDERS' MEETING DATE: November, in Bellevue, Washington

VIPs AFFILIATED WITH THE COMPANY: Steve Ballmer—President ▪ Bill Gates—Chairman and CEO ▪ Robert J. Herbold—Executive Vice President and COO ▪ John Connors—Senior Vice President and CFO ▪ Deborah N. Willingham—Vice President, Human Resources ▪ Rick Devenuti—Vice President and CIO ▪ Paul G. Allen (Chairman, Vulcan Northwest, Inc.)—Board Member ▪ Jill Barad (President and CEO, Mattel, Inc.)—Board Member ▪ Wm. G. Reed, Jr. (Former Chairman, Simpson Investment Company)—Board Member ▪ Jon A. Shirley (Former President and COO, Microsoft Corporation)—Board Member ▪ Richard A. Hackborn (Chairman Elect, Hewlett-Packard Company)—Board Member ▪ David F. Marquardt (General Partner, August Capital and Technology Venture Investors)—Board Member

CHARITIES SUPPORTED: United Way ▪ SeniorNet ▪ Green Thumb ▪ National Council on Aging ▪ National Foundation for Teaching Entrepreneurship ▪ American Lung Association ▪ American Red Cross ▪ America's Promise—The Alliance for Youth ▪ Boys and Girls Clubs of America ▪ Habitat for Humanity ▪ International Youth Foundation ▪ Lions Club ▪ National Multiple Sclerosis Society ▪ Salvation Army ▪ World Wildlife Fund ▪ Youth Service America ▪ New York University ▪ Seattle Art Museum ▪ Seattle Symphony Orchestra ▪ Boy Scouts of America ▪ Mothers Against Violence in America ▪ The Nature Conservancy ▪ World Affairs Council

■ University of Texas at Austin ■ University of California at Berkeley ■ UCLA ■ University of Illinois ■ University of Michigan ■ MIT ■ Big Brothers Big Sisters of America ■ AIDS Project ■ Easter Seals Society ■ Goodwill Industries ■ United Cerebral Palsy ■ Junior Achievement ■ Domestic Abuse Women's Network ■ YMCA ■ YMCA ■ Volunteers of America ■ Save the Children ■ Starlight Children's Foundation

Minnesota Mining and Manufacturing

CONTACT:

3M Corporation
3M Center
St. Paul, MN 55144

TELEPHONE: (651) 733-1110

WEB: *www.3m.com*

BUSINESS FOCUS: Product innovation

COMPANY BACKGROUND: In addition to Post-it notes, 3M is into manufacturing electronics and insulation. The auto industry is their main focus.

NETWORKING SPECIFICS: Contacts in the automotive industry are strong ways into 3M. The charity/shareholder route is strong as well.

SHAREHOLDERS' MEETING DATE: Mid-May in St. Paul, Minnesota

VIPs AFFILIATED WITH THE COMPANY: L. D. Simone—Chairman and CEO ■ Ronald O. Baukel—EVP Internal Operations ■ Kay Grenz—VP, Human Resources ■ Edward Brennan (Former Chairman and CEO, Sears)—Board Member ■ Allen Murry (Former Chairman and CEO, Mobil)—Board Member ■ Rozanne Ridgeway (Former Assistant Secretary of State)—Board Member ■ Frank Shrontz (Former Chairman and CEO, Boeing)—Board Member ■ Lewis Sullivan (President, Moorehouse School of Medicine)—Board Member

CHARITIES SUPPORTED: Carleton College ■ Junior Achievement ■ Cornell University ■ Duke University ■ Massachusetts Institute of Technology ■ Vanderbilt University ■ University of Texas at Austin ■ American Red Cross ■ Goodwill Industries ■ Habitat for Humanity ■ Meals On Wheels ■ Project HOPE ■ Salvation Army ■ Second Harvest Food Bank ■ Special Olympics ■ YMCA ■ YWCA ■ Big Brothers Big Sisters ■ Boys and Girls Clubs of America ■ Boys Scouts of America ■ Camp Fire Boys and Girls ■ Girl Scouts ■ United Way ■ Smithsonian Institution ■ Make-A-Wish Foundation

Morgan Stanley Dean Witter

CONTACT:

Morgan Stanley Dean Witter & Co.
1585 Broadway
New York, NY 10036

TELEPHONE: (212) 761-4000

WEB: *www.msdw.com*

BUSINESS FOCUS: Financial services

COMPANY BACKGROUND: Morgan Stanley Dean Witter & Co. provides financial services in the areas of asset management, credit services, and securities in twenty-five countries worldwide. It also owns the Discover brand consumer credit card.

NETWORKING SPECIFICS: Business schools are the best way in.

SHAREHOLDERS' MEETING DATE: March

VIPs AFFILIATED WITH THE COMPANY: Philip J. Purcell—Chairman and CEO ▪ John J. Mack—President and COO ▪ Donald G. Kempf, Jr.—Chief Legal Officer and Secretary ▪ John J. Schaefer—Chief Strategic and Administrative Officer ▪ Robert G. Scott—CFO ▪ Joanne Pace—Controller and Principal Accounting Officer ▪ Robert P. Bauman (Former CEO, SmithKline Beecham plc)—Board Member ▪ Edward A. Brennan (Former Chairman and CEO, Sears, Roebuck and Co.)—Board Member ▪ Diana D. Brooks (President and CEO, Sotheby's Holdings, Inc.)—Board Member ▪ Daniel B. Burke (Former CEO, President, and COO, Capital Cities/ABC, Inc.)—Board Member ▪ C. Robert Kidder (Chairman and CEO, Borden, Inc.)—Board Member ▪ Charles F. Knight (Chairman and CEO, Emerson Electric Co.)—Board Member ▪ John W. Madigan (Chairman, President, and CEO, Tribune Company)—Board Member ▪ Miles L. Marsh (Chairman and CEO, Fort James Corporation)—Board Member ▪ Michael A. Miles (Special Limited Partner, Forstmann Little & Co.)—Board Member ▪ Allen E. Murray (Former Chairman and CEO, Mobil Corporation)—Board Member ▪ Clarence B. Rogers, Jr. (Former Chairman of the Board and CEO, Equifax Inc.)—Board Member ▪ Laura D'Andrea Tyson (Dean, Walter A. Haas School of Business, University of California at Berkeley)—Board Member

CHARITIES SUPPORTED: America's Promise—The Alliance for Youth ▪ The Metropolitan Museum of Art ▪ Museum of Modern Art ▪ Partnership for a Drug-Free America ▪ Make-A-Wish Foundation ▪ Project A.L.S.

Motorola

CONTACT:
Motorola
1303 East Algonquin Road
Schaumburg, IL 60196

TELEPHONE: (847) 576-5000

WEB: *www.motorola.com*

BUSINESS FOCUS: Communications

COMPANY BACKGROUND: Motorola is in the communications business—everything from cellular telephones to land mobile communications. They are also in the semiconductor and auto components business.

NETWORKING SPECIFICS: Networking through charitable functions is the strongest way in. They are big supporters of Junior Achievement.

SHAREHOLDERS' MEETING DATE: May

VIPs AFFILIATED WITH THE COMPANY: Gary Tooker—Chairman of the Board ▪ Christopher Galvin—CEO ▪ Robert Growney—President and COO ▪ Keith Bane—EVP ▪ Glenn A. Gienko—EVP, Human Resources ▪ Carl Koenemann—CFO ▪ Lawrence Fuller (CEO of Amoco)—Board Member ▪ Ann Jones (FCC Retired)—Board Member ▪ Judy Lewent (CFO of Merck Co., Inc.)—Board Member ▪ Walter Massy (President, Morehouse College)—Board Member ▪ Nicholas Negroponte (MIT)—Board Member ▪ John Pepper (Chairman and CEO, Procter & Gamble)—Board Member ▪ John White (Chancellor, University of Arkansas)—Board Member

CHARITIES SUPPORTED: Junior Achievement ▪ The American Red Cross ▪ Boys and Girls Club ▪ The Art Institute of Chicago ▪ National Law Enforcement Officers Memorial Fund ▪ World Wildlife Fund ▪ Elton John AIDS Foundation

EVENTS SPONSORED: Spirit Awards

New York Life Insurance

CONTACT:
New York Life Insurance Company
51 Madison Avenue
New York, NY 10010

TELEPHONE: (212) 576-2000

WEB: www.newyorklife.com

BUSINESS FOCUS: Insurance

COMPANY BACKGROUND: New York Life Insurance offers life insurance and annuities, stable value products, long-term care insurance, institutional asset management, trust services, and securities products and services. It is a mutual life insurance company rather than a public one, and so has no shareholders. Some of its clients include General Motors, the National Basketball Association, the Air Line Pilots Association, and The American Institute of Architects.

NETWORKING SPECIFICS: In addition to the conventional routes, any connections in Major League Soccer will get you in the door. New York Life is a major sponsor of MLS and its youth efforts.

VIPs AFFILIATED WITH THE COMPANY: Sy Sternberg—Chairman of the Board, President, and CEO ▪ Gary G. Benanav—Vice Chairman ▪ Frederick J. Sievert—Vice Chairman ▪ Howard I. Atkins—Executive Vice President and CFO ▪ Richard M. Kernan, Jr.—Executive Vice President and Chief Investment Officer ▪ Judith E. Campbell—Senior Vice President and CIO ▪ James L. Broadhead (Chairman of the Board and CEO, FPL Group, Inc.; Chairman and CEO, Florida Light and Power Company)—Board Member ▪ William G. Burns (Former Vice Chairman, NYNEX Corporation)—Board Member ▪ Betty C. Alewine (President and CEO, COMSAT Corporation)—Board Member ▪ Kent B. Foster (Retired President, GTE Corporation)—Board Member ▪ Leslie G. McCraw, Jr. (Retired Chairman and CEO, Fluor Corporation)—Board Member ▪ Richard R. Pivarotto (Retired Chairman, Associated Dry Goods Corporation)—Board Member ▪ Harry G. Hohn (Retired Chairman and CEO, New York Life)—Board Member ▪ Robert M. Baylis (Former Vice Chairman, CS First Boston, Inc.)—Board Member ▪ Patricia T. Carbine (Cofounder and President, Ms. Foundation for Education and Communication, Inc.; Cofounder, Ms. Foundation for Women, Inc.)—Board Member ▪ David W. Mitchell (Retired Chairman and CEO, Avon Products, Inc.)—Board Member ▪ Conrad K. Harper (Partner, Law Firm of Simpson Thatcher & Bartlett; Former Legal Advisor, Department of the State; Former Member, Court of Arbitration at The Hague)—Board Member

CHARITIES SUPPORTED: United Way ▪ Goodwill Industries ▪ Big Brothers Big Sisters ▪ Boys and Girls Clubs of America ▪ Girl Scouts ▪ National Junior Achievement ▪ YMCA ▪ City Harvest ▪ Heart-to-Heart International ▪ American Red Cross ▪ Women's Bar Association of the State of New York ▪ PBS ▪ The Metropolitan Museum of Art ▪ National AIDS Fund

The New York Times Company

CONTACT:
The New York Times Company
229 West Forty-third Street, 10th Floor
New York, NY 10036

TELEPHONE: (212) 556-3660

WEB: www.nytco.com

BUSINESS FOCUS: Communications

COMPANY BACKGROUND: The New York Times Company is one of the most important media companies in the world. It runs numerous media outlets including the *New York Times*, the *Boston Globe*, New York Times Digital, The New York Times Broadcast Group, The New York Times Magazine Group. The *New York Times* has won seventy-seven Pulitzer Prizes, the most of any newspaper, and is circulated among over 2.5 million subscribers. The New York Times Broadcasting Group also owns four CBS, two NBC, and two ABC television stations.

NETWORKING SPECIFICS: The major journalism schools are strong routes in.

SHAREHOLDERS' MEETING DATE: April in New York, New York

VIPs AFFILIATED WITH THE COMPANY: Arthur Sulzberger, Jr.—Chairman and Publisher, The New York Times Company ▪ Russell T. Lewis—President and CEO, The New York Times Company ▪ Cynthia H. Augustine—Senior Vice President, Human Resources, The New York Times Company ▪ John M. O'Brien—Senior Vice President and CFO, The New York Times Company ▪ Janet L. Robinson—President and General Manager, the *New York Times* ▪ Joseph Lelyveld—Executive Editor, the *New York Times* ▪ Richard H. Gilman—Publisher, the *Boston Globe* ▪ William B. Huff—President, the *Boston Globe* ▪ Matthew V. Storin—Editor, the *Boston Globe* ▪ C. Frank Roberts—Chairman, The New York Times Broadcast Group ▪ Cynthia H. Augustine—President, The New York Times Broadcast Group ▪ Leonard P. Forman—President and CEO, The New York Times Magazine Group ▪ Keith M. Levitt—COO, The New York Times Magazine Group ▪ Martin A. Nisenholtz—CEO, New York Times Digital ▪ David A. Thurm—COO, New York Times Digital ▪ Ellen Taus—CFO, New York Times Digital ▪ Muriel R. Watkins—Vice President, Human Resources and Communications, New York Times Digital ▪ Richard L. Gelb (Chairman Emeritus, Bristol-Myers Squibb Company)—Board Member ▪ William O. Taylor (Chairman Emeritus, Globe Newspaper Company, Inc.)—Board Member

CHARITIES SUPPORTED: The Metropolitan Museum of Art ▪ World Wildlife Fund

EVENT SPONSORED: Spirit Awards

Nike

CONTACT:
Nike World Headquarters
One Bowerman Drive
Beaverton, OR 97005-6453

TELEPHONE: (800) 806-6453

WEB: *www.nike.com*

BUSINESS FOCUS: Athletic shoes and apparel manufacturing

COMPANY BACKGROUND: Nike is a leading manufacturer of athletic shoes and apparel. Cole Haan, a subsidiary of Nike, makes men's and women's shoes and accessories.

NETWORKING SPECIFICS: If you're looking to network with Nike brass, the Super Show in Atlanta is a great place to start. In addition, any major sporting event would be strong. Last time we were at the U.S. Open Tennis tournament, we ran into Phil Knight. Elliot's brother sat down and had drinks with him.

SHAREHOLDERS' MEETING DATE: September

VIPs AFFILIATED WITH THE COMPANY: Thomas E. Clarke—President, New Business Ventures, and COO ▪ Philip H. Knight—Chairman, President, and CEO ▪ Donald Blair—Vice President and CFO ▪ Michael Jordan (President, the Michael Jordan Foundation)—Advisory Council Member ▪ John R. Thompson, Jr. (Former Head Basketball Coach, Georgetown University)—Board Member ▪ Jill K. Conway (Visiting Scholar, Massachusetts Institute of Technology)—Board Member ▪ Ralph D. DeNunzio (President, Harbor Point Associates, Inc.)—Board Member ▪ Richard K. Donahue (Vice Chairman of the Board, Lowell, Massachusetts) ▪ Delbert J. Hayes—Board Member ▪ Douglas G. Houser (Assistant Secretary, Nike Inc.; Partner, Bullivant, Houser, Bailey, Pendergrass & Hoffman, Attorneys)—Board Member ▪ John E. Jaqua (Secretary, Nike Inc.; Partner, Jacqua & Wheatley, P.C., Attorneys)—Board Member ▪ Charles W. Robinson (President, Robinson & Associates, Venture Capital)—Board Member ▪ William J. Bowerman (Director Emeritus)—Board Member ▪ A. Michael Spence (Dean, Stanford University Graduate School of Business)—Board Member ▪ Tiger Woods—Member of Nike Golf's Design and Development Team ▪ Charles Barkley—Host of On-line Charles Barkley Network (sponsored by Nike) ▪ Heather Locklear

NIKE ATHLETES: Lance Armstrong ▪ Dale Jarrett ▪ Randy Johnson ▪ Donna Richardson ▪ Ken Griffey, Jr. ▪ Mia Hamm ▪ Greg Maddux ▪ Roy Jones, Jr. ▪ U.S. Women's Soccer Team ▪ Alex Rodriguez ▪ Casey Martin ▪ Chan Ho Park ▪ Alberto Salazar ▪ L.A. Lakers ▪ Pete Sampras ▪ Tom Glavine ▪ Mark McGuire ▪ Derek Jeter ▪ Carl Lewis ▪ Deion Sanders

CHARITIES SUPPORTED: International Youth Foundation ▪ Tuck School of Business at Dartmouth College ▪ University of North Carolina's School of Public Health ▪ Boys and Girls Clubs of America ▪ Women's Sports Foundation ▪ Let Us Play Girls Sport Camp ▪ Sportsbridge ▪ WNBA Be Active ▪ 100 Black Men of America ▪ America's Promise—The Alliance for Youth ▪ YWCA

EVENT SPONSORED: Nike U.S. Women's Cup (Soccer)

Oracle Corporation

CONTACT:
Oracle Corporation
500 Oracle Parkway
Redwood City, CA 94065

TELEPHONE: (650) 506-7000

WEB: *www.oracle.com*

BUSINESS FOCUS: Software

BACKGROUND INFORMATION: Oracle's business is supplying corporations with software that deals with information management. The two areas of focus are systems software and business applications software. There are over 43,000 people that work for Oracle.

NETWORKING SPECIFICS: Trade shows are king.

SHAREHOLDERS' MEETING DATE: May

VIPs AFFILIATED WITH THE COMPANY: Lawrence Ellison—CEO and Chairman ▪ Jeffrey Henley—Executive Vice President and CFO ▪ Gary Bloom—Executive Vice President ▪ Randy Baker—Executive Vice President, Support Services ▪ Jay Nussbaum—Executive Vice President, Service Industries ▪ Jeffrey Berg (Chairman and CEO, International Creative Management)—Board Member ▪ Dr. Michael J. Boskin (Professor of Economics, Stanford University; President, Boskin & Co.)—Board Member ▪ Jack F. Kemp (Codirector, Empower America)—Board Member ▪ Kay Koplovitz (Founder, USA Networks)—Board Member ▪ Donald L. Lucas (Venture Capitalist)—Board Member ▪ Richard A. McGinn (Chairman and CEO, Lucent Technologies)—Board Member ▪ George Roberts—Executive Vice President, North America Sales ▪ Edward (Sandy) Sanderson—Executive Vice President, Consulting

CHARITIES SUPPORTED: Project HOPE ▪ St. Jude's Research Hospital ▪ World Wildlife Fund ▪ Boys and Girls Club ▪ Junior Achievement ▪ YMCA ▪ The Breast Cancer Fund ▪ Juvenile Diabetes Foundation

PepsiCo

CONTACT:
PepsiCo, Inc.
700 Anderson Hill Road
Purchase, NY 10577

TELEPHONE: (914) 253-2000

WEB: *www.pepsico.com*

BUSINESS FOCUS: Prepackaged foods

COMPANY BACKGROUND: PepsiCo, Inc., produces and markets snack foods and beverages for Pepsi, Frito Lay, and Tropicana, and also partners with Starbucks and Lipton to produce other bottled beverages. It also provides its products to Kentucky Fried Chicken, Taco Bell, and Pizza Hut.

NETWORKING SPECIFICS: Inroads into Pepsi can come in many forms. They are a large sponsor of numerous sporting events and festivals. You can't hold a weenie roast anywhere in America without Pepsi or Coca-Cola competing for sponsorship. This is a fantastic way in at a local level.

SHAREHOLDERS' MEETING DATE: May

VIPs AFFILIATED WITH THE COMPANY: Roger A. Enrico—Chairman of the Board and CEO ▪ Margret D. Moore—Senior Vice President, Personnel ▪ Indra K. Nooyi—Senior Vice President, CFO ▪ Steven S. Reinemund—President and COO ▪ Stephen Schuckenbrock—Senior Vice President, Information Technology, and CIO ▪ Franklin D. Raines (Chairman of the Board and CEO, Fannie Mae)—Board Member ▪ Arthur C. Martinez (Chairman of the Board, President, and CEO, Sears, Roebuck and Co.)—Board Member ▪ Jeff Gordon ▪ Shaquille O'Neal

CHARITIES SUPPORTED: YWCA ▪ MENC: The National Association for Music Education ▪ Habitat for Humanity ▪ The Metropolitan Museum of Art ▪ Partnership for a Drug-Free America ▪ Sierra Club ▪ YMCA ▪ Susan G. Komen Foundation

ORGANIZATION SPONSORED: NASCAR

Pfizer, Inc.

CONTACT:
Pfizer, Inc.
235 East Forty-second Street
New York, NY 10017-5755

TELEPHONE: (212) 573-2323

WEB: *www.pfizer.com*

BUSINESS FOCUS: Pharmaceuticals

COMPANY BACKGROUND: Pfizer is one of the world's leading research-based pharmaceutical companies with products that can be found in 150 countries across the globe and a workforce of almost 50,000 employees. Their most recognized product is Viagra.

NETWORKING SPECIFICS: Medical schools and business schools are strong ways in.

SHAREHOLDERS' MEETING DATE: April in New York City

VIPs AFFILIATED WITH THE CORPORATION: William C. Steere, Jr.—Chairman and CEO ▪ Henry A. McKinnell—President and COO ▪ John F. Niblack—Vice Chairman ▪ C. L. Clemente—Executive Vice President and Secretary ▪ David L. Shedlarz—Executive Vice President and CFO ▪ M. Anthony Burns (Chairman and CEO, Ryder System, Inc.)—Board Member ▪ W. Don Cornwell (Chairman and CEO, Granite Broadcasting Corp.)—Board Member ▪ George B. Harvey (Former Chairman, President, and CEO, Pitney Bowes, Inc.)—Board Member ▪ Constance J. Horner (Guest Scholar, The Brookings Institution; Former Assistant to the President of the U.S.)—Board Member ▪ Stanley O. Ikenberry (President, American Council on Education)—Board Member ▪ Harry P. Kamen (Former President, Chairman, and CEO, Metropolitan Life Insurance Company)—Board Member ▪ Thomas G. Lebrecque (Former Chairman, The Chase Manhattan Corporation)—Board Member ▪ Dana G. Mead (Chairman, Tenneco Automotive, Inc., and Pactiv Corporation)—Board Member ▪ Franklin D. Raines (Chairman and CEO, Fannie Mae)—Board Member ▪ Ruth J. Simmons (President, Smith College)—Board Member ▪ Jean Paul Valles (Chairman and CEO, Minerals Technologies, Inc.)—Board Member

SPONSORING ACTIVITY: Senior Olympics

CHARITIES SUPPORTED: International Trachoma Initiative ▪ United Way ▪ Community Health Ventures ▪ The Metropolitan Museum of Art ▪ America's Promise—The Alliance for Youth ▪ American Diabetes Association ▪ National AIDS Fund ▪ Partnership for a Drug-Free America ▪ Project HOPE

Philip Morris

CONTACT:
Philip Morris
120 Park Avenue
New York, NY 10017

TELEPHONE: (212) 880-5000

WEB: *www.philipmorris.com*

BUSINESS FOCUS: Consumables

COMPANY BACKGROUND: In addition to their cigarette business, Philip Morris owns Kraft Foods, Jell-O, and Miller Brewing. Also, Philip Morris recently purchased Nabisco. The onslaught of lawsuits has prompted many shareholdes to want the food and tobacco businesses to be broken apart, but at this point they have not done it.

NETWORKING SPECIFICS: Ways into big Mo start with sports. Top execs from Miller and Phillip Morris can be found everywhere from prizefights to ladies' tennis. If people are playing with a ball professionally, chances are Big Tobacco or Big Beer are funding it.

SHAREHOLDERS' MEETING DATE: Late April

VIP'S AFFILIATED WITH THE COMPANY: Geoffery Bible—Chairman and CEO ▪ Murray Bring—Vice Chairman ▪ William Webb—COO ▪ Louis Camilleri—CRO ▪ Timothy Sompolski—Senior Vice President, Human Resources ▪ Michael Szymanczyk—President ▪ Robert Eckert—CEO, Kraft Foods ▪ John MacDonough—CEO,

Miller Brewing Company ▪ Elizabeth Bailey (Wharton School of Business)—Board Member ▪ William Donaldson (Cofounder, Donaldson, Lufkin, and Jenrette)—Board Member ▪ Rupert Murdoch (Billionaire)—Board Member ▪ Lucio Noto (Vice Chairman, Exxon Mobil Corporation)—Board Member ▪ Richard Parsons (President, Time Warner)—Board Member ▪ John Reed (Chairman and DEO, US Air)—Board Member ▪ Billie Jean King—Board Member

CHARITIES SUPPORTED: Richmond Ballet ▪ Washington, D.C., Ballet ▪ Habitat for Humanity ▪ American Red Cross ▪ Meals On Wheels ▪ The Art Institute of Chicago ▪ The Metropolitan Museum of Art ▪ Museum of Modern Art ▪ America's Second Harvest ▪ American Diabetes Association ▪ Literacy Volunteers of America ▪ National AIDS Fund ▪ World Wildlife Fund

Phillips Petroleum Company

CONTACT:
Phillips Petroleum Company
Phillips Building
Bartlesville, OK 74004

TELEPHONE: (918) 661-6600

WEB: *www.phillips66.com*

BUSINESS FOCUS: Oil, gas, and energy

COMPANY BACKGROUND: The products created by Phillips Petroleum Company are widely used throughout thirty-six states. Phillips Petroleum is divided into four specific groups: exploration and production; gas gathering, processing and marketing; refining, marketing and transportation; and chemicals. The workforce that drives Phillips is 15,900 employees strong.

NETWORKING SPECIFICS: Bartlesville, Oklahoma, is a company town. Fifteen minutes at a local eatery, and you have begun your networking journey.

SHAREHOLDERS' MEETING DATE: May in Bartlesville, Oklahoma

VIPs AFFILIATED WITH THE COMPANY: J. J. Mulva—Chairman and CEO ▪ T. C. Morris—Senior Vice President and CFO ▪ E. L. Batchelder—Vice President and CIO ▪ Norman R. Augustine (Chairman, Executive Committee, Lockheed Martin Corporation)—Board Member ▪ David L. Boren (President, University of Oklahoma)—Board Member ▪ Larry D. Horner (Chairman, Pacific USA Holdings Corporation)—Board Member ▪ Robert E. Chappell, Jr. (Self-employed Management and Investment Consultant)—Board Member ▪ Robert M. Devlin (Chairman, President, and CEO, American General Corporation)—Board Member ▪ Kathryn C. Turner (Chairperson and CEO, Standard Technology, Inc.)—Board Member

SPONSORING ACTIVITIES: NASCAR Driver Todd Bodine ▪ USA Swimming ▪ NCAA Conferences: Big Twelve Conference, Big Ten Conference, Big South Conference, Rocky Mountain Athletic Conference, Missouri Valley Conference, Conference USA, Mountain West Conference

CHARITIES SUPPORTED: Boys and Girls Clubs ▪ Boy Scouts ▪ Junior Achievement

Procter & Gamble

CONTACT:
The Procter & Gamble Company
PO Box 599
Cincinnati, OH 45201-0599

TELEPHONE: (513) 983-1100

BUSINESS FOCUS: Manufactures beauty care, food, beverage, health care, laundry and cleaning, and paper products

COMPANY BACKGROUND: Procter & Gamble sells its products in over 140 countries. Some of P&G's more than 100 brands include Secret, Pantene Pro-V, Pert Plus, Noxzema, Hugo Boss, Ivory, Cover Girl, Crisco, Folgers, Jif, Pringles, Sunny Delight, NyQuil, Crest, Dawn, Cheer, Mr. Clean, Downy, Comet, Pampers, Charmin, Bounty, and Always. Procter & Gamble owns *The Guiding Light* and *As the World Turns*, two daytime soap operas. In addition to the charities that Procter & Gamble directly supports, they give money to their customers (Kroger, Target, etc.) to be used for charitable giving.

NETWORKING SPECIFICS: The conventional routes in are strong.

SHAREHOLDERS' MEETING DATE: October

VIPs AFFILIATED WITH THE COMPANY: Durk I. Jager—President, Chairman, and CEO ▪ Clayton C. Daley, Jr.—CFO ▪ G. Gilbert Cloyd—CTO ▪ Charles R. Lee (Chairman and CEO, GTE Corporation)—Board Member ▪ John F. Smith, Jr. (Chairman and CEO, General Motors Corporation)—Board Member ▪ Edwin L. Artzt (Retired Chairman of the Board and Chief Executive, Spalding Sports Worldwide, Inc.)—Board Member ▪ Norman R. Augustine (Chairman of the Executive Committee, Lockheed Martin Corporation)—Board Member ▪ Donald R. Beall (Retired Chairman and CEO, Rockwell International Corporation; Chairman of the Executive Committee, Rockwell International Corporation)—Board Member ▪ Richard B. Cheney (CEO, Halliburton Company)—Board Member ▪ Richard J. Ferris (Retired Cochairman, Doubletree Corporation)—Board Member ▪ Joseph I. Gorman (Chairman and CEO, TRW Inc.)—Board Member ▪ Lynn M. Martin (Professor, J. L. Kellogg Graduate School of Management, Northwestern University)—Board Member ▪ Ralph Snyderman (Chancellor for Health Affairs, Executive Dean, School of Medecine at Duke University; President/CEO, Duke University Health System)—Board Member ▪ Robert D. Storey (Partner, Law Firm of Thompson, Hine, and Flory, LLP)—Board Member ▪ Marina v.N. Whitman (Professor of Business Administration and Public Policy, University of Michigan)—Board Member

CHARITIES SUPPORTED: Project HOPE ▪ CARE's Primary Education Project ▪ Second Harvest ▪ American Red Cross ▪ United Way ▪ Milwaukee School of Engineering ▪ Western Michigan University ▪ Juvenile Diabetes Foundation ▪ The Nature Conservancy ▪ America's Promise—The Alliance for Youth ▪ American Diabetes Association ▪ Partnership for a Drug-Free America ▪ Save the Children ▪ World Wildlife Fund

Prudential Insurance Company of America

CONTACT:

The Prudential Insurance Company of America
751 Broad Street
Newark, NJ 07102

TELEPHONE: (973) 802-2589

WEB: *www.prudential.com*

BUSINESS FOCUS: Financial services and insurance

COMPANY BACKGROUND: Prudential is the largest insurance company in North America. It is not publicly traded but instead controlled by its policyholders.

NETWORKING SPECIFICS: Trade conferences and business schools are where we would start.

POLICYHOLDERS' MEETING DATE: July

VIPs AFFILIATED WITH THE COMPANY: Arthur F. Ryan—Chairman and CEO ▪ Michele S. Darling—Executive Vice President, Human Resources ▪ William M. Bethke—CIO ▪ Richard J. Carbone—CFO ▪ John M. Liftin— Senior Vice President and General Counsel ▪ James G. Cullen (President and COO, Bell Atlantic Corporation)—Board Member ▪ Roger A. Enrico (Chairman and CEO, PepsiCo, Inc.)—Board Member ▪ Allan D. Gilmour (Former Vice Chairman, Ford Motor Company)—Board Member ▪ Glen H. Hiner (Chairman and CEO, Owens Corning)—Board Member ▪ Constance J. Horner (Guest Scholar, The Brookings Institution)— Board Member ▪ Charles R. Sitter (Former President, Exxon Corporation)—Board Member ▪ Donald L. Staheli (Retired Chairman and CEO, Continental Grain Company)—Board Member ▪ P. Roy Vagelos (Former Chairman and CEO, Merck & Co., Inc.)—Board Member

CHARITIES SUPPORTED: Child Welfare League of America, Inc. ▪ Children Defense Fund ▪ Children's Television Workshop ▪ United Negro College Fund ▪ Habitat for Humanity ▪ The Metropolitan Museum of Art ▪ America's Promise—The Alliance for Youth

RadioShack Corporation

CONTACT:

RadioShack
100 Throckmorton Street, Suite 1800
Fort Worth, TX 76102

TELEPHONE: (817) 415-3700

WEB: *www.radioshack.com*

BUSINESS FOCUS: Electronics

COMPANY BACKGROUND: There are approximately 7,100 RadioShack stores spread throughout the U.S. They are striving to become America's favorite place to buy electronics.

NETWORKING SPECIFICS: RadioShack is very involved with the Fort Worth community. Local charities are a great place to start. Their strong support of Junior Achievement and the public school system are your best bets.

SHAREHOLDERS' MEETING DATE: May in Fort Worth, Texas.

VIPs AFFILIATED WITH THE COMPANY: Leonard H. Roberts—Chairman, President, and CEO ▪ Evelyn Follit— Senior Vice President and CIO ▪ Dwain H. Hughes—Senior Vice President and CFO ▪ David Edmondson— Executive Vice President and COO ▪ Francesca Spinelli—Senior Vice President of People ▪ Frank J. Belatti (Chairman, AFC Enterprises, Inc.)—Board Member ▪ Jack L. Messman (President and CEO, Cambridge Technology Partners, Inc.)—Board Member ▪ Ronald E. Elmquist (Chairman, CEO, and President, Keystone Automotive, Inc.)—Board Member ▪ William G. Morton, Jr. (Chairman and CEO, Boston Stock Exchange, Inc.)—Board Member ▪ Edwina D. Woodbury (President, The Chapel Hill Press, Inc.)—Board Member ▪ Lewis F. Kornfield, Jr. (Retired Vice Chairman, RadioShack Corporation)—Board Member ▪ William E. Tucker (Chancellor Emeritus, Texas Christian University)—Board Member

CORPORATE PARTNERSHIPS: Compaq Computer ▪ NorthPoint Communications ▪ Microsoft ▪ RCA ▪ Sprint

CHARITIES SUPPORTED: American Lung Association ▪ Operation FireSafe ▪ RadioShack National Teacher Awards ▪ United Against Crime (A charitable partnership formed between RadioShack, National Crime Prevention Council, and the National Sheriff's Association) ▪ Junior Achievement

Raytheon

CONTACT:

Raytheon Company
141 Spring Street
Lexington, MA 02173

TELEPHONE: (781) 862-6600

WEB: *www.raytheon.com*

BUSINESS FOCUS: Defense

COMPANY BACKGROUND: Raytheon is one of the key players in the defense industry. Its core businesses are aircraft, defense, and commercial electronics. It employs 100,000 individuals worldwide, and it serves customers in more than seventy countries.

NETWORKING SPECIFICS: The key to making yourself valuable to Raytheon is emphasizing your relationships with people in government, both foreign and domestic. Any contacts at the Pentagon, no matter how small or insignificant, are a gold key in.

SHAREHOLDERS' MEETING DATE: May

VIPs AFFILIATED WITH THE COMPANY: Daniel Burnham—Chairman and CEO ▪ Kenneth Dahlberg—Executive Vice President, Business Development ▪ Franklin Caine—Senior Vice President and CFO ▪ Dennis M. Donovan—Senior Vice President, Human Resources ▪ James L. Infinger—Vice President and CIO ▪ Stephen Dorman (Vice Chairman, Hughes Electronics)—Board Member ▪ Thomas Everhart (President Emeritus, California Institute of Technology)—Board Member ▪ John Galvin (Dean, Fletcher School at Tufts)—Board Member ▪ Richard Hill (Former Chairman, Bank of Boston)—Board Member ▪ Alfred M. Zeien (Chairman and CEO, Gillette)—Board Member

CHARITIES SUPPORTED: United Way ▪ United Negro College Fund

Reebok International

CONTACT:

Reebok International Ltd.
100 Technology Center Drive
Stoughton, MA 02072

TELEPHONE: (781) 401-5000

WEB: *www.reebok.com*

BUSINESS FOCUS: Sports apparel

COMPANY BACKGROUND: Reebok International not only makes Reebok shoes, but it also makes Rockport, the Greg Norman Collection, and Ralph Lauren Footwear.

NETWORKING SPECIFICS: The Super Show in Vegas is a great place to meet the Reebok elite.

SHAREHOLDERS' MEETING DATE: May in Boston, Massachusetts

VIPs AFFILIATED WITH THE COMPANY: Paul Fireman—President, CEO, and Chairman, Reebok International Ltd. ▪ Kenneth Watchmaker—Executive Vice President and CFO, Reebok International Ltd. ▪ Paul R. Duncan—Executive Vice President, Reebok International Ltd. ▪ James R. Jones III—Senior Vice President and Chief Human Resources Officer, Reebok International Ltd. ▪ Anthony J. Tiberii—President and CEO, The Rockport Company, Inc. ▪ Carl Yankowski—President and CEO, Reebok Unlimited ▪ Angel Martinez—

Executive Vice President CMO, Reebok Unlimited ▪ M. Katherine Dwyer (President, Revlon Consumer Products of USA Revlon, Inc.)—Board Member ▪ Mannie L. Jackson (Chairman and CEO, Harlem Globetrotters International, Inc.)—Board Member ▪ Richard G. Lesser (Executive Vice President and COO, TJX Companies, Inc.)—Board Member ▪ Geoffrey Nunes (Former Senior Vice President and General Counsel, Millipore Corp.)—Board Member ▪ Thomas M. Ryan (President and CEO, CVS Corporation)—Board Member ▪ Peter Gabriel ▪ Greg Norman

CHARITIES SUPPORTED: Reebok Human Rights Foundation ▪ Amnesty International

Royal Dutch/Shell Group

CONTACT:
David Sexton
Shell Oil Company
GSDF Division
630 Fifth Avenue, Suite 1970
New York, NY 10111

TELEPHONE: (212) 218-3113

WEB: *www.shell.com*

BUSINESS FOCUS: Oil, gas, coal, and chemicals

BACKGROUND INFORMATION: The entire unit of the Royal Dutch/Shell Group, which is made up of numerous smaller companies, has operations in over 130 countries around the world with a staff exceeding 100,000 individuals. Shell is divided into five main sectors: exploration and production, oil products, chemicals, gas and power, and renewables.

NETWORKING SPECIFICS: Top petroleum engineering programs around the country will yield valuable contacts.

SHAREHOLDERS' MEETING DATE: May

VIPs AFFILIATED WITH THE COMPANY: Harry Roels—Managing Director, Royal Dutch Petroleum Company; Group Managing Director, the Royal Dutch/Shell Group of Companies ▪ Paul Skinner—Managing Director, The Shell Petroleum Company; Group Managing Director, the Royal Dutch/Shell Group; CEO, Oil Products ▪ Mark Moody-Stuart—Chairman, Committee of Managing Directors, Royal Dutch/Shell Group of Companies; Chairman, The Shell Petroleum Company ▪ Jeroen van der Veer—Vice Chairman, Committee of Managing Directors, Royal Dutch/Shell Group of Companies; President, Royal Dutch Petroleum Company ▪ Phil Watts—Managing Director, The Shell Petroleum Company; Group Managing Director, Royal Dutch/Shell Group of Companies

CHARITIES SUPPORTED: America's Promise—The Alliance for Youth ▪ Juvenile Diabetes Foundation

The Seagram Company Ltd.

CONTACT:
The Seagram Company Ltd.
1430 Peel Street
Montreal, Quebec
H3A 1S9, Canada

TELEPHONE: (514) 987-5200

BUSINESS FOCUS: Alcoholic beverages, music, filmed entertainment, and recreation

COMPANY BACKGROUND: Seagram is huge. Their alcohol division focuses on such beverages as whiskey, cognac, brandy, gin, vodka, rum, tequila, liqueur, coolers, sparkling wine, sherry, port, wine, and selected brands such as Absolut and Jim Beam. Their music division includes numerous record labels including Def Jam Recordings, Geffen Records, MCA Records, Interscope Records, and Universal Records. Artists signed to these labels include Sheryl Crow, Elton John, ABBA, Jay-Z, George Strait, Vince Gill, and U2. Seagram's filmed entertainment division consists of such divisions as Universal Pictures, Universal Studios Home Video, and Universal Television and Networks Group. The Universal Studios Recreation Group makes up Seagram's recreation division. It includes ten theme parks across the globe. Other businesses that Seagram is involved in include such retail businesses as Spencer Gifts, Universal Studios Consumer Products Group, and such on-line departments as Universal Studios Online, and Universal Interactive Studios.

NETWORKING SPECIFICS: The networking possibilities within Seagram are endless. There are numerous divisions within Seagram, and it would be best to focus networking efforts on one particular segment. Any connections within the music or film industry could prove to be beneficial to networking in Seagram. Other routes into Seagram are through shareholder events or through connections with the charities that Seagram supports.

SHAREHOLDERS' MEETING DATE: November in Montreal, Quebec

VIPs AFFILIATED WITH THE COMPANY: Edgar Bronfman—Chairman ▪ Edgar Bronfman, Jr.—President, CEO, and Director ▪ Charles Bronfman—Cochairman ▪ Robert W. Matschullat—Vice Chairman and CFO ▪ John Borgia—Executive Vice President, Human Resources ▪ Steven J. Kalagher—Executive Vice President, President, and Chief Executive Officer, The Seagram Spirits and Wine Group ▪ Ron Meyer—COO and President, Universal Studios, Inc. ▪ Stacey Snider—Chairman, Universal Pictures ▪ Doug Morris—Chairman and CEO, Universal Music Group ▪ Samuel Bronfman II (President, The Seagram Chateau and Estate Wines Company; Chairman, Seagram Beverage Company)—Board Member ▪ Matthew W. Barrett (Group Chief Executive, Barclay PLC)—Board Member ▪ Laurent Beaudoin (Chairman of Board and Chairman of Executive Committee, Bombadier, Inc.)—Board Member ▪ Richard H. Brown (Chairman and CEO, Electronic Data Systems Corporation)—Board Member ▪ Barry Diller (Chairman and CEO, USA Networks, Inc.)—Board Member ▪ E. Leo Kolber (Member of the Senate of Canada)—Board Member ▪ Samuel Minzberg (Chairman and CEO, Claridge, Inc.)—Board Member ▪ John S. Weinberg (Managing Director, Goldman, Sachs & Co.)—Board Member

CHARITIES SUPPORTED: United Way ▪ Life Force ▪ Children's Hope Foundation ▪ Elton John AIDS Foundation ▪ Make-A-Wish Foundation ▪ Project A.L.S.

Sears, Roebuck and Co.

CONTACT:
Sears, Roebuck and Co.
3333 Beverly Road
Hoffman Estates, IL 60179

TELEPHONE: (847) 286-2500

WEB: *www.sears.com*

BUSINESS FOCUS: Retail

COMPANY BACKGROUND: Sears, Roebuck and Co. is famous for its extensive catalog, which launched its business. Today, Sears sells merchandise from both its catalog and in stores at 2,000 malls nationwide.

NETWORKING SPECIFICS: The conventional routes in are strong.

SHAREHOLDERS' MEETING DATE: May in Hoffman Estates, Illinois

VIPs AFFILIATED WITH THE COMPANY: Arthur C. Martinez—Chairman, President, and CEO ▪ Julian C. Day— Executive Vice President and COO ▪ Jeffrey N. Boyer—CFO ▪ James R. Clifford—CMO ▪ Gerald N. Miller— Senior Vice President and CIO ▪ John T. Sloan—Executive Vice President, Human Resources ▪ Brenda C. Barnes (Former President and CEO, Pepsi-Cola North America)—Board Member ▪ Warren L. Batts (Former Chairman and CEO, Tupperware Corporation)—Board Member ▪ Michael A. Miles (Former Chairman and CEO, The Philip Morris Companies, Inc.)—Board Member ▪ Richard C. Notebaert (Former Chairman, CEO, and President, Ameritech Corporation)—Board Member ▪ Hugh B. Price (President and CEO, National Urban League, Inc.)—Board Member ▪ Patrick G. Ryan (Chairman and CEO, AON Corporation)—Board Member

SPONSORING ACTIVITY: Backstreet Boys Millenium Tour

CHARITIES SUPPORTED: America's Promise—The Alliance for Youth ▪ You Can Make A Difference ▪ Partnership for a Drug-Free America

ORGANIZATION SPONSORED: NASCAR

SFX Corporation

CONTACT:
SFX Corporation
650 Madison Avenue, 16th Floor
New York, NY 10022

TELEPHONE: (212) 838-3100

WEB: *www.sfx.com*

COMPANY BACKGROUND: SFX is the organization that puts on the American Century Celebrity Golf Championshiop. This is one of the best events in the United States. SFX is one of the leading promoters, producers, and presenters of live entertainment in the world. It organizes concerts, theater performances, arena motor sports events, and family entertainment. Its clients include some of the biggest names in sports and entertainment.

VIPs AFFILIATED WITH THE COMPANY: Robert F. X. Sillerman—Chairman ▪ Michael G. Ferrel—President and CEO ▪ Brian Becker—Executive Vice President ▪ Howard J. Tytel—Executive Vice President and Secretary ▪ Thomas P. Benson—Senior Vice President and CFO ▪ Edward F. Dugan (President, Dugan Associates, Inc.)—Board Member

EVENT: The American Century Celebrity Golf Championship (Held in July, this three-day-long event is attended by many of the leaders in the world of sports as well as some politicians and entertainers. The event is sponsored by such corporations as Hewlett-Packard, Beck's, American Airlines, and American Century Investments.)

VIPs ATTENDING THE GOLF CHAMPIONSHIP: Jim McMahon ▪ Carlton Fisk ▪ John Smoltz ▪ Al Del Greco ▪ Oscar de la Hoya ▪ Marcus Allen ▪ Marshall Faulk ▪ Bruce Jenner ▪ Mario Lemieux ▪ Kevin Nealon ▪ Jerry Rice ▪ Joe Theismann ▪ Rollie Fingers ▪ Johnny Bench ▪ Bryant Gumbel ▪ Maury Povich ▪ Steve Bartkowski ▪ Lenny Dykstra ▪ George Brett ▪ Michael Jordan ▪ Wayne Gretzky ▪ Dan Quayle ▪ Mike Schmidt ▪ Billy Joe Tolliver

- John Elway ▪ Brett Hull ▪ Damon Wayans ▪ Chris Webber ▪ Clyde Drexler ▪ Charles Barkley ▪ Dan Jansen ▪ Matt Lauer ▪ Dan Majerle ▪ Ahmad Rashad ▪ Emmitt Smith

CLIENTS: Adidas ▪ American Airlines ▪ Amway Corporation ▪ AT&T ▪ Charles Schwab ▪ Chevrolet ▪ Country Music Association ▪ ESPN ▪ Florida Panthers ▪ GTE ▪ Kansas City Royals ▪ Lotus Development Corp. ▪ Miami Dolphins ▪ Morgan Stanley Dean Witter ▪ New England Patriots ▪ Northwest Airlines ▪ Oracle Corporation ▪ Reebok ▪ San Francisco Giants ▪ St. Louis Rams ▪ VH-1 ▪ Yahoo! ▪ Rock and Roll Hall of Fame and Museum ▪ Adobe Systems ▪ American Bar Association ▪ Anheuser-Busch, Inc. ▪ Boeing Company ▪ CBS Television Network ▪ Coca-Cola Company ▪ Delta Air Lines ▪ Excite ▪ Florida Marlins ▪ IBM ▪ KPMG ▪ Major League Baseball ▪ Miami Heat ▪ National Football League ▪ Nike ▪ Ocean Spray ▪ Pacific Bell ▪ Revlon ▪ Southwest Airlines ▪ Sun Microsystems ▪ Visa ▪ Boys and Girls Club of America ▪ Aetna ▪ American Red Cross ▪ Apple Computers ▪ Boston Red Sox ▪ Cisco Systems ▪ Compaq Computers ▪ Easter Seals ▪ First Union Bank ▪ Fox Television Network ▪ Indianapolis Colts ▪ Lehman Brothers ▪ MCI WorldCom ▪ Miller Brewing Company ▪ New Balance ▪ Nissan ▪ Oppenheimer Funds ▪ Ralston-Purina ▪ Rolls-Royce ▪ St. Louis Blues ▪ Toyota ▪ Volvo ▪ Indianapolis Motor Speedway

Sony Corporation of America

CONTACT:
Sony Corporation of America
550 Madison Avenue, 9th Floor
New York, NY 10022-3211

TELEPHONE: (212) 833-6849

WEB: *www.sony.com*

BUSINESS FOCUS: Electronics and entertainment

COMPANY BACKGROUND: Sony is one of the leading audiovisual electronics, and motion picture and television production companies in the world. Sony was cocreator of the compact disk and DVD technology. In America, their workforce totals 25,500 employees, and 189,700 employees worldwide. Sony's American subsidiaries, besides Sony Corporation of America, are Sony Capital Corporation, Sony Electronics Inc., Sony Music Entertainment Inc., Sony Pictures Entertainment Inc., and Sony Magnetic Products Inc. of America.

NETWORKING SPECIFICS: Start at the COMDEX show. It will be a winner.

SHAREHOLDERS' MEETING DATE: June

VIPs AFFILIATED WITH THE COMPANY: Nobuyuki Idei—Chairman and CEO, Sony Corporation ▪ Kunitake Ando—President and COO ▪ Howard Stringer—Chairman and CEO, Sony Corporation of America ▪ Yang Hun Lee—Executive Vice President, Sony Corporation of America ▪ John Calley—President and CEO, Sony Pictures Entertainment ▪ Bob Wynne—Copresident and COO, Sony Pictures Entertainment

CORPORATE PARTNERSHIPS: Warner Music Group ▪ EMI ▪ General Instrument ▪ Loews Cineplex Entertainment ▪ Time-Warner (Formation of Columbia House) ▪ Microsoft Corporation

CHARITIES SUPPORTED: America's Promise—The Alliance for Youth ▪ The Glenn Gould Foundation ▪ The Metropolitan Museum of Art

Sotheby's Holdings, Inc.

CONTACT:
Sotheby's Holdings, Inc.
1334 York Avenue
New York, NY 10021

TELEPHONE: (212) 606-7000

WEB: *www.sothebys.com*

BUSINESS FOCUS: Auctioning and real estate

COMPANY BACKGROUND: Sotheby's is one of the two largest auctioneers across the globe. They auction numerous items in the categories of fine arts, antiques, and collectibles. The real estate division of Sotheby's handles luxury residential real estate. Their client list is a veritable who's who in the world.

NETWORKING SPECIFICS: Sniff the money and you will find success at working into Sotheby's.

SHAREHOLDERS' MEETING DATE: April in New York

VIPs AFFILIATED WITH THE COMPANY: Michael Sovern—Chairman ▪ Max Fisher—Vice Chairman and Director ▪ William Ruprecht—President, CEO, and Director ▪ William Sheridan—Senior Vice President and CFO ▪ Robin Woodhead—Executive Vice President; Director, and CEO, Sotheby's Europe and Asia ▪ Hon. Conrad M. Black, P.C., O.C.—Board Member ▪ Viscount Blakenham—Board Member ▪ Diana D. Brooks—Board Member ▪ Ambassador Walter J. P. Curley—Board Member ▪ Max M. Fisher—Board Member ▪ Marquess of Hartington—Board Member ▪ Henry R. Kravis—Board Member ▪ Jeffrey H. Miro—Board Member ▪ Sharon Percy Rockefeller—Board Member ▪ Robin Woodhead—Board Member ▪ Deborah Zoullas—Board Member ▪ A. Alfred Taubman—Board Member ▪ Giovanni Agnelli—Advisory Board Member ▪ Her Royal Highness, The Infanta Pilar de Borbon—Advisory Board Member ▪ Duchess of Badajoz—Advisory Board Member ▪ Ann Getty—Advisory Board Member ▪ Alexis Gregory—Advisory Board Member ▪ Sir Q. W. Lee—Advisory Board Member ▪ John L. Marion—Advisory Board Member ▪ The Rt. Honorable Sir Angus Ogilvy, K.C.V.O—Advisory Board Member ▪ Carroll Petrie—Advisory Board Member ▪ Carol Price—Advisory Board Member ▪ Baron Hans Heinrich Thyssen Bornemisza de Kaszon—Advisory Board Member

CHARITIES SUPPORTED: MOUSE (Making Opportunities for Upgrading Schools and Education) ▪ Elizabeth Glaser Pediatric AIDS Foundation ▪ National Black Child Development Institute ▪ Reading is Fundamental ▪ The Metropolitan Museum of Art ▪ Project HOPE

Sprint

CONTACT:
Sprint Corporation
2330 Shawnee Mission Parkway
Westwood, KS 66205

TELEPHONE: (913) 624-3000

WEB: *www.sprint.com*

BUSINESS FOCUS: Telecommunications

COMPANY BACKGROUND: Sprint is a completely integrated global communications company. Sprint has over 17 million business and residential customers, and it is one of the world's largest mediums through which the Internet is accessed. Their PCS division heads the cellular business.

NETWORKING SPECIFICS: Charities, especially those based in the Kansas City metropolitan area, are strong ways in.

SHAREHOLDERS' MEETING DATE: April, in Westwood, Kansas

VIPs AFFILIATED WITH THE COMPANY: William Esrey—Chairman and CEO ▪ Ronald LeMay—President and COO ▪ Arthur Krause—Executive Vice President and CFO

SPONSORING ACTIVITIES: U.S. Ski Team ▪ PGA ▪ Spirit Awards

CHARITIES SUPPORTED: Junior Achievement ▪ United Way ▪ The Carter Center ▪ YMCA ▪ YWCA ▪ Harvard University ▪ University of Michigan ▪ University of Pennsylvania ▪ Penn State University ▪ Texas A&M University ▪ University of Virginia ▪ Boy Scouts of America ▪ Boys and Girls Clubs of America ▪ Big Brothers Big Sisters of America ▪ Camp Fire Boys and Girls ▪ Girl Scouts ▪ Elton John AIDS Foundation ▪ American Cancer Society ▪ Juvenile Diabetes Foundation

State Farm Insurance

CONTACT:
State Farm Insurance
One State Farm Plaza
Bloomington, IL 61710

TELEPHONE: (309) 766-2311

WEB: *www.statefarm.com*

BUSINESS FOCUS: Insurance

COMPANY BACKGROUND: State Farm Insurance is the leading insurance company in America and one of the largest financial institutions in the world. State Farm's workforce exceeds 92,000 employees.

NETWORKING SPECIFICS: Attending sporting events where State Farm is the title sponsor is a great way in.

SHAREHOLDERS' MEETING DATE: Second Monday of June in Bloomington, Illinois

VIPs AFFILIATED WITH THE COMPANY: Edward B. Rust, Jr.—Chairman and CEO ▪ Roger Joslin—Vice Chairman, Treasurer, and CFO ▪ Vincent J. Trocino—Vice Chairman, President, and COO ▪ W. H. Knight, Jr. (Vice Provost, University of Iowa)—Board Member ▪ George L. Perry (Senior Fellow, The Brookings Institution)—Board Member ▪ Susan M. Phillips (Dean, George Washington University)—Board Member ▪ Paul T. Stecko (Chairman and CEO, Packaging Corporation of America)—Board Member

SPONSORING ACTIVITIES: This Old House ▪ The Victory Garden (PBS Series) ▪ State Farm Women's Tennis Classic ▪ State Farm Women's Basketball Tip-Off Classic ▪ State Farm U.S. Figure Skating Championships ▪ State Farm Rail Classic ▪ State Farm Women's Volleyball Classic ▪ Women's Golf Championship ▪ State Farm Senior Classic ▪ State Farm Bayou Classic ▪ The Gold Cup

CHARITIES SUPPORTED: The Children's Hospital of Philadelphia ▪ National Board for Professional Teaching Standards ▪ National Domestic Violence Hotline ▪ State Domestic Violence Coalitions ▪ American Red Cross ▪ Partnership for a Drug-Free America

Sun Microsystems

CONTACT:
Sun Microsystems, Inc.
901 San Antonio Road
Palo Alto, CA 94303

TELEPHONE: (800) 801-7869
(650) 960-1300

WEB: *www.sun.com*

BUSINESS FOCUS: Computer innovation

COMPANY BACKGROUND: Sun Microsystems is one of the new economy leaders. They are a leader in computer innovations with such creations as Java, a web enhancer, and Jini, a business and networking enhancer. Sun's corporate partner list is a who's who of the new economy, including Motorola, 3Com Corp., Nokia, America Online, and Netscape. Their customer list includes Ericsson, Siemens, AT&T, Pixar Animation Studios, Exodus Communication, Inc., Colgate Palmolive Company, CDNow, Inc., GO Network, Enron Communications, Excite, eBay, CNN, and Stanford University, to name a few.

NETWORKING SPECIFICS: Trade shows and Stanford Business School are good ways in.

SHAREHOLDERS' MEETING DATE: November at Menlo Park, California.

VIPs AFFILIATED WITH THE COMPANY: Scott McNealy—CEO, Chairman, and Cofounder ▪ Edward J. Zander—President and COO ▪ Michael E. Lehman—CFO and Corporate Executive Officer ▪ Bill Joy—Corporate Executive Officer and Cofounder ▪ H. William Howard—Vice President and CIO ▪ Greg Papadopoulos—CTO ▪ William J. Raduchel—CSO ▪ Edward Saliba—Vice President, Human Resources ▪ Judith L. Estrin (CTO and Senior Vice President, Cisco Systems, Inc.)—Board Member ▪ Robert J. Fisher (Executive Vice President and Director, The Gap, Inc; President, the Gap Division)—Board Member ▪ M. Kenneth Oshman (Chairman, President, and CEO, Echelon Corporation)—Board Member

CHARITIES SUPPORTED: Worldwide Volunteer Week ▪ Girl's Club ▪ Winner of Disabilities Act Eagle Award given by Disability Rights Advocates ▪ YWCA ▪ Friends for Youth, Inc. ▪ HOPE Rehabilitation Foundation ▪ The Metropolitan Education Foundation ▪ Sacred Heart Community Service ▪ Children's Hospital Foundation ▪ AIDS Action Community ▪ United Way ▪ Family Giving Tree ▪ Share-A-Gift ▪ America's Promise—The Alliance for Youth

Target Corporation

CONTACT:
Target Corporation
777 Nicollet Mall
Minneapolis, MN 55402

TELEPHONE: (612) 370-6948

WEB: *www.targetcorp.com*

BUSINESS FOCUS: Retail stores

COMPANY BACKGROUND: Target Corporation, formerly known as Dayton Hudson, owns and operates Target, Mervyn's California, Dayton's, Hudson's, and Marshall Field's stores. Target also owns Rivertown

Trading Company, which produces catalogs, and Associated Merchandising Corporation, which studies trends in retailing. Target has more than 900 stores in forty-five states.

NETWORKING SPECIFICS: Target is very involved in the local Minneapolis community. Civic events around Minneapolis are a great place to start.

SHAREHOLDERS' MEETING DATE: May, in Minneapolis, Minnesota

VIPs AFFILIATED WITH THE COMPANY: Robert J. Ulrich—Chairman and CEO ▪ Paul L. Singer—Technology Services and CIO ▪ Douglas A. Scovanner—Executive Vice President, Finance, and CFO ▪ Livio D. DeSimone (Chairman and CEO, 3M)—Board Member ▪ Roger A. Enrico (Chairman and CEO, PepsiCo, Inc.)—Board Member ▪ William W. George (Chairman and CEO, Medtronic, Inc.)—Board Member ▪ Michele J. Hooper (President and CEO, Voyager Expanded Learning)—Board Member ▪ James A. Johnson (Chairman, Executive Committee of the Board, Fannie Mae)—Board Member ▪ Richard M. Kovacevich (President and CEO, Wells Fargo & Company)—Board Member ▪ Susan A. McLaughlin (President, Consumer Services, BellSouth Telecommunications, Inc.)—Board Member ▪ Anne M. Mulcahy (President and COO, Xerox)—Board Member ▪ Stephen W. Sanger (Chairman and CEO, General Mills, Inc.)—Board Member ▪ George W. Tamke (Former Chairman and Co-CEO, Emerson Electric Co.)—Board Member ▪ Solomon D. Trujillo (Chairman, President, and CEO, US West, Inc.)—Board Member

CHARITIES SUPPORTED: American Red Cross ▪ March of Dimes ▪ National Wildlife Federation ▪ St. Jude's Research Hospital ▪ United Way ▪ Women's Sports Foundation ▪ Walker Art Center ▪ Art Institute of Chicago ▪ The Metropolitan Museum of Art ▪ America's Promise—The Alliance for Youth

Texaco

CONTACT:
Texaco
2000 Westchester Avenue
White Plains, NY 10650

TELEPHONE: (914) 253-4000

WEB: *www.texaco.com*

BUSINESS FOCUS: Petroleum

COMPANY BACKGROUND: Texaco has a history of over 100 years, and it is located in over 150 countries around the globe. It is mainly focused on providing people with energy and the operations that are included in that: exploration, production, distribution, refining, and marketing.

NETWORKING SPECIFICS: Texaco is a sponsor of racers of NASCAR, CART, and Formula One events. They also are involved with the Olympic Games and the U.S. Tennis Open. Events where they are the title sponsor are great places to network.

SHAREHOLDERS' MEETING DATE: Late April in Purchase, New York

VIPs AFFILIATED WITH THE COMPANY: Peter I. Bijur—Chairman and CEO ▪ Patric J. Lynch—CFO ▪ Elizabeth Smith—Vice President, Investor Relations ▪ Janet Stoner—Vice President, Human Resources ▪ James Link—Treasurer ▪ John Brademas (President Emeritus, NYU)—Board Member ▪ Willard Butcher (Former Chairman and CEO, Chase Manhattan)—Board Member ▪ Michael C. Hawley (President and COO, Gillette)—Board Member ▪ Franklyn G. Jenifer (President, University of Texas at Dallas)—Board Member ▪ Thomas Murphy (Former Chairman and CEO, Capital Cities ABC)—Board Member ▪ Sam Nunn (Former U.S. Senator of Georgia)—Board Member ▪ Robin B. Smith (Chairman and CEO, Publishers Clearing

House)—Board Member ▪ William C. Steere, Jr. (Chairman and CEO, Pfizer)—Board Member ▪ William Wrigley (President and CEO, Wrigley Company)—Board Member

SPONSORING ACTIVITIES: 2002 Olympics ▪ U.S. Olympic Team ▪ U.S. Tennis Open ▪ Robert Yates Racing ▪ Newman-Haas Racing ▪ Texaco Grand Prix of Houston ▪ Metropolitan Opera

CHARITIES SUPPORTED: Early Notes: The Sound of Children Learning ▪ Touch Science: Hands-on Learning for Kids and Communities ▪ Musical Roots ▪ Peter F. Drucker Foundation for Non-Profit Management ▪ Americans for Indian Opportunity ▪ Jackie Robinson Foundation ▪ Leadership America ▪ Mexican American Legal Defense and Education Fund ▪ National Asian Pacific American Legal Consortium ▪ National Council of La Raza ▪ National Council of Negro Women ▪ National Minority Supplier Development Council ▪ Ronald H. Brown Foundation ▪ Metropolitan Opera ▪ The Metropolitan Museum of Art ▪ Juvenile Diabetes Foundation

Tiffany & Co.

CONTACT:
Tiffany & Co.
727 Fifth Avenue
New York, NY 10022

TELEPHONE: (212) 755-8000

WEB: *www.tiffany.com*

BUSINESS FOCUS: High-end retail

COMPANY BACKGROUND: Tiffany & Co. is one of the most recognized name brands in the world. Tiffany & Co. focuses its business efforts in the selling of high-end luxury items; these items include fine jewelry, timepieces, sterling silver goods, china, crystal, stationery, writing instruments, fragrances, and personal accessories.

NETWORKING SPECIFICS: Shareholders' meeting is a great place to start.

SHAREHOLDERS' MEETING DATE: Mid-May in New York, New York.

VIPs AFFILIATED WITH THE COMPANY: William Chaney—Chairman ▪ James Quinn—Vice Chairman ▪ Michael Kowalski—President, CEO, and Director ▪ James Fernandez—Executive Vice President and CFO ▪ Beth Canavan—Executive Vice President ▪ David Eisenhower—Vice President, Human Relations ▪ Rose Marie Bravo (Worldwide Chief Executive, Burberry Limited)—Board Member ▪ Samuel L. Hayes III (Harvard Business School)—Board Member ▪ Charles K. Marquis (Senior Advisor, Investcorp International, Inc.)—Board Member ▪ Geraldine Stutz (Principal Partner, GSG Group)—Board Member ▪ Paloma Picasso—Jewelry Designer and Daughter to Pablo Picasso

TROPHIES DESIGNED: NBA Finals Trophy ▪ Superbowl Trophy

CHARITY SUPPORTED: The Metropolitan Museum of Art

Toys "R" Us

CONTACT:
Toys "R" Us
461 From Road
Paramus, NJ 07652

TELEPHONE: (201) 262-7800

Bret and George W. Bush,
forty-third U.S. President

Elliot and George Bush,
former U.S. President

Bret and Michael Eisner, chairman of Disney

Elliot and the late Alan Shepard, first American to orbit the earth

Elliot and Lady Bird Johnson, former First Lady

Elliot and Chief Justice William Renquist

Elliot and Walter Annenburg, publishing magnate and billionaire philanthropist

Elliot and Ross Perot

Elliot and Sandra Day
O'Connor, first female
Supreme Court Justice

Elliot and John Major,
former Prime Minister
of England

Bret and Cindy Crawford

Elliot and Mohammed Ali

Bret and Sir Elton John

Bret and Bono, lead singer of U2

Elliot and Heather Mack, supermodel, and Troy Aikman, three-time Super Bowl winner and Dallas Cowboys quarterback

Bret with John Travolta and Kelly Preston

WEB: *www.toysrus.com*

BUSINESS FOCUS: Toys

COMPANY BACKGROUND: Toys "R" Us is one of the largest toy stores in the world with over 1,450 stores across the globe, and over 60,000 employees. Toys "R" Us has expanded into other children-based markets with Kids "R" Us and Babies "R" Us.

NETWORKING SPECIFICS: Children's charities are a route in.

SHAREHOLDERS' MEETING DATE: June

VIPs AFFILIATED WITH THE COMPANY: Michael Goldstein—Chairman ▪ Charles Lazarus—Chairman Emeritus ▪ Robert C. Nakasone—CEO ▪ Louis Lipschitz—Executive Vice President and CFO ▪ Michael G. Shannon—Executive Vice President and President, U.S. Toy Stores ▪ John Holohan—Senior Vice President and CIO ▪ Warren F. Kornblum—Senior Vice President and CMO, U.S. Toy Stores ▪ Roger C. Gaston—Senior Vice President, Human Relations ▪ Robert A. Bernhard (Real Estate Developer)—Board Member ▪ Roann Costin (President, Reservoir Capital Management, Inc.)—Board Member ▪ Arthur B. Newman (Senior Managing Director, the Blackstone Group)—Board Member ▪ Calvin Hill (Consultant)—Board Member ▪ Norman S. Matthews (Consultant)—Board Member ▪ Howard W. Moore (Consultant)—Board Member

CHARITIES SUPPORTED: Children Affected by AIDS Foundation, ▪ Children's Memorial Hospital—Chicago ▪ Cure Autism Now ▪ Children's National Medical Center—Washington, D.C. ▪ Juvenile Diabetes Foundation International ▪ The Institute for Child Development at Hackensack University Medical Center ▪ PENCIL (Public Education Needs Civic Involvement in Learning) ▪ The Institute for Neurology and Neurosurgery at Beth Israel Medical Center ▪ Make-A-Wish Foundation ▪ Starlight Children's Foundation

UAL

CONTACT:
UAL World Headquarters
1200 E. Algonquin Road
Elk Grove Township, IL 60007

TELEPHONE: (847) 700-4000

WEB: *www.ual.com*

BUSINESS FOCUS: Air travel

COMPANY BACKGROUND: UAL is the holding company that owns United Airlines. United flies to more than twenty-five countries and is the largest airline in the world in terms of passenger miles flown. United has a connection with many professional sports teams, as it is the official carrier of the Chicago Bears, the Denver Broncos, the New York Giants, the San Francisco 49ers, and the Chicago Blackhawks. United is also the official carrier of the U.S. Olympic Committee.

NETWORKING SPECIFICS: Shareholders and Chicago-based charities are strong ways in.

SHAREHOLDERS' MEETING DATE: May, in Chicago, Illinois

VIPs AFFILIATED WITH THE COMPANY: Rono J. Dutta—President ▪ James E. Goodwin—Chairman and CEO ▪ Douglas A. Hacker—Executive Vice President and CFO ▪ Andrew P. Studdert—Executive Vice President and COO ▪ John W. Creighton, Jr. (Director and Advisor, Weyerhaeuser Company)—Board Member ▪ Richard D. McCormick (Retired Chairman of the Board, US West, Inc.)—Board Member ▪ John F. Mc-Gillicuddy (Retired Chairman and CEO, Chemical Banking Corporation)—Board Member ▪ James J. O'Connor (Retired Chairman and CEO, Unicom Corporation)—Board Member ▪ Hazel R. O'Leary (President, O'Leary & Associates)—Board Member ▪ Deval L. Patrick (Vice President and General Counsel, Texaco Inc.)—Board Member ▪ John F. Peterpaul (Retired General Vice President, International Association of Machinist District #141)—Board Member ▪ Paul E. Tierney, Jr. (Managing Member, Development Capital, LLC)—Board Member ▪ John K. Van de Kamp (President, Thoroughbred Owners of California)—Board Member

CHARITIES SUPPORTED: Art Institute of Chicago ▪ American Ballet Theatre ▪ AIDS Project Los Angeles ▪ American Red Cross ▪ Muscular Dystrophy Association ▪ Salvation Army ▪ Special Olympics ▪ Make-A-Wish Foundation ▪ Breast Cancer Research Foundation ▪ Habitat for Humanity ▪ NAACP ▪ National Urban League ▪ Smithsonian Museum ▪ Alzheimer's Association ▪ America's Promise—The Alliance for Youth ▪ Cystic Fibrosis Foundation

EVENT SPONSORED: Webby Awards

United Technologies

CONTACT:
United Technologies Corporation
One Financial Plaza
Hartford, CT 06103

TELEPHONE: (860) 728-7000

WEB: *www.utc.com*

BUSINESS FOCUS: Manufactures aerospace and building products

COMPANY BACKGROUND: United Technologies' major business operations are Pratt & Whitney aircraft engines, Carrier heating and air-conditioning systems, Otis elevators and escalators, Hamilton Sundstrand aerospace systems, Sikorsky helicopters, and International Fuel Cells. It also has a Research Center to research and develop products for its businesses. United Technologies Corporation sells many of its products to government agencies such as NASA.

NETWORKING SPECIFICS: The traditional routes in will work well.

SHAREHOLDERS' MEETING DATE: April

VIPs AFFILIATED WITH THE COMPANY: George David—Chairman and CEO ▪ Karl J. Krapek—President and COO ▪ David J. Fitzpatrick—Senior Vice President and CFO ▪ William L. Bucknall, Jr.—Senior Vice President, Human Resources and Organization ▪ Robert S. Harris—Vice President and Chief Learning Officer ▪ Antonia Handler Chayes (Senior Advisor and Board Member, Conflict Management Group)—Board Member ▪ Jean-Pierre Garnier (COO, SmithKline Beecham plc)—Board Member ▪ Jamie S. Gorlick (Vice Chair, Fannie Mae)—Board Member ▪ Charles R. Lee (Chairman and CEO, GTE Corporation)—Board Member ▪ Richard D. McCormick (Chairman Emeritus, US West, Inc.)—Board Member ▪ William J. Perry (Michael and Barbara Berberian Professor, Stanford University; Fellow at the Hoover Institute; Codirector, Stanford-Harvard Defense Project)—Board Member ▪ Frank P. Popoff (Chairman, The Dow Chemical Company)—Board Member ▪ André Villenueve (Executive Director, Reuters Holding plc)—Board Member ▪ Harold A. Wagner (Chairman and CEO, Air Products and Chemicals Inc.)—Board Member ▪ Sanford I. Weill (Chairman and CEO, Citigroup, Inc.)—Board Member

CHARITIES SUPPORTED: United Way ▪ Special Olympics ▪ Toys for Tots ▪ Junior Achievement ▪ Boys and Girls Club ▪ YMCA ▪ YWCA ▪ Nature Conservancy ▪ Big Brothers Big Sisters ▪ Salvation Army ▪ United Negro College Fund

UPS

CONTACT:
United Parcel Service, Inc.
55 Glenlake Parkway NE
Atlanta, GA 30328

TELEPHONE: (404) 828-6000

WEB: *www.ups.com*

BUSINESS FOCUS: The delivery of documents and packages

COMPANY BACKGROUND: UPS is the world's largest express carrier and package delivery company, delivering more than 12 million packages each day to more than 200 countries. UPS is a supporter of the Great American Book Drive, founded by Chicago Bear Jim Flanigan.

NETWORKING SPECIFICS: UPS likes to sponsor golf tournaments. A trip to your local PGA tour stop will yield strong results.

SHAREHOLDERS' MEETING DATES: May, in Wilmington, Delaware

VIPs AFFILIATED WITH THE COMPANY: James P. Kelly—Chairman of the Board and CEO ▪ Charles L. Schaffer—Senior Vice President and COO ▪ Robert J. Clanin—Senior Vice President, Treasurer, and CFO ▪ Kenneth W. Lacy—Senior Vice President and CIO ▪ Lea N. Soupata—Senior Vice President, Human Resources ▪ William H. Brown III (Partner, Schnader Harrison Segal & Lewis LLP)—Board Member ▪ Ann Livermore (Vice President, Hewlett-Packard)—Board Member ▪ Gary E. MacDougal (Former Chairman of the Board and CEO, Mark Controls Corporation)—Board Member ▪ Kent C. Nelson (Former Chairman of the Board and CEO, UPS)—Board Member ▪ Victor A. Pelson (Senior Advisor, Warburg Dillon Read, LLC)—Board Member ▪ John W. Rogers (Former Chairman of the Board and CEO, UPS)—Board Member ▪ Robert M. Teeter (President, Coldwater Corporation)—Board Member

CHARITIES SUPPORTED: Welfare to Work ▪ School to Work ▪ Orphan Foundation of America ▪ The Great American Book Drive ▪ Big Brothers Big Sisters of America ▪ Junior Achievement ▪ 100 Black Men of America ▪ Points of Light Foundation ▪ United Way of America ▪ Habitat for Humanity ▪ YWCA ▪ YMCA ▪ Police Athletic League ▪ Boys and Girls Clubs of America ▪ Boy Scouts ▪ Special Olympics ▪ Goodwill ▪ American Cancer Society ▪ NAACP ▪ Spelman College ▪ Morehouse College ▪ Clark Atlanta University ▪ National Council of La Raza ▪ National Urban League ▪ Organization of Chinese Americans ▪ U.S. Hispanic Chamber of Commerce ▪ America's Promise—The Alliance for Youth ▪ Partnership for a Drug-Free America

US West

CONTACT:
US West
1801 California Street
Denver, CO 80202

TELEPHONE: (303) 672-2700

WEB: *www.uswest.com*

BUSINESS FOCUS: Communications

COMPANY BACKGROUND: US West is a communications company that delivers its services to states in the Midwest. Its subsidiary, US West Communications, Inc., serves close to 74 percent of the businesses and residences within its region. US West is divided into four operational segments: retail services, wholesale services, network services, and directory services.

NETWORKING SPECIFICS: US West's heavy sponsorship of pro sports is one way in.

SHAREHOLDERS' MEETING DATE: May in New York City

VIPs AFFILIATED WITH THE COMPANY: Solomon D. Trujillo—Chairman, President, and CEO ▪ Mark D. Roellig—Executive Vice President of Public Policy, Human Resources, Law, General Counsel, and Secretary ▪ Allan Spies—Executive Vice President and CFO ▪ David R. Laube—Vice President and CIO ▪ Linda G. Alavarado (President and CEO, Alvarado Construction, Inc.)—Board Member ▪ Craig R. Barrett (President and CEO, Intel Corporation)—Board Member ▪ Jerry J. Colangelo (President, CEO, and Owner, the Phoenix Suns; Chairman and CEO, the Arizona Diamondbacks)—Board Member ▪ Manny Fernandez (Chairman, Gartner Group)—Board Member ▪ George J. Harad (Chairman and CEO, Boise Cascade Corporation)—Board Member ▪ Peter S. Hellman (Former President and CEO, TRW, Inc.)—Board Member ▪ Marilyn C. Nelson (President, CEO, and Vice Chair, Carlson Companies, Inc.)—Board Member ▪ Frank Popoff (Chairman, The Dow Chemical Company)—Board Member

SPONSORING ACTIVITIES: U.S. Olympic Team ▪ Arizona Diamondbacks ▪ Phoenix Suns ▪ Colorado Rockies ▪ Colorado Avalanche ▪ Denver Nuggets ▪ Minnesota Timberwolves ▪ Portland Trailblazers ▪ Seattle Supersonics

CHARITY SUPPORTED: America's Promise—The Alliance for Youth

Verizon Communications

CONTACT:
Verizon Communications
1095 Avenue of the Americas
New York, NY 10036

TELEPHONE: (212) 395-2121
(800) 621-9900

WEB: *www.verizon.com*

BUSINESS FOCUS: Telecommunications

COMPANY BACKGROUND: Verizon Communications was formed by the merger between Bell Atlantic and GTE. It is the largest provider of wireless and wire-line voice and communications services in the United States, and the world's largest provider of directory information. Verizon Wireless is a combination of Bell Atlantic, GTE, and Vodafone AirTouch's wireless operations. Verizon has operations in approximately forty countries worldwide.

NETWORKING SPECIFICS: Attend the Byron Nelson PGA tour stop. The top GTE brass can be found everywhere.

VIPs AFFILIATED WITH THE COMPANY: Charles R. Lee—Chairman and Co-CEO ▪ Ivan Seidenberg—President and Co-CEO ▪ Frederic V. Salerno—Vice Chairman and CFO ▪ J. Randall MacDonnell—Executive Vice President, Human Resources ▪ James R. Barker (Chairman, The Interlake Steamship Co.; Vice Chairman, Mormac ▪ Marine Group, Inc. and Moran Towing Company)—Board Member ▪ Edward H. Budd (Retired Chairman, The Travelers Corporation)—Board Member ▪ Richard L. Carrion (Chairman, President, and CEO, Banco Popular de Puerto Rico and Popular, Inc.)—Board Member ▪ Robert F. Daniell (Retired Chairman, United Technologies Corporation)—Board Member ▪ Helene L. Kaplan (Of Counsel to the Law Firm Skadden, Arps, Slate, Meagher & Flom LLP)—Board Member ▪ Sandra O. Moose (Senior Vice President and Director, The Eoston Consulting Group, Inc.)—Board Member ▪ Joseph Neubauer (Chairman and CEO, ARAMARK Corporation)—Board Member ▪ Thomas H. O'Brien (Chairman and CEO, The PNC Financial Services Group, Inc.)—Board Member ▪ Russell E. Palmer (Chairman and CEO, The Palmer Group)—Board Member ▪ Hugh B. Price (President and CEO, National Urban League)—Board Member ▪ Walter V. Shipley (Retired Chairman and CEO, The Chase Manhattan Corporation)—Board Member ▪ John W. Snow (Chairman, President, and CEO, CSX Corporation)—Board Member ▪ John R. Stafford (Chairman, President, and CEO, American Home Products Corporation)—Board Member ▪ Robert D. Storey (Partner, Law Firm of Thompson, Hine & Flory LLP)—Board Member ▪ James Earl Jones—Spokesperson

CHARITIES SUPPORTED: American Cancer Society ▪ American Diabetes Association ▪ American Red Cross ▪ ASPCA ▪ Boy Scouts of America ▪ Big Brothers Big Sisters ▪ Boys and Girls Club ▪ Girl Scouts of America ▪ Habitat for Humanity ▪ Hugh O'Brian Youth Foundation ▪ Junior Achievement ▪ Leukemia Society of America ▪ Little League Baseball, Inc. ▪ Make-A-Wish Foundation ▪ March of Dimes ▪ Meals On Wheels ▪ NAACP ▪ Salvation Army ▪ Special Olympics ▪ United Way ▪ YMCA ▪ United Negro College Fund ▪ Susan G. Komen Race for the Cure ▪ National Institute for Literacy ▪ PBS ▪ Carnegie Hall ▪ National PTA ▪ American Foundation for the Blind ▪ The Metropolitan Museum of Art ▪ America's Promise—The Alliance for Youth ▪ Volunteers of America ▪ Literacy Volunteers of America ▪ National AIDS Fund ▪ YWCA ▪ Elizabeth Glaser Pediatric AIDS Foundation

EVENTS SPONSORED: Bell Atlantic Jazz Festival ▪ U.S. Luge Team ▪ Atlantic 10 Collegiate Athletic Conference ▪ GTE Byron-Nelson Classic ▪ Republican National Convention

Viacom, Inc.

CONTACT:
Viacom, Inc.
1515 Broadway
New York, NY 10036

TELEPHONE: (212) 258-6000

WEB: *www.viacom.com*

BUSINESS FOCUS: Entertainment and media

COMPANY BACKGROUND: Viacom, Inc., is a media and entertainment company that merged with CBS in May 2000. Viacom's television networks are CBS, MTV, MTV2, Nickelodeon, TV Land, VH1, Comedy Central (jointly owned), Showtime, The Movie Channel, Flix, Sundance Channel (jointly owned), Noggin, and UPN. It owns the television production companies Spelling Television and Paramount Television, and Paramount Pictures, Paramount Home Entertainment, Simon & Schuster, and Paramount Parks theme parks.

NETWORKING SPECIFIES: Because of Viacom's prominence in the industry, entertainment events would be a great place to network with Viacom executives.

SHAREHOLDERS' MEETING DATE: June, in New York City

VIPs AFFILIATED WITH THE COMPANY: Sumner M. Redstone—Chairman and CEO ▪ Mel Karmazin—President and COO ▪ George S. Abrams (Attorney, Winer and Abrams)—Board Member ▪ George H. Conrades (Chairman and CEO, Akamai Technologies, Inc.)—Board Member ▪ Philippe P. Dauman (Former Deputy Chairman, Viacom)—Board Member ▪ Thomas E. Dooley (Former Deputy Chairman, Viacom)—Board Member ▪ William H. Gray III (President and CEO, The College Fund/UNCF)—Board Member ▪ Jan Leschly (Retired Chief Executive, SmithKline Beecham)—Board Member ▪ David T. McLaughlin (Chairman and CEO, Orion Safety Products)—Board Member ▪ Ken Miller (Vice Chairman, Credit Suisse First Boston Corp.)—Board

Member ▪ Leslie Moonves (President and CEO, CBS Television)—Board Member ▪ Brent D. Redstone (Attorney)—Board Member ▪ Shari Redstone (President, National Amusements, Inc.)—Board Member ▪ Frederic V. Salerno (Senior Executive Vice President and CFO/Strategy and Business Development, Bell Atlantic Corp.)—Board Member ▪ William Schwartz (Counsel to Cadwalader, Wickersham & Taft)—Board Member ▪ Ivan Seidenberg (Chairman and CEO, Bell Atlantic Corp.)—Board Member ▪ Patty Stonesifer (Cochair and President, Bill and Melinda Gates Foundation)—Board Member ▪ Robert D. Walter (Chairman and CEO, Cardinal Health, Inc.)—Board Member ▪ Robert Redford—Creative Director, Sundance Film Channel

CHARITIES SUPPORTED: Habitat for Humanity ▪ Meals on Wheels ▪ Second-Harvest ▪ Big Brothers Big Sisters ▪ Boys and Girls Clubs ▪ Easter Seals ▪ Girl Scouts ▪ Keep America Beautiful ▪ March of Dimes ▪ National 4-H Council ▪ The National PTA ▪ National Wildlife Federation ▪ Points of Light Foundation ▪ YMCA ▪ Youth Service America ▪ YWCA ▪ The Metropolitan Museum of Art ▪ America's Promise—The Alliance for Youth ▪ The Hunger Project ▪ Project A.L.S

EVENT SPONSORED: The Kennedy Center Honors

Visa

CONTACT:
Visa
3155 Clearview Way
San Mateo, CA 94402

TELEPHONE: (650) 432-3200

WEB: *www.visa.com*

BUSINESS FOCUS: Payment cards

BACKGROUND INFORMATION: Visa is the most widely used payment card in the world; it has recently reached its one billionth card point. There are approximately 21,000 member financial institutions across the globe that offer Visa cards. Visa's cards are accepted in over 300 countries at over nineteen million locations. And over 50 percent of all transactions on the Internet are made with Visa.

SHAREHOLDERS' MEETING DATE: Contact Shareholders Relations for date

VIPs AFFILIATED WITH THE COMPANY: Malcolm Williamson—President and CEO ▪ Carl F. Pascarella—President, Visa USA ▪ William P. Boardman (Senior Executive Vice President, Bank One)—Chairman, Visa International Board of Directors ▪ Paul J. Vessey—COO, Visa USA ▪ Mark MacCarthy—Senior Vice President for Public Policy ▪ David F. Demarest—Head of Corporate Relations and Corporate Communications ▪ James D. Dixon (BankofAmerica.com Executive at Bank of America)—Board Member ▪ G. Kennedy Thompson (President, First Union Corporation)—Board Member

CORPORATE PARTNERSHIPS: Sun Microsystems ▪ Cisco Systems ▪ Nokia ▪ eBay ▪ Marriott

SPONSORING ACTIVITIES: Olympic Games ▪ NASCAR ▪ Rugby World Cup ▪ Tony Awards ▪ Women's Sports Foundation ▪ The Visa Triple Crown: The Kentucky Derby, The Preakness Stakes, and The Belmont Stakes ▪ Operation Bass ▪ NFL

CHARITIES SUPPORTED: Reading Is Fundamental, Inc. ▪ United Way ▪ Big Brothers Big Sisters of America

Walt Disney

CONTACT:
Walt Disney
500 S. Buena Vista Street
Burbank, CA 91521

TELEPHONE: (818) 560-1000

WEB: www.go.disney.com

BUSINESS FOCUS: Entertainment

COMPANY BACKGROUND: Disney is an entertainment conglomerate that holds many of the major players in the entertainment industry. In addition to their world-famous theme parks and animation studio, they own ABC and Walt Disney Pictures. They own the NHL's Mighty Ducks. Other entities owned by Disney include ESPN, ESPN the Magazine, Miramax, A&E, Lifetime, and The History Channel.

NETWORKING SPECIFICS: Disney is in the entertainment business. The best place to catch these executives is at award shows and movie openings that are specific to their business units: Miramax at a premier or The History Channel at the Cable Ace Awards. The ESPYs held in New York City is another great event for hard-core networking. Their shareholders' meeting is the stronger of the two shareholders/charity standbys.

SHAREHOLDERS' MEETING DATE: February

VIPs AFFILIATED WITH THE COMPANY: Michael Eisner—Chairman and CEO ▪ Roy Disney—Vice Chairman ▪ Sanford M. Litvack—Vice Chairman ▪ Robert Iger—President and COO ▪ Thomas Staggs—Senior Executive Vice President and CFO ▪ Peter E. Murphy—Senior Executive Vice President and Chief Strategic Officer ▪ Judith Estrin (CTO and Senior Vice President, Cisco Systems, Inc.)—Board Member ▪ Stanley P. Gold (President and CEO, Shamrock Holdings, Inc.)—Board Member ▪ Ignacio E. Lozano, Jr. (Chairman, Lozano Communications)—Board Member ▪ George J. Mitchell (Special Counsel, Verner, Liipfert, Bernard, McPherson and Hand)—Board Member ▪ Thomas S. Murphy (Former Chairman, Capital Cities/ABC Inc.)—Board Member ▪ Leo J. O'Donovan, S. J. (President, Georgetown University)—Board Member ▪ Sidney Poitier (CEO, Verdon-Cedric Products, Ltd.)—Board Member ▪ Irwin E. Russell (Attorney at Law)—Board Member ▪ Robert A. M. Stern (Senior Partner, Robert A. M. Stern Architects)—Board Member ▪ Andrea L. Van de Kamp (Chairman, Sotheby's West Coast)—Board Member ▪ Raymond L. Watson (Vice Chairman, The Irvine Company)—Board Member ▪ Gary L. Wilson (Chairman, Northwest Airlines Corporation)—Board Member

CHARITIES SUPPORTED: Walt Disney Family Foundation ▪ Various teachers and schools ▪ The Metropolitan Museum of Art ▪ America's Promise—The Alliance for Youth ▪ ASPCA ▪ Children's Miracle Network ▪ World Wildlife Fund ▪ Make-A-Wish Foundation ▪ Project A.L.S.

EVENTS SPONSORED: American Teacher Awards ▪ Spirit Awards

CHAPTER FOUR

Trade Shows

Trade shows are one of the best places to network. They are rich with opportunity and access. They were originally set up in an efficient market system as a market-place for large buyers of a product to buy in a particular category. Over the years, they have evolved into much more. Today, buyers and sellers meet, competition scopes each other out, experts in a field give seminars, colleagues visit, and dedicated networkers are getting farther and farther ahead. For job searching, sales growth, free tickets for the Kentucky Derby, or research and development of new products and ideas, the trade show is the place to network. Before you can be successful at networking at a trade show, you must know how to work a trade show. This section will describe the inner workings of the trade show and discuss and demonstrate the various trade show networking techniques and opportunities.

TRADE SHOW BASICS

Trade shows are designed to offer a meeting place for companies and individuals of a particular industry to get together. A clear concept of the players involved in setting up and producing a trade show is invaluable to the networker. Additionally, knowing staff positions and job functions of trade show personnel can ensure that you know all the best floor times, the VIP gatherings, the seminars, and the special roundtable discussions. When you identify a trade show in your networking plan, the first step is to call and ask for the show brochure. The brochure will list everything from the dates of the event to the suggested hotels to the times of special events.

This will help you identify the structure of the show and the best networking opportunities.

Dissect the brochure, looking for any insight into the players at the trade show. The preferred hotel will be a natural spot to meet industry insiders. The brochure will also list the major sponsors of the show. You can be sure that these sponsors will be throwing parties at the show, which are great networking opportunities. Also look for the education and roundtable sessions. These sessions will have as a speaker or panel participants some of the most influential attendees at the conference. Note the time, date, and location of these sessions, and you'll know the key information needed for meeting these industry VIPs.

After analyzing the brochure, you must get yourself registered. You can either pay to attend or network in through the media office. To get media credentials, call a local newspaper, speak with an editor, and offer to write an article about the trade show—for free. The editor will usually tell you to go ahead and submit it, and they will review it. Make sure you let the editor know that you don't expect to be paid, you just want to be able to submit the article to him. Once the editor tells you to go ahead and submit the article, you can call the trade organization and tell them you are writing an article for that paper. You certainly aren't lying. Just make sure that after the conference, you actually write the article and submit it to the editor. Bret and Elliot have done this many, many times, and they always follow through with the writing of the article. An added bonus to the process is that if the article is actually published, you have made yourself valuable to the trade show by bringing them media. You will be treated very well at the next conference of that organization.

Once at the trade show, you will be issued a badge. There are different badges for different types of show attendees. There are badges for exhibitors—companies who have booths at the show—attendees, media, staff, and speakers. The media badges are terrific, because everyone wants to speak with you in hopes that you will offer media exposure for their product or company. Another very valuable badge is that of speaker. These are the people who sit on the session panels or speak at the opening sessions. These badges tend to give the wearer the aura of expertise. The feeling is that you wouldn't have been invited to speak if you weren't a major player or expert in the industry. The bottom line is to try to get the best badge you can. If you come in through the media angle, you have it made. If you are simply attending, when you register and pick up your badge, ask the person processing your registration for a media or speaker badge. They will very often assume you are supposed to have the badge you are asking for and give it to you. It never hurts to ask.

So you have your badge, you know the major sponsors, you know the hotel that most of the attendees are staying in, and you know the show schedule. It is time to begin networking.

TRADE SHOW NETWORKING TECHNIQUES

At trade shows, you should always employ the networking techniques discussed earlier in this book. Research is exceptionally important at trade shows. As just mentioned, the brochure is a great place to start your research. To go deeper, look on the Internet for both information on the show itself, as well as information about the major companies attending the show. It is also very helpful to talk with people who are veterans of the trade show you attend. They can give you insight into where the important parties were, where the influential people congregated, and how the show flowed. It is also valuable to network with members of the media who are covering the show. They will certainly know the ins and outs of the show, especially if they have covered it in a previous year.

There are many specific tricks that should be used when networking at trade shows. The most important thing to keep in mind is that you should create a well-thought-out plan for meeting the key attendees of the trade show. There are two ways to do this: You can approach them at the trade show, or schedule an appointment before the show.

When approaching a target at a trade show, you first need to identify the best opportunity to meet. The show brochure will identify if the target is on any panels or speaking in any sessions. This will tell you when and where the person will be. You don't want to approach your target before a scheduled appearance, as he will most likely be in the middle of mentally preparing for it. However, it is perfectly acceptable to approach him after his appearance. Remember to be confident, try to find some common ground quickly, and then get to the point. Another opportunity to approach someone is at their booth on the trade show floor. Typically, trade shows run for two or three days. The first day is always very, very busy. People are running around trying to talk to everyone, exhibitors are getting a feel for the traffic, and attendees are getting their bearings. By the second day, and certainly the third day, boredom begins to set in at many of the booths. This is the time when you can approach executives of major corporations and spend some real time. They are looking for opportunities and conversations to eliminate the boredom of smiling at the same people as they walk by for the third straight day.

Another tactic is to try to set up appointments with key players. When trying to set appointments with people at trade shows, it is key to remember that the week before they go, they are generally extremely busy. They protect their show schedule because they usually feel as if they will be pressed for time. As a result, they will be hesitant to commit to an appointment. As just discussed, by three P.M. on day two of the trade show, they will set an appointment for day three or for lunch or dinner the next day. Do not get caught by the anticipatory block-out timing issue. Also remember that company representatives are specifically attending the trade show to create business. Do some research and identify the trade show goals of the company that you want to network with. This information will help you craft your request when you call for an appointment.

You will find trade shows to be truly unique networking opportunities. In addition to the access to companies that the show provides, the show also overcomes a geographic obstacle. As mentioned in the section on corporations, trade shows offer the opportunity to meet with many companies in the same industry, in the same geographic location: the trade show floor. So if you wanted to work in the computer industry, you might need to travel to Seattle to visit Microsoft, Texas to visit Dell, and California to visit companies in the Silicon Valley. Or you can visit them all at the COMDEX trade show in Las Vegas. Use trade shows for the access they provide. The aggregation of an industry into one place is invaluable for a networker. Don't forget to ask around on the trade show floor about the corporate parties that are held after the trade show closes each evening. This is another golden opportunity to meet with the industry power players in a social situation.

CASE STUDY: NETWORKING AT A TRADE SHOW

The best way to understand how networking can be valuable at trade shows is to follow along with an actual example. Like the case study in the previous section, this example will demonstrate how the techniques in this book work together to achieve a networking goal.

To demonstrate the power of the trade show, Bret devised a networking test case. He wanted to see if he could pitch a concept for a new type of sole for sneakers to the CEO of Nike, Phillip Knight.

Bret began by identifying the key steps:

Step 1: What do I want? Bret wanted to secure some time with Nike CEO Phil Knight in order to pitch him a new idea for sneakers. Bret wrote down his goal, to personally pitch the sneaker idea to Knight.

Step 2: How do I get there? The next step for Bret was to develop a plan. As this book points out, to answer that question, you have to answer the five Ws: Who do I network with? What do I want from the networking? Where do I go to network? When is the best time to network? How do I best network?

The *Who do I network with* question would ultimately be answered with Phil Knight, but Bret knew that preliminary research would require networking with others within Nike. Bret identified two other networking targets: The first was corporate communication personnel who could tell Bret which trade shows Knight would be attending, and the second target was someone in Nike product development who could give Bret the lay of the land so he was prepared when he spoke to Knight. As a result, Bret had a list of three people to network with: Phil Knight, personnel at corporate communications, and personnel in product development.

The next question, *What do I want from the networking plan,* was identified: a personal pitch of a sneaker idea to Phil Knight. The next question, *Where do I network*, required some research. Bret began by studying the listing on Nike provided in this book. This is that listing:

Nike

CONTACT:
Nike World Headquarters
One Bowerman Drive
Beaverton, OR 97005-6453

TELEPHONE: 1-800-806-6453

WEB: *www.nike.com*

BUSINESS FOCUS: Athletic shoes and apparel manufacturing

COMPANY BACKGROUND: Nike is a leading manufacturer of athletic shoes and apparel. Cole Haan, a subsidiary of Nike, makes men's and women's shoes and accessories.

NETWORKING SPECIFICS: If you're looking to network with Nike brass, the Super Show in Atlanta is a great place to start. In addition, any major sporting event would be strong. Last time we were at the U.S. Open Tennis tournament, we ran into Phil Knight. Elliot's brother sat down and had drinks with him.

SHAREHOLDERS' MEETING DATE: September

VIPs AFFILIATED WITH THE COMPANY: Thomas E. Clarke—President of New Business Ventures and COO ▪ Philip H. Knight—Chairman, President, and CEO ▪ Donald Blair—Vice President and CFO ▪ Michael Jordan (President, the Michael Jordan Foundation)—Advisory Council Member ▪ John R. Thompson, Jr. (Former Head Basketball Coach, Georgetown University)—Board Member ▪ Jill K. Conway (Visiting Scholar, Massachusetts Institute of Technology)—Board Member ▪ Ralph D. DeNunzio (President, Harbor Point Associates, Inc.)—Board Member ▪ Richard K. Donahue (Vice Chairman of the Board Lowell, Massachusetts) ▪ Delbert J. Hayes—Board Member ▪ Douglas G. Houser (Assistant Secretary, NIKE Inc.; Partner, Bullivant, Houser, Bailey, Pendergrass & Hoffman, Attorneys)—Board Member ▪ John E. Jaqua (Secretary, NIKE Inc.; Partner—Jacqua & Wheatley, P. C., Attorneys)—Board Member ▪ Charles W. Robinson (President, Robinson & Associates, venture capital)—Board Member ▪ William J. Bowerman (Director Emeritus)—Board Member ▪ A. Michael Spence (Dean, Stanford University Graduate School of Business)—Board Member ▪ Tiger Woods—Member of Nike Golf's design and development team ▪ Charles Barkley—Host of online Charles Barkley Network (sponsored by Nike) ▪ Heather Locklear

NIKE ATHLETES: Lance Armstrong ▪ Dale Jarrett ▪ Randy Johnson ▪ Donna Richardson ▪ Ken Griffey, Jr. ▪ Mia Hamm ▪ Greg Maddux ▪ Roy Jones, Jr. ▪ U.S. Women's Soccer Team ▪ Alex Rodriguez ▪ Casey Martin

■ Chan Ho Park ■ Alberto Salazar ■ L.A. Lakers ■ Pete Sampras ■ Tom Glavine ■ Mark McGuire ■ Derek Jeter ■ Carl Lewis ■ Deion Sanders

CHARITIES SUPPORTED: International Youth Foundation ■ Tuck School of Business at Dartmouth College ■ University of North Carolina's School of Public Health ■ Boys and Girls Clubs of America ■ Women's Sports Foundation ■ Let Us Play Girls Sport Camp ■ Sportsbridge ■ WNBA Be Active ■ 100 Black Men of America ■ America's Promise—The Alliance for Youth ■ YWCA

EVENTS SPONSORED: Nike U.S. Women's Cup (soccer)

The Corporate listing was discussed in the previous section on corporations. But it is important to note that the section on networking specifics points out that Nike brass attends the Super Show in Las Vegas. That seemed to be the best starting point for Bret.

He next called the corporate communications department at Nike, using the phone number on the Nike listing. When he spoke with the communications office, he asked at which sessions Mr. Knight would be speaking during the Super Show. The communications office said they hadn't determined his final schedule, but Bret was able to confirm that Knight would be attending the show.

Bret then pulled up the trade show listing for the Super Show.

Super Show

CONTACT:
The Super Show
1450 NE 123 Street
N. Miami, FL 33161

TELEPHONE: 305-893-8771
800-327-3736

DATE HELD: January

LOCATION: Las Vegas, NV

INDUSTRY: Sporting Goods

NETWORKING SPECIFICS: Every major player in sporting goods and fitness are here. This is a great place to network with the top brass of Reebok, Nike, Fila, Ray Ban, Adidas, Everlast, and every other manufacturer of sporting goods and athletic apparel. In the past this has been a fantastic place to sit down and visit with Bill Russell. It is a sports fan's networking paradise.

NUMBER OF CORPORATIONS ATTENDING: Close to 3,000

MAJOR CORPORATE HIGHLIGHTS: Nike ■ Nautica ■ CBS Sportsline ■ Logo Athletic ■ Starter ■ NHL ■ Reebok ■ Tommy Hilfiger ■ Wilson ■ Ray Ban ■ Spalding ■ Major League Baseball ■ Adidas ■ Coleman ■ Plano ■ Everlast ■ NFL Properties ■ NBA

VIPs: Cindy Crawford ■ Jenny McCarthy ■ Joe Montana ■ Troy Aikman ■ Wade Boggs ■ Julius Erving ■ Phil Esposito ■ Chris Evert ■ Bjorn Borg ■ Evander Holyfield, ■ Kathy Ireland ■ Richard Simmons ■ Emmitt Smith

■ Hank Aaron ■ Bill Russell ■ Kareem Abdul Jabbar ■ Mary Lou Retton ■ Monica Seles ■ Muhammad Ali ■ Lee Haney ■ Jane Fonda ■ Kenny Rogers ■ Dan Marino ■ John Smoltz ■ Magic Johnson ■ Mario Lemieux ■ Nadia Comaneci ■ Jimmy Connors ■ Lennox Lewis

The listing gives information that immediately helps formulate the plan. Bret used the listed phone number to call and speak with the Super Show personnel. They faxed him the conference brochure, told him about the hotel of choice, and mentioned many of the company-sponsored parties. They also gave Bret a tip on two sessions that Phil Knight was expected to attend. By the end of this research, Bret had identified a number of possible answers to the *where* question. The opportunities were the Nike booth, preferably on day three, the sessions that the Super Show expected Knight, and the Nike company party.

The question of *When do I network* was answered during the research. The Super Show seemed to offer many good opportunities to find Phil Knight.

The final question, *How do I network,* was Bret's next consideration. He called Nike and got to a product development person and spent about fifteen minutes learning about what Nike looks for in new product opportunities and how presentations are generally made. Bret was able to learn buzzwords that are typical in the industry, as well as some insight into Knight's personality. The only thing left for the *how* question was to find Knight at the Super Show and complete the goal of making the pitch.

At the Super Show, Bret was able to secure a media badge through the techniques described earlier. Once inside, Bret familiarized himself with the lay of the land. He spoke with people at the Nike booth and got confirmations about Knight's scheduled appearances at sessions, as well as the Nike party that evening. The first opportunity came at one of the sessions. Following the tips in this book, Bret didn't approach Knight when he saw him in the ballroom just before he was about to speak. In the thirty minutes before a speaker goes onstage, there are many mental preparations going on, and even if you were able to engage the speaker in conversation, you wouldn't get much focus. After the session, a crowd swarmed Knight, as he was the biggest celebrity in the room. Bret decided to wait for a quieter time. That evening, the Nike party was very exciting; many sports celebrities attended, and the entertainment was fun. While Bret had a great time at the party, he never saw Knight. The next day, Bret wandered by the Nike booth and noticed that things were beginning to calm down from the frantic pace of the day before. He decided to spend some time at the booth toward the end of the day. When Bret returned to the Nike booth around 4:30 on day two of the trade show, he immediately saw Knight speaking with two other Nike employees. Bret waited patiently until he had the chance to introduce himself. After a brief bit of relationship building, Bret discussed a recent visit Knight had with media personality Michael Moore, when Moore was creating a stir complaining about Nike policies. When Bret thought the timing was right, he mentioned casually that he had an idea for a new type of sole for sneakers. Bret launched into the pitch, smiling in the knowledge that he had once again successfully completed a networking challenge.

The key to this case study is that VIPs are accessible at trade shows. There are many opportunities to network with them as they are in town to mingle and do business for two to three days.

Trade Show Events

What follows are the entries for some of the biggest trade shows that repeat on an annual basis. Each piece of information contained in the listing can help with your networking goals. The information can help you identify who is likely to be in attendance, which companies are supporters of the show, which companies are exhibitors, and contact information. The Internet is a great source when researching trade shows, and the listings post the Internet address wherever possible.

American Bar Association Annual Meeting

CONTACT:
American Bar Association
Service Center
541 N. Fairbanks Connecticut
Chicago, IL 60611

TELEPHONE: (312) 988-5522

WEB: *www.abanet.org*

DATES HELD: Every July or August

LOCATION: Rotating

INDUSTRY: Legal

NETWORKING SPECIFICS: The ABA Annual Meeting is held consecutively with the ABA Expo. This is the largest lawyer-attended conference in the world, and it is attended by many of the movers and shakers in the law industry. If you are interested in networking within the world of law, attend this event.

NUMBER OF CORPORATIONS ATTENDING: Over 150

MAJOR CORPORATE HIGHLIGHTS: The Affiliates ▪ Bose Corporation ▪ The Hertz Corporation ▪ Mercedes-Benz USA, Inc. ▪ Saks Fifth Avenue ▪ Xerox Corporation ▪ Blumberg Excelsior, Inc. ▪ DaimlerChrysler ▪ International Bar Association ▪ The Ritz-Carlton ▪ Sony Electronics, Inc. ▪ Lexis-Nexis ▪ 3M ▪ Delta Air Lines ▪ IBM ▪ Sprint ▪ UPS

VIPs: Several Supreme Court Justices and some of the top lawyers and top firms in the legal world

American International TOY FAIR

CONTACT:
Managed by:
Toy Manufacturers of America, Inc. (TMA®)
1115 Broadway, Suite 400
New York, NY 10010

TELEPHONE: (212) 675-1141

Owned and Sponsored by:
American International TOY FAIR®
A TMA® Event
1115 Broadway, Suite 400
New York, NY 10010

TELEPHONE: (212) 675-1141

WEB: *www.toy-tma.com/AITF/index.html*

DATES HELD: Every February

LOCATION: New York, New York

INDUSTRY: Toys

NETWORKING SPECIFICS: This toy show is the king of all toy shows. If you have a new board game or idea for a toy, this is the place to shop it.

NUMBER OF CORPORATIONS ATTENDING: Over 1,700

MAJOR CORPORATE HIGHLIGHTS: Ferrari Classics Corp. ▪ Houghton Mifflin Co. ▪ McGraw Hill Consumer Products ▪ Binney & Smith, Inc. ▪ Fisher-Price Brands ▪ Hoyle Products ▪ Time Warner Trade Publishing ▪ Toymax ▪ Hasbro, Inc. ▪ Mattel, Inc. ▪ Ty, Inc.

Bakersfield Business Conference

CONTACT:
Owned and Sponsored by:
Borton, Petrini & Conron, LLP Attorneys at Law
PO Box 2026
Bakersfield, CA 93303

TELEPHONE: (661) 322-4001

Hosted by:
California State University, Bakersfield
9001 Stockdale Highway
Bakersfield, CA 93311-1099

TELEPHONE: (661) 664-2011

WEB: *www.bpcbakbusconf.com*

DATES HELD: Every October

LOCATION: Bakersfield, California

INDUSTRY: Business and finance

NETWORKING SPECIFICS: This event has been voted the best one-day conference in the nation two times in the past five years. There is a long list of business leaders, entertainers, and politicians that attend the conference every year. This event offers up unlimited networking possibilities for those interested in the state of business affairs, or those simply interested in meeting some of today's biggest names.

VIPs: Ann-Margret ▪ William Bennett (Former Secretary of Education) ▪ James Carville (Political Consultant) ▪ Robert Crandall (Former CEO, American Airlines) ▪ Hugh Downs (Television News Anchor) ▪ Mikhail Gorbachev ▪ Wayne Gretzky ▪ Robert Kennedy, Jr. (Environmental Activist) ▪ Colin Powell ▪ Benjamin Netanyahu (Former Prime Minister of Israel) ▪ Bob Newhart ▪ Queen Noor (Queen of Jordan) ▪ John Sununu (Presidential Chief of Staff) ▪ Lily Tomlin ▪ Tom Hanks ▪ Jack Kemp (Former Secretary, HUD, and 1992 Running Mate with Bob Dole) ▪ James E. Oesterreicher (Chairman and CEO, JCPenney, Inc.) ▪ Ronald Reagan ▪ Jimmy Carter ▪ Gerald Ford ▪ George Bush ▪ Margaret Thatcher ▪ Helmut Schmidt ▪ Neil Armstrong ▪ Norman Schwarzkopf ▪ Mike Wallace ▪ Dan Rather ▪ Tom Brokaw ▪ Rush Limbaugh ▪ Paul Harvey ▪ Reba McEntire ▪ Jay Leno ▪ Burt Bacharach

BookExpo America

CONTACT:
Sponsored by:
American Booksellers Association
828 South Broadway
Tarrytown, NY 10591

TELEPHONE: (800) 637-0037

Produced by:
Reed Exhibition Companies
383 Main Avenue
Norwalk, CT 06851

TELEPHONE: (208) 910-7878

Association of American Publishers
71 Fifth Avenue
New York, NY 10003-3004

TELEPHONE: (212) 255-0200

The Association of Authors' Representatives, Inc.
PO Box 237201
Ansonia Station, New York, NY 10003

Publishers Weekly
245 W. 17th St.
New York, NY 10011

TELEPHONE: (212) 463-6758

WEB: *www.bookexpoamerica.com/SingleGateway.asp*

DATES HELD: Every June

LOCATION: Rotates

INDUSTRY: Books

NETWORKING SPECIFICS: The BookExpo is the largest gathering of book publishers in the country. Shopping a book idea? Start here.

NUMBER OF CORPORATIONS ATTENDING: 2,100

MAJOR CORPORATE HIGHLIGHTS: Pendleton Books ▪ 3D Artworks, Inc. ▪ Alfred A. Knopf, Inc. ▪ Artisan ▪ Bantam Books ▪ Bloomberg Press ▪ Book$MART ▪ Cato Institute ▪ *Consumer Reports* Books ▪ Cornell University Press ▪ Dell ▪ Disney Publishing Worldwide ▪ Duke University Press ▪ FedEx Ground ▪ Harbor Press, Inc. ▪ Harcourt ▪ HarperCollins ▪ Hearst Books ▪ IBM Corporation ▪ Kinko's CDS ▪ The Lerner Publishing Group ▪ McGraw Hill ▪ Microsoft Press ▪ The New York Times ▪ Penguin Putnam, Inc. ▪ Princeton University Press ▪ Random House ▪ Rutledge Hill Press ▪ Simon & Schuster, Inc. ▪ Sotheby's Post Auction Catalogs ▪ Time Life Trade Publishing ▪ United States Postal Service ▪ Xerox Corporation ▪ HAYDEN Publishing, Inc. ▪ Academic Press and Publishers Limited ▪ Amazon.com ▪ Audio Publishers Association ▪ Beckett Publications ▪ Book Club of America, Inc. ▪ Brookings Institution Press ▪ Columbia University Press ▪ Copper Canyon Press ▪ DC Comics/*MAD* Magazine ▪ Daimler Chrysler/Inter One Marketing Group ▪ Doubleday ▪ eBay, Inc. ▪ Georgetown University Press ▪ Guinness World Record c/o Mint Publishers ▪ Harlequin Enterprises Ltd. ▪ Harvard University Press ▪ Houghton Mifflin ▪ Johns Hopkins University Press ▪ Klutz ▪ Marvel Entertainment Group ▪ Merck & Company, Inc. ▪ National Geographic Books ▪ Oxford University Press ▪ Prentice Hall ▪ Rand McNally ▪ Reader's Digest ▪ Sierra Club Books ▪ Smithsonian Institution Press ▪ Stanford University Press ▪ UPS ▪ *Variety* Magazine ▪ Zagat Survey

COMDEX (Computer Dealer Expo)

CONTACT:
Produced by:
Key3 Media Group Inc.
300 First Avenue
Needham, MA 02194-2722

TELEPHONE: (781) 433-1500

WEB: *www.zdevents.com/comdex/*

DATES HELD: Every November and every April

LOCATION: Las Vegas, Nevada, and Chicago, Illinois

INDUSTRY: Information technology

NETWORKING SPECIFICS: COMDEX is one of the largest computer and E-commerce shows in the United States. Senior government officials attend to discuss information technology with key leaders in the industry. It is often the starting place for new products and technology.

MAJOR CORPORATE HIGHLIGHTS: Qualcomm ▪ Novell ▪ Toshiba ▪ Cisco ▪ Microsoft ▪ 3Com ▪ Ericsson ▪ Hewlett-Packard ▪ Kodak

VIPs: Bill Clinton ▪ Bill Gates ▪ Larry Ellison ▪ Dick Brown

Consumer Electronics Show

CONTACT:
Sponsored, Produced and Managed by:
Consumer Electronics Association sector of the Electronic Industries Alliance
2500 Wilson Boulevard
Arlington, VA 22201

TELEPHONE: (703) 907-7500

WEB: *www.cesweb.org*

DATES HELD: Every January

LOCATION: Las Vegas, Nevada

INDUSTRY: Consumer technology

NETWORKING SPECIFICS: This is the largest consumer electronics show in the world. This is the show! Want a job with a major player in the world of electronics? This is the place to start. Sit down with the heads of Lucent Technologies, Hewlett-Packard, or Cisco Systems. Never met Bill Gates? Stop by Microsoft's presentation that he is giving.

NUMBER OF CORPORATIONS ATTENDING: Over 1,500

MAJOR CORPORATE HIGHLIGHTS: 3Com Corporation ▪ Arista Enterprises, Inc. ▪ Boston Acoustics, Inc. ▪ Cerwin-Vega, Inc. ▪ Clarion Sales Corp. ▪ Details Magazine ▪ Ericsson, Inc. ▪ Hewlett-Packard ▪ Kenwood USA Corporation ▪ Lucas Film/THX ▪ Luxor Enterprises, Inc. ▪ Owens-Corning ▪ Pioneer Electronics ▪ Rand McNally & Company ▪ Samsung America, Inc. ▪ Southwestern Bell ▪ Texas Instruments, Inc. ▪ U.S. Census Bureau ▪ Agfa Corporation ▪ AT&T ▪ Canon USA, Inc. ▪ CES-Wireless Networking ▪ Compaq Computer ▪ Eastman Kodak Company ▪ Fuji Photo Film USA, Inc. ▪ JBL Consumer Products, Inc. ▪ Klipsch, LLC ▪ Lucent Technology ▪ MCI WorldCom ▪ Panasonic Company ▪ Qualcomm, Inc. ▪ Rockford Fosgate ▪ The Sharper Image ▪ Sun Microsystems, Inc. ▪ Toshiba American Electronic Components, Inc. ▪ *Vibe* Magazine ▪ AMD ▪ BIC America ▪ Casio, Inc. ▪ Cisco Systems ▪ DirecTV, Inc. ▪ Elektra Audio ▪ IBM ▪ JL Audio, Inc. ▪ Microsoft ▪ Motorola ▪ Polk Audio ▪ Sara Lee ▪ Sony ▪ Yahoo! ▪ Yamaha Corp. ▪ Zenith Corp.

VIPs: Bill Gates ▪ Eric A. Benhamou (Chairman and CEO, 3M Corp.) ▪ Scott McNealy (Chairman and CEO, Sun Microsystems) ▪ Rob Glaser (Chairman and CEO, RealNetworks Inc.) ▪ Brad Anderson (President, Best Buy) ▪ Alan McCullough (President, Circuit City) ▪ Leonard Roberts (President, RadioShack) ▪ Megadeth (Musical Group) ▪ Jeff Cook (Lead Singer of Country Band Alabama) ▪ Barbara Eden (Actress on *I Dream of Jeannie*)

Fort Lauderdale International Boat Show

CONTACT:
  Managed and Produced by:
  Yachting Promotions, Inc.

TELEPHONE: (800) 940-7642
         (954) 764-7642

For more event info:
Show Management, Inc.
1115 NE Ninth Avenue
Fort Lauderdale, FL 33304

TELEPHONE: (954) 764-7642
         (800) 940-7642

WEB: *www.showmanagement.com/ftlauderdaleinternational_frame.htm*

DATES HELD: Every October

LOCATION: Fort Lauderdale, Florida

INDUSTRY: Boating

NETWORKING SPECIFICS: This is *the* boat manufacturers' event. Attending this event is a must if you want to break into the boating industry.

NUMBER OF CORPORATIONS ATTENDING: More than 1,400

MAJOR CORPORATE HIGHLIGHTS: Chris Craft ▪ Aquasport ▪ Carver ▪ Fountain ▪ Pro-Line ▪ Rybovich Spencer ▪ Novurania ▪ Silverton ▪ Contender ▪ Bayliner ▪ Donzi ▪ Grand Banks ▪ Sea Ray ▪ Intrepid ▪ Wellcraft ▪ Hatteras ▪ Cruisers ▪ Bluewater ▪ Dusky ▪ Glastron ▪ Regal ▪ Luhrs ▪ Mainship ▪ Maxum

International Hotel/Motel & Restaurant Show

CONTACT:
Managed by:
George Little Management, Inc.
10 Bank Street
White Plains, NY 10606-1954

TELEPHONE: (914) 421-3200

Sponsored by:
Hotel Association of New York City
437 Madison Avenue, 36th Floor
New York, NY 10022-7398

TELEPHONE: (212) 754-6700

Sponsored by:
New York State Hospitality & Tourism Association, Inc.
11 North Pearl Street, 11th Floor
Albany, NY 12207

TELEPHONE: (518) 465-2300

Sponsored by:
American Hotel & Motel Association
1201 New York Avenue NW, #600
Washington, DC 20005-3931

TELEPHONE: (202) 289-3100

WEB: *www.ihmrs.com*

DATE HELD: Every November

LOCATION: New York, New York

INDUSTRY: Restaurant

NETWORKING SPECIFICS: This is the event where networking within the hotel and restaurant field can be conducted with a great amount of ease. All of the major players in both industries attend.

NUMBER OF CORPORATIONS ATTENDING: Approximately 1,870

MAJOR CORPORATE HIGHLIGHTS: Amtrak ▪ Marriott International ▪ Doubletree Hotels Corp. ▪ Grand Casinos, Inc. ▪ Howard Johnson International ▪ MGM Grand Hotel ▪ PGA National Resort & Spa ▪ Ritz-Carlton ▪ Waldorf-Astoria ▪ Bally's Park Place ▪ Deloitte & Touche ▪ Ethan Allen Inn ▪ Holiday Inn ▪ Motel 6 ▪ Prudential Real Estate Co. ▪ Royal Carribean Cruise Lines ▪ Walt Disney World ▪ Caesar's Hotel Casino ▪ Disneyland ▪ Four Seasons Hotels ▪ Hyatt Hotels and Resorts ▪ La Quinta Inns ▪ Omni Hotels ▪ Raddison Hotels ▪ Yale University

CORPORATE PARTNERS: Network of Executive Women in Hospitality ▪ United States Air Force ▪ American Culinary Federation

International Housewares Show

CONTACT:
Sponsored by:
National Housewares Manufacturers Association
6400 Shafer Court, Suite 650
Rosemont, IL 60018

TELEPHONE: (847) 292-4200

WEB: *www.nhma.com/ihshow/default.asp*

DATES HELD: Every January

LOCATION: Chicago, Illinois

INDUSTRY: Housewares

NETWORKING SPECIFICS: This is the premier show for the housewares industry. There are many celebrities who attend. For years the best place to meet Joe DiMaggio was at the Mr. Coffee booth during the IHS.

NUMBER OF CORPORATIONS ATTENDING: Approximately 1,900

MAJOR CORPORATE HIGHLIGHTS: Hefty ▪ Bemis Company, Inc. ▪ Calflawn ▪ Rubbermaid Home Products ▪ Sunbeam ▪ Hitachi ▪ Krups ▪ Panasonic

VIPs: Norman Schwarzkopf ▪ General Colin Powell

Magic Apparel Show

CONTACT:
Magic Corporate
6200 Canoga Ave., Suite 303
Woodland Hills, CA 91367

TELEPHONE: (818) 593-5000

WEB: *www.magiconline.com*

DATES HELD: February and August

LOCATION: Las Vegas, Nevada, at the Las Vegas Convention Center, Sands Expo and Convention Center, and the Las Vegas Hilton

INDUSTRY: Fashion

NETWORKING SPECIFICS: MAGIC (Men's Apparel Guild In California) International is the largest and most prestigious of the apparel trade shows. The show is divided into MAGIC (men's apparel), WWDMAGIC (women's apparel, also sponsored by *Women's Wear Daily*), MAGIC kids, and The Edge (progressive apparel trends). It is a great place to network with buyers as well as representatives from more than 20,000 product lines. Every major player in the apparel business attends this show. The boys from FUBU got their start here. The Opening Night party kicks off the MAGIC Show and features well-known musical performers, such as past performers Melissa Ethridge and the B-52s.

NUMBER OF CORPORATIONS ATTENDING: More than 3,000

VIP STAFF: Joe Loggia—President ▪ Cindy Adams—Group Marketing Director ▪ Theresa Allen—Group Show Director ▪ Nora Ellingwood—Show Manager: MAGIC ▪ Cathy Austin—Show Manager: WWDMAGIC ▪ Gwyn A. Chafetz—Special Events Manager

MAJOR CORPORATE HIGHLIGHTS: BCBG Max Azria ▪ Calvin Klein Jeans ▪ Christian Dior ▪ Cole Haan ▪ DKNY ▪ Fossil ▪ Guess Leather ▪ Izod ▪ K-Swiss ▪ Levi Strauss & Co. ▪ Marithe & Francois Girbaud ▪ Ocean Pacific ▪ Perry Ellis ▪ Puma ▪ Speedo Authentic Fitness ▪ Todd Oldham ▪ Van Heusen ▪ Bill Blass ▪ Chaps Ralph Lauren ▪ The Coca-Cola Co. ▪ Cutter and Buck ▪ Fila ▪ Fruit of the Loom ▪ Haggar Clothing Co. ▪ Jones New York ▪ Kenneth Cole New York ▪ London Fog ▪ Nautica ▪ Pepe Jeans London ▪ Polo Jeans Company ▪ Saucony ▪ The Timberland Company ▪ Tommy Jeans ▪ Versace Neckwear ▪ 9 & Co. ▪ Candie's ▪ Urban Outfitters ▪ Z Cavaricci, Inc. ▪ Mattel, Inc. ▪ *GQ* Magazine ▪ FUBU ▪ Brighton ▪ Mia Shoes, Inc. ▪ XOXO ▪ Disney Enterprises, Inc. ▪ Warner Brothers Consumer Products ▪ *Esquire* Magazine

CHARITY SUPPORTED: Fashion Institute of Technology

National Association of TV Program Executives Annual Program Conference

CONTACT:
NATPE
2425 Olympic Boulevard, Suite 600E
Santa Monica, CA 90404

TELEPHONE: (310) 453-4440

WEB: *www.napte.com/conference/*

DATES HELD: Every January

LOCATION: Rotating

INDUSTRY: Television

NETWORKING SPECIFICS: The NATPE Annual Program Conference is one of the best ways to network into the television industry. Connections with corporate sponsors, important television executives, or television personalities would be the best ways to get in the door. The value of networking at this convention is immeasurable.

NUMBER OF CORPORATIONS ATTENDING: Around 780

MAJOR CORPORATE HIGHLIGHTS: ABC International ▪ BBC Worldwide Americas ▪ CBS News Archives ▪ Cisco Systems, Inc. ▪ Columbia Tristar International ▪ Discovery Communications ▪ Enron Communications ▪ Hallmark Entertainment ▪ MGM Worldwide Television Group ▪ Motorola ▪ NBC Inc. ▪ Nielsen Media Research ▪ Pricewaterhouse Coopers ▪ St. Jude Children's Research Hospital ▪ Target ▪ Troma Entertainment, Inc. ▪ Universal Studios ▪ World Wrestling Federation ▪ Academy of Television Arts & Sciences ▪ Bloomberg Information Television ▪ CBS Broadcast International ▪ Columbia Tristar Television Distribution ▪ Columbia Tristar Television Group ▪ E! Entertainment Television ▪ Fuji Television Network, Inc. ▪ *Variety* Magazine ▪ Microsoft ▪ MTV Networks ▪ New Line Television ▪ Paramount Television ▪ Public Broadcasting Service ▪ Sun Microsystems ▪ Trimark Television ▪ United Nations ▪ Warner Brothers International Television ▪ Bernie Brillstein (Partner of Brillstein-Grey, One of Hollywood's Most Powerful Production and Management Firms) ▪ Bill Maher ▪ Roger King (Creator, King World Productions) ▪ Eric McCormack and Debra Messing (Stars, NBC's *Will and Grace*) ▪ Robin Givens ▪ Jerry Springer ▪ Louie Anderson ▪ Kweisi Mfume (President and CEO, NAACP) ▪ Larry King ▪ Howard Stern ▪ Leeza Gibbons ▪ Gene Simmons ▪ Angie Everheart

NATPE SPONSORING ACTIVITY: The Webby Awards

National Confectioners Association All-Candy Expo

CONTACT:
National Confectioners Association
7900 Westpark Drive, Suite A-320
McLean, VA 22102

TELEPHONE: (703) 790-5750
(800) 433-1200

WEB: www.nca-cma.org/index.html

DATES HELD: Every June

LOCATION: Chicago, Illinois

INDUSTRY: Candy

NETWORKING SPECIFICS: If candy is your thing, this is the show to be at.

NUMBER OF CORPORATIONS ATTENDING: Over 175

MAJOR CORPORATE HIGHLIGHTS: BF Goodrich Hilton Davis, Inc. ▪ Brach and Brock Confections ▪ Charms Company ▪ Ferrara Pan Candy Company ▪ Judson-Atkinson Candies, Inc. ▪ Leaf ▪ Nestlé USA ▪ Simply Lite ▪ Tootsie Roll Industries ▪ BonBons Associes 2000, Inc. ▪ Certs ▪ Clark Bar ▪ Haribo of America, Inc. ▪ Kellogg Specialty Ingredients ▪ M&M/Mars ▪ Pez Candy, Inc. ▪ The Topps Company ▪ Wm. Wrigley Jr. Company

VIPs: Salvatore Ferrara II (President and COO, Ferrara Pan Candy Company) ▪ Larry Graham (President, National Confectioners Association)

National Hardware Show

CONTACT:
Sponsored by:
American Hardware Manufacturers Association
801 North Plaza Drive
Schaumburg, IL 60173

TELEPHONE: (847) 605-1025

Produced by:
Association Exposition and Services
383 Main Avenue
Norwalk, CT 06851

TELEPHONE: (203) 840-5622

WEB: www.nationalhardwareshow.com

DATES HELD: Every August

LOCATION: Chicago, Illinois

INDUSTRY: Hardware

NETWORKING SPECIFICS: This is the show to network with the major players in the hardware and lawn and garden business. Everyone from Rubbermaid to Kohler to Ortho attend. In addition, they bring in a heavyweight speaker every year as well as major celebrities attracting buyers to booths. Past attendees include President Bush, Elizabeth Dole, and Brooks Robinson.

NUMBER OF CORPORATIONS ATTENDING: Approximately 3,300

MAJOR CORPORATE HIGHLIGHTS: ACE Hardware Corporation ▪ The Clorox Company ▪ Energizer ▪ Howard Johnson's Enterprises ▪ The Dow Chemical Company ▪ Black and Decker ▪ Acme Lawn and Garden ▪ DeWitt Company ▪ Lincoln Motors ▪ Red Devil, Inc. ▪ Zenith Products Corporation ▪ Ortho ▪ Anheuser-Busch ▪ Disney Paint ▪ Owens-Corning ▪ Rubbermaid ▪ Kohler

North American International Auto Show

CONTACT:
Owned and Sponsored by:
NAIAS LLC
1900 West Big Beaver Road
Troy, MI 48084

TELEPHONE: (248) 643-0250

WEB: *www.naias.com*

DATES HELD: Every January

LOCATION: Cobo Center, Detroit, Michigan

INDUSTRY: Automobile

NETWORKING SPECIFICS: The North American International Auto Show is the longest-running auto show in the United States, making it an important event for major car manufacturers worldwide. Top-ranking auto industry officers attend the show to observe reactions to their cars and make presentations. Before the show opens, there is a black-tie charity event that benefits many national and local charities. This event is a great place to network and meet many business leaders and celebrities. Ticket requests begin nearly a year in advance for the black-tie event.

NUMBER OF CORPORATIONS ATTENDING: More than 1,100

MAJOR CORPORATE HIGHLIGHTS: Toyota Motor Corp. ▪ Ford Motor Company ▪ Honda ▪ Pontiac ▪ Porsche ▪ Audi ▪ Hyundai ▪ Nissan ▪ Audi ▪ General Motors ▪ DaimlerChrysler ▪ Daewoo ▪ Saab ▪ Volkswagen ▪ BMW ▪ Mitsubishi ▪ Dodge ▪ Kia

VIPs: Fujio Cho (President, Toyota) ▪ Bob Eaton (Chairman, DaimlerChrysler) ▪ Dennis Archer (Detroit Mayor) ▪ Carlos Ghosn (President, Nissan Motor Corporation) ▪ James O'Connor (President, Ford Division) ▪ Rick Suzuki (President, American Suzuki Motor Corporation) ▪ Hiroyuki Yoshino (President and CEO, Honda Motor Co.) ▪ Richard Anderson (Executive Vice President and COO, Northwest Airlines) ▪ Jack Smith (Chairman and CEO, General Motors) ▪ Bill Nye (The Science Guy) ▪ Aretha Franklin ▪ Thomas Hearns ▪ Grant Hill ▪ Marvin Hamlisch ▪ Dave Brubeck ▪ Joan Lunden ▪ Mel Gibson ▪ Isaiah Thomas ▪ Anita Baker ▪ Jeff Daniels ▪ Robin Leach ▪ Robert Ulrich ▪ Lynda Carter ▪ Bill Clinton ▪ Bill Richardson (Energy Secretary)

CHARITIES SUPPORTED: Boys and Girls Club ▪ March of Dimes ▪ Easter Seals

Retail Advertising and Marketing Association's Retail Advertising Conference

CONTACT:
Retail Advertising and Marketing Association
333 N. Michigan Avenue
Suite 3000
Chicago, IL 60601

TELEPHONE: (312) 251-7262

WEB: *www.rama-nrf.org*

DATES HELD: Mid-February

LOCATION: Chicago, Illinois

INDUSTRY: Advertising

NETWORKING SPECIFICS: This event is where many of the advertising and marketing heavies come to interact with one another, discuss new business ideas, and to determine the status of advertising in America.

NUMBER OF CORPORATIONS ATTENDING: Almost 50

CORPORATE HIGHLIGHTS: America Online ▪ Newspaper Association of America ▪ Mastercard/TDS ▪ The Newspaper Network (TNN)

VIPs: Bernie Marcus (Founder and Chairman, The Home Depot) ▪ Dick Hammill (Senior Vice President of Marketing, The Home Depot) ▪ Cynthia Cohen (President, Strategic Mindshare) ▪ Roy Spence (President and CEO, GSD&M Advertising) ▪ Paul Higham (Senior Vice President of Marketing, Wal-Mart) ▪ Carol Cone (President, Cone, Inc.) ▪ Derrick Ungliss (Executive Vice President and Creative Director, Brooks Brothers) ▪ Chris Ohlinger (CEO, SIDS)

ShowBiz Expo West

CONTACT:
Produced by:
Reed Exhibition Companies
383 Main Avenue
Norwalk, CT 06851

TELEPHONE: (208) 910-7878

WEB: *www.showbiz.reedexpo.com/*

DATES HELD: Every June

LOCATION: Los Angeles, California

INDUSTRY: Entertainment production

NETWORKING SPECIFICS: This is the top event bringing together the big names in entertainment production. If you have an interest in networking with those involved in the technical aspect of the entertainment industry, you cannot afford to miss this event.

NUMBER OF CORPORATIONS IN ATTENDANCE: Over 500

MAJOR CORPORATE HIGHLIGHTS: Canon ▪ General Motors ▪ Sony Pictures Studios ▪ Paine Webber ▪ Paramount Pictures Technical Services ▪ Eastman Kodak Company ▪ Marriott International ▪ Morgan Stanley Dean Witter ▪ Motion Picture Editors Guild ▪ Fuji Photo Film ▪ Monster.com ▪ Motel 6

VIPs: Gerry Byrne (Vice President and Publisher, *Variety*) ▪ Russell Goldsmith (Chairman and CEO, City National Bank) ▪ Frank J. Biondi (Chairman and CEO, MCA, Inc.) ▪ Eddy W. Hartenstein (President, DirecTV) ▪ Avram Miller (Vice President of Business Development, Intel Corporation) ▪ Russell Schwartz (President, Gramercy Pictures) ▪ Raymond W. Smith (CEO and Chairman, Bell Atlantic Corporation) ▪ Mitch Horowits (President, Spelling Films) ▪ Kiki Washington (Vice President, Human Resources and Administration, Home Box Office) ▪ Dave Zemelman (Senior Vice President, Human Resources, Westinghouse Electric)

ShoWest

CONTACT:
ShoWest
244 West 49th Street
New York, NY 10019

TELEPHONE: (212) 246-5897
(323) 525-2290

WEB: *www.showest.com*

DATES HELD: Every March

LOCATION: Las Vegas, Nevada

INDUSTRY: Motion pictures

NETWORKING SPECIFICS: This is a great place to network. All of the A-list celebrities attend this convention to promote their movies to the theater owners in attendance. It is a regular who's who of Hollywood.

NUMBER OF CORPORATIONS ATTENDING: Over 650

MAJOR CORPORATE HIGHLIGHTS: American Express ▪ Colgate-Palmolive Co. ▪ Hershey Chocolate USA ▪ Kraft Foods/Oscar Mayer ▪ Motorola ▪ Paramount Pictures ▪ Sara Lee/Ball Park Franks ▪ Tootsie Roll Industries ▪ Coca-Cola Co. ▪ Dr Pepper/7UP ▪ JBL Professional ▪ M&M/Mars ▪ Universal Cinema Services ▪ Pepsi-Cola Co. ▪ Sony Cinema Products ▪ Dolby Laboratories ▪ Häagen-Daz Co. ▪ Lucasfilm/THX ▪ Merrill Lynch ▪ Panasonic ▪ Yamaha Electronics ▪ Nestlé USA

VIPs: Dan Ackroyd ▪ Drew Barrymore ▪ Kim Basinger ▪ Warren Beatty ▪ Jeff Bridges ▪ Jerry Bruckheimer ▪ Sandra Bullock ▪ Edward Burns ▪ Tim Burton ▪ James Caan ▪ Nicholas Cage ▪ James Cameron ▪ Jim Carrey ▪ George Clooney ▪ Glen Close ▪ Sean Connery ▪ Kevin Costner ▪ Michael Crichton ▪ Tom Cruise ▪ Billy Crystal ▪ Ice Cube ▪ Johnny Depp ▪ Danny DeVito ▪ Kirk Douglas ▪ Michael Douglas ▪ Clint Eastwood ▪ Bobby and Peter Farrelly ▪ Bridget Fonda ▪ Harrison Ford ▪ Jodie Foster ▪ Morgan Freeman ▪ Andy Garcia ▪ David Geffen ▪ Mel Gibson ▪ Danny Glover ▪ Whoopi Goldberg ▪ Cuba Gooding, Jr. ▪ Heather Graham ▪ Hugh Grant ▪ Tom Hanks ▪ Salma Hayek ▪ Ron Howard ▪ Elizabeth Hurley ▪ LL Cool J ▪ James Earl Jones ▪ Jeffrey Katzenberg ▪ Nicole Kidman ▪ Greg Kinnear ▪ Al Kopelson ▪ Martin Lawrence ▪ Spike Lee ▪ Jack Lemmon ▪ Jennifer Jason Leigh ▪ Sophia Loren ▪ George Lucas ▪ William H. Macy ▪ John Madden ▪ Penny Marshall ▪ Steve Martin ▪ Dylan MeDermott ▪ Mike Myers ▪ Demi Moore ▪ Rupert Murdoch ▪ Eddie Murphy ▪ Leslie Nielson ▪ Chris O'Donnell ▪ Gwyneth Paltrow ▪ Matthew Perry ▪ Michelle Pfeiffer ▪ Brad Pitt ▪ Tom Pollock ▪ Dennis Quaid ▪ Keanu Reeves ▪ Rob Reiner ▪ Julia Roberts ▪ Geoffrey Rush ▪ Meg Ryan ▪ Winona Ryder ▪ Adam Sandler ▪ Arnold Schwarzenegger ▪ Gary Shandling ▪ William Shatner ▪ Brooke Shields ▪ Joel Silver

Super Show

CONTACT:
The Super Show
1450 NE 123 Street
N. Miami, FL 33161

TELEPHONE: (305) 893-8771
(800) 327-3736

DATE HELD: January

LOCATION: Las Vegas, Nevada

INDUSTRY: Sporting goods

NETWORKING SPECIFICS: Every major player in sporting goods and fitness is here. This is a great place to network with the top brass of Reebok, Nike, Fila, Ray Ban, Adidas, Everlast, and every other manufacturer of sporting goods and athletic apparel. In the past, this has been a fantastic place to sit down and visit with Bill Russell. It is a sports fan's networking paradise.

NUMBER OF CORPORATIONS ATTENDING: Close to 3,000

MAJOR CORPORATE HIGHLIGHTS: Nike ▪ Nautica ▪ CBS Sportsline ▪ Logo Athletic ▪ Starter ▪ NHL ▪ Reebok ▪ Tommy Hilfiger ▪ Wilson ▪ Ray Ban ▪ Spalding ▪ Major League Baseball ▪ Adidas ▪ Coleman ▪ Plano ▪ Everlast ▪ NFL Properties ▪ NBA

VIPs: Cindy Crawford ▪ Jenny McCarthy ▪ Joe Montana ▪ Troy Aikman ▪ Wade Boggs ▪ Julius Erving ▪ Phil Esposito ▪ Chris Evert ▪ Bjorn Borg ▪ Evander Holyfield ▪ Kathy Ireland ▪ Richard Simmons ▪ Emmitt Smith ▪ Hank Aaron ▪ Bill Russell ▪ Kareem Abdul Jabbar ▪ Mary Lou Retton ▪ Monica Seles ▪ Muhammad Ali ▪ Lee Haney ▪ Jane Fonda ▪ Kenny Rogers ▪ Dan Marino ▪ John Smoltz ▪ Magic Johnson ▪ Mario Lemieux ▪ Nadia Comaneci ▪ Jimmy Connors ▪ Lennox Lewis

CHAPTER FIVE

Charities

Charities offer unique opportunities that aren't found anywhere else. On one hand, charity events are prime networking ground. On the other hand, by supporting the charity, attending the events, and even becoming a part of the charity, you do a service for yourself and those who the charity supports. This book has discussed manners at the table, how to conduct yourself when networking, posture, and attitude. The concept of taking the high ground—of behaving honorably—is particularly important when dealing with charities. These are organizations that are set up to help those who are less fortunate. They provide you terrific opportunities for networking, they provide celebrities opportunities for boosting their public image, and they provide corporations with a vehicle to look like they are giving back. But they also perform their core function, which is to help others. When networking through a charity, make sure to keep your promises, try to offer some type of contribution for the charity's help, whether financially or through service or even media exposure. The point is, don't just use the charity as a networking vehicle and forget the purpose of the vehicle. If you are sincere, you will be that much better at networking, not to mention that much better as a person.

Charities are terrific opportunities for networking. When you meet someone at a charity event, you have an automatic bond, as you are on the same social level as the person you are meeting, and you have a common interest, supporting the charity. The key to charities is that they draw very high-quality VIPs. From celebrities to corporate executives, charities can create prime networking opportunities. Charities are typically most powerful in the city in which they have their headquarters. For instance, the Camp Fire Girls are very important in Kansas City, Missouri. However, local chapters can also create powerful local opportunity. For instance, the United Way in Silicon Valley or in Seattle would be a great entrée to Bill Gates, while the national headquarters in New York might not be as direct.

Each charity is very different. They have different goals, raise money in different ways, put on different events, and attract different celebrities and VIPs. If you are trying to network with someone specific, call the person's publicist and ask what charity he supports. You can then call the charity and find out its marquee events. You are likely to find the person you want to network with at the event. At the end of this chapter is a list of major charities and the VIPs who support them. This is a great starting point to identify events that would help with your networking goals.

When looking at how you can make yourself valuable to a nonprofit institution, continue to focus on what you can do to help the institution to prosper and grow. Financial contributions, media exposure, volunteering time, and being a valuable resource for contacts are all ways to ingratiate yourself to a charity.

Case Study: Networking Through a Charity

As with the last two sections, the best way to understand how networking can be valuable through a charity is to follow along with an actual example. This example will demonstrate how the techniques in this book work together to achieve a networking goal.

Bret and Elliot both enjoy meeting people. Bret tends to move in Hollywood circles, while Elliot enjoys politics. One person, however, that they both agree is fascinating is Paul McCartney. McCartney is interesting to them not just because of his success but because of the effect on society he has created through his career with the Beatles and on his own. With the exception of Elvis Presley, McCartney is arguably one of the most influential entertainers in history. Because of his significant place in history, he was also someone who Bret and Elliot decided they should meet. The two decided that they would begin a networking plan to meet Paul McCartney.

First, they began by identifying the key steps:

Step 1: What do I want? Bret and Elliot's goal was simple, to meet Paul McCartney. To focus on the task at hand, they wrote down their goal and remembered to stay on course throughout the process.

Step 2: How do I get there? The next step required the two to develop a plan. A good networking plan requires the answering of the Ws: Who do I network with? What do I want from the networking? Where do I go to network? When is the best time to network? How do I best network?

The first question is *Who do I network with?* Many times, when attempting to meet celebrities, the best methods to accomplishing your goal is through a charity or at an awards show. McCartney rarely attends award shows any longer, he wasn't on tour, and his projects were varied but secretive. As for charities, McCartney is known for his philanthropic endeavors, and Bret and Elliot decided that the *who* would be answered with a person at a charity.

The next is *What do I want*, which was answered when setting up the goal: to meet Paul McCartney. As always, it is important to be as specific as possible when creating your goal. Next on the list of five *W*s is *Where do I network?* This required research. The authors began scanning through the charity listings until they found the following:

People for the Ethical Treatment of Animals

CONTACT:
People for the Ethical Treatment of Animals
501 Front St.
Norfolk, VA 23510

TELEPHONE: (757) 622-PETA

WEB: *www.peta-online.org*

BACKGROUND INFO: PETA's main goal is to establish and protect the rights of all animals. PETA has caused many large corporations, such as Benetton, Avon, Revlon, Estee Lauder, L'Oreal, and Gillette, to cease testing their products on animals. PETA teams up with celebrities of film, music, and sports to promote the safety of animals.

EVENT: Millenium Gala (Event celebrating the success of PETA is attended by some of the major names in both the music and the movie industries. Do not wear fur to this event.)

VIP STAFF: Ingrid Newkirk-President

VIP WHO SUPPORT THE ORGANIZATION: Richard Pryor ▪ Jennie Garth ▪ Rob Reiner ▪ Michael Stipe ▪ Sheryl Lee ▪ Belinda Carlisle ▪ Alec Baldwin ▪ Montel Williams ▪ Jamie Lee Curtis ▪ Alicia Silverstone ▪ Oliver Stone ▪ Paul McCartney ▪ James Cromwell ▪ Kathy Najimy ▪ Indigo Girls ▪ Sarah MacLachlan ▪ Grace Slick ▪ Bill Maher ▪ Martina Navratilova ▪ Martin Scorsese ▪ Stella McCartney ▪ Pamela Anderson Lee ▪ Steven Seagal ▪ Gillian Anderson ▪ Woody Harrelson ▪ Ellen DeGeneres

CORPORATE SPONSOR: Paul Mitchell Professional Salon Products

The charity listing shows McCartney to be a VIP supporter. A quick call to the phone number listed proved invaluable, as the PETA people told Bret that McCartney was not only scheduled to be there, but he would be performing for the crowd as well. Bret was also able to get PETA to fax over information about the upcoming event, including date, time, and where it was to be held—on the back lot of Paramount Studios. Bret and Elliot had answered the *Where* and *When* question. They were going to a PETA event at Paramount Studios.

The final question to be answered was *How do I best network?* This analysis fit hand in hand with the next step of the process:

Step 3: How do I make myself valuable? By making themselves valuable, Bret and Elliot could increase the effectiveness of their networking plan. They knew they would attend the PETA event, but they didn't want to get lost in the crowd; they wanted to become VIPs so they would increase their chances of meeting McCartney. On the fax that was sent over from PETA, Elliot noticed that there was to be a silent auction to raise money at the event. The two realized that if they could round up some high-end auction items, they could make themselves valuable to PETA while actually helping the cause. As Bret and Elliot are serious networkers, their Rolodexes are full of contacts. They began making calls and were able to round up five very provocative donations, including a signed script by the cast of *Seinfeld*. When they called PETA and offered the donations, PETA was ecstatic. Each of the donated items was displayed that evening with a placard listing the individual who donated the item. Bret and Elliot were given a grand tour by a PETA executive and offered passes that allowed them to go anywhere the entire evening. After attending a star-studded cocktail party that hosted Alicia Silverstone, Monica Lewinsky, Steven Seagal, and many other celebs, the PETA exec walked up to Bret and Elliot and asked if they would like to say hi to Paul McCartney. The two were taken to a private waiting area where McCartney was lounging with a half-dozen people. The PETA executive introduced Bret and Elliot as good friends of the organization. For the next twenty minutes, Bret and Elliot chatted with Paul. Another successful networking plan completed.

Charity Resources

What follows are the entries for the some of the larger charity organizations and charitable foundations. The information contained in the listing can help with your networking goals by identifying which VIPs support the charity, what events they hold, and contact information. The Internet is a great place to keep up to date on a charity's ongoing endeavors and special events.

AIDS Project Los Angeles

CONTACT:
AIDS Project Los Angeles
1313 N. Vine Street
Los Angeles, CA 90028

TELEPHONE: (323) 993-1600

WEB: *www.apla.org.*

BACKGROUND INFO: The APLA is the largest AIDS organization in California and the second largest in the United States. APLA's focus is to provide victims suffering from HIV and AIDS in the Los Angeles community with different types of assistance to make living with the disease easier. Since the celebrity-to-civilian ration in Los Angeles is higher than normal, the APLA is supported by many big names.

EVENTS: AIDS Marathon ▪ AIDS Walk Los Angeles ▪ Black Tie Gala (Held in November, this event usually honors a clothing designer who has donated time and money to the APLA.)

VIP PERSONNEL: Craig E. Thompson—Executive Director ▪ Jack Corwin—Cochair ▪ Kevin James—Cochair ▪ Jeffrey Haber—Co–Vice Chair ▪ Time Aldrete—Treasurer ▪ Mark Juhas—Secretary

VIPs SUPPORTING THE CHARITY: Madonna ▪ Nathan Lane ▪ Numerous politicians ▪ Jasmine Guy ▪ Jennifer Aniston ▪ Calvin Klein ▪ Tom Hanks ▪ Kevin Bacon ▪ Carrie Fisher ▪ Bronson Pinchot ▪ Christine Baranski

CORPORATE SPONSORS: UAL ▪ Anheuser-Busch

America's Promise

CONTACT:
America's Promise—The Alliance for Youth
909 N. Washington Street, Suite 400
Alexandria, VA 22314-1556

TELEPHONE: (703) 684-4500

WEB: *www.americaspromise.org*

ORGANIZATIONAL FOCUS: Youth guidance

BACKGROUND INFO: America's Promise focuses on networking with corporations, nonprofit organizations, community groups, colleges and universities, arts and culture organizations, federal agencies, state and local governments, and individuals. America's Promise provides at-risk youth with caring adults, safe places, healthy starts, marketable skills, and opportunities to serve. Network within America's Promise, and you will be networking within one of the most widely supported organizations in the world.

VIP PERSONNEL: General Colin Powell—Chairman ▪ Linda J. Robb—Vice Chairman ▪ Sharhara Ahmad-Llewellyn—Vice Chairman ▪ William H. Shore—Secretary and Treasurer ▪ Peter A. Gallagher—President and CEO ▪ Gregg Petersmeyer—Senior Vice President ▪ Chris Keppler—Vice President for Planning and Special Events ▪ E. Renee Ingram—CFO and Chief of Administration ▪ Becky Quinn—Senior Vice President ▪ Melinda Hudson—Senior Vice President ▪ Joanne Giordano—Senior Vice President ▪ Betty S. Beene (President and CEO, United Way of North America)—Board Member ▪ Charles M. Cawley (President, MBNA Corporation)—Board Member ▪ Jamie Gorelick (Vice Chairman, Fannie Mae)—Board Member ▪ Michael Jordan (President, Basketball Operations, Washington Wizards)—Board Member ▪ Edward M. Liddy (President, CEO, and Chairman, The Allstate Corporation)—Board Member ▪ Tim Russert (Senior Vice President and Washington Bureau Chief, NBC News)—Board Member ▪ Jim Hayes (President and CEO, Junior Achievement, Inc.)—Advisory Board Member ▪ Brian Murrow (Principal Consultant, Pricewaterhouse Coopers)—Advisory Board Member ▪ Roxanne Spillett (President, Boys and Girls Clubs of America)—Advisory Board Member ▪ Judy Vredenburgh (President and CEO, Big Brothers Big Sisters of America)—Advisory Board Member

VIPs SUPPORTING THE ORGANIZATION: Faith Hill ▪ Janet Jackson

CORPORATIONS SUPPORTING THE ORGANIZATION: Aetna ▪ America Online ▪ AT&T ▪ Bell Atlantic ▪ BP Amoco ▪ British Airways North America ▪ Cisco Systems ▪ The Coca-Cola Foundation ▪ Columbia/HCA Healthcare Corporation ▪ Costco Companies, Inc. ▪ Denny's, Inc. ▪ Fannie Mae Foundation ▪ Federated Department Stores ▪ General Electric Company ▪ General Motors Corporation ▪ Hallmark Cards ▪ The Home Depot ▪ Howard Johnson International, Inc. ▪ Intel Corporation ▪ Kellogg Company ▪ Kmart Corporation ▪ MBNA America ▪ MCI WorldCom ▪ Morgan Stanely Dean Witter ▪ NBA ▪ Oracle ▪ Pfizer, Inc. ▪ Procter & Gamble Company ▪ Sears, Roebuck and Co. ▪ Sony ▪ Sun Microsystems, Inc. ▪ Ticketmaster Corporation, Time Warner, Inc. ▪ UPS ▪ VH1 ▪ The Walt Disney Company ▪ Allstate Corporation ▪ American Express Company ▪ Barnes & Noble Superstores ▪ Best Buy Co., Inc. ▪ Brinks Home Security ▪ Chase Manhattan Corporation ▪ Citigroup Foundation ▪ Colgate-Palmolive Company ▪ Yahoo! ▪ DaimlerChrysler Corporation ▪ Enron ▪ Farmers Insurance Group ▪ Freddie Mac Foundation ▪ General Mills, Inc. ▪ H&R Block ▪ Hasbro, Inc. ▪ Honeywell, Inc. ▪ IBM ▪ Kaiser Permanente ▪ Kimberly-Clark Corporation ▪ KPMG ▪ The McGraw-Hill Companies ▪ Microsoft Corporation ▪ MTV ▪ Nike, Inc. ▪ *People* Magazine ▪ The Pillsbury Company ▪ Prudential Insurance ▪ Shell Oil Company ▪ Southwest Airlines ▪ Target Corporation ▪ Timberland Company ▪ United Airlines ▪ US West, Inc. ▪ Wal-Mart, Inc. ▪ Wyeth-Ayerst Pharmaceuticals

OTHER SUPPORTERS: Minnesota Twins ▪ Florida State University ▪ Museum of Modern Art ▪ Ohio State University ▪ Trinity College ▪ University of Notre Dame ▪ University of Southern California ▪ U.S. Department of Labor ▪ U.S. Department of Treasury ▪ Department of the Air Force ▪ Department of the Army ▪ U.S. Department of Agriculture ▪ U.S. Department of Commerce ▪ U.S. Department of Education ▪ U.S. Department of Energy ▪ U.S. Department of Housing & Urban Development ▪ U.S. Department of Interior ▪ U.S. Department of Justice ▪ U.S. Department of Transportation ▪ U.S. Department of Veterans Affairs ▪ Department of the Navy—U.S. Marines ▪ Department of the Navy—U.S. Navy

NOT-FOR-PROFIT PARTNERS: American Cancer Society ▪ American Red Cross ▪ Big Brothers Big Sisters of America ▪ Boy Scouts of America ▪ Camp Fire Boys and Girls ▪ Habitat for Humanity International ▪ March of Dimes Birth Defects Foundation ▪ National Urban League ▪ Rotary International ▪ United Cerebral Palsy Associations ▪ Volunteers of America ▪ YWCA ▪ Ronald McDonald House Charities ▪ United States Peace Corps ▪ American Lung Association ▪ AMVETS ▪ Bill and Melinda Gates Foundation ▪ Boys and Girls Clubs of America ▪ Girl Scouts of the USA ▪ Junior Achievement, Inc. ▪ National Easter Seals Society ▪ The Nature Conservancy ▪ Special Olympics International ▪ United Way ▪ YMCA ▪ The Salvation Army ▪ Special Olympics International

America's Second Harvest

CONTACT:
America's Second Harvest
116 S. Michigan Ave., #4
Chicago, IL 60603

TELEPHONE: (312) 263-2303

WEB: *www.secondharvest.org*

BACKGROUND INFO: America's Second Harvest is the leading hunger relief organization in America. It runs over 200 food banks and food-rescue programs that enable twenty-six million Americans to eat.

EVENTS: Annual Conference, early September

VIP STAFF: Deborah Leff—President and CEO ▪ Sandra L. Hensley—Secretary ▪ Roberta Lane—Treasurer ▪ Martha Pickett—Vice President ▪ Glen Crawford (Vice President of Engineering, Pillsbury Company)—Chairman ▪ Marsh Blackburn (Chairman and CEO, Plato Partners)—Board Member ▪ Mary Burczyk—Board Member ▪ Tom W. Christal, Jr. (President and CEO, Advantage/Christal Sales & Marketing Company)—Board Member ▪ Irving Cramer—Board Member ▪ David Nasby (Director of Community Affairs and Vice President, The General Mills Foundation)—Board Member ▪ Chuck O'Dell—Board Member ▪ Michael Mudd (Vice President of Corporate Affairs, Kraft Foods)—Board Member ▪ Mark Schar (Vice President and Chief Learning Officer, Global Learning & Leadership Development, Procter & Gamble Worldwide)—Board Member ▪ Barry F. Scher (Vice President of Public Affairs, Giant Food Inc.)—Board Member

VIP SUPPORTING THE ORGANIZATION: Susan Lucci

CORPORATIONS SUPPORTING THE ORGANIZATION: Albertson's ▪ Nestlé ▪ Quaker Oats ▪ Kellogg's ▪ Supervalu ▪ Cisco Systems ▪ Kroger ▪ Sara Lee ▪ Humana, Inc. ▪ Borden, Inc. ▪ Macy's ▪ Loews ▪ Northwest Airlines ▪ ConAgra ▪ Kraft Foods ▪ Pillsbury Company ▪ Hewlett-Packard ▪ The Pampered Chef, Ltd. ▪ Compaq Computer ▪ Procter & Gamble ▪ William Randolph Hearst Foundation ▪ William Wrigley Jr. Company, Foundation ▪ FreeShop.com ▪ General Mills ▪ 3M ▪ Viacom

American Cancer Society

CONTACT:
American Cancer Society
1599 Clifton Road
Atlanta, GA 30329–4251

TELEPHONE: (800) ACS-2345

WEB: *www.cancer.org*

BACKGROUND INFO: The ACS is one of the largest charities in America with over two million individuals volunteering their time and money to the organization. It is a nationwide, community-based, voluntary health organization dedicated to eliminating cancer as a health risk. Deals with public policy issues concerning regulation of tobacco, improving access of cancer patients to all types of health care, raising money for cancer research, while fighting for the rights of cancer survivors.

EVENTS: Each local chapter presents its own events. Check the web site for contact information for the chapter nearest you.

VIP STAFF: John R. Seffrin—CEO ▪ Gerald L. Woolam—President ▪ John R. Kelly—Chairman of the Board ▪ Dileep G. Bal—President Elect ▪ John C. Baity, Esq.—Chairman Elect ▪ H. Fred Mickelson—Vice Chairman ▪ David M. Zacks—Treasurer ▪ Sally West Brooks—Secretary

VIPs SUPPORTING THE SOCIETY: Christy Turlington ▪ Cindy Crawford ▪ Hillary Clinton ▪ Pete Sampras ▪ Jim Boeheim (Head Basketball Coach, Syracuse University) ▪ Denny Crum (Head Basketball Coach, University of Louisville) ▪ Jerry Dunn (Head Basketball Coach, Penn State University) ▪ Fran Dunphy (Head Basketball Coach, University of Pennsylvania) ▪ Rob Evans (Head Basketball Coach, Arizona State University) ▪ Jeff Gamber (Head Basketball Coach, York College) ▪ Michael Jarvis (Head Basketball Coach, St. John's University) ▪ Mike Krzyzewski (Head Basketball Coach, Duke University) ▪ Kelvin Sampson (Head Basketball Coach, University of Oklahoma) ▪ Roy Williams (Head Basketball Coach, University of Kansas) ▪ Gary Williams (Head Basketball Coach, University of Maryland)

CORPORATE SPONSORS: General Mills ▪ National Association of Basketball Coaches ▪ General Motors ▪ Honeywell ▪ Sprint ▪ Bristol-Myers Squibb ▪ Supervalu ▪ Verizon Communications ▪ Amazon.com ▪ Women's Basketball Coaches Association ▪ Dell Computer ▪ IBM ▪ American Express ▪ Lockheed Martin ▪ UPS ▪ Anheuser-Busch

American Diabetes Association

CONTACT:

American Diabetes Association
1701 North Beauregard Street
Alexandria, VA 22311

TELEPHONE: (800) DIABETES

WEB: *www.diabetes.org*

BACKGROUND INFO: The Association is the largest nonprofit organization in the nation that focuses on preventing and curing diabetes, while improving the lives of people affected by diabetes. The association is sponsored by some of America's largest corporations.

EVENTS: America's Walk for Diabetes (Held across the country, the Walk for Diabetes is the American Diabetes Association's largest fund-raising activity ▪ Other events are held at the local level. Contact local chapters for more information.

VIP STAFF: Mayer B. Davidson—President ▪ John H. Graham IV—Chief Executive Officer ▪ Bruce R. Zimmerman—Vice President ▪ Elizabeth A. Walker—Vice President ▪ Christine A. Beebe—President, Health Care & Education ▪ Stephen J. Satalino—Chair of the Board ▪ Edward T. Hawthorne—Vice Chair of the Board ▪ James A. Horbowicz—Secretary-Treasurer

VIPs SUPPORTING THE ORGANIZATION: Gladys Knight ▪ Earvin "Magic" Johnson ▪ Kevin Bacon ▪ Dick Vitale ▪ Tony Randall

CORPORATE SPONSORS: Pfizer, Inc. ▪ Bayer Corporation ▪ Chase Enterprises ▪ Compaq Computers ▪ Amtrak ▪ Bristol-Myers Squibb Company ▪ Procter & Gamble ▪ Kraft Foods ▪ American Airlines ▪ Merrill Lynch ▪ Kaiser Permanente ▪ Honeywell ▪ Ronald McDonald House Charities ▪ *People Weekly* ▪ Harley-Davidson Motorcycles ▪ Campbell's Center for Nutrition and Wellness ▪ *Ebony Magazine*/ Johnson Publishing Company ▪ Verizon Communications ▪ Ocean Spray Cranberries, Inc. ▪ Sam Adams

American Foundation for AIDS Research

CONTACT:

amfAR
120 Wall Street, 13th Floor
New York, NY 10005

TELEPHONE: (212) 806–1600

WEB: *www.amfar.org*

BACKGROUND INFO: The goal of amfAR is to prevent infection of and death by HIV while protecting the rights of those suffering from HIV. The foundation brings together many celebrities for many of its events, and it is also sponsored and supported by some big-name businesses.

EVENTS: 25 Years of #1 Hits: Arista's Anniversary Celebration (Concert benefiting amfAR with performances or appearances by some of today's best-known artists) ▪ Cinema Against AIDS 2000 (Held annually at large festivals like Sundance and Cannes, events include the Victoria's Secret Fashion Show (which is also broadcast live at *www.VictoriasSecret.com*, a Miramax movie preview, and a black-tie gala. In the past, an auction of celebrity items or the opportunity to spend time with a celebrity has been held. This event is amfAR's largest fund-raiser, having raised a total of over five million dollars for AIDS research.) ▪ Seasons of Hope Awards Dinner (Held annually, this event honors those who have given selflessly to AIDS research. Past award recipients include some of today's top entertainers.) ▪ World AIDS Day events, December 1 (Addresses the state of the world and the effects of AIDS upon it.)

VIP STAFF: Sharon Stone—Chairman, amfAR's campaign for AIDS research

VIPs SUPPORTING THE ORGANIZATION: Mira Sorvino ▪ Gregory Peck ▪ Sela Ward ▪ Harvey Weinstein ▪ Pat Riley ▪ Daniela Pestova ▪ Claudia Schiffer ▪ Robin Williams ▪ Elizabeth Hurley ▪ Billy Crystal ▪ Elizabeth Taylor ▪ Cast/Producers of TV's *Frasier* ▪ Clive Davis (Arista Records) ▪ Angelica Huston ▪ Demi Moore ▪ Santana ▪ Patti Smith ▪ Annie Lennox ▪ Monica ▪ Carly Simon ▪ James Caan ▪ Jared Leto ▪ Joaquin Phoenix ▪ Nelson Mandela ▪ Tyra Banks ▪ Stephanie Seymour ▪ Naomi Campbell ▪ Sharon Stone ▪ Ben Affleck ▪ Catherine Zeta Jones ▪ Christian Slater ▪ Margaret Cho ▪ Salma Hayek ▪ Jerry Hall ▪ Linda Fiorentino ▪ Sarah McLachlan ▪ Kenny G ▪ Brooks & Dunn ▪ Alan Jackson ▪ Archbishop Desmond Tutu ▪ Sean Penn ▪ Milla Jovovitch ▪ Kenneth Branaugh ▪ Heidi Klum ▪ Karen Mulder ▪ Laetitia Casta ▪ Gisele ▪ Elton John ▪ Uma Thurman ▪ Michael Douglas, ▪ Quincy Jones ▪ TLC ▪ Angie Everheart ▪ Elle McPherson ▪ Ringo Starr ▪ Whitney Houston ▪ Aretha Franklin ▪ Puff Daddy ▪ Barry Manilow

SPONSORS: Victoria's Secret ▪ *Interview* Magazine ▪ Neiman Marcus ▪ Continental Airlines ▪ Gap, Inc. ▪ Miramax ▪ Miadora ▪ artnet.com ▪ Bank of America ▪ Gift for Life ▪ DuPont ▪ Christie's ▪ Saks Fifth Avenue

American Foundation for the Blind

CONTACT:
American Foundation for the Blind
11 Penn Plaza, Suite 300
New York, NY 10001

TELEPHONE: (212) 502–7600

WEB: *www.afb.org*

BACKGROUND INFO: The AFB is the big kahuna of charitable organizations serving visually impaired individuals. The foundation is nationally recognized as Helen Keller's cause, and its goal is to allow the blind to reach a level of access and opportunity that allows them total freedom in their lives. The foundation works closely with the nation's government to achieve their goals.

EVENTS: Josephine L. Taylor Leadership Institute (A three-day-long event that features lectures from leaders in the field of advocacy for the blind) ▪ Helen Keller Achievement Awards Honor Gala (Held in May, this event honors individuals and corporations who have made a contribution to the foundation.)

VIP STAFF: Carl R. Augusto—President

VIPs SUPPORTING THE ORGANIZATION: Harold McGraw III (Chairman/President/CEO, The McGraw-Hill Companies) ▪ Kiyoshi Kawakami (President/CEO, Mitsubishi Electronics America, Inc.) ▪ F. Duane Ackerman (Chairman/CEO, BellSouth Corporation) ▪ Michael J. Critelli (Chairman/CEO, Pitney Bowes, Inc.) ▪ Ahmet Ertegun (Cochairman/Co-CEO, Atlantic Records Group) ▪ Leonard J. Fassler (Cochairman, Interliant) ▪ George Packard (President, US/Japan Foundation)

CORPORATE SPONSORS: The McGraw-Hill Companies ▪ Mitsubishi Electronics America, Inc. ▪ BellSouth Corporation ▪ Pitney Bowes, Inc. ▪ Atlantic Records Group ▪ Interliant ▪ U.S./Japan Foundation ▪ Verizon

American Heart Association

CONTACT:
American Heart Association
National Center
7272 Greenville Avenue
Dallas, TX 75231

TELEPHONE: (214) 706–1173

WEB: *www.americanheart.org*

BACKGROUND INFO: The AHA is a nonprofit organization that focuses on eliminating heart disease and stroke, and it is funded by private contributions. AHA is one of the worlds premier health organizations with over 2,000 state and metropolitan affiliates, divisions, and branches throughout the U.S. and Puerto Rico. The AHA works closely with Congress to pass certain public policy proposals.

EVENTS: Heart Throb Ball (Held annually at the International Trade Center at the Ronald Reagan Building in Washington, D.C., this event draws 1,700 guests from D.C.'s legal, medical, financial, and government communities; sponsored by Capital One Financial Corporation and Lockheed Martin.) ▪ Metro-Wide Heart Gala (Held annually, Washington Hilton and Towers, Washington, D.C.)

VIP STAFF: M. Cass Wheeler—CEO ▪ Valentin Fuster—President ▪ Edward F. Hines, Jr.—Chairman of the Board

CORPORATE SPONSORS: Campbell Soup Company ▪ General Motors ▪ Federated Department Stores ▪ General Mills ▪ American Express ▪ Supervalu ▪ Capital One Financial Corporation ▪ Deloitte & Touche ▪ Honeywell ▪ Chevron ▪ Aetna ▪ Archer Daniels Midland ▪ USX ▪ Lockheed Martin

American Red Cross

CONTACT:
American Red Cross
Attn: Public Inquiry Office
431 Eighteenth Street NW
Washington, DC 20006

TELEPHONE: (202) 639-3520

WEB: *www.redcross.org*

BACKGROUND INFO: The American Red Cross is a division of the International Red Cross. The goal of the American Red Cross is to provide relief for those affected by disasters and to assist people in the prevention, preparation for, and response to emergencies.

EVENTS: Lifesavers Ball (Held annually) ▪ National Convention (Held annually)

DISTINGUISHED STAFF: Bernadine Healy—President/CEO

VIPs SUPPORTING THE ORGANIZATION: Alan Jackson ▪ George Strait ▪ Trisha Yearwood ▪ Elizabeth Dole ▪ Reba McEntire ▪ Wynonna Judd

CORPORATE SPONSORS: State Farm Insurance ▪ AT&T ▪ IBM ▪ Safeway ▪ A&P ▪ Aetna ▪ Albertson's ▪ Coca-Cola ▪ First Union Corporation ▪ Allstate ▪ Kmart ▪ Motorola ▪ Philip Morris ▪ JC Penny ▪ Citigroup ▪ Chevron ▪ Target ▪ General Mills ▪ AMR ▪ Home Depot ▪ New York Life Insurance ▪ UAL ▪ Delta Air Lines ▪ Ernest & Julio Gallo ▪ CNN ▪ Lowe's Home Improvement Warehouse ▪ Food Lion ▪ Winn-Dixie ▪ The Learning Channel ▪ Cisco Systems ▪ Compaq Computers ▪ Honeywell ▪ Johnson & Johnson ▪ Microsoft ▪ Northwest Airlines ▪ Procter & Gamble ▪ Bristol-Myers Squibb ▪ Intel Corporation ▪ Lockheed Martin ▪ Verizon ▪ American Express ▪ BellSouth ▪ J.P. Morgan & Co. ▪ 3M ▪ Anheuser-Busch

American Society for the Prevention of Cruelty to Animals

CONTACT:
ASPCA
424 East Ninety-Second Street
New York, NY 10128

TELEPHONE: (212) 876-7700

WEB: *www.aspca.org*

BACKGROUND INFO: The ASPCA was the first humane organization in existence in the Western Hemisphere. The goal of the ASPCA is to save animal lives and to improve the way they are treated by society.

EVENTS: Bergh Ball (Held annually to raise money to aid in ASPCA operations; previous guests include leaders in the entertainment industry.)

VIP STAFF: Larry M. Hawk—President and CEO ▪ Stephen Musso—Senior Vice President and Chief of Operations ▪ Stephen Eudene—Senior Vice President and CFO ▪ Tatyana D. Olyphant—Senior Vice President and General Counsel ▪ Peter Paris—Vice President of Public Affairs

VIPs SUPPORTING THE ORGANIZATION: Roy E. Disney—Vice Chairman, Walt Disney Company ▪ Mary Tyler Moore ▪ Bernadette Peters

CORPORATE SPONSORS: Walt Disney Company ▪ Verizon

Amnesty International of the U.S.A.

CONTACT:
Amnesty International
322 Eighth Avenue
New York, NY 10001

TELEPHONE: (212) 807-8400

WEB: *www.amnesty-usa.org*

BACKGROUND INFO: Amnesty International is a Nobel Prize–winning grassroots campaign with a membership of over one million individuals. The goal of Amnesty International is to enforce human rights of individuals the world over.

EVENTS: Annual General Meeting (Attracts over 500 Amnesty members and civil rights activists from all over the globe) ▪ Seattle Human Rights Film Festival (Three-day-long event showcasing documentaries covering the injustices of the world; all proceeds go to Amnesty International.)

VIP STAFF: Julianne Cartwright Traylor—Chair, Amnesty International USA ▪ Susan Waltz—United States of America Representative, International Executive Committee

VIPs SUPPORTING THE ORGANIZATION: Peter Gabriel ▪ Jimmy Page ▪ Sarah Jessica Parker ▪ Cindy Lauper ▪ Tom Morello (guitarist, Rage Against the Machine) ▪ Bruce Springsteen ▪ Robert Plant ▪ Radiohead ▪ Suzanne Vega ▪ Tracy Chapman ▪ Alanis Morissette ▪ Tim Robbins

CORPORATE SPONSORS: Excite ▪ Virgin Records ▪ Reebok

AMVETS National Service Foundation

CONTACT:
AMVETS National Headquarters
4647 Forbes Boulevard
Lanham, MD 20706-4380

TELEPHONE: (301) 459-9600

WEB: *www.amvets.org*

BACKGROUND INFO: The goals of the foundation are to promote peace, preserve the American way of life, and enable veterans to live well. The foundation works with the government to protect and preserve the entitlements of honorably discharged veterans.

EVENT: National Convention (Held in August, AMVETS throughout the nation gather once a year to discuss concerns and issues facing the American Veteran.)

VIP STAFF: Charles L. Taylor—National Commander ▪ Dave Woodbury—Executive Director ▪ Howie De-Wolf—National Service Director ▪ Peter Gaytan—National Legislative Director ▪ Don Coffman—National Programs Director ▪ Dick Flanagan—Public Relations Director ▪ John Powell—Membership Director

VIP SUPPORTING THE ORGANIZATION: Heather French (Miss America 2000)

Arthritis Foundation

CONTACT:
Arthritis Foundation National Office
1330 West Peachtree Street
Atlanta, GA 30309

TELEPHONE: (404) 872-7100

WEB: *www.arthritis.org*

BACKGROUND INFO: The foundation focuses mainly on finding a cure for arthritis. It was the first arthritis organization in America, and it has led to a great increase in the amount of arthritis research that is conducted.

EVENTS: In addition to their national walk-a-thon called the Joint Walk, they also hold an annual dinner.

VIP STAFF: Don L. Riggin—President and CEO ▪ William J. Mulvihill—Chair

VIPs SUPPORTING THE ORGANIZATION: Bob Hope (First Chair) ▪ Charlton Heston (Chairman of the NRA)

SPONSORS: General Motors ▪ Honeywell

Big Brothers Big Sisters of America

CONTACT:
Big Brothers Big Sisters of America
230 North Thirteenth Street
Philadelphia, PA 19107

TELEPHONE: (215) 567-7000

BACKGROUND INFO: The BBBSA is the expert organization when it comes to youth mentoring. The purpose of BBBSA is to provide adult mentors who are willing to spend time with the youth who need them most.

EVENTS: National Conference (Held in June, this is an event where big brothers and big sisters and the children they support are given an opportunity to discuss issues concerning them with a Congressional representative.)

VIP STAFF: Judy Vredenburgh—CEO ▪ Thomas M. McKenna—National Executive Director

VIP SUPPORTING THE ORGANIZATION: Mark Martin (NASCAR Driver)

CORPORATE SPONSORS: IBM ▪ Hewlett-Packard ▪ Arby's Inc. ▪ Northwest Airlines ▪ Kellogg Foundation ▪ Pillsbury Company ▪ AMC Entertainment Inc. ▪ NASCAR ▪ Cisco Systems ▪ Lucent Technologies ▪ Unilever Home & Personal Care—USA ▪ JCPenney ▪ United Technologies ▪ Sprint ▪ BellSouth ▪ New York Life Insurance ▪ UPS ▪ Aetna ▪ Anheuser-Busch ▪ Digital ▪ Hardware Wholesalers, Inc. ▪ American Express ▪ Frito-Lay ▪ Annie E. Casey Foundation ▪ De Witt-Wallace/Readers Digest Fund ▪ Valvoline ▪ eBay ▪ Dell Computers ▪ Microsoft ▪ Intel Corporation ▪ Verizon ▪ General Mills ▪ Home Depot ▪ 3M ▪ Viacom ▪ J. P. Morgan & Co. ▪ Visa

Bill and Melinda Gates Foundation

CONTACT:
Bill & Melinda Gates Foundation
PO Box 23350
Seattle, WA 98102

TELEPHONE: (206) 709-3100

WEB: *www.gatesfoundations.org*

ORGANIZATIONAL FOCUS: Donations to promote health and learning

BACKGROUND INFO: The Bill and Melinda Gates Foundation and the Gates Learning Foundation awarded well over three billion dollars in grants in 1999 alone. The foundation is largely financed by Bill and Melinda Gates. Grants are primarily given to support educational programs, scholarships, technology in schools, public libraries, and world health problems.

EVENTS: Check presentations

VIP STAFF: Bill Gates III—Founder ▪ Melinda Gates—Founder ▪ William H. Gates, Sr.—Cochair and CEO ▪ Patty Stonesifer—Cochair and President ▪ Allan C. Golston—Chief Financial and Administrative Officer ▪ Terry Meersman—Senior Program Officer

VIP SUPPORTING THE ORGANIZATION: Nelson Mandela

CHARITIES SUPPORTED: American Red Cross ▪ Save the Children Federation ▪ Ronald McDonald House Charities ▪ Boys and Girls Clubs ▪ YWCA ▪ American Cancer Society ▪ United Way ▪ Planned Parenthood ▪ University of California at Berkeley ▪ Duke University ▪ United Negro College Fund ▪ Cystic Fibrosis Foundation ▪ UNICEF ▪ Camp Fire Boys and Girls ▪ Helen Keller International ▪ Harvard University ▪ Goodwill Industries ▪ United Nations Foundations ▪ University of Texas at Austin ▪ Columbia University ▪ Make-A-Wish Foundation ▪ CARE ▪ YMCA ▪ University of Pennsylvania ▪ Habitat for Humanity ▪ Rotary Foundation ▪ MIT ▪ CityYear

Boy Scouts of America

CONTACT:

Boy Scouts of America
1325 West Walnut Hill Lane
PO Box 152079
Irving, TX 75015-2079

TELEPHONE: (972) 580-2401

WEB: *www.bsa.scouting.org*

BACKGROUND INFO: The goal of the Boy Scouts of America is to prepare young people to lead an ethical life following the Scout Law. Many government officials are associated with the Boy Scout of America.

EVENTS: Boy Scouts Report to the Nation (Five-day tour of Washington, D.C.: The Boy Scouts of America choose seven delegates from across the nation to travel to Washington, D.C., to speak to the president, the Senate, and the House of Representatives.)

VIP STAFF: Roy L. Williams—Chief Scout Executive ▪ Edward E. Whitacre, Jr.—President

VIPs SUPPORTING THE ORGANIZATION: Willie Banks (Former World Record Holder in the Triple Jump and the Long Jump) ▪ Lloyd Bentsen, Jr. (Former Secretary of the Treasury; Former Senator, Texas) ▪ Bill Bradley (Former Senator, New Jersey; Former NBA Star; Former Presidential Hopeful) ▪ Thomas Foley (Former Speaker of the House; Former Congressman) ▪ Gerald Ford (Former President of the United States) ▪ James A. Lovell, Jr. (Apollo Astronaut) ▪ Richard Lugar (Senator, Indiana) ▪ J. Willard Marriott, Jr. (Chairman and President, Marriott Corporation) ▪ Sam Nunn (Former Senator, Georgia) ▪ H. Ross Perot (Businessman; Former Presidential Hopeful; Founder of the Reform Party) ▪ Steven Spielberg ▪ Togo West (Secretary of the Army)

CORPORATE SPONSORS: Coca-Cola ▪ Honeywell ▪ Microsoft ▪ Phillips Petroleum ▪ Wal-Mart ▪ Chevron ▪ Citigroup ▪ Verizon ▪ SBC ▪ Sprint ▪ Colgate-Palmolive ▪ AMR Corporation ▪ Cigna ▪ 3M ▪ USX ▪ Home Depot ▪ Delta Air Lines ▪ American Express ▪ BellSouth ▪ Kimberly-Clark ▪ UPS ▪ General Mills ▪ Anheuser-Busch

Boys and Girls Clubs of America

CONTACT:

Boys and Girls Clubs of America
1230 W. Peachtree Street NW
Atlanta, GA 30309

TELEPHONE: (404) 815-5700

WEB: *www.bgca.org*

BACKGROUND INFO: The Boys and Girls Clubs of America were created to give children with working parents a safe place to go after school. Many leaders in the fields of entertainment, politics, and business are former members of the B&GCA.

EVENT: Boys and Girls Clubs of America National Conference

VIP STAFF: Roxanne Spillett—President ▪ Bill Clinton—Honorary Chairman ▪ Rick Goings—Chairman Emeritus ▪ Peter L. Haynes—Chairman of the Board ▪ Arnold I. Burns—Chairman Elect ▪ Jean C. Crystal—Vice Chairman, Secretary ▪ Ronald J. Gidwitz—Vice Chairman ▪ Harvey W. Schiller—Vice Chairman ▪ Edward M. Liddy (President, Chairman, and CEO, The Allstate Corporation)—Treasurer

VIPs SUPPORTING THE ORGANIZATION: Bonnie Raitt ▪ Walter Anderson (Editor, *Parade* Magazine) ▪ Bill Cosby ▪ Walter Matthau ▪ Joe Piscopo ▪ Bob Ueker ▪ Robin Williams ▪ Jack Kemp ▪ John F. Smith (Chairman &

CEO, General Motors Corp.) ▪ C. J. Silas (Retired Chairman and CEO, Phillips Petroleum Co.) ▪ Wayne Allen (Chairman and CEO, Phillips Petroleum Co.) ▪ Kenneth T. Stevens (Chairman and CEO, Banc One Retail Group) ▪ John Antioco (Chairman and CEO, Blockbuster Entertainment) ▪ Ronald T. LeMay (President and COO, Sprint Corp.) ▪ Dan Rather ▪ Dick Clark ▪ George Lucas ▪ Danny Devito ▪ Denzel Washington ▪ Gen. Wesley Clark (NATO Military Commander) ▪ George Mitchell (Former Senate Majority Leader) ▪ Bernard Shaw ▪ Shaquille O'Neal ▪ John Mellencamp ▪ Leonard Nimoy ▪ Cuba Gooding, Jr. ▪ Jennifer Lopez

CORPORATE SPONSORS: Coca-Cola ▪ Fender Guitars ▪ Major League Baseball ▪ Nike ▪ Sports Illustrated ▪ Cisco Systems ▪ Honeywell ▪ Motorola ▪ Phillips Petroleum ▪ Chevron ▪ Coors ▪ Metropolitan Life ▪ United Tehnologies ▪ Sprint ▪ General Mills ▪ American Express ▪ ConAgra ▪ Enron ▪ Kimberly-Clark ▪ New York Life Insurance ▪ USX ▪ Anheuser-Busch ▪ Delta Air Lines ▪ Compaq Computer Corporation ▪ L'Oreal ▪ MasterCard ▪ Post Cereal ▪ Allstate Insurance ▪ Electronic Data Systems ▪ Microsoft ▪ Northwest Airlines ▪ Bristol-Myers Squibb ▪ Citigroup ▪ Intel Corporation ▪ SBC ▪ Verizon ▪ Colgate-Palmolive ▪ Bank of America ▪ Cigna ▪ E.I. du Pont de Nemours ▪ Home Depot ▪ 3M ▪ UPS ▪ Viacom ▪ Oracle

Breast Cancer Fund

CONTACT:
Breast Cancer Fund
282 Second Street, 2nd Floor
San Francisco, CA 94105

TELEPHONE: (415) 543-2979
(800) 487-0492

WEB: *www.breastcancerfund.org*

BACKGROUND INFO: The Breast Cancer Fund is a national nonprofit organization whose focus is to end breast cancer and to ensure that all women receive the best medical care, support services, and information available. The fund deals with Congress to increase research on the effect of the environment on breast cancer.

EVENTS: Sexuality & Cancer Conference (With appearances from experts in the field of breast cancer and the leaders of the Breast Cancer Fund)

VIP STAFF: Andrea Martin—Founder, Executive Director ▪ Elizabeth Cain—Board Member ▪ Connie George—Chair of the Board ▪ Joanne Hagopian—Board Member ▪ Nicole Schapiro—Board Member ▪ Susan Shinagawa—Board Member ▪ Ioana Petrou—Board Member ▪ Maida B. Taylor—Board Member ▪ Donna Westmoreland—Board Member ▪ Wanna Wright—Board Member

VIPs SUPPORTING THE ORGANIZATION: Sharon Stone ▪ Mary Chapin Carpenter ▪ Indigo Girls ▪ Judy Bloom ▪ Paula Cole ▪ Celine Dion ▪ k.d. lang

CORPORATE SPONSORS: Pacific Bell ▪ Warner Brothers Records ▪ Bristol-Myers Squibb ▪ American Cancer Society ▪ Sun Microsystems Foundation ▪ Macy's West ▪ Genentech ▪ Oracle ▪ Charles Schwab Corporation Foundation ▪ Merrill Lynch ▪ Farmers Insurance ▪ Susan G. Komen Foundation

ORGANIZATIONS SUPPORTED BY THE BREAST CANCER FUND: Greenpeace ▪ AMC Cancer Research Center ▪ Tulane University ▪ University of Michigan

Camp Fire Boys and Girls

CONTACT:
Camp Fire Boys and Girls
4601 Madison Avenue
Kansas City, MO 64112-1278

TELEPHONE: (816) 756-1950

WEB: *www.campfire.org*

BACKGROUND INFO: Camp Fire Boys and Girls is a nonprofit, youth development organization with 129 councils and over 625,000 participants nationwide.

EVENT: Camp Fire Boys and Girls National Convention

VIP STAFF: Rosie Mauk—President ▪ Stewart Smith—National Executive Director ▪ Bunnie Curtis—Vice President of Youth Leadership

CORPORATE SPONSORS: Honeywell ▪ Sprint ▪ Colgate-Palmolive ▪ ConAgra ▪ 3M

Childhelp USA

CONTACT:
Childhelp USA National Headquarters
15757 North Seventy-eighth Street
Scottsdale, AZ 85260

TELEPHONE: (480) 922-8212

WEB: *www.childhelpusa.org*

BACKGROUND INFO: Childhelp USA is dedicated to aiding neglected and abused children by meeting their physical, spiritual, emotional, and educational needs.

EVENTS: Angel Award Gala (Held in Tennessee in May) ▪ Spirit of the Children Gala (Held in October in Arizona)

VIP STAFF: Yvonne Fedderson—President ▪ Sara O'Meara—CEO/Chairman

National Advisory Board: General & Mrs. James Abrahamson ▪ Joseph Barbera ▪ Hon. Thomas J. Bliley ▪ Hon. Bill Bradley ▪ Barbara Bush ▪ Rosalyn Carter ▪ Hon. Dan Coats ▪ Hon. James C. Corman ▪ Hon. Christopher Cox ▪ Hon. Bud Cramer ▪ Hon. John C. Danforth ▪ Hon. Dennis DeConcini ▪ Father Ralph DiOrio ▪ Hon. Christopher Dodd ▪ Hon. Elizabeth Dole ▪ Hon. David Drier ▪ Dr. Vincent J. Fontana ▪ Rev. Billy Graham ▪ Hon. James M. Inhofe ▪ Hon. Jack Kemp ▪ C. Everett Koop, M.D. ▪ Gen. Robert F. McDermott ▪ Hon. Barbara Milkulski ▪ Adm. William Owens ▪ Hon. Harry Pregerson ▪ Nancy Reagan ▪ Hon. Charles Robb ▪ Dale Evans Rogers ▪ Hon. Paul Sarbanes ▪ Willard Scott ▪ Robert Sigholtz, Ph.D. ▪ Allen E. Susman ▪ Hon. Strom Thurmond ▪ Hon. John Warner ▪ Hon. & Mrs. Paul Wellstone ▪ Governor & Mrs. Pete Wilson ▪ Hon. Frank Wolf

VIPs SUPPORTING THE ORGANIZATION: Pat Boone ▪ Glenn Frey ▪ Kathy Lee Gifford ▪ Chris O'Donnell ▪ Collin Raye ▪ Jane Seymour ▪ Norm Crosby ▪ Leeza Gibbons ▪ Melissa Gilbert ▪ Merlin Olson ▪ Jack Scalia ▪ John Stamos ▪ Mary Hart ▪ Kathleen Turner ▪ Florence Henderson ▪ Barbara Bush

CORPORATE SPONSORS: International House of Pancakes ▪ Discount Tire Co.

Children's Wish Foundation International

CONTACT:
Children's Wish Foundation International, Inc.
8615 Roswell Road
Atlanta, GA 30350-7526

TELEPHONE: (770) 393-WISH
(800) 323-WISH

WEB: *www.childrenswish.com*

BACKGROUND INFO: The Children's Wish Foundation International focuses its energy on fulfilling wishes of seriously ill children.

EVENT: Midnight Ball (Held annually, this event raises a large amount of money for the foundation. It is attended by over 500 of the foundation's most generous supporters as well as comedians and musicians.)

VIP STAFF: Linda Dozoretz—Exec. Director and Cofounder ▪ Arthur J. Stein—President/CEO

VIPs SUPPORTING THE ORGANIZATION: Pope John Paul ▪ Newt Gingrich ▪ LL Cool J ▪ Olivia Newton John ▪ David Copperfield ▪ Lorna Luft (Sister of Liza Minelli) ▪ George Lucas ▪ Dolly Parton ▪ Pat Summerall ▪ Jean-Claude Van Damme ▪ Helen Hunt

Cystic Fibrosis Foundation

CONTACT:
The Cystic Fibrosis Foundation
6931 Arlington Road
Bethesda, MD 20814

TELEPHONE: (301) 951-4422
(800) FIGHT-CF

WEB: *www.cff.org*

BACKGROUND INFO: The foundation focuses on developing the means to control and cure cystic fibrosis while improving the life of those individuals suffering from the disease.

EVENT: American Airlines Celebrity Ski (Held annually, the event, hosted by American Airlines, raises money to aid in the fight against cystic fibrosis. It brings together celebrities and entertainers to raise money.)

VIP STAFF: Robert J. Beall—President and CEO

VIPs SUPPORTING THE FOUNDATION: Boomer and Cheryl Esiason (Honorary Cochairs, Building Bridges to a Cure) ▪ Garth Brooks ▪ Billy Dean ▪ Faith Hill ▪ Olivia Newton-John ▪ Rosie O'Donnell ▪ Dan and Marilyn Quayle ▪ Buzz Aldrin ▪ Dan Jansen

SPONSORS: American Air Lines ▪ Delta Air Lines ▪ Genentech, Inc. ▪ Nationwide Express ▪ Scandipharm, Inc. ▪ Targeted Genetics ▪ Honeywell ▪ The Alfred Hitchcock Memorial Fund ▪ Bristol-Myers Squibb ▪ Alaska Airlines ▪ Falcon Cable TV ▪ Heilig-Meyers ▪ Patho Genesis ▪ Solvay Pharmaceuticals ▪ United Airlines ▪ Warner/Elektra/Atlantic Corporation

Easter Seals

CONTACT:
Easter Seals
230 West Monroe Street, Suite 1800
Chicago, IL 60606

TELEPHONE: (312) 726-6200

WEB: *www.easter-seals.org*

ORGANIZATIONAL FOCUS: Health and human services provider

BACKGROUND INFO: Easter Seals was a leader in creating and implementing the Americans with Disabilities Act. Easter Seals focuses on improving the lives of disabled children and adults so that they may gain independence. Throughout its life, the organization has enabled over one million disabled individuals to achieve a higher level of independence.

EVENT: Annual EDI Awards (Held in early October, these awards recognize individuals and corporations who promote the equality, dignity, and independence of individuals with disabilities.)

VIP PERSONNEL: James E. Williams—President and CEO ▪ Jeanne Sowa—Senior Vice President, Marketing and Corporate Relations

VIPs SUPPORTING THE ORGANIZATION: John Hockenberry ▪ Sally Jesse Raphael ▪ Phylicia Rashad ▪ Cliff Robertson ▪ Marlee Matlin ▪ Heather Whitestone (1995 Miss America)

CORPORATIONS SUPPORTING THE ORGANIZATION: Safeway, Inc. ▪ Century 21 Real Estate Corporation ▪ U.S. Rotary Clubs ▪ American Express ▪ JCPenny ▪ American Express Foundation ▪ Paine Webber ▪ Viacom ▪ Amway Corporation ▪ Microsoft ▪ Domino's Pizza ▪ Pearle Vision ▪ Allstate Foundation ▪ Bank of America ▪ General Mills ▪ Anheuser-Busch

Elizabeth Glaser Pediatric AIDS Foundation

CONTACT:
Elizabeth Glaser Pediatric AIDS Foundation
2950 Thirty-first Street, #125
Santa Monica, CA 90405

TELEPHONE: (310) 314-1459

WEB: *www.pedaids.org/homefrm/html*

BACKGROUND INFO: The foundation is the world leader in conducting pediatric AIDS research and treatment. Events held by the foundation usually bring in a high number of entertainers, athletes, and politicians.

EVENTS: Glaser Foundation Picnic (Held annually, the picnic benefit is successful at raising money for AIDS research and bringing together big names from the entertainment and sports world.) ▪ A Night to Unite (This event unites politicians for the sole purpose of benefiting the foundation.) ▪ Kids for Kids (Held annually, the foundation turns select streets in New York into a carnival. Past guests include supermodels and actresses.)

VIP STAFF: Paul Glaser—Chairman ▪ Susie Zeegen—Cofounder ▪ Susan DeLaurentis—Cofounder ▪ James Carville—Cochair ▪ Mary Matalin—Cochair

VIPs SUPPORTING THE FOUNDATION: Brooke Shields ▪ Christie Brinkley ▪ Tyra Banks ▪ Jack Nicholson ▪ James Carville ▪ Senator Barbara Boxer ▪ Sanita Jackson (Daughter of Rev. Jesse Jackson) ▪ Natalie Portman ▪ Kevin Costner ▪ Kobe Bryant ▪ Sandy Koufax ▪ Senator Orrin Hatch ▪ Carol Kane

Elton John AIDS Foundation

CONTACT:
Elton John AIDS Foundation
PO Box 17139
Beverly Hills, CA 90209-3139

TELEPHONE: (310) 535-1775

WEB: *www.ejaf.org*

BACKGROUND INFO: The mission of the Elton John AIDS Foundation is to to educate the public on AIDS prevention methods, to eliminate both prejudice and discrimination of AIDS victims, and to assist those with AIDS and their families. The foundation is very widely supported by stars of stage, screen, and music, as well as large, influential corporations.

EVENTS: Elton John AIDS Foundation/InStyle Magazine Academy Awards Dinner and After Party (Held annually, this event is attended by numerous musicians and movie stars.) ▪ Broadway Cares/Equity Fights AIDS Concert (Elton John as well as a supporting cast of stars from Broadway, Hollywood, and the recording industry team up to raise money for the Elton John Aids Foundation.)

VIP STAFF: Elton John—Chairman ▪ John Scott—Executive Director and President ▪ Michelle Burns—Treasurer ▪ Virginia Banks—Secretary

VIPs SUPPORTING THE FOUNDATION: Gerald Levin (Time-Warner CEO) ▪ Chris O'Donnell ▪ Fran Drescher ▪ Keri Russell ▪ k.d. lang ▪ Janine Turner ▪ Bernie Taupin ▪ Ellen DeGeneres ▪ Whitney Houston ▪ Jim Carrey ▪ Alec Baldwin ▪ Goldie Hawn ▪ Kevin Costner ▪ Helen Hunt ▪ Dylan MacDermott ▪ Puff Daddy ▪ Jay Leno ▪ Janet Jackson ▪ Tim Allen ▪ Sarah Michelle Gellar ▪ Rebecca Gayhart ▪ Antonio Sabato, Jr. ▪ William H. Macy ▪ Robert Wagner ▪ Anne Heche ▪ Lisa Marie Presley ▪ Mariah Carey ▪ Kim Basinger ▪ Kurt Russell ▪ Val Kilmer ▪ Geena Davis ▪ Natalie Cole ▪ Rod Stewart ▪ Melissa Ethridge

CORPORATE SPONSORS: Motorola ▪ Seagram/Absolut Vodka ▪ Jaguar ▪ Sprint

Girl Scouts of America

CONTACT:
Girl Scouts of the U.S.A.
420 Fifth Avenue
New York, NY 10018-2798

TELEPHONE: (212) 852-6548

WEB: *www.gsusa.org*

BACKGROUND INFO: The Girl Scouts is the world's largest organization just for girls. The goal of Girl Scouting is to inspire girls with the highest ideals of character, conduct, patriotism, and service so that they may become resourceful citizens. Their famous cookie drive is anticipated yearly by many Americans.

EVENT: Girl Scouts National Convention

VIP STAFF: Marsha Johnson Evans—National Executive Director ▪ Connie Matsui—President ▪ Hillary Rodham Clinton—National Honorary President

VIP ASSOCIATED WITH THE INSTITUTION: Madeleine Albright (Secretary of State)

CORPORATE SPONSORS: Cisco ▪ AT&T ▪ Honeywell ▪ Wal-Mart ▪ SBC ▪ Sprint ▪ General Mills ▪ Kimberly-Clark ▪ New York Life Insurance ▪ Viacom ▪ Bristol-Myers Squibb ▪ Chevron ▪ Citigroup ▪ Lockheed Martin ▪ Verizon ▪ Colgate-Palmolive ▪ BellSouth ▪ 3M ▪ USX ▪ Anheuser-Busch

Goodwill Industries

CONTACT:
Goodwill Industries International, Inc.
9200 Rockville Pike
Bethesda, MD 20814

TELEPHONE: (301) 530-6500

WEB: *www.goodwill.org*

BACKGROUND INFO: The goal of Goodwill Industries is to enable people with disabilities and other individuals with special needs to expand their opportunities and occupational capabilities through a collection of independent, nonprofit, community-based organizations.

EVENT: Delegate Assembly (Held annually)

VIP STAFF: Fred Grandy (Former Gopher on *Love Boat*)—President/CEO, Goodwill Industries International ▪ Carl E. Hansen—Chairman ▪ Paul Foster—Vice Chairman ▪ Lawrence Wheat—Treasurer ▪ J. Clay Murphy—Secretary

CORPORATE SUPPORTERS: *Bride's* Magazine ▪ U.S. Census Bureau ▪ Paul Harris Stores, Inc. ▪ Cisco Systems ▪ Microsoft ▪ American Express ▪ General Mills ▪ Natural Wonders, Inc. ▪ Hewlett-Packard ▪ Bank of America ▪ Honeywell ▪ New York Life Insurance ▪ 3M ▪ UPS

Habitat for Humanity International

CONTACT:
Partner Service Center
Habitat for Humanity International
121 Habitat St.
Americus, GA 31709

TELEPHONE: (912) 924-6935, ext. 2551 or 2552

WEB: *www.habitat.org*

BACKGROUND INFO: Habitat for Humanity has built over 95,000 houses across the globe, allowing over 475,000 individuals to obtain shelter. Habitat for Humanity International is a Christian ministry that has helped needy families build houses in over 1,500 U.S. cities and sixty other countries. Jimmy Carter is one of its most well-known supporters.

EVENT: Jimmy Carter Work Project (Former President Carter and his wife and thousands of other volunteers go on a week-long house-building spree.)

VIP STAFF: Millard Fuller—President and Founder ▪ Linda Fuller—Cofounder ▪ Sister Maria de Lourdes Turueno (Mexico City)—Board Member ▪ Bonnie McElveen-Hunter (Greensboro, N.C.)—Board Member ▪ Jim Copeland (Washington, D.C.)—Board Member

VIPs SUPPORTING THE ORGANIZATION: Jimmy and Rosalynn Carter ▪ Jack Kemp (Former Secretary of Housing and Urban Development and former HFHI Board Member)

CORPORATE SPONSORS: Charles Schwab ▪ General Motors ▪ Mobil Oil Corporation ▪ Cisco Systems ▪ Dell Computer ▪ Federated Department Stores ▪ Freddie Mac ▪ Lucent Technologies ▪ PepsiCo ▪ Philip Morris ▪ Bristol-Myers Squibb ▪ Duke Energy ▪ Metropolitan Life ▪ General Mills ▪ Dow Chemical ▪ Home Depot ▪ Whirlpool Corporation ▪ Arthur Andersen ▪ Eastman Kodak ▪ First Union Corporation ▪ Honeywell ▪ Microsoft ▪ Northwest Airlines ▪ Prudential ▪ Citigroup ▪ Intel Corporation ▪ Verizon ▪ BellSouth ▪ Viacom ▪ Aetna ▪ AMR Corporation ▪ Pricewaterhouse Coopers ▪ UPS ▪ 3M ▪ American Express ▪ J. P. Morgan & Co. ▪ UAL ▪ Delta Air Lines

Junior Achievement

CONTACT:
Junior Achievement Inc.
National Headquarters and Service Center
One Education Way
Colorado Springs, CO 80906

TELEPHONE: (719) 540-8000

WEB: *www.ja.org/*

BACKGROUND INFO: Junior Achievement currently reaches over 3.5 million students in an attempt to secure their well-being in the real world. The Junior Achievement program is concerned with familiarizing every child in America with the fundamentals of the free-enterprise system so they may succeed in a global economy. It is the world's largest and fastest growing nonprofit organization focusing on economic education. Many Junior Achievement alumni are leaders in both business and political arenas.

EVENT: Junior Achievement National Business Hall of Fame Induction Ceremony (This event takes place in New York City, and it recognizes those business leaders who have made enormous contributions to the free-enterprise system.)

VIP STAFF: James B. Hayes—President and CEO ▪ Jerome T. Loeb (Chairman of the Board, The May Department Stores Company)—National Chairman ▪ Arte Johnson—National Board Member

VIPs SUPPORTING THE ORGANIZATION: Bob Clement (U.S. Congressman, D-Tenn.) ▪ Frederick A. Deluca (Founder and CEO, Subway) ▪ Dick De Vos (President, Amway Corporation) ▪ Arte Johnson (Actor and Junior Achievement National Board Member) ▪ Marshall Loeb (Editor, *Columbia Journalism Review*) ▪ Thomas S. Monaghan (President and CEO, Domino's Pizza, Inc.) ▪ Dan Rather (Anchor and Managing Editor, CBS Evening News) ▪ Dr. Donna Shalala (U.S. Secretary of Health and Human Services) ▪ Katie Couric ▪ Matt Lauer ▪ Al Rocher ▪ Bill Cosby

CORPORATE SPONSORS: Lycos ▪ Monster.com ▪ bizE.com ▪ Cisco Systems ▪ UPS Foundation ▪ Cracker Barrel Restaurants ▪ Albertson's ▪ Dell Computer ▪ Fluor Corporation ▪ Microsoft ▪ Northwest Airlines ▪ MCI WorldCom ▪ Chevron ▪ Intel Corporation ▪ Verizon ▪ General Mills ▪ Kimberly-Clark ▪ USX ▪ Bank of America ▪ RadioShack ▪ Anheuser-Busch ▪ Delta Air Lines ▪ Honeywell ▪ Motorola ▪ Phillips Petroleum ▪ JC Penney ▪ Citigroup ▪ United Technologies ▪ Sprint ▪ BellSouth ▪ New York Life Insurance ▪ American Express ▪ J. P. Morgan & Co. ▪ 3M ▪ Oracle

Juvenile Diabetes Foundation

CONTACT:

Juvenile Diabetes Foundation
120 Wall Street
New York, NY 10005

TELEPHONE: (800) JDF-CURE
(212) 785-9500

WEB: *www.jdfcure.org*

BACKGROUND INFO: The Juvenile Diabetes Foundation International is the leading nonprofit, nongovernmental supporter of diabetes research throughout the world.

EVENT: Walk to Cure Diabetes (A year-round event held in 170 locations, this event raises tens of millions of dollars for diabetes research, and it includes the participation of individuals from over 5,000 large corporations.)

VIP STAFF: Robert Wood Johnson IV—Chairman, JDF International ▪ John J. McDonough—Chairman of the Board ▪ Samuel D. Ewing, Jr.—Treasurer ▪ Penn Payne, Esq.—Secretary ▪ Captain James Lovell (Former Astronaut)—Board Member ▪ Newt Gingrich—Board Member ▪ Leeza Gibbons—Honorary Chair

VIPs SUPPORTING THE FOUNDATION: Leeza Gibbons ▪ Larry King ▪ Sugar Ray Leonard (Chair of Walk to Cure Diabetes) ▪ Leigh Stanley ▪ Newt Gingrich ▪ Margaret Thatcher

COPORATE SPONSORS: Bayer Corporation ▪ Coca-Cola ▪ Delta Air Lines ▪ Procter & Gamble ▪ Paine Webber ▪ Walgreens ▪ Toys "R" Us ▪ Andersen Consulting ▪ Ernst & Young ▪ Deloitte & Touche ▪ Shell ▪ American Airlines ▪ Cigna ▪ Dell Computer ▪ Honeywell ▪ Johnson & Johnson ▪ Northwest Airlines ▪ Marshalls ▪ Sprint ▪ Anheuser-Busch ▪ NFL Properties ▪ Texaco ▪ Oracle

Literacy Volunteers of America

CONTACT:

Literacy Volunteers of America
635 James Street
Syracuse, NY 13203-2214

TELEPHONE: (315) 472-0001

WEB: *www.literacyvolunteers.org*

BACKGROUND INFO: LVA's main focus is improving the literacy of Americans. There are many powerful executives and celebrities that are members of the LVA National Advisory Board.

EVENT: National Conference (Held annually; Literacy Volunteers of America teams up with the U.S. Department of Education and the American Library Association.)

VIP STAFF: Marsha L. Tait—President

National Board of Directors: Vikki Jo Stewart—Chair ▪ Shan Atkins—Vice Chair ▪ Donald Chiappetta—Secretary ▪ Thomas V. Fiscoe—Treasurer ▪ Ruth Colvin—Founder, Board of Directors, New York

VIPs SUPPORTING THE ORGANIZATION: Walter Anderson (Editor, *Parade Magazine*)—National Advisory Board Member ▪ Barbara Bush (Former First Lady)—National Advisory Board Honorary Member ▪ Tom Curley (President and Publisher, *USA Today*)—National Advisory Board Member ▪ Jim Davis (Cartoonist, *Gar-*

field)—National Advisory Board Member ▪ Robert Fulghum (Author)—National Advisory Board Member ▪ Tom Harken (Tom Harken Associates)—National Advisory Board Member ▪ Tara Harken (Miss America 1997)—National Advisory Board Member ▪ J. Richard Munro (Chairman, Executive Committee, Time Warner Inc.)—National Advisory Board Member ▪ Arnold Palmer (Professional Golfer)—National Advisory Board Member ▪ Paul Simon (Senator, Ill.)—National Advisory Board Member ▪ Alex Trebek (Host of TV's *Jeopardy*)—National Advisory Board Member ▪ Ted Turner (Chairman of the Board, Turner Broadcasting System)—National Advisory Board Member

CORPORATE SPONSORS: GTE ▪ Philip Morris Companies ▪ Time Warner ▪ Conoco ▪ Fannie Mae Foundation ▪ General Mills ▪ Honeywell

Los Angeles Police Memorial Foundation

CONTACT:
Los Angeles Police Memorial Foundation
Los Angeles Police Department
150 North Los Angeles Street
Los Angeles, CA 90012

TELEPHONE: (213) 485-3281

WEB: *www.lapdonline.org/get_involved/memorial_foundation/memorial_foundation_main.htm*

BACKGROUND INFO: The L.A. Police Memorial Foundation gives money to aid those families who have lost a family member in the line of duty. It raises money through its Police-Celebrity Golf Tournament, which has been held for the past twenty-eight years. There is a very high turnout of celebrities at this fundraising event.

EVENT: The Police-Celebrity Golf Tournament (held in May in California)

VIP STAFF: John McMahon (President, Wilshire Court Productions)—President ▪ Robert S. Gil (Deputy Chief, LAPD)—First Vice President ▪ Bernard C. Parks (Chief, LAPD)—Second Vice President ▪ Alan Atkins (Retired, LAPD)—Executive Director ▪ Peter O'Malley (President, Los Angeles Dodgers)—Board Member ▪ Keith Renken (Deloitte and Touche)—Board Member ▪ Edith R. Perez (President, Los Angeles Board of Police Commissioners)—Board Member ▪ Donald Ohlmeyer (President, NBC West)—Board Member

VIPs SUPPORTING THE ORGANIZATION: Craig T. Nelson ▪ Robert Stack ▪ Jack Lemmon ▪ Pat Boone ▪ Kenny G ▪ James Woods ▪ Billy Bob Thornton ▪ Rick Schroeder ▪ Joe Pesci ▪ Leslie Nielsen ▪ Dennis Quaid ▪ Cheech Marin ▪ Dennis Franz ▪ Jason Alexander ▪ Dennis Hopper ▪ Jack Nicholson ▪ Jane Seymour ▪ Dennis Miller ▪ Richard Dreyfuss ▪ Samuel L. Jackson ▪ Burt Reynolds

Make-A-Wish Foundation

CONTACT:
Make-A-Wish Foundation
4000 North Central Ave, Suite 2200
Phoenix, AZ 85012

TELEPHONE: (800) 722-WISH

WEB: *www.wish.org*

BACKGROUND INFO: The goal of the Make-A-Wish Foundation is to grant wishes to people under the age of eighteen years who are afflicted with life-threatening illnesses. Many corporations sponsor the foundation, and many celebrities are involved in helping to fulfill children's wishes.

VIP STAFF: Paula Van Ness—President/CEO ▪ Tony Leal, Jr.—Chairman of the Board

VIPs SUPPORTING THE FOUNDATION: Emilio and Gloria Estefan ▪ Jeff Gordon ▪ Mike Piazza ▪ Drew Bledsoe ▪ Dale Earnhardt ▪ Colin Powell

CORPORATE SPONSORS: American Airlines ▪ Wal-Mart ▪ Sea World ▪ Delta Air Lines ▪ Allstate Insurance ▪ Zale Corporation ▪ Sammy Sosa Charitable Foundation ▪ Walt Disney Company ▪ Bassett Furniture Industries, Inc. ▪ British Airways ▪ Chief Auto Parts Inc. ▪ Bristol-Myers Squibb ▪ Toys "R" Us/Children's Benefit Fund ▪ Union of Auto Workers—General Motors ▪ Verizon ▪ Discover Financial Services, Inc. ▪ The Walt Disney World Company ▪ United Airlines ▪ Universal Studios, Inc. ▪ Northwest Airlines ▪ 3M Stationery and Office Supplies Division ▪ Saks Incorporated ▪ Lipton ▪ Ty Inc. ▪ Mazda Foundation, Inc. ▪ Honeywell ▪ Chevron

Maranatha Baptist Church

CONTACT:

> Maranatha Baptist Church
> 148 Old GA Hwy. 45
> PO Box 307
> Plains, GA 31780-0307

TELEPHONE: (912) 824-7896

WEB: *http://sowega.net/~alcrump/maranatha/*

EVENT: Former President Carter's Sunday School Class (Selected Sundays at 10 A.M. The church opens its doors at 9 A.M. Space is limited, and the class fills quickly.)

VIPs SUPPORTING THE INSTITUTION: Jimmy Carter ▪ Rosalynn Carter ▪ Millard and Linda Fuller (Founders of Habitat for Humanity)

March of Dimes

CONTACT:

> March of Dimes Birth Defects Foundation
> 1275 Mamaroneck Avenue
> White Plains, NY 10605

TELEPHONE: (888) MODIMES (663-4637)

WEB: *www.modimes.org*

BACKGROUND INFO: The goal of the organization is to improve the health of babies by raising money to aid in the prevention of birth defects and infant mortality. They are the creator of the Birth Defects Prevention Act, which was signed into a law by President Clinton.

EVENTS: Air Awards (Held throughout the year, this awards ceremony recognizes the best radio personalities throughout America. Many radio personalities are in attendance, and all of the proceeds benefit the March of Dimes.) ▪ March of Dimes Golf Tournaments (Celebrities and key community leaders gather for this fund-raiser to save babies.) ▪ Walk America (Occurs all over the country; the nation's largest walk-a-thon. Famous celebrities participate in the walk.)

VIP STAFF: Jennifer L. Howse—March of Dimes President ▪ James E. Oesterreicher (Chairman and CEO, JCPenney Company, Inc.)—Chairman of the Board of Trustees ▪ Susan Molinari (Former Congresswoman, New York)—Board Member ▪ Jean Sherman Chatzky (Editor at Large, *Money Magazine*)—Board Member

• John Woodruff (Independent Investor and Philanthropist)—Board Member ▪ Gary White (President/CEO The Gymboree Corporation)—Board Member ▪ Michael M. Sears (President, The Boeing Company in McDonnell Aircraft and Missile Systems in St. Louis)—Board Member ▪ Calvin Hill (Former Dallas Cowboy)—Board Member ▪ Susan Lucci—Spokesperson ▪ Kathy Ireland—Honorary WalkAmerica 2000 Chair

VIPs SUPPORTING THE ORGANIZATION: Kathy Ireland ▪ Kathy Smith ▪ Susan Lucci

CORPORATE SPONSORS: Kmart ▪ Canon, U.S.A. ▪ Dell Computer ▪ Honeywell ▪ JCPenney ▪ Verizon ▪ Viacom ▪ AMR Corporation ▪ Delta Air Lines ▪ Cigna HealthCare ▪ The Health Network ▪ First Union Corporation ▪ Northwest Airlines ▪ Target ▪ General Mills ▪ American Express ▪ Anheuser-Busch

Meals On Wheels Association of America

CONTACT:
Meals On Wheels Association of America
1414 Prince Street, Suite 202
Alexandria, VA 22314

TELEPHONE: (703) 548-5558

WEB: *www.projectmeal.org*

BACKGROUND INFO: The Meals On Wheels Association of America was created to supply nutritious meals to those individuals who are unable to cook for themselves. It consists of nineteen chapters in Texas, California, Minnesota, Rhode Island, Ohio, New York, Maryland, Florida, Maine, Pennsylvania, Tennessee, and Arkansas.

EVENTS: MOWAA Annual Training Conference & Trade Expo (Held in September) ▪ Contact your local chapter for other events on a local level.

VIP STAFF: Richard Lipner—President, MOW of San Francisco, Inc. ▪ Margot Clark—President Elect, MOW of Northwest Indiana ▪ Jackie Smith—Vice President, MOW of Sheboygan County, Inc., Sheboygan, Wisconsin ▪ Javier Garza—Secretary, MOW and More/UAE, Inc., Austin, Texas ▪ Linda Netterville—Treasurer, Johnson County Nutrition Program, Olathe, Kansas ▪ Enid A. Borden—Executive Director

CORPORATE SUPPORTERS: Cisco Systems ▪ Honeywell ▪ Philip Morris ▪ Verizon ▪ General Mills ▪ 3M ▪ Viacom ▪ Aetna ▪ American Express ▪ AMR Corporation

MADD—Mothers Against Drunk Driving

CONTACT:
MADD
PO Box 541688
Dallas, TX 75354-1688

TELEPHONE: (800) GET-MADD

WEB: *www.madd.org*

BACKGROUND INFO: MADD is a nonprofit, grassroots organization with more than 600 chapters nationwide focused on finding solutions to drunk driving and underage drinking, while supporting families victimized by drunk drivers.

VIP STAFF: Millie Webb—MADD National President ▪ Robert S. Driegert—Treasurer ▪ Patricia Eichhorn—Chairman of the Board ▪ Wendy J. Hamilton—Vice President, Victim Issues ▪ Ralph Hingson, Sc.D.—Vice

President, Public Policy ▪ Karroll Ann Searcy—Vice President, Field Issues ▪ Jan Blaser-Upchurch—Secretary

VIPs SUPPORTING THE INSTITUTION: Nancy Kerrigan ▪ Dennis Green (Coach, Minnesota Vikings)

CORPORATE SPONSORS: Kmart ▪ Autobytel.com ▪ Allstate Insurance ▪ Citibank USA ▪ Daimler Chrysler ▪ Honeywell

Muscular Dystrophy Association

CONTACT:

Muscular Dystrophy Association—USA
National Headquarters
3300 E. Sunrise Dr.
Tucson, AZ 85718

TELEPHONE: (800) 572-1717

WEB ADDRESS: *www.mdausa.org*

BACKGROUND INFO: The MDA is the organization that is responsible for the telecast of the Jerry Lewis MDA Telethon. The MDA is an organization combining the efforts of scientists and citizens to eliminate neuromuscular diseases that plague over one million Americans. Jerry Lewis is the biggest supporter as well as the national chairman.

EVENT: Jerry Lewis MDA Telethon (Held annually, the telethon lasts 21½ hours, with entertainment from many major celebrities.)

VIP STAFF: Robert M. Bennett—President ▪ Robert Ross—Senior Vice President and Executive Director ▪ Victor R. Wright—Treasurer ▪ Timmi Masters—Secretary ▪ Jerry Lewis—National Chairman, Board of Directors ▪ Ed McMahon—National Vice President ▪ Bart Conner—National Vice President ▪ Casey Kasem—National Vice President

VIPs SUPPORTING THE ORGANIZATION: Jerry Lewis ▪ Jerry Springer ▪ James Caan ▪ Rosie O'Donnell ▪ Kathie Lee Gifford ▪ Phil Collins ▪ Aretha Franklin ▪ Tony Bennett ▪ Helen Hunt ▪ Mary Tyler Moore ▪ Regis Philbin ▪ Mel Torme ▪ Kirk and Michael Douglas ▪ Garth Brooks ▪ Tony Danza ▪ Will Smith ▪ Celine Dion ▪ Clint Black ▪ Billy Crystal ▪ Dennis Franz ▪ Drew Carey ▪ David Alan Grier ▪ Michael Jackson ▪ Jack Lemmon ▪ Ronald Reagan ▪ Steve Young ▪ Jason Alexander ▪ Edward James Almos ▪ Robin Williams ▪ Angela Lansbury ▪ Harry Connick, Jr. ▪ Michael J. Fox ▪ Ed Asner ▪ Robert DeNiro ▪ Kareem Abdul Jabbar ▪ B. B. King ▪ Willie Nelson ▪ Martin Scorsese

CORPORATE SPONSORS: Harley-Davidson ▪ Dr Pepper/7UP ▪ American Express ▪ AT&T ▪ AMR Corporation ▪ Service Merchandise ▪ National Child Care Association ▪ Anheuser-Busch, Inc. ▪ United Airlines

National AIDS Fund

CONTACT:

National AIDS Fund
1400 I Street NW, 1220
Washington, DC 20005

TELEPHONE: (888) 234-AIDS
(202) 408-4848

WEB: *www.aidsfund.org*

ORGANIZATIONAL FOCUS: HIV/AIDS

BACKGROUND INFO: The National AIDS Fund allocates money to local and national programs that deal with the HIV/AIDS epidemic. In 1998, grants totaled over nine million dollars. The National AIDS Fund helps sponsor the AmeriCorps program and the Ryan White National Youth Conference on HIV/AIDS.

EVENTS: Virginia Slims Women's Legends of Tennis Tour (Raises funds for HIV/AIDS and honors local leaders against AIDS)

VIP STAFF: Mary Wilson-Byrom—President and CEO ▪ Kandy Ferree—Senior Program Officer

VIPs SUPPORTING THE ORGANIZATION: Elton John ▪ Billie Jean King ▪ Kate Shindle (Miss America 1998)

CORPORATIONS SUPPORTING THE ORGANIZATION: Phillip Morris ▪ Metropolitan Life Foundation ▪ Chevron ▪ AMR Corporation ▪ AT&T ▪ Gap, Inc. ▪ Bank of America ▪ BellAtlantic ▪ The Body Shop ▪ Elton John Foundation ▪ Ford Foundation ▪ Gund Foundation ▪ Levi Strauss Foundation ▪ Merck ▪ Merrill Lynch and Co. ▪ Nations Bank ▪ New York Life ▪ Pfizer ▪ DuPont

Partnership for a Drug-Free America

CONTACT:
Partnership for a Drug-Free America
405 Lexington Avenue
New York, NY 10174

TELEPHONE: (212) 922-1560

WEB: *www.drugfreeamerica.org*

ORGANIZATIONAL FOCUS: Preventing drug use among children

BACKGROUND INFO: The Partnership for a Drug-Free America is formed from professionals in the communications industry who are trying to reduce the demand for illegal drugs in America through media exposure and advertising campaigns. Partnership for a Drug-Free America hopes that by exposing the negative effects of illegal drugs, they will change society's attitudes, which will in turn change behavior.

VIP STAFF: James E. Burke—Chairman ▪ Richard D. Bonnette—President and CEO ▪ Daniel B. Burke (Retired President and CEO, ABC, Inc.)—Board Member ▪ Steven J. Heyer (President and COO, Turner Broadcasting Systems, Inc.)—Board Member

VIPs SUPPORTING THE ORGANIZATION: Mary J. Blige ▪ Dixie Chicks ▪ Lauryn Hill ▪ Everclear ▪ Meredith Brooks ▪ Lorrie Morgan ▪ KISS ▪ Chuck Negron (Former Lead Singer of Three Dog Night) ▪ Venus and Serena Williams

CORPORATIONS SUPPORTING THE ORGANIZATION: Bayer Corporation ▪ Bristol-Myers Squibb Foundation ▪ Chrysler Corporation Fund ▪ Eastman Kodak Company ▪ William Randolph Hearst Foundation ▪ H. J. Heinz Company Foundation ▪ Johnson and Johnson ▪ Metropolitan Life Foundation ▪ The Procter & Gamble Company ▪ SmithKline Beecham Consumer Healthcare ▪ The UPS Foundation ▪ BankAmerica Foundation ▪ BellSouth Corporation ▪ BMG Entertainment ▪ Capitol Records ▪ Chevron Corporation ▪ Exxon Corporation ▪ Ford Motor Company ▪ General Electric Foundation ▪ General Motors Foundation ▪ Kimberly-Clark Foundation ▪ Merck Company Foundation ▪ Merrill Lynch & Co. Foundation ▪ Morgan Stanley Group ▪ Sears Roebuck and Co. ▪ State Farm Companies Foundation ▪ The Xerox Foundation ▪ Chase Manhattan Bank ▪ Citigroup ▪ Hallmark Corporate Foundation ▪ The Pfizer Foundation, Inc. ▪ Caterpillar Foundation ▪ Colgate-Palmolive Company ▪ John Deere Foundation ▪ *Forbes* Magazine ▪ Hershey Foods ▪ Home Box Office ▪ PepsiCo, Inc. ▪ Simon and Schuster

People for the Ethical Treatment of Animals

CONTACT:
People for the Ethical Treatment of Animals
501 Front St.
Norfolk, VA 23510

TELEPHONE: (757) 622-PETA

WEB: *www.peta-online.org*

BACKGROUND INFO: PETA's main goal is to establish and protect the rights of all animals. PETA has caused many large corporations, such as Benetton, Avon, Revlon, Estee Lauder, L'Oreal, and Gillette, to cease testing their products on animals. PETA teams up with celebrities of film, music, and sports to promote the safety of animals.

EVENT: Millenium Gala (Event celebrating the success of PETA is attended by some of the major names in both the music and the movie industries. Do not wear fur to this event.)

VIP STAFF: Ingrid Newkirk—President

VIPs SUPPORTING THE ORGANIZATION: Richard Pryor ▪ Jennie Garth ▪ Rob Reiner ▪ Michael Stipe ▪ Sheryl Lee ▪ Belinda Carlisle ▪ Alec Baldwin ▪ Montel Williams ▪ Jamie Lee Curtis ▪ Alicia Silverstone ▪ Oliver Stone ▪ Paul McCartney ▪ James Cromwell ▪ Kathy Najimy ▪ Indigo Girls ▪ Sarah MacLachlan ▪ Grace Slick ▪ Bill Maher ▪ Martina Navratilova ▪ Martin Scorsese ▪ Stella McCartney ▪ Pamela Anderson Lee ▪ Steven Seagal ▪ Gillian Anderson ▪ Woody Harrelson ▪ Ellen DeGeneres

CORPORATE SPONSORS: Paul Mitchell Professional Salon Products

Project A.L.S.

CONTACT:
Project A.L.S.
511 Avenue of the Americas, PMB#341
New York, NY 10011

TELEPHONE: (212) 969-0329

WEB: *www.projectals.org*

BACKGROUND INFO: Project A.L.S. works to increase awareness about amyotropic lateral sclerosis, commonly known as Lou Gehrig's disease, and to raise money to find a treatment for the disease. At present, there is no known treatment or cure for A.L.S.

EVENT: Project A.L.S. Gala (October, in New York)

VIP STAFF: Jenifer Estess—President

VIPs SUPPORTING THE INSTITUTION: Kristen Johnson ▪ George Clooney ▪ Gina Gershon ▪ Jesse L. Martin ▪ Molly Shannon ▪ Marisa Tomei ▪ William Baldwin ▪ Katie Couric ▪ Richard Kind ▪ Rob Morrow ▪ Jon Stewart ▪ Scott Wolf

CORPORATE SPONSORS: Nordstrom ▪ American Airlines ▪ AOL ▪ The Carsey-Werner Company ▪ Continental Airlines ▪ Entertainment Weekly ▪ Goldman Sachs ▪ Merrill Lynch ▪ The New York Stock Exchange ▪ Paramount Pictures ▪ Saks Fifth Avenue ▪ Vogue ▪ ABC ▪ American Express ▪ Bank of America ▪ Citigroup ▪ David E. Kelley Productions ▪ Fox Filmed Entertainment ▪ InStyle ▪ Morgan Stanley Dean Witter ▪ Paine Webber ▪ Paramount Television ▪ Universal Studios ▪ Disney

Project New Hope

CONTACT:
Project New Hope
3325 Wilshire Blvd., Suite 800
Los Angeles, CA 90010

TELEPHONE: (213) 580-9977

WEB: *www.projectnewhope.org*

BACKGROUND INFO: Project New Hope promotes opportunity, self-sufficiency, and dignity for low-income and homeless people, focused primarily on those living with HIV/AIDS and other disabilities. Through collaboration, Project New Hope develops supportive, affordable housing and provides comprehensive vocational services and opportunities.

EVENT: Rick Weiss Humanitarian Awards

VIP STAFF: Michael-Jon Smith—Board Chair ▪ Scott Figenshow—Executive Director ▪ Earl Greenburg—Honorary Chair

MAJOR SPONSORS: Home Shopping Network ▪ Transactional Marketing Partners ▪ Pacific Bell ▪ American Telecast ▪ Emson ▪ Guthy-Renker ▪ U.S. Trust Company ▪ Bank of America ▪ California Federal Bank ▪ Cmedia ▪ Dick Prochnow ▪ ERA ▪ Jack Kirby ▪ Mercury Media ▪ MSG ▪ *Response* Magazine ▪ Robert Blagman ▪ Steve Breimer ▪ Thane Entertainment

Public Broadcasting Service

CONTACT:
Public Broadcasting Service
1320 Braddock Place
Alexandria, VA 22314

TELEPHONE: (703) 739-5000

WEB: *www.pbs.org*

ORGANIZATIONAL FOCUS: Public programming

BACKGROUND INFO: The Public Broadcasting Service is a nonprofit, private organization whose affiliates include 348 noncommercial stations that serve all fifty states, and also Puerto Rico, the U.S. Virgin Islands, Guam, and American Samoa. The 348 stations are run by 171 noncommercial licensees that include 87 community organizations, 55 colleges and universities, 21 state authorities, and 8 local educational and local authorities.

EVENTS: Antique Road Show stops

VIP STAFF: Ervin S. Duggan—President and CEO ▪ Elizabeth A. Wolfe—Executive Vice President and CAO ▪ John C. Hollar—Executive Vice President ▪ Robert C. Altman—Senior Vice President ▪ Edward P. Caleca—Senior Vice President ▪ M. Peter Downey—Senior Vice President ▪ Carole L. Feld—Senior Vice President ▪ Gregory Farenbach—Senior Vice President and General Counsel ▪ John F. Wilson—Senior Vice President and Chief Programming Executive ▪ Colin G. Campbell (President, Rockefeller Brothers Fund, New York, New York)—Chairman ▪ Sonia Perez (Executive Director of External Affairs of Southwestern Bell)—Board Member ▪ Catharine R. Stimpson (Dean of Graduate School of Arts & Science at NYU)—Board Member

CORPORATIONS SUPPORTING THE ORGANIZATION: AT&T ▪ Metropolitan Life ▪ Norwest ▪ State Farm Insurance Companies ▪ The Saturn Corporation ▪ Fannie Mae ▪ Kellogg Company ▪ New York Life Insurance ▪ Lockheed Martin ▪ Verizon ▪ IBM ▪ Ace Hardware ▪ Archer Daniels Midland ▪ ThompsonMinwax Company ▪ Gateway, Inc.

Ronald McDonald House Charities

CONTACT:
Ronald McDonald House Charities
One Kroc Drive
Oak Brook, IL 60523

TELEPHONE: (630) 623-7048

WEB: *www.rmhc.com*

ORGANIZATIONAL FOCUS: Places to stay for families of seriously ill children

BACKGROUND INFO: The Ronald McDonald House Charities are supported by McDonald's, which is one of the most easily recognizable companies in the world. The McDonald's Corporation funds the general and administrative costs of running the more than 200 Ronald McDonald Houses located in almost twenty countries. More than 3,000 bedrooms are available each night for families to stay in. Ronald McDonald House donates money to other charitable organizations and runs a camp for disabled children, Camp Ronald McDonald.

EVENT: Annual Awards of Excellence gala to recognize winners for their contributions to charity

VIP STAFF: Ken Barun—President and CEO ▪ Jack Greenberg—Chairman and CEO, McDonald's ▪ Joan Kroc—Honorary Chairperson

VIPs SUPPORTING THE ORGANIZATION: Dr. David Satcher—U.S. Surgeon General ▪ Third Eye Blind ▪ Oprah Winfrey ▪ Joan Kroc ▪ Dr. Antonio Novello (Former U.S. Surgeon General) ▪ Jimmy Carter ▪ Betty Ford ▪ General Colin Powell ▪ Barbara Bush ▪ Fred Rogers

CORPORATIONS SUPPORTING THE ORGANIZATION: AT&T ▪ The Coca-Cola Company ▪ Department 56 ▪ Dillard's ▪ USA Today ▪ Georgia Pacific ▪ Nestlé ▪ Southwest Airlines ▪ Ty, Inc. ▪ Cisco ▪ Honeywell ▪ Lucent Technologies ▪ McDonald's ▪ Bristol-Myers Squibb ▪ SBC Communications ▪ Alpha Delta Pi Sorority ▪ Enron ▪ LPGA Tour

Salvation Army

CONTACT:
The Salvation Army
615 Slaters Lane
PO Box 269
Alexandria, VA 22313

TELEPHONE: (703) 684-5500

WEB: *www.salvationarmyusa.org*

BACKGROUND INFO: The Salvation Army is interested in serving those in need of assistance throughout the world. The Salvation Army's busiest time of the year is Christmas. Salvation Army representatives can be found at almost every grocery store and shopping mall across the country.

VIP STAFF: Commissioner John Busby—National Commander ▪ Donald V. Fites—Chairman, National Advisory Board of the Salvation Army

VIPs SUPPORTING THE ORGANIZATION: Bill Clinton ▪ Governor Hunt (North Carolina)

CORPORATE SPONSORS: Albertson's ▪ Cisco Systems ▪ Kmart ▪ Northwest Airlines ▪ Bristol-Myers Squibb ▪ Intel Corporation ▪ Verizon ▪ 3M ▪ Aetna ▪ Anheuser-Busch ▪ UAL ▪ Chase Manhattan ▪ Honeywell ▪ Microsoft ▪ JCPenney ▪ Citigroup ▪ United Technologies ▪ General Mills ▪ USX ▪ American Express ▪ SBC Communications ▪ National Association of Broadcasters

Southern Poverty Law Center

CONTACT:
Southern Poverty Law Center
400 Washington Avenue
Montgomery, AL 36104

TELEPHONE: (334) 241-0726

WEB: *www.splcenter.org*

BACKGROUND INFO: The Southern Poverty Law Center is an organization that focuses on the application of civil rights. It promotes tolerance education and works against white supremacist groups and hate groups. The SPLC is paid through contributions from supporters, as it accepts no money from its clients.

VIP STAFF: Morris Dees—Cofounder ▪ Joe Levin—Cofounder ▪ Julian Bond—President Emeritus

VIPs SUPPORTING THE ORGANIZATION: Maya Lin (Designer of the Civil Rights Memorial) ▪ Rosa Parks (Cochair of the SPLC's National Campaign for Tolerance)

Sovereign Military Order of Malta

CONTACT:
Joe Dempsy
1730 M Street NW, Suite 403
Washington, DC 20036

TELEPHONE: (202) 331-2494

WEB: *www.smom.org*

ORGANIZATIONAL FOCUS: This international Catholic humanitarian organization is primarily focused on "defining the faith and servicing the poor."

BACKGROUND INFO: Formed in 1099, the Knights of Malta were formed during the Crusades to run a hospice and infirmary and to serve the poor. The Knights of Malta maintain diplomatic relations between the Vatican and individual countries and support hospitals and residences for the elderly, such as the Malta House in Washington, D.C., and Malta Park in New Orleans. The Knights of Malta are a permanent, nongovernment observer in the United Nations. Branches of the organization in the United States are the Federal Association, in Washington, D.C., the American Association, in New York, and the Western Association, in San Francisco. There are regional gatherings of the Knights throughout the country. Membership is attained through sponsorship by two current members and through the payment of a "small" passage fee of $3,000. There are on average 650 members in each of the domestic associations.

EVENTS: International Annual Pilgrimage to Lourdes (May) ▪ Other events are held by specific associations. Contact local association.

VIP STAFF: Andrew Bertie—Prince and Grand Master ▪ Ludwig Hoffmann von Rumerstein—Grand Commander ▪ Count Don Carlo Marullo di Condojanni, Prince of Casalnuovo—Grand Chancellor ▪ Albrecht Freiherr von Boeselager—Grand Hospitaller ▪ Joe Dempsey—Executive Director, Federal Association ▪ Jack Shine—Executive Director, American Association ▪ Bob Bond—President, Western Association

CHARITIES SUPPORTED: Christmas in April ▪ Project SHARE ▪ Central America Feed Program ▪ Missions of Charity

Special Olympics

CONTACT:

Special Olympics, Inc.
1325 G Street NW, Suite 500
Washington, DC 20005–3104

TELEPHONE: (202) 628-3630

WEB: *www.specialolympics.org*

ORGANIZATIONAL FOCUS: Athletic training and competition for adults and children with mental retardation

BACKGROUND INFO: Special Olympics was created by the Joseph P. Kennedy, Jr., Foundation for Mental Retardation. More than one million people participate in Special Olympics events each year throughout the United States and in more than 140 other countries. Sports such as basketball, bowling, soccer, golf, softball, tennis, and volleyball are offered as training programs or competitive events.

EVENT: World Games (Every four years)

VIP STAFF: Eunice Kennedy Shriver—Founder and Honorary Chairman ▪ Sargent Shriver—Chairman of the Board ▪ Timothy P. Shriver, Ph.D.—President and CEO, Special Olympics, Inc. ▪ Maria Shriver—Board Member ▪ Arnold Schwarzenegger—Global Torch Bearer and International Weight Training Coach ▪ Antonia C. Novello, M.D., M.P.H (Commissioner of Health, New York State Health Department; Former Surgeon General of the U.S.)—Board Member ▪ Bart Conner (Sports Broadcaster; Olympic Gymnastics Gold Medalist; Member, Gymnastics Hall of Fame)—Board Member ▪ Susan Saint James (Actress)—Board Member ▪ Anne Sweeney (President, Disney/ABC Cable Networks; President, Disney Channel)—Board Member ▪ Keiko Sofia Fujimori Higuchi (First Lady of the Republic of Peru; President, Foundation for the Children of Peru)—Board Member ▪ Calvin Hill (Professional Sports Consultant; Former Vice President of Baltimore Orioles; Former NFL player for the Dallas Cowboys, Washington Redskins, and Cleveland Browns)—Board Member ▪ Walther Troeger (President, Germany National Olympic Committee; Member, International Olympic Committee)—Board Member ▪ Rafer Johnson (Sports Announcer and Consultant; Olympic Decathlon Gold Medalist)—Board Member ▪ Stacey Johnson (Sports Announcer and Consultant; Olympic Decathlon Gold Medalist)—Board Member ▪ LeRoy T. Walker, Ph.D. (Former President, U.S. Olympic Committee; Chancellor Emeritus, North Carolina Central University; President, 1999 Special Olympics World Summer Games)—Board Member ▪ HRH Prince Ra'ad bin Zeid (Lord Chamberlain to His Majesty the King; Chairman, Special Olympics, Jordan)—Board Member

VIPs SUPPORTING THE ORGANIZATION: Melba Moore (Actress/Singer) ▪ Stevie Wonder ▪ Maya Angelou ▪ Billy Crystal ▪ Sugar Ray ▪ Kirk Franklin ▪ Morgan Heritage ▪ Rev. Billy Graham ▪ Grant Hill ▪ Muhammad Ali ▪ Bon Jovi ▪ Kathy Ireland ▪ Kimberley Pressler (Former Miss U.S.A.)

CORPORATIONS SUPPORTING THE ORGANIZATION: America Online ▪ American Express ▪ AMF Bowling, Inc. ▪ The Coca-Cola Compmany ▪ Oracle ▪ Phoenix ▪ First USA ▪ ABB, Inc. ▪ Clark Retail Enterprises, Inc. ▪ Eastman Kodak Company ▪ Flooring America ▪ Knights of Pythias ▪ Midwest Trophy Manufacturing ▪ Otis Elevator Company ▪ Columbia Sportswear ▪ Human-i-Tees ▪ Red Lobster Restaurants ▪ Saturn Corporation ▪ SnowSports Industry America ▪ United Airlines ▪ Dell Computers ▪ Honeywell ▪ Chevron ▪ Intel ▪ SBC Communications ▪ United Technologies ▪ Verizon Communications ▪ AMR Corporation ▪ Caterpillar ▪ UPS ▪ General Mills ▪ Minnesota Mining and Manufacturing

St. Jude Children's Research Hospital

CONTACT:
St. Jude Children's Research Hospital
332 N. Lauderdale Street
Memphis, TN 38105

TELEPHONE: (901) 495-3300

WEB: *www.stjude.org*

BACKGROUND INFO: The St. Jude Children's Research Hospital is dedicated to the treatment of children afflicted with severe diseases. St. Jude has a close relationship with the country music industry.

EVENTS: St. Jude Las Vegas Gala (This event is attended by numerous celebrities.) ▪ St. Jude Golf Tournaments ▪ Up All Night (Fund-raising event held at college campuses throughout the nation; includes performances by artists in the music industry.)

VIP STAFF: Arthur W. Nienhuis, M.D.—Director of St. Jude Children's Research Hospital ▪ Marlo Thomas— National Outreach Director for St. Jude Hospital, Daughter of Founder Danny Thomas

VIPs SUPPORTING THE ORGANIZATION: Clint Black ▪ Garth Brooks ▪ Faith Hill ▪ Rita Rudner ▪ Martina McBride ▪ Lorrie Morgan ▪ Travis Tritt ▪ Phil Donahue ▪ Anthony Quinn ▪ Ray Romano ▪ Tony Orlando

CORPORATE SPONSORS: Target Stores ▪ Northwest Airlines ▪ Oracle

Starlight Children's Foundation

CONTACT:
Starlight Children's Foundation
5900 Wilshire Blvd., Suite 2530
Los Angeles, CA 90036

TELEPHONE: (323) 634-0080

WEB: *www.starlight.org*

BACKGROUND INFO: The Starlight Children's Foundation allows terminally ill children all over the world between the ages of four and eighteen to live out their dreams. Sponsors of the foundation include leaders of the Internet industry and the entertainment industry.

EVENT: Los Angeles Gala (Held annually, this event honors those who have supported the Starlight Children's Foundation over the past years and is attended by numerous celebrities.)

VIP STAFF: Peter Samuelson (President, Samuelson Productions)—Chairman and Cofounder ▪ Warren Kornblum (Chief Marketing Officer, Toys "R" Us)—President ▪ Katherine Culpepper—Executive Director ▪ Kip Crennan (President and CEO, Starlight Candles)—Exec. Vice President ▪ Kenneth Forkos—Chief Financial Officer ▪ Jacqueline Carlish—Secretary ▪ Bruce Hendricks (Exec. VP of Motion Picture Production, Walt Disney Co.)—Director ▪ Clifton E. Rodgers (Vice President, The Real Estate Roundtable)—Director ▪ Roger Shiffman (President, Tiger Electronics, Ltd.)—Director ▪ Joseph Wessely (Executive VP, Business Banking, Fleet Bank, N.A.)—Director ▪ Richard Spencer (President, The Crossroads Group)—Director ▪ Shari Belafonte—International Spokesperson

VIPs SUPPORTING THE ORGANIZATION: Tyra Banks ▪ Michael Jordan ▪ Shari Belafonte ▪ Hillary Clinton ▪ Gordon Elliot ▪ Joey Lawrence (Actor) ▪ Daisy Fuentes ▪ Rosie O'Donnell ▪ Will Smith ▪ Faith Hill ▪ Mike Myers ▪ Gillian Anderson ▪ David Hasselhoff ▪ Tom Hanks ▪ Ed McMahon ▪ Hanson ▪ Lance Burton (Magician) ▪ Drew Barrymore ▪ Jada Pinkett Smith ▪ Cindy Crawford ▪ Kevin Kline ▪ Bette Midler

CORPORATE SPONSORS: Colgate-Palmolive Company ▪ American Airlines ▪ Artisan Entertainment ▪ Compaq Computers ▪ Nestlé ▪ Hasbro ▪ Lycos ▪ Armani Exchange ▪ Toys "R" Us ▪ Nintendo of America ▪ Wal-Mart ▪ Microsoft ▪ Kodak ▪ Yahoo ▪ Kellogg's ▪ Hollywood Entertainment

Susan G. Komen Foundation

CONTACT:

Susan G. Komen Foundation
5005 LBJ Freeway, Suite 370
Dallas, TX 75244

TELEPHONE: (972) 855-1600

WEB: *www.komen.org*

BACKGROUND INFO: The Susan G. Komen Foundation is America's largest private provider for research dedicated solely to breast cancer. Many large corporations donate money to the foundation, and community leaders contribute their time and energy to the events held by the foundation.

EVENT: Komen Race for the Cure (Held annually; largest series of 5K runs held across the nation. City leaders across the nation are involved in the race.)

VIP STAFF: Linda Kay Peterson—Chairman ▪ Nancy Brinker (Has been appointed by Presidents Reagan and Bush and Vice President Quayle to serve on National Cancer Advisory Boards)—Founding Chairman ▪ Norman Brinker (Chairman and CEO, Brinker International)—Board Member

VIPs SUPPORTING THE FOUNDATION: Roger Staubach ▪ Betty Ford ▪ Lance Armstrong ▪ Al and Tipper Gore ▪ Dan and Marilyn Quayle

CORPORATE SPONSORS: Lee ▪ BMW ▪ Gillette ▪ JCPenny ▪ OxyChem ▪ Tropicana ▪ FootJoy ▪ The Carlisle Collection, Ltd. ▪ Charles Schwab & Co. ▪ Chevron ▪ Hoya Crystal ▪ LPGA ▪ Kellogg's ▪ American Airlines ▪ Ford ▪ Harrah's ▪ New Balance ▪ Pier 1 Imports ▪ Titleist ▪ Brinker International ▪ Bristol-Meyers Squibb Oncology ▪ Hallmark ▪ Verizon ▪ Johnson & Johnson ▪ NFL ▪ Samsung ▪ MCI WorldCom ▪ Texas Monthly ▪ Albertson's ▪ Federated Department Stores ▪ Wyndham Hotels and Resorts ▪ Zeta Tau Alpha Fraternity ▪ Roman, Inc. ▪ Yoplait ▪ Cigna ▪ General Motors

Toys for Tots Foundation

CONTACT:

Toys Foundation
PO Box 30883
Greenwood Station
Seattle, WA 98103-0883

TELEPHONE: (206) 762-2229

WEB: *www.toys4tots.org*

BACKGROUND INFO: The Toys for Tots Foundation believes that every child should have a Christmas, and they focus on making Christmas happen for thousands of needy children.

EVENTS: The Toys for Tots Foundation is supported by many Seattle professional, semiprofessional, and minor league sports teams, which aid the foundation through charitable activities both on and off the job.

VIP STAFF: Stan Sober—Officer in Charge ▪ Michael R. Stine—Officer in Charge

VIPs SUPPORTING THE FOUNDATION: Bob Hope ▪ Barbara Bush ▪ Jay Buhner (Seattle Mariner) ▪ Brooke Shields ▪ Johnny Carson

CORPORATE SPONSORS: AirTouch Cellular ▪ AT&T ▪ JCPenney ▪ Federated Department Stores ▪ Northwest Airlines ▪ Chevron ▪ United Technologies

UNICEF

CONTACT:
UNICEF Headquarters
UNICEF House
3 UN Plaza
New York, NY 10017

TELEPHONE: (212) 824-6724

WEB: *www.unicef.org*

ORGANIZATIONAL FOCUS: Advancement of children

BACKGROUND INFO: The goal of UNICEF is to end the poverty of children. UNICEF, which is mandated by the United Nations General Assembly and is the only UN organization dedicated specifically to children, focuses on supplying children all around the world with primary health care, nutrition, basic education, safe water, and sanitation.

VIP STAFF: Carol Bellamy—Executive Director

VIPs SUPPORTING THE ORGANIZATION: Judy Collins ▪ Susan Sarandon ▪ Ted Turner ▪ Harry Belafonte ▪ Roger Moore ▪ Vanessa Redgrave ▪ Nelson Mandela

CORPORATIONS SUPPORTING THE ORGANIZATION: Lockheed Martin ▪ AMR Corporation ▪ Kiwanis International ▪ Merck ▪ Sheraton Hotels and Resorts ▪ Rotary International ▪ British Airlines

United Negro College Fund

CONTACT:
United Negro College Fund
8260 Willow Oaks Corporate Drive
Fairfax, VA 22031

TELEPHONE: (800) 331-2244

WEB: *www.uncf.org*

ORGANIZATIONAL FOCUS: Funding college for African Americans

BACKGROUND INFO: Through their generous assisance, the United Negro College Fund has enabled over 300,000 African Americans to obtain a college education. The UNCF has ties to thirty-nine universities across America and sponsors more than 450 educational programs.

EVENT: Annual Evening of Stars (Early January; this telethon raises money for the UNCF with the participation of numerous athletes, musicians, and other public figures.)

VIP STAFF: William H. Gray III—President and CEO ▪ Michael H. Jordan (Retired Chairman and CEO, CBS Corporation)—Chairman ▪ Virgil E. Ecton—Senior Executive Vice President for Development ▪ Sydney M. Avent—Executive Vice President, General Counsel, and Secretary of the Corporation ▪ Steven L.

Pruitt—Executive Vice President, Operations ▪ Liz H. Lowe—Executive Vice President, Federal Programs ▪ Sydney R. Storr—Vice President and Chief Financial Officer ▪ Dr. Frederick D. Patterson—Founder

VIPs SUPPORTING THE ORGANIZATION: General Colin Powell ▪ Michael Jackson ▪ Whitney Houston ▪ Lauryn Hill ▪ Barry White ▪ The O'Jays ▪ Chaka Khan ▪ Quincy Jones ▪ Barry Bonds ▪ Lou Rawls

CORPORATIONS SUPPORTING THE ORGANIZATION: American Airlines ▪ Chase Manhattan ▪ KFC ▪ Exxon Mobil Corporation ▪ Northwest Airlines ▪ Chevron ▪ Lockheed Martin ▪ AT&T ▪ Daimler-Chrysler ▪ Prudential ▪ Federated Department Stores ▪ Bristol-Myers Squibb ▪ Coors ▪ United Technologies

United Way of America

CONTACT:

United Way of America
701 North Fairfax Street
Alexandria, VA 22314

TELEPHONE: (703) 836-7112

WEB: *www.unitedway.org*

BACKGROUND INFO: The United Way is one of the most widely supported organizations in the world. Its goal is to meet health and human care needs within the community. The United Way of America has formed a partnership and a close relationship with the National Football League and works with Congress, as well as federal, state, and local governments to implement policies and programs.

EVENT: United Way of America's Quality Awards (Reward United Way organizations demonstrating substantial progress in customer satisfaction, productivity, and accountability)

VIP STAFF: Betty Stanley Beene—President and CEO

VIPs SUPPORTING THE ORGANIZATION: Bill Gates ▪ Bruce Smith (Buffalo Bills) ▪ Troy Aikman (Dallas Cowboys) ▪ Ed McCaffrey (Denver Broncos) ▪ Randy Moss (Minnesota Vikings) ▪ Paul Tagliabue (NFL Commissioner) ▪ Dennis Green (Coach, Minnesota Vikings) ▪ Dan Marino (Miami Dolphins) ▪ Nate Newton (Carolina Panthers)

CORPORATE SPONSORS: Bank of America Foundation ▪ National Football League ▪ Albertson's ▪ Dell Computer ▪ Coca-Cola ▪ First Union Corporation ▪ Ford Motor Company ▪ Hershey's ▪ IBM ▪ Kmart ▪ Lucent Technologies ▪ Boeing ▪ Procter & Gamble ▪ The Seagram Company Ltd. ▪ Time Warner ▪ Sprint ▪ Delta Air Lines ▪ Visa ▪ Chase Manhattan ▪ Eastman Kodak ▪ Federated Department Stores ▪ Fluor Corporation ▪ General Electric ▪ Honeywell ▪ J. P. Morgan ▪ Kroger ▪ Microsoft ▪ Pfizer, Inc. ▪ Raytheon ▪ Sun Microsystems ▪ Wal-Mart ▪ JCPenney ▪ Intel Corporation ▪ Chevron ▪ Coors ▪ United Technologies ▪ Ingram Micro ▪ General Mills ▪ New York Life Insurance ▪ Aetna ▪ UPS ▪ AT&T ▪ E. I. du Pont de Nemours ▪ Home Depot ▪ Metropolitan Life Insurance Company ▪ Target ▪ Bristol-Myers Squibb ▪ Citigroup ▪ Lockheed Martin ▪ Verizon ▪ SBC ▪ 3M ▪ USX ▪ American Express ▪ AMR Corporation ▪ Caterpillar ▪ Enron ▪ International Paper ▪ Supervalu Inc.

Volunteers of America

CONTACT:
Volunteers of America
National Office
1660 Duke Street
Alexandria, VA 22314-3421

TELEPHONE: (800) 899-0089
(703) 341-5000

WEB: *www.voa.org*

BACKGROUND INFO: The VOA is one of the largest service organizations in America, helping an estimated 1,500,000 people annually. The Volunteers of America is a Christian service organization focusing on assisting people in need.

EVENTS: Volunteers of America Century of Miracles Gala (Held annually in Washington, D.C., major news personalities have been in attendance.) ▪ Annual Conference (All the leaders of the Volunteers of America are in attendance.)

VIP STAFF: Charles Gould—President ▪ Walter C. Patterson—Chair, National Board of Directors ▪ Rubye E. Noble—Vice Chair, National Board of Directors ▪ Shahab Dadjou—Vice Chair, National Board of Directors ▪ Mark T. Flaten—Treasurer ▪ Ronald S. Kareken—Secretary

VIPs SUPPORTING THE ORGANIZATION: Phyllis Coors ▪ Cokie Roberts

CORPORATE SPONSORS: AARP ▪ Fannie Mae Foundation ▪ Forbes Foundation ▪ GTE Foundation ▪ Microsoft Corporation

World Wildlife Fund

CONTACT:
World Wildlife Fund
1250 Twenty-fourth Street NW
PO Box 97180
Washington, DC 20037

TELEPHONE: (800) CALL-WWF

WEB: *www.worldwildlife.org*

ORGANIZATIONAL FOCUS: Endangered species and habitats

BACKGROUND INFO: The World Wildlife Fund is the largest privately funded conservation group on the globe. WWF works to protect endangered habitats, save endangered species, and address global threats. It has more than one million members in the U.S. alone and works to save wildlife in more than 150 countries.

VIP STAFF: Roger Sant—Chairman ▪ Kathryn S. Fuller—President ▪ James P. Leape—Senior Vice President

VIPs SUPPORTING THE ORGANIZATION: Dixie Chicks ▪ Kathleen Turner ▪ R.E.M.

CORPORATIONS SUPPORTING THE ORGANIZATION: American Express ▪ Bank of America ▪ Chiquita Brands International, Inc. ▪ Chrysler Corporation Fund ▪ Citicorp Foundation ▪ The Coca-Cola Company ▪ E. I. du Pont de Nemours and Company ▪ Eastman Kodak Company ▪ The Home Depot, Inc. ▪ Johnson & Johnson

• Chevron • Mobil • Lucent Technologies, Inc. • Merrill Lynch & Company Foundation, Inc. • Microsoft Corporation • J. P. Morgan Charitable Trust • Motorola, Inc. • New York Times Company Foundation • Philip Morris Companies, Inc. • The Procter & Gamble Fund • Sony Electronics, Inc. • The Walt Disney Company Foundation • Intel • Bristol-Myers Squibb • Xerox • Oracle • Delta Air Lines

YMCA

CONTACT:
YMCA of the USA
101 North Wacker Drive
Chicago, IL 60606

TELEPHONE: (312) 977-0031

WEB: *www.ymca.com*

ORGANIZATIONAL FOCUS: Health and social service in communities

BACKGROUND INFO: The YMCA is the largest not-for-profit community service organization in America, with more than 2,000 Ys serving over 16 million people. Outside the U.S., Ys serve over 30 million people in more than 120 countries. Each individual Y offers varying programs, from swimming lessons to child care. The YMCA has a long and illustrious history, claiming to have invented volleyball, basketball, and student work-study, and to have had a part in the origins of racquetball, the Gideons, Father's Day, professional football, softball, the term *bodybuilding,* Boy Scouts, and Jazzercize. Both Dave Thomas, the founder of Wendy's, and Malcolm X once stayed at YMCAs.

VIP STAFF: David Mercer—CEO • Gary Clarke—COO • Kathleen Spencer—CFO • Bill Bradley (Former U.S. Senator, New Jersey)—Board Member • Lattie Coor (President, Arizona State University)—Board Member • Elizabeth Dole (Former President, American Red Cross)—Board Member • Daniel K. Inouye (U.S. Senator, Hawaii)—Board Member • Jack F. Kemp (Former Secretary, U.S. Department of Housing and Urban Development)—Board Member • Gary Michael (CEO and Chairman of the Board, Albertson's, Inc.)—Board Member • Hon. Eleanor Holmes Norton (District of Columbia Delegate, U.S. House of Representatives)—Board Member • Lewis E. Platt (President, Chairman, and CEO, The Hewlett-Packard Company)—Board Member • George Rupp (President, Columbia University)—Board Member • Louis W. Sullivan M.D. (President, Morehouse University School of Medicine)—Board Member

VIPs SUPPORTING THE ORGANIZATION: Al Gore • Richard W. Riley (U.S. Secretary of Education)

CORPORATIONS SUPPORTING THE ORGANIZATION: Bristol-Myers Squibb • Chevron • Citigroup • SBC Communications • United Technologies • Verizon Communications • Aetna • AMR Corporation • ConAgra • Home Depot • J. P. Morgan • Kimberly-Clark • New York Life Insurance • UPS • USX • JCPenney • PepsiCo, Inc. • Viacom • Sprint • General Mills • 3M • American Express • Anheuser-Busch • Chase Manhattan • Cisco Systems • Kodak • Honeywell • Microsoft • Paine Webber Group • Time Warner • Aetna • Oracle

YWCA

CONTACT:
YWCA of the U.S.A.
Empire State Building
350 Fifth Avenue, Suite 301
New York, NY 10118

TELEPHONE: (212) 273-7800

WEB: *www.ywca.org*

ORGANIZATIONAL FOCUS: To support women and children and end racism

BACKGROUND INFO: More than 300 YWCAs in the U.S. provide shelter for women and children, provide child care, offer violence prevention programs, offer athletic programs, and act as employment training and placement agencies.

EVENT: Race Against Racism (April, in Washington, D.C.)

VIP STAFF: Alexine Clement Jackson—President ▪ Anita Andersson—World President ▪ Musimbi Kanyoro, Ph.D.—World General Secretary

CORPORATIONS SUPPORTING THE ORGANIZATION: U.S. Olympic Committee ▪ The Chase Manhattan Foundation ▪ Bell Atlantic Foundation ▪ GTE Foundation ▪ Nike, Inc. ▪ USA Networks ▪ Merrill Lynch & Co. Foundation, Inc. ▪ Allstate Insurance Company ▪ Exxon Corporation ▪ Citigroup ▪ SBC Communications ▪ United Technologies ▪ AMR Corporation ▪ Kimberly-Clark ▪ PepsiCo ▪ UPS ▪ American Express ▪ Lifetime Television ▪ Viacom ▪ Sprint ▪ General Mills ▪ 3M ▪ Anheuser-Busch ▪ Cisco Systems ▪ Federated Department Stores ▪ Honeywell ▪ Microsoft ▪ Sun Microsystems ▪ Delta Air Lines

CHAPTER SIX

Government

Government Basics

In government, the key to success is definitely who you know. Almost every job awarded in government is given out to somebody's contact. As a result, to be successful in government, networking is particularly crucial. In fact, even once you are working in government, your success will depend on how well you network outside of the office. Government institutions, in fact politics itself, function on one thing: votes. All other activities are related to achieving the goal of aggregating votes. The money that is raised is simply an instrument in the game of getting votes. Politicians need votes to get elected and to retain power, which is always their ultimate objective. As a networker, in order to make yourself valuable, you must show a politician that you can help them hold on to the power they have or even attain more. Since most people don't have enough money to donate anything of significance themselves, they must show their value by demonstrating relationships to institutions that deliver large blocks of votes or affiliations to groups who infuse campaigns with money. Politics is a big-money game, and you must think big. While a donation of $1,000 would seem like a lot of money to most people, it is a drop in the ocean when compared to the amount of money a national office candidate must raise. These days, candidates have to spend nearly $50,000,000 dollars in order to attain a $200,000 job as senator from New York.

As a result, the networker must think on a large scale. The question becomes how you can show that you are an important player. You can do this with an affiliation. For example, the AARP is an organization that delivers twelve to thirty million votes on election day, and the National Rifle Association has members who are very diligent about voting. Politicians pay attention to people affiliated with these large voting blocks. If you are not tied in to a large organization, you can show that you can influence PAC dollars or PAC coalition dollars. PAC is an acronym for Political Action Committee, a legal organization that can contribute up to $5,000 to an individual campaign. This is five times what an individual can contribute. PAC dollars start to become significant in smaller federal elections where $1,000,000 will win a race. The dollar amounts get exponentially bigger when dealing with a PAC coalition. A PAC coalition is a group of PACs that get together and basically swap donation support. For example, a PAC can only contribute $5,000 to any one race, but if it joins a PAC coalition that is comprised of 100 PACs interested in 100 different races, then each PAC can contribute to each other's race. The effective result is that the PAC coalition in this example could donate $500,000 dollars to each race. If you can position yourself as affiliated with a PAC coalition, the candidate and the campaign will see you as an asset. Never forget that to politicians, money is nothing more than a means of getting votes. Votes are the key.

Another thing you can do to create value is volunteer your time. If volunteering your time means votes, you have just made yourself valuable. If you can drive supporters to the polls on Election Day to vote, you are valuable. If you can help hand out yard signs and thus ultimately contribute to vote count, you are valuable.

There are many different types of government institutions. Some of the lesser-known ones are very interesting for the opportunities they offer to networkers.

PRESIDENTIAL LIBRARIES

The presidential libraries host terrific events that are high-end networking opportunities. Recently, the Lyndon B. Johnson Library hosted an event and brought in Presidents Ford and Carter. The events are typically intimate gatherings where you can get in some quality time with major political players. The libraries also hold great lecture series with top politicians as guest speakers. Bret and Elliot have found presidential libraries to be extremely strong networking grounds. They hold many events throughout the year, and many VIPs support these institutions. The Lyndon B. Johnson Library has been the institution that has drawn the most civil rights leaders, like Jesse Jackson. This is a natural since one of the focuses of the Johnson presidency was civil rights. The Ronald Reagan Library attracts speakers and those involved in the end of the Cold War, such as Mikhail Gorbachev.

The biggest event at a presidential library is the opening ceremony. Elliot heard about the opening of the George Bush Presidential Library a few years back. Elliot knew this would be a great event and started rounding up library tickets and passes to special events. When he was finished, he had seven tickets to all of the opening events. He only needed three, but he had asked everyone he had contacts with and ended up with seven. Elliot was then able to pass out his extra tickets to others, ingratiating himself to the lucky four who got his extra tickets.

The networking opportunities were endless. The attendees included every living former president and first lady except President Reagan. They were all accessible at a casual barbecue the evening before the official opening. In addition, major heads of state from George Bush's era attended, as well as Bush's cabinet members.

The weekend started with the arrival ceremony of the president by train from Houston to College Station. This was followed by the casual evening barbecue. When Elliot and his two guests arrived at the barbecue, it was clear they were in a networker's paradise. You couldn't walk fifty feet without bumping into a VIP. Elliot started the evening by having a quick chat with President and Mrs. Ford. This was cut short because England's former prime minister, John Major, walked up to join the conversation. Elliot and the prime minister started visiting about Major's last trip to Washington, D.C., in 1992, which included a stop in to a Tower Records down the street from the White House. This was the first time Elliot had met Prime Minister Major. They continued talking for about fifteen minutes, until Elliot excused himself to go say hello to President and Mrs. Bush. After spending time having a beer with President Bush, the group went over to visit with billionaire philanthropist Walter Annenberg. Being in his late eighties and extremely wealthy, Mr. Annenberg is not the most accessible individual in the country, although, for this occasion, he was pleased to sit down and visit with Elliot.

The evening went on with Elliot visiting with governors, generals, political consultants, and entertainers. Some were old friends, others were friends of friends, and still others were new acquaintances. The evening was a huge success, and the main event wouldn't even start until the following day.

The next day was the official library opening ceremony and lunch. The ceremony was covered by all the major media outlets, which proved to be a good time for Elliot to visit with Matt Lauer. Elliot was also able to meet former Secretary of State James Baker before it was time for the opening lunch. The lunch turned out to be one of the biggest VIP events Elliot had ever attended. Everyone from the previous evening's barbecue attended, as well as celebrities and VIPs who flew in for the day, such Arnold Schwarzenegger and many sitting members of the United States Senate. Elliot ended up in the buffet line with Kevin Costner. Later, he spoke with the ambassador from Australia and two state governors. It is obvious that if political networking is your goal, a presidential library opening is a must. Watch for President Clinton's Library in 2003.

THINK TANKS

Think tanks in Washington are set up to help create policy. The think tanks employ world authorities, influential people, and high-end politicians. Many former cabinet secretaries join think tanks after they leave office. Former Attorney General Edwin Meese is an example of a high-level official who joined a think tank. These are great organizations for networking because of the caliber of people who are a part of them. The networking opportunities span both political parties, as the think tank's focus is on policy. They hold lectures very often, which are great events to meet senators or cabinet secretaries.

CONGRESSIONAL AND SENATORIAL COMMITTEES

These organizations, such as the Republican Senatorial Committee, are responsible for raising money. The door is open for volunteers. They often have receptions for people who contribute large donations, so this is a good place to network if you want to be in a room with people who can afford to donate $100,000 and more to a political organization. As a volunteer or supporter of one of these organizations, you create value for yourself because you help support the political party, which helps support the candidates. They are a great conduit to meet government VIPs.

HISTORICAL SOCIETIES

Historical societies are charged with the function of preserving the history behind major government institutions, such as the Supreme Court and the White House. The major historical societies hold functions that host VIPs associated with their institution. For instance, the Capitol Hill Historical Society hosts events that are heavily attended by senators and congressmen. If you are looking to network with a particular individual in Washington, do some research and see which historical society he might support. By supporting the historical society, you make yourself valuable to the VIP because you are helping to preserve the history of the institution of which they are a member.

LOBBYING ORGANIZATIONS

Lobbying organizations are created to represent a particular agenda to lawmakers. The lobbyists will work diligently to convince lawmakers to pass laws that are favorable to their causes. The National Rifle Association (NRA) is a powerful gun lobby that works to convince lawmakers not to pass gun control laws. The AARP lobbies for the elderly. The NAACP lobbies for minority rights. These are examples of lobbying organizations, and these organizations wield incredible power. They represent very large, special-interest voting blocks, as well as large money donations. The AARP is said to influence as many as one out of every four votes in the United States. They have over 30,000,000 members who are diligent in their voting. Since these institutions are very powerful, an affiliation you have with one of them will help you become valuable, especially to a lawmaker who courts that particular vote.

Government Strategies

The federal government is divided into three branches, and opportunities to network are available in all three. In the Executive Branch, the presidential libraries are great networking institutions. The presidential libraries include: Harry Truman, Lyndon Johnson, George Bush, Ronald Reagan, Gerald Ford, Jimmy Carter, Richard Nixon, Dwight Eisenhower, and John F. Kennedy. Another great networking institution for the Executive Branch is the White House Historical Society.

The legislative branch also offers networking opportunities. A great one is by going down to the underground subway that takes senators and congressmen from their offices to the Capitol. The subway is more like the people mover at Disneyland, and it is open to the public. On days when there are roll call votes, nearly every senator and congressman will exit the subway to ride the elevator upstairs to the Capitol chambers. In an hour you could meet dozens of senators without ever moving from one spot. An additional institution is the Capitol Hill Historical Society.

In the judicial branch, there are three great networking opportunities. The Supreme Court Historical Society is a great resource for Supreme Court justices. Legal trade shows offer opportunities to meet judicial VIPs. The third opportunity comes at law school conferences, where the law school community gets together to meet on issues of the day. Another possibility is through law schools themselves, as they often host Supreme Court justices and federal appellate judges for speeches and receptions.

Networking directly through political parties can be accomplished through the Republican and Democratic National Committees, the Capitol Hill Club, and the other methods described above.

The key in politics is to remember that it is who you know. This concept is paramount to your success. Use the techniques in this book to drop names, ask for what you want quickly, dress the part, and be up on customs and buzzwords. As you begin circulating, networking will get easier and easier as you have more contacts, more names to drop, more conversation topics to pull from, and more ease in your mannerisms.

Government Resources

What follows are the entries for the some of the governmental institutions that have been discussed in this chapter. From presidential libraries to historical societies to lobbying organizations, the entries will provide important networking information.

AARP

CONTACT:
AARP
601 E Street NW
Washington, DC 20049

TELEPHONE: (800) 424-3410

WEB: *www.aarp.org*

ORGANIZATION'S FOCUS: The concerns and needs of people over fifty

BACKGROUND INFO: The AARP is the most powerful lobbying organization in the United States. With thirty million members who are over fifty (generally tending to vote early and often), they can truly sway legislation. They are well funded and highly organized. AARP lobbies on both a federal and state level. In addition to lobbying on behalf of its members, it arranges discounts on airlines, car rentals, hotels, cruise lines, flowers, Internet service, on-line shopping, personal finance, sightseeing and travel tours, and vacation packages. AARP also offers financial and legal services, health and medical services, insurance and travel safety services, and life consultation services to its members. *Modern Maturity* is AARP's magazine, which features articles on over-fifty celebrities like Judith Krantz, Paul Newman, Dr. Laura Schlessinger, and Judge Judy, as well as aging issues.

EVENT: National Convention (Held biennially; past speakers and performers include Maya Angelou, Bill Cosby, Liza Minelli, Harry Belafonte, Dr. Deepak Chopra, Robert F. Kennedy, Jr., and C. Michael Armstrong, Chairman and CEO of AT&T.)

VIP STAFF: Esther Canja—President ▪ James G. Parkel—President Elect ▪ Joseph S. Perkins—Immediate Past President ▪ Jane O'Dell Baumgarten—Board Member ▪ Beatrice S. Braun, M.D.—Board Member ▪ Rutherford Brice—Board Member ▪ C. Keith Campbell—Board Member ▪ Lavada E. DeSalles—Board Member ▪ Douglas C. Holbrook—Board Member ▪ J. Kenneth Huff, Sr.—Board Member ▪ Chris Lambert—Board Member ▪ Charles Leven—Board Member ▪ Charles J. Mendoza—Board Member ▪ Mary Jane O'Gara—Board Member ▪ Erik Olsen—Board Member ▪ Otto H. Schultz—Board Member ▪ Betty J. Severyn—Board Member ▪ Kenneth B. Smith, Sr.—Board Member ▪ Marie Smith—Board Member ▪ Virginia L. Tierney—Board Member ▪ Arnulfo Zamora—Board Member

VIP MEMBER: Al Gore

CHARITIES SUPPORTED: PBS ▪ American Society on Aging ▪ Gerontological Society of America ▪ Duke University ▪ Northwestern University ▪ Volunteers of America

Alfalfa Club

CONTACT:

Richard Pearson
Secretary of the Alfalfa Club
PO Box 75785
Washington, DC 20035-5785

TELEPHONE: (202) 857-7450

ORGANIZATION'S FOCUS: Absolutely nothing (and proud of it)

BACKGROUND INFO: The Alfalfa Club is an elite social club consisting of 220 members. These members get together once a year to have an annual dinner and roast. Everyone is in attendance: the president of the United States, the vice president of the United States, all of the Cabinet secretaries, the entire Supreme Court, VIP members of Congress, key business leaders, and the Joint Chiefs of Staff. The dinner lasts four hours, and they nominate a member for president as a humorous portion of the program. The total guest list to the dinner is 550 people, and they only let in six or seven new members a year. The dinner is one of the premier events in the United States.

EVENTS: Dinner, held late January or early February in Washington, DC.

VIPs AFFILIATED WITH THE ORGANIZATION: Senator John Breaux—President ▪ Carl H. Linder (Chairman of the Board and CEO, American Financial Group) ▪ Robert L. Albritton (Executive Vice President and COO, Albritton Communications Company) ▪ Ronald Reagan ▪ Senator John McCain ▪ Fred Kleisner (CEO, Wyndham International) ▪ Senator Jay Rockefeller ▪ Former President Bill Clinton ▪ Lee H. Hamilton (Director, Woodrow Wilson International Center for Scholars; Commissioner, U.S. Commission on National Security) ▪ Senator Ted Stephens ▪ Joint Chiefs ▪ Jack Welch ▪ Rep. John Dingle ▪ President George W. Bush

American Enterprise Institute

LOCATION:

American Enterprise Institute
1150 Seventeenth Street, NW
Washington, DC 20036

TELEPHONE: (202) 862-5800

WEB: *www.aei.org*

BACKGROUND INFORMATION: The institution is made up of America's foremost economists, legal scholars, political scientists, and foreign policy experts. AEI publishes position papers that intend to influence policy. This is a great place to meet major players in many policy fields.

EVENTS: AEI Annual Dinner (February, at Washington Hilton Hotel) ▪ AEI Bradley Lecture Series (Held monthly)

VIP STAFF: Christopher C. DeMuth—President ▪ David Gerson—Executive Vice President ▪ John R. Bolton—Senior Vice President

VIPs SUPPORTING THE INSTITUTION: Gerald R. Ford (Former President of the United States of America; FBA) ▪ Henry A. Kissinger (FBA) ▪ Ronald Reagan (Former President of the United States of America; FBA) ▪ Antonin Scalia (Supreme Court Associate Justice; FBA) ▪ Irving Kristol (Father of Modern Conservatism; FBA) ▪ Richard B. Cheney (Former Secretary of Defense; FBA) ▪ George F. Will (FBA) ▪ Robert H. Bork (Federal Judge; FBA) ▪ Alan Greenspan (Chairman of the Federal Reserve; FBA) ▪ Jeane J. Kirkpatrick

(Former Ambassador of the United Nations; FBA) ▪ Michael Novak (FBA) ▪ Paul A. Volcker (FBA) ▪ Lynn Chaney (Former Head of the National Endowment for the Arts)

The Francis Boyer Award is the top award given out by the AEI each year.

Brookings Institution

CONTACT:
The Brookings Institution
1775 Massachusetts Avenue NW
Washington, DC 20036

TELEPHONE: (202) 797-6000

WEB: *www.brook.edu/*

BACKGROUND INFO: The Brookings Institution is an independent foundation supported by philanthropic foundations, corporations, and private individuals. It focuses mainly on public policy issues. Many corporate leaders, as well as leaders of foundations and universities, sit on the board of trustees.

EVENTS: Public Policy Conference (Attended by members of the board of trustees as well as members of the Brookings Council, those individuals and corporations in the community who have donated large sums of money to the institution) ▪ Brookings Board of Trustees Dinners (Attended by members of both the board of trustees and the Brookings Council, and featuring political speakers)

VIP STAFF: Michael H. Armacost—President and CEO, The Brookings Institution ▪ James A. Johnson, Chairman, The Brookings Institution; (Chairman, Executive Committee of the Board, Fannie Mae)—Trustee ▪ Elizabeth E. Bailey (Chair and John C. Hower Professor of Public Policy and Management, The Wharton School at the University of Pennsylvania)—Trustee ▪ Zoe Baird (President, The Markle Foundation)—Trustee ▪ Alan R. Batkin (Vice Chairman, Kissinger Associates, Inc.)—Trustee ▪ Alan M. Dachs (President and CEO, The Fremont Group)—Trustee ▪ D. Ronald Daniel (Director, McKinsey & Company, Inc.)—Trustee ▪ Robert A. Day (Chairman and CEO, Trust Company of the West)—Trustee ▪ Lawrence K. Fish (Chairman, Citizens Financial Group, Inc.)—Trustee ▪ Teresa Heinz (Chairman, Heinz Family Philanthropies)—Trustee ▪ Marie L. Knowles (Executive Vice President and CFO, Atlantic Richfield Company)—Trustee ▪ Thomas G. Labrecque (Former Chairman, The Chase Manhattan Corporation)—Trustee ▪ Jessica Tuchman Matthews (President, Carnegie Endowment for International Peace)—Trustee ▪ David O. Maxwell (Retired Chairman and CEO, Fannie Mae)—Trustee ▪ Constance Berry Newman (Under Secretary, The Smithsonian Institution)—Trustee ▪ Judith Rodin (President, University of Pennsylvania)—Trustee ▪ Joan E. Spero (President, Doris Duke Charitable Foundation)—Trustee ▪ Vincent J. Trosino (President, COO, and Vice Chairman of the Board, State Farm Mutual Automobile Insurance Company)—Trustee ▪ Stephen M. Wolf (Chairman, US Airways Group, Inc.)—Trustee ▪ Barton M. Biggs (Chairman, Morgan Stanley Asset Management, Inc.)—Honorary Trustee ▪ Frank T. Cary (Retired Chairman and CEO, IBM Corporation)—Honorary Trustee ▪ A. W. Clausen (Retired Chairman and CEO, Bank of America Corporation)—Honorary Trustee ▪ John L. Clendenin (Chairman Emeritus, BellSouth Corporation)—Honorary Trustee ▪ Robert F. Erbubu (Former Chairman of the Board, The Times Mirror Company)—Honorary Trustee ▪ Robert D. Haas (Chairman and CEO, Levi Strauss & Co.)—Honorary Trustee ▪ Nannerl O. Keohane (President, Duke University)—Honorary Trustee ▪ Robert S. McNamara (Former President, The World Bank)—Honorary Trustee ▪ Mary Patterson McPherson (Vice President, The Andrew W. Mellon Foundation)—Honorary Trustee ▪ Arjay Miller (Dean Emeritus, Graduate School of Business, Stanford University)—Honorary Trustee ▪ Maconda Brown O'Connor, Ph.D. (President, The Brown Foundation, Inc.)—Honorary Trustee ▪ Donald S. Perkins (Former Chairman, Jewel Cos.)—Honorary Trustee ▪ David Rockefeller, Jr. (Chairman, Rockefeller Financial Services, Inc.)—Honorary Trustee ▪ Howard D. Samuel (Senior Fellow, National Policy Association)—Honorary Trustee ▪ Ralph S. Saul (Former Chairman, CIGNA Corporation)—Honorary

Trustee ▪ Morris Tanenbaum (Retired Vice Chairman and CFO, AT&T)—Honorary Trustee ▪ James D. Wolfensohn (President, The World Bank)—Honorary Trustee ▪ Breene M. Kerr (President, Brookside Company)—Honorary Trustee

VIPs SUPPORTING THE INSTITUTION: Robert Rubin (Secretary of the Treasury under President Bill Clinton) ▪ Hillary Rodham Clinton ▪ Thomas Friedman (Foreign Affairs Columnist, *New York Times*)

CORPORATE SUPPORTER: Chase Manhattan

Cato Institute

CONTACT:
The Cato Institute
1000 Massachusetts Avenue NW
Washington, DC 20001-5403

TELEPHONE: (202) 842-0200

WEB: *www.cato.org*

BACKGROUND INFO: The Cato Institute was created twenty-three years ago for the purpose of conducting nonpartisan public policy research. The Cato Institute is supported and run by many of the nation's leading advocates of free markets and limited government.

EVENTS: Annual Benefactor Summit (Includes lectures from senior Cato policy directors, as well as internationally renowned speakers) ▪ Cato Conferences (In addition, Cato holds many conferences and city seminars. Call for specifics.)

VIP STAFF: Edward H. Crane—President ▪ David Boaz—Executive Vice President ▪ William A. Niskanen—Chairman ▪ Peter Ackerman (Managing Director, Rockport Financial Ltd.)—Board Member ▪ K. Tucker Andersen (Managing Partner, Cumberland Associates)—Board Member ▪ Richard J. Dennis (President, Dennis Trading Group)—Board Member ▪ David H. Koch (Executive Vice President, Koch Industries, Inc.)—Board Member ▪ John C. Malone (Chairman, Liberty Media Corporation)—Board Member ▪ Rupert Murdoch (Chairman and CEO, The News Corp. Ltd.)—Board Member ▪ David H. Padden (President, Padden & Company)—Board Member ▪ Howard S. Rich (President, U.S. Term Limits)—Board Member ▪ Frederick W. Smith (Chairman and CEO, FDX Corporation)—Board Member

VIPs SUPPORTING THE INSTITUTION: Alan Greenspan (Chairman, Federal Reserve Board) ▪ Don Nickles (Senator, OK) ▪ Rod Grams (Senator, MN) ▪ Robert L. Bartley (Editor, *The Wall Street Journal*)

Centers for Disease Control and Prevention

CONTACT:
Centers for Disease Control and Prevention
1600 Clifton Road
Atlanta, GA 30333

TELEPHONE: (404) 639-3311

WEB: *www.cdc.gov*

INSTITUTION'S FOCUS: Monitor the health of the United States and provide national health statistics

BACKGROUND INFO: The CDC works with the national government and individual states to promote good health, immunizations, and conduct research. The CDC has six centers: the National Center for Chronic

Disease Prevention and Health Promotion, the National Center for Environmental Health, the National Center for Health Statistics, the National Center for HIV, STD, and TB Prevention, the National Center for Infectious Diseases, and the National Center for Injury Prevention and Control. It also has one institute, the National Institute for Occupational Safety and Health, and four offices: the Epidemiology Program Office, the National Immunization Program, the Office of Global Health, and the Public Health Practice Program Office. Together, these centers, offices, and an institute, which are located across the U.S., make up the Centers for Disease Control and Prevention. The CDC Foundation cooperates with CDC to create programs to address threats to public health.

NETWORKING SPECIFICS: Government contacts could be a great way to network within CDC.

EVENT: Advisory Committee to the Director Meeting (August, in Atlanta)

VIP STAFF: Jeffrey P. Koplan, M.D., M.P.H.—Director, CDC; Administrator, Agency for Toxic Substances and Disease Registry ▪ Claire V. Broome, M.D.—Senior Advisor to the Director, Integrated Health Information Systems ▪ Stephen M. Ostroff, M.D.—Acting Deputy Director, Science and Public Health ▪ Martha F. Katz—Deputy Director, Policy and Legislation ▪ Virginia Shankle Bales—Deputy Director, Program Management

Center for the Study of Popular Culture

CONTACT:
Center for the Study of Popular Culture
9911 W. Pico Blvd., Suite 1290
Los Angeles, CA 90035

TELEPHONE: (310) 843-3699

The Wednesday Morning Club
PO Box 67398
Los Angeles, CA 90067

TELEPHONE: (310) 843-3692

WEB: *www.cspc.org*

BACKGROUND INFORMATION: The Center for the Study of Popular Culture is one of the leading Republican organizations in the U.S. The CSPC focuses mainly on the roles that individual rights, education, and media play in the U.S.

EVENTS: Wednesday Morning Club (Held at the Beverly Hills Hotel, the goal of this club is to introduce entertainment leaders to political leaders so that each may understand the components of each respective industry.) ▪ Annual Image of Ourselves Conference (Held in March, the movers and shakers of the entertainment and computer industry meet with individuals of Congress to discuss the effect of legislation on their respective industries.) ▪ Restoration Weekend (Held annually, the Restoration Weekend is to the Republicans as the Renaissance Weekend is to the Democrats. A large number of Republican politicians, columnists, and satirists attend.)

VIP STAFF: Peter Collier—Founder and Operator ▪ David Horowitz—Founder and Operator; Executive Director, Wednesday Morning Club ▪ Lionel Chetwynd—Chairman, Wednesday Morning Club

VIPs SUPPORTING THE INSTITUTION: Jack Kemp (Vice Presidential Nominee) ▪ Anne Volokh (President and Executive Publisher, *Movieline* Magazine) ▪ Henry Hyde (Chairman, House Judiciary Committee) ▪ Fred Thompson (Senator, R-TN) ▪ Dore Gold (Israeli Ambassador to the United Nations) ▪ Newt Gingrich (Former Speaker of the House) ▪ Arlen Specter (Senator, R-PA) ▪ Bill Schneider (Political Consultant) ▪ Rick Sartorum (Senator, R-PA) ▪ Byron Dorgan (Senator, D-ND) ▪ J. C. Watts (Representative, R-OK) ▪ John Kasich

(Representative, R-OH) ▪ Billy Tauzin (Representative, R-LA) ▪ David Dreier (Representative, R-CA) ▪ Ed Royce (Representative, R-CA) ▪ Dana Rohrabacher (Representative, R-CA) ▪ Jim Rogan (Representative, R-CA) ▪ Frank Riggs (Representative, R-CA) ▪ Tom DeLay (Representative, R-TX) ▪ Sky Dayton (Founder and Chairman, Earthlink Network, Inc.) ▪ Chris Cox (Representative, R-CA) ▪ Sam Nunn (Former Senator, D-GA) ▪ Jeffrey I. Cole (Director, UCLA's Center for Communication Policy) ▪ Dan Coats (Senator, R-IN) ▪ Dick Cheney (Former Secretary of Defense) ▪ Les Moonves (President, CBS Entertainment Division) ▪ Paul Maslin (Political Consultant) ▪ Frank Luntz (Political Consultant) ▪ Bill Carrick (Political Consultant) ▪ Sam Brownback (Senator, R-KS) ▪ Joe Leiberman (Senator, D-CT) ▪ Christine La Monte (Executive Vice President, Motion Picture Group, Rogers and Cowan) ▪ Fred Barnes (Editor, *The Weekly Standard*) ▪ Bill Kristol (Political Consultant and Editor, *The Weekly Standard*) ▪ Spencer Abraham (Senator, R-MI) ▪ Ken Khachigian (Political Consultant) ▪ John McCain (Senator, R-AZ) ▪ George Pataki (Governor of New York) ▪ Ward Connerly (Equality Activist) ▪ John Irving (Author, *The Cider House Rules*) ▪ Bill O'Reilly (Newscaster) ▪ George F. Will (Columnist) ▪ Ben Nighthorse Campbell (Senator, R-CO) ▪ Bill Frist (Senator, R-TN) ▪ George W. Bush (Governor of Texas) ▪ Jim Greenwood (Congressman, R-PA) ▪ Orrin Hatch (Senator, R-UT) ▪ G. Gordon Liddy ▪ Rudolph Giuliani (Mayor of New York City)

Congressional Medal of Honor Society

CONTACT:
National Headquarters and Museum
40 Patriots Point Road,
Mt. Pleasant, SC 29464

TELEPHONE: (843) 884-8862

WEB: *www.cmohs.com*

BACKGROUND INFO: The Medal of Honor is the highest honor awarded to an individual member of the United States Armed Services. It is given for bravery in combat against an enemy and is presented by the president in the name of Congress. More than 3,400 Medals of Honor have been given since the award's inception in 1861.

VIP STAFF: Barney Barnum—President (Medal Recipient) ▪ Nick D. Bacon—Vice President (Medal Recipient) ▪ Michael Lindquist—Executive Director ▪ Admiral James Stockdale—Medal Recipient

Democratic Congressional Campaign Committee

CONTACT:
Democratic Congressional Campaign Committee
430 South Capitol Street SE
Washington, DC 20003

TELEPHONE: (202) 863-1500

WEB: *www.dccc.org*

BACKGROUND INFO: The Democratic Congressional Campaign Committee helps to recruit, train, and support Democratic congressional candidates. The goal of the DCCC is to help the Democratic party gain a majority in the U.S. House of Representatives.

EVENTS: Annual Congressional Dinner (Held in March, this is the DCCC's largest fund-raising event. Expect some of the DCCC's most generous donors to be in attendance.)

VIP STAFF: Patrick J. Kennedy (U.S. Representative, RI)—Chairman ▪ Ellen Tauscher (U.S. Representative, CA)—Cochair ▪ Charles Rangel (U.S. Representative, NY)—Cochair ▪ Frank Pallone (U.S. Representative, NJ)—Cochair ▪ Richard A. Gephardt (U.S. Representative, MO)—House Democratic Leader

Democratic National Committee

CONTACT:
Democratic National Committee
430 S. Capitol St. SE
Washington, DC 20003

TELEPHONE: (202) 863-8000

WEB: *www.democrats.org/index.html*

BACKGROUND INFO: The Democratic National Committee focuses on promoting the beliefs and views of the Democratic party by supporting Democrats that are running for public office. It aids those Democrats running at the national, state, and local level. The Democratic National Committee has a membership of 450 individuals.

EVENTS: Democratic National Convention (Held in August) ▪ Democratic National Committee Full Committee Meeting (Held in August) ▪ These meetings are both attended by a large number of Democrats holding public office.

VIP STAFF: Joe Andrew—National Chair Terry McAuliffe ▪ Dennis W. Archer—General Cochair ▪ Loretta Sanchez—General Cochair ▪ Linda Chavez-Thompson—Vice Chair ▪ Bill Lynch—Vice Chair ▪ Joan M. Menard—Vice Chair ▪ Gloria Molina—Vice Chair ▪ Lottie Shackelford—Vice Chair ▪ Andrew Tobias—Treasurer ▪ Kathleen M. Vick—Secretary ▪ Mazie Hirono—Deputy Chair ▪ Joe Cari—Finance Chair ▪ Joel Hyatt—Finance Chair ▪ Carol Pensky—Finance Chair

Democratic Senatorial Campaign Committee

CONTACT:
Democratic Senatorial Campaign Committee
430 South Capitol Street SE
Washington, DC 20003

TELEPHONE: (202) 224-2447

WEB: *www.dscc.org*

ORGANIZATIONAL FOCUS: To help the Democratic party gain a majority in the U.S. Senate

BACKGROUND INFO: The Democratic Congressional Campaign Committee helps to recruit, train, and support Democratic congressional candidates.

EVENTS: Call for specific events.

VIP STAFF: Patty Murray—Chairman ▪ Bill Nelson (U.S. Senator, FL)—Vice Chairman

Dwight D. Eisenhower Library & Museum

CONTACT:

The Dwight D. Eisenhower Library & Museum
200 Southeast Fourth Street
Abilene, KS 67410

TELEPHONE: (785) 263-4751

WEB: *www.eisenhower.utexas.edu*

BACKGROUND INFO: The Dwight D. Eisenhower Library & Museum focuses mainly on World War II and the role that Eisenhower played in the postwar politics of America. Many of the events are ones dealing with military recognition.

EVENTS: Herbert Brownall Memorial Lecture ▪ Former Chiefs of Staff Wreath Laying Ceremony ▪ Presidential Wreath Laying Ceremony ▪ Paul H. Royer Film Series

VIP STAFF: Dr. Dan Holt—Executive Director

George Bush Presidential Library

CONTACT:

The George Bush Presidential Library and Museum
1000 George Bush Drive West
College Station, TX 77845

TELEPHONE: (409) 260-9552

WEB: *bushlibrary.tamu.edu*

BACKGROUND INFO: This presidential library is dedicated to providing information about the politics surrounding Bush's rise through the ranks of America's political system. The site is located near the Bush residence, and George Bush and his wife Barbara Bush, as well as their son George Bush, Jr., are involved in the activities of the library.

EVENTS: Vary from year to year; usually include Christmas festivities and art exhibits

VIP STAFF: Dave Alsobrook—Executive Director

VIPs SUPPORTING THE LIBRARY: George Bush ▪ Barbara Bush ▪ George W. Bush ▪ John Major (Former Prime Minister, England) ▪ Kevin Costner ▪ James Baker ▪ Walter Annenberg ▪ Arnold Schwarzenegger ▪ Dan Quayle ▪ Michael Milken

Gerald R. Ford Library

CONTACT:

Gerald R. Ford Library
1000 Beal Avenue
Ann Arbor, MI 48109

TELEPHONE: (734) 741-2218

Gerald R. Ford Foundation
303 Pearl St. NW
Grand Rapids, MI 49504

TELEPHONE: (616) 451-9263

WEB: *www.ford.utexas.edu/*

BACKGROUND INFO: The Gerald R. Ford Library is dedicated to promoting an interest in the history of domestic policy and foreign affairs during the era of the Cold War with a special focus on Ford's presidency.

EVENTS: Gerald R. Ford Colloquium ▪ William E. Simon Public Affairs Lectures (Past guests include Henry Kissinger and Alan Greenspan.)

VIP STAFF: Richard Norton Smith—Director ▪ Martin J. Allen—Chairman, Gerald R. Ford Foundation

VIP SUPPORTERS: Gerald R. Ford ▪ Betty Ford

Gridiron Club

Contact the Capital Hilton for information.

ORGANIZATION'S FOCUS: Journalism

BACKGROUND INFO: The Gridiron Club is made up of 135 active and retired journalists and some special limited members who take part in the skits performed at the organization's annual Gridiron Club Dinner. The club invites around 600 celebrities, politicians, journalists, lobbyists, and judges to a white-tie dinner featuring skits mocking current events. Democrats and Republicans are roasted equally, although it is a tradition of the club that the president never be represented by a cast member onstage, in keeping with the organization's motto, "We may singe, but we never burn."

EVENT: Gridiron Club Dinner (March, at the Capitol Hilton in Washington, D.C.)

VIPs AFFILIATED WITH THE ORGANIZATION: William Raspberry (*Washington Post*)—President ▪ Robert Novak (Columnist)—Past President

VIPs ATTENDING: Bill Clinton ▪ Al Gore ▪ Sen. John Kerry ▪ Ken Burns ▪ Sen. Daniel Patrick Moynihan ▪ Tim Russert (NBC Journalist) ▪ Jim Lehrer ▪ Janet Reno ▪ Sen. John Glenn ▪ Madeleine Albright ▪ Pete Wilson (Governor of California) ▪ Mike McCurry (White House Press Secretary) ▪ Vernon Jordan ▪ Frank McCourt ▪ Donna Shalala (Health and Human Services Secretary) ▪ Rep. Bill Paxon ▪ James Gilmore (Governor of Virginia) ▪ Rahm Emanuel (Clinton Aide) ▪ Lamar Alexander ▪ Pat Robertson ▪ Jim and Sarah Brady ▪ Alan Greenspan ▪ Jimmy Hoffa, Jr. ▪ Steve Forbes ▪ Newt Gingrich ▪ Sam Donaldson ▪ Hillary Rodham Clinton ▪ Mike Wallace ▪ Ann Landers ▪ Abigail Van Buren ▪ Charlene Barshefsky ▪ Alexis Herman ▪ Aida Alvarez ▪ Sen. John McCain

Harry Truman Presidential Library

CONTACT:
Truman Library
500 W. U.S. Hwy. 24
Independence, MO 64050

TELEPHONE: (816) 833-1400

WEB: *www.trumanlibrary.org/*

BACKGROUND INFO: The role of the Harry Truman Presidential Library is to celebrate Truman's presidency and to communicate the role of the presidency in a nation recovering from World War II.

EVENTS: Good Neighbor Award Presentations ▪ Bess Truman Day Lecture Series ▪ The Truman Music Series

The Heritage Foundation

CONTACT:

The Heritage Foundation
214 Massachusetts Ave. NE
Washington, DC 20002-4999

TELEPHONE: (202) 546-4400

WEB: *www.heritage.org/*

BACKGROUND INFO: The foundation focuses on conservative public policy such as limited government, free enterprise, and a strong national defense. The foundation shares the information it finds primarily with members of Congress, key congressional staff members, policymakers in the executive branch, the nation's news media, and the academic and policy communities. As one of the nation's largest public policy research organizations with over 200,000 contributors, it is the most broadly supported research organization in America.

EVENTS: Annual Heritage Foundation Resource Bank Meeting ▪ Semi-Annual President's Club Meetings (Washington, D.C. Some of the most well-known politicians speak at these meetings.) ▪ Mandate for Leadership (A series of publications and conferences designed to guide the next presidential administration in successfully running America. Political insiders attend.) ▪ Leadership for America Lectures (Influential politicians speak at this lecture series.)

VIP STAFF:

Board of Trustees: David R. Brown, M.D.—Chairman ▪ Richard M. Scaife (Publisher and Owner, Tribune-Review Publishing Co., Inc.)—Vice Chairman ▪ J. Frederic Rench—Secretary ▪ Douglas F. Allison (Chairman and Chief Executive Officer, Allison-Fisher, Inc., Southfield, Michigan) ▪ Holland H. "Holly" Coors (Related to the Coors Brewing Company) ▪ Frank Shakespeare (Former President, RKO General Inc.; Director, U.S. Information Agency; President, CBS Television Services) ▪ Jay Van Andel (Cofounder and Senior Chairman, Amway Corp.) ▪ Barb Van Andel-Gaby (Vice President, Corporate Affairs, Amway Corp.)

Staff: Dr. Edwin J. Feulner—President ▪ Phillip Truluck—Executive Vice President ▪ Herbert Berkowitz—Vice President, Communications, and Director, Center for Media and Public Policy ▪ Dr. Stuart Butler—Vice President, Domestic and Economic Policy Studies ▪ Becky Norton Dunlop—Vice President, External Relations ▪ Michael Franc—Vice President, Government Relations ▪ Lewis Gayner—Vice President, Finance and Operations ▪ Dr. Kim R. Holmes—Vice President and Director, The Kathryn and Shelby Cullom Davis Institute for International Studies ▪ Dr. Bernard P. Lomas—Counselor to the President ▪ Adam Meyerson—Vice President, Educational Affairs ▪ Hugh G. Newton—Senior Counsel, Public Relations ▪ Robert E. Russell, Jr.—Counselor to the President ▪ John Von Kannon—Vice President and Treasurer

VIPs SUPPORTING THE ORGANIZATION: Ronald Reagan ▪ Nobel Laureate Milton Friedman ▪ Newt Gingrich ▪ Steve Forbes ▪ Dick Armey ▪ Phil Gramm ▪ Margaret Thatcher ▪ Trent Lott ▪ Hon. Edwin Meese III (Former Attorney General of the United States, Former Counselor to President Ronald Reagan) ▪ Hon. Leon Panetta (Former Member of Congress, Former Chief of Staff to President Bill Clinton) ▪ Kelly D. Johnston (Former Secretary of the United States Senate) ▪ Zbigniew Brzezinski (Former National Security Advisor to President Jimmy Carter) ▪ Caspar Weinberger (Former Secretary of Defense to President Ronald Reagan) ▪ George Will ▪ Clarence Thomas ▪ Steve Forbes ▪ Jeane Kirkpatrick ▪ William J. Bennett ▪ James Q. Wilson

Jimmy Carter Library

CONTACT:
Jimmy Carter Library
441 Freedom Parkway
Atlanta, GA 30307-1498

TELEPHONE: (404) 331-3942

WEB: *carterlibrary.galileo.peachnet.edu/*

BACKGROUND INFO: The Jimmy Carter Library was created to allow the public to gain a closer, more detailed look at the roles and duties of the modern president through the presidency of Jimmy Carter.

VIP STAFF: Dr. Jay E. Hakes

VIPs SUPPORTING THE INSTITUTION: Jimmy and Rosalynn Carter

John F. Kennedy Presidential Library

CONTACT:
John F. Kennedy Presidential Library
Columbia Point
Boston, MA 02125

TELEPHONE: (617) 929-4500

John Fitzgerald Kennedy Library Foundation
Columbia Point
Boston, MA 02125

TELEPHONE: (617) 929-1200

WEB: *www.cs.umb.edu/jfklibrary/*

BACKGROUND INFO: The John F. Kennedy Presidential Library is dedicated to preserving the memory of JFK, as well as his goals for and views on America.

EVENTS: Distinguished Foreign Visitors Series (The library foundation invites leaders of foreign countries to come and visit the John F. Kennedy Presidential Library. Past visitors include Mikhail Gorbachev, former President, Soviet Union; Nelson Mandela, Deputy Director of African National Congress; Corazon Aquino, former President, Philippines; Benazir Butto, former Prime Minister, Pakistan; Mary Robinson, President, Republic of Ireland; Arpad Goncz, President, Hungary; Albert Reynolds, Prime Minister, Ireland; Vaclav Havel, President, Czech Republic; Rafael Caldera, President, Venezuela; Ion Iliescue, President, Romania. ▪ Distinguished American Series (Conversations with influential members of society such as George Bush)

VIP STAFF: Paul Kirk—Chairman of the Board ▪ Charles W. Daly—Executive Director ▪ Brad Gerratt—Director, Library

VIPs SUPPORTING THE INSTITUTION: Sen. Ted Kennedy ▪ Caroline Kennedy

Lyndon B. Johnson Library

CONTACT:
LBJ Library
2313 Red River Street
Austin, TX 78705

TELEPHONE: (512) 916-5136;
 (512) 478-7829, Ext. 296 (Event Information)

BACKGROUND INFO: The library celebrates the presidency of Lyndon Baines Johnson. One of LBJ's main concerns while he was in office was civil rights. This is an excellent resource for meeting civil rights leaders.

EVENTS: Lectureship Series (Presented by the Friends of the LBJ Library)

VIP STAFF: Harry Middleton—Executive Director

VIPs SUPPORTING THE ORGANIZATION: Lady Bird Johnson ▪ Liz Carpenter ▪ Jesse Jackson

National Aeronautics and Space Association

CONTACT:
NASA Headquarters
300 E Street SW
Washington, DC 20546

TELEPHONE: (202) 358-0000

WEB: *www.nasa.gov*

ORGANIZATIONAL FOCUS: Exploring space and developing technology to travel and do research in space

BACKGROUND INFO: NASA is the administrative body behind the U.S. Space Program. NASA hopes to expand the frontier into space and to use this knowledge of space to benefit the earth. It works closely with the White House and the vice president to develop space technology and plan missions. Other government agencies NASA works with include the Department of Commerce, the Department of Defense, the Department of the Interior, the Department of Transportation, and the National Science Foundation. NASA has fifteen space centers throughout the U.S.

EVENTS: Shuttle launches from Kennedy Space Center in Florida

VIP STAFF: Daniel S. Goldin—Administrator ▪ Arnold G. Holtz—CFO ▪ W. Brian Keegan—Chief Engineer ▪ Lee B. Holcomb—CIO ▪ Dr. Kathie L. Olson—Chief Scientist ▪ Vicki A. Novak—Associate Administrator, Office of Human Resources and Education

National Association for the Advancement of Colored People

CONTACT:
NAACP
4805 Mt. Hope Drive
Baltimore, MD 21215

TELEPHONE: (410) 521-4939

WEB: *www.naacp.com*

ORGANIZATIONAL FOCUS: Equality

BACKGROUND INFO: The NAACP is the largest organization in the nation that focuses on the promotion of civil rights.

EVENTS: Annual Convention (Early July)

VIP STAFF: Kweisi Mfume—President, CEO, and Spokesperson ▪ Julian Bond—Chairman ▪ Bishop William H. Graves—Vice Chairman ▪ Carolyn Q. Coleman—Assistant Secretary ▪ Francisco L. Borges—Treasurer ▪ Jesse H. Turner, Jr.—Assistant Treasurer ▪ Hon. Fred L. Banks, Jr.—Board Member ▪ Roslyn L. McCallister-Brock—Board Member ▪ Sally G. Carroll—Board Member ▪ James E. Ghee, Esq.—Board Member ▪ Nancy L. Lane—Board Member ▪ William Lucy—Board Member ▪ Reverend Raymond Scott—Board Member ▪ Maxine Smith—Board Member ▪ LaRoddric C. Theodule—Board Member ▪ Menola N. Upshaw—Board Member ▪ Charles Whitehead—Board Member ▪ Roy L. Williams—Board Member ▪ Henry Aaron—Trustee

CORPORATIONS SUPPORTING THE ORGANIZATION: NBC ▪ FOX ▪ Freddie Mac ▪ Verizon ▪ Anheuser-Busch ▪ CBS ▪ Allstate Insurance ▪ Federated Department Stores ▪ General Mills

National Republican Congressional Committee

CONTACT:
National Republican Congressional Committee
320 First Street SE
Washington, DC 20003

TELEPHONE: (202) 479-7000

WEB: *www.nrcc.org*

ORGANIZATIONAL FOCUS: To help the Republican party maintain a majority in the U.S. House of Representatives

BACKGROUND INFO: The NRCC supports congressional candidates through financial contributions, voter awareness programs, and technical and research assistance.

EVENT: Annual Congressional Dinner (Held in March)

VIP STAFF: Tom Davis (U.S. Representative, VI)—Chairman, Ex Officio Member ▪ Henry Bonilla (U.S. Representative, TX)—Vice Chairman, Communications ▪ John Doolittle (U.S. Representative, CA)—Vice Chairman, Coalitions/Outreach ▪ Bob Ehrlich (U.S. Representative, MD)—Vice Chairman, Finance ▪ Jim McCrery (U.S. Representative, LA)—Vice Chairman, Incumbent Retention ▪ John Shadegg (U.S. Representative, AZ)—Vice Chairman, Member Training ▪ Dennis Hastert (Speaker of the House)—Ex Officio Member ▪ Dick Armey (House Majority Leader)—Ex Officio Member ▪ Tom DeLay (House Majority Whip)—Ex Officio Member ▪ J. C. Watts (Chairman, House Republican Conference)—Ex Officio Member ▪ Chris Cox (Chairman, House Republican Policy Committee)—Ex Officio Member ▪ Tillie Fowler (Conference Vice Chair)—Ex Officio Member ▪ Deborah Pryce (Conference Secretary)—Ex Officio Member

National Republican Senatorial Committee

CONTACT:
NRSC
Ronald Reagan Republican Center
425 Second Street NE
Washington, DC 20002

TELEPHONE: (202) 478-4447

WEB: *www.nrsc.org*

ORGANIZATIONAL FOCUS: To help the Republican party maintain a majority in the U.S. Senate

BACKGROUND INFO: The National Republican Senatorial Committee supports Republican candidates in their senatorial campaigns. The Inner Circle, a subset of NRSC, is an active group in the Republican party that is composed of past and present Republican senators, as well as civic leaders, business executives, and celebrities who have been nominated for membership. The Republican Presidential Roundtable is a forum of 400 prominent business and community leaders.

EVENTS: Spring National Briefing (Held for Inner Circle members in Washington, D.C., in March) ▪ Special events: Please contact Senatorial Committee for dates and times.

VIP STAFF: Bill Frist (U.S. Senator, TN)—Chairman ▪ Sam Brownback (U.S. Senator, KS)—Chairman, Inner Circle

National Rifle Association

CONTACT:
NRA Headquarters
11250 Waples Mill Road
Fairfax, VA 22030

TELEPHONE: (703) 267-1000

WEB: *www.nrahq.org*

ORGANIZATIONAL FOCUS: Firearms education

BACKGROUND INFO: The NRA is the leading firearms education organization in the world with a membership totaling nearly 3,000,000 individuals. When it comes to training civilians, the NRA is the leader of firearms education. There are over 50,000 NRA Certified Trainers that educate upwards of 750,000 gun owners a year.

EVENTS: Annual Meeting and Exhibits (May)

VIP STAFF: Charlton Heston—President ▪ Wayne R. LaPierre—Executive Vice President ▪ Brenda Potterfield—Vice President ▪ John R. Woods—President Emeritus ▪ Wilson H. Phillips, Jr.—Treasurer ▪ Steven C. Anderson—Executive Director ▪ Robert E. Hodgdon—Trustee ▪ Marion P. Hammer—Trustee ▪ Bill Miller—Trustee ▪ Robert A. Nosler—Trustee ▪ William K. Brewster—Trustee ▪ James W. Porter II—Trustee ▪ Sandy S. Elkin—Secretary

CORPORATIONS SUPPORTING THE NRA: Alliant Techsystems ▪ Beretta USA Corporation ▪ Butterfield & Butterfield ▪ Goodyear Rubber & Supply ▪ Olin Corporation—Winchester Group ▪ Raytheon Aircraft Company

SPONSORING ACTIVITY: Blue Ridge Racing Team and NASCAR Busch race car driver Philip Morris

Republican National Committee

CONTACT:
Republican National Committee
310 First Street SE
Washington, DC 20003

TELEPHONE: (202) 863-8500

WEB: *www.rnc.org*

BACKGROUND INFO: The goal of the Republican National Committee is to promote and achieve the missions and goals of the Republican party.

EVENTS: Republican National Convention (Held in late July and early August) ▪ Winter and Summer Meetings ▪ Not only are these events attended by numerous Republicans in office, but they are also attended by some of the GOP's most generous donors.

VIP STAFF: Jim Nicholson—Chairman ▪ Pat Harrison—Cochair ▪ Alec Poitevint—Treasurer ▪ Linda Shaw—Secretary ▪ Michael Grebe—General Counsel ▪ Mel Sembler—Finance Chairman ▪ Ron Carlson—Chairman, Budget Committee ▪ Mike McDaniel—Chairman, Republican State Chairmen's Advisory Committee ▪ Gov. Jim Gilmore—RNC Chairman ▪ Ann Wagner—Co-Chairman ▪ Robert M. "Mike" Duncan (NCM, KY)—Treasurer ▪ Linda Shaw (NCW, NC)—Secretary ▪ Tom Sansonetti (NCM, WY)—General Counsel ▪ Al Hoffman, Jr.—Finance Chairman

The Richard Nixon Library & Birthplace

CONTACT:
The Richard Nixon Library & Birthplace
18001 Yorba Linda Boulevard
Yorba Linda, CA 92886

TELEPHONE: (714) 993-3393
(800) USA-8865 (Event Information)

WEB: *www.nixonfoundation.org*

BACKGROUND INFO: The goal of The Richard Nixon Library and Birthplace is to celebrate both the presidential and the personal aspects of Richard Nixon.

VIP STAFF: John H. Taylor—Executive Director

VIP SUPPORTING THE FOUNDATION: Henry Kissinger

Ronald Reagan Presidential Library

CONTACT:
Ronald Reagan Presidential Library
40 Presidential Drive
Simi Valley, CA 93065

TELEPHONE: (800) 410-8354
(805) 522-8444

Ronald Reagan Presidential Foundation
40 Presidential Drive
Simi Valley, CA 93065

TELEPHONE: (805) 522-2977

WEB: *www.reagan.utexas.edu/*

BACKGROUND INFO: The goal of the library is to preserve dignity of the American president and to celebrate the achievements of Ronald Reagan's presidency. Leaders from government, business, media, and academia are brought in to discuss public affairs.

EVENTS: The Reagan Lecture Series ▪ The Reagan Forum (Guests include Ward Connerly, Chairman of the American Civil Rights Institute.)

VIP STAFF: R. Duke Blackwood—Director

VIPs SUPPORTING THE INSTITUTION: Nancy Reagan ▪ C. Michael Armstrong (CEO, AT&T) ▪ John Ashcroft (Senator, MO) ▪ Howard Baker (Former Senator and White House Chief of Staff) ▪ James Baker (Former Treasury Secretary and Secretary of State) ▪ Haley Barbour (Former Chairman, National Republican Committee) ▪ Tom Brokaw ▪ George W. Bush ▪ John McCain ▪ James Carville (Clinton Political Consultant) ▪ Sam Donaldson ▪ Michael Dukakis ▪ Edwin Feulner, Jr. (President, Heritage Foundation) ▪ New Gingrich ▪ Charlton Heston ▪ Rudolph Giuliani ▪ Steve Forbes ▪ Mikhail Gorbechev ▪ Jack Kemp

The Supreme Court Historical Society

CONTACT:

Supreme Court Historical Society
Operman House
224 East Capitol Street NE
Washington, DC 20003

TELEPHONE: (202) 543-0400

WEB: *www.supremecourthistory.org/*

BACKGROUND INFO: This is one of the three finest institutions in the United States. This society was created twenty-seven years ago in order to extend the public awareness of both the history and the heritage of the Supreme Court. Membership includes the current members of the Supreme Court as well as influential politicians.

EVENTS: Society's Annual Meeting (Held in June, the meeting includes an annual lecture, a formal reception, and dinner. It is held in the Supreme Court.) ▪ Lecture Series (Call the society for dates and times.)

VIP STAFF: David T. Pride—Executive Director ▪ Kathy Schulteff

SUPPORTERS: Leon Silverman—President ▪ Virginia Warren Daly (Daughter of Chief Justice Earl Warren)—Secretary ▪ Kenneth Starr ▪ Dwight Operman (Billionaire) ▪ Justice Byron White ▪ William H. Rehnquist—Chief Justice ▪ Antonin Scalia—Associate Justice ▪ John Paul Stevens—Associate Justice ▪ Sandra Day O'Connor—Associate Justice ▪ Anthony M. Kennedy—Associate Justice ▪ Ruth Bader Ginsburg—Associate Justice ▪ David H. Souter—Associate Justice ▪ Clarence Thomas—Associate Justice ▪ Stephen G. Breyer—Associate Justice

United States Capitol Historical Society

CONTACT:

U.S. Capitol Historical Society
200 Maryland Ave. NE
Washington, DC 20002

TELEPHONE: (202) 543-8919

WEB: *www.uschs.org*

ORGANIZATIONAL FOCUS: Historical preservation

BACKGROUND INFO: The purpose of the U.S. Capitol Historical Society is to preserve and strengthen the history of the Capitol and those people who have served in Congress and the Capitol. The USCHS creates educational programs for educational institutions, they hold numerous symposia, they add to the Capitol's collection of art and artifacts, and they create Capitol memorabilia. They do this all for the preservation of the United States Capitol.

EVENTS: Reception for Retiring Members of Congress (In mid-July, members of Congress that are retiring are honored at this event.) ▪ House Judiciary Committee Dinner (This event in September is a great place to meet the members of the House Judiciary Committee.)

VIP STAFF: Robert L. Breeden—Chairman ▪ Ronald A. Sarasin—President ▪ Suzie Dicks—General Secretary ▪ Neale Cosby—Treasurer ▪ Rebecca Evans—Director of Development ▪ Scott Hollins—Operations Manager ▪ J. Charles Bruse (Vice President and Assistant General Counsel, Allstate Insurance Company)—Trustee ▪ Kenneth W. Cole (Corporate Vice President, Allied-Signal)—Trustee ▪ Curtis C. Deane (CAE and President, American Society of Civil Engineers Foundation)—Trustee ▪ Deborah Dingell (President, General Motors Foundation)—Trustee ▪ Jane Fawcett-Hoover (Vice President, National Government Relations for Procter & Gamble)—Trustee ▪ Porter J. Goss (U.S. House of Representatives)—Trustee ▪ Holly Hassett (Director, Government Relations, Hershey Foods Corporation)—Trustee ▪ H. Thomas Greene (Executive Director, Legislative Affairs, National Automobile Dealers Association)—Trustee ▪ James C. May (Executive Vice President, Government Relations, National Association of Broadcasters)—Trustee ▪ Daniel Patrick Moynihan (United States Senate)—Trustee ▪ Robert B. Okun (Vice President, Washington Office, National Broadcasting Co.)—Trustee ▪ Norman J. Ornstein (Resident Scholar, American Enterprise Institute)—Trustee ▪ Barbara L. Phillips (Vice President, Federal Relations, AirTouch Communications, Inc.)—Trustee ▪ Barclay T. Resler (Assistant Vice President, Government Relations, The Coca-Cola Company)—Trustee ▪ Cokie Roberts (ABC News)—Trustee ▪ Lee J. Stillwell (Senior Vice President, Advocacy, American Medical Association)—Trustee ▪ William R. Sweeney, Jr. (Executive Director, Government Relations, EDS Corp.)—Trustee ▪ Thomas J. Tauke (Senior Vice President, Bell Atlantic Corp.)—Trustee ▪ Susan M. Walter (Vice President, Government Relations, General Electric Company)—Trustee

United States House of Representatives

CONTACT:
United States House of Representatives
Washington, DC 20515

TELEPHONE: (202) 224-3121

WEB: *www.house.gov*

ORGANIZATIONAL FOCUS: Governmental functions

BACKGROUND INFO: The House of Representatives makes up half of the U.S. Congress, with the Senate making up the other half. The amount of representatives which is allotted for each state is determined by the population of the state. There are 435 members of the House of Representatives. Each member is up for election every two years, making them the elected representative most responsive to the voters.

VIP STAFF: Dennis Hastert (R-IL)—Speaker ▪ Dick Armey (R-TX)—Majority Leader ▪ Tom DeLay (R-TX)—Majority Whip ▪ Richard Gephardt (D-Mo)—Minority Leader ▪ David E. Bonior (D-M)—Minority Whip ▪ J. C. Watts, Jr. (R-OK)—House Republican Conference Chairman ▪ Martin Frost (D-TX)—Democratic Caucus Chairman ▪ Robert Menendez (D-NJ)—Democratic Caucus Vice Chairman ▪ Christopher Cox (R-CA)—House Republican Policy Committee Chairman

COMMITTEES:

Committee on Agriculture: Larry Combest (R-TX)—Chairman ▪ Charles Stenholm (D-TX)—Ranking Member
Committee on Appropriations: C. W. Bill Young (R-FL)—Chairman ▪ David R. Obey (D-TX)—Ranking Member
Committee on Armed Services: Bob Stump (R-AZ)—Chairman ▪ Ike Skelton (D-MT)—Ranking Member
Committee on the Budget: Jim Nussle (R-OH)—Chairman ▪ John Spratt (D-SC)—Ranking Member

Committee on Education and the Workforce: John Boehner (R-OH)—Chairman ▪ George Miller (D-CA)—Ranking Member

Committee on Energy and Commerce: W. J. "Billy" Tauzin (R-LA)—Chairman ▪ Richard Burr (R-NC)—Vice Chairman Hon. John D. Dingell (D-MI)—Ranking Member

Committee on Government Reform: Dan Burton (R-ID)—Chairman ▪ Henry A. Waxman (D-CA)—Ranking Member

Committee on Financial Services: Michael G. Oxley (R-OH)—Chairman ▪ Hon. John J. LaFalce (D-NY)—Ranking Member

Committee on House Administration: Robert W. Ney (R-OH)—Chairman

Committee on International Relations: Henry Hyde (R-IL)—Chairman ▪ Tom Lantos (D-CA)—Ranking Member

Committee on the Judiciary: F. James Sensenbrenner, Jr. (R-WI)—Chairman ▪ John Conyers, Jr. (D-MI)—Ranking Member

Committee on Resources: James V. Hansen (R-UT)—Chairman ▪ Dan Young (R-AK)—Vice Chairman

Committee on Rules: David Dreier (R-CA)—Chairman ▪ John Joseph Moakley (D-MA)—Ranking Member

Committee on Science: Sherwood L. Boehlert (R-NY)—Chairman ▪ Ralph M. Hall (D-TX)—Ranking Member

Committee on Small Business: Dan Manzullo (R-IL)—Chairman ▪ Nydia Velazquez (D-NY)—Ranking Member

Committee on Standards of Official Conduct: Joel Hefly (R-CO)—Chairman ▪ Howard L. Berman (D-CA)—Ranking Member

Committee on Transportation and Infrastructure: Dan Young (R-AK)—Chairman ▪ James L. Oberstar (D-MN)—Ranking Member

Committee on Veterans Affairs: Chris Smith (R-NJ)—Chairman ▪ Lane Evans (D-IL)—Ranking Member

Committee on Ways and Means: Hon. Bill Thomas (R-CA)—Chairman

Joint Economic Committee: Sen. Connie Mack (R-FL)—Chairman ▪ Jim Saxton (R-NJ)—Vice Chairman ▪ Pete Fortney Stark (D-CA)—Ranking Member

Joint Committee on Printing: Bill Thomas (R-CA)—Chairman ▪ Sen. Mitch McConnell (R-KY)—Vice Chairman ▪ Sen. Dianne Feinstein (D-CA)—Ranking Member

Joint Committee on Taxation: Bill Archer (R-TX)—Chairman

United States Senate

CONTACT:

For Member inquiries:
Office of Senator (Name)
United States Senate
Washington, DC 20510

For Committee inquiries:
(Name of Committee)
United States Senate
Washington, DC 20510

TELEPHONE: (202) 224–3121

WEB: *www.senate.gov*

BACKGROUND INFO: The United States Senate makes up half of the U.S. Congress. It has 100 members, 2 from each of the fifty states. The Senators serve six-year terms. The vice president of the United States is president of the Senate. The U.S. Senate is responsible for many things, including confirmation of the president's appointments. Their confirmations include the president's Supreme Court nominees.

VIP STAFF: Trent Lott (R-MS)—Majority Leader ▪ Don Nickles (R-OK)—Majority Whip ▪ Thomas Daschle (D-SD)—Democratic Leader; Chairman; Democratic Policy Committee ▪ Harry Reid (D-NV)—Democratic Whip ▪ Larry Craig (R-ID)—Chairman, Republican Policy Committee ▪ Strom Thurmond (R-SC)—President Pro Tempore ▪ Gary Sisco—Secretary of the Senate ▪ James Ziglar—Sargeant at Arms ▪ Elizabeth B. Letchworth—Secretary for the Majority ▪ Martin P. Paone—Secretary for the Minority ▪ Dr. Lloyd J. Ogilvie—Senate Chaplain ▪ Dick Cheney—President of Senate (Vice President of United States)
Rick Santorum—Chairman, Republic Conference

COMMITTEES:

Standing:
Agriculture, Nutrition, and Forestry Committee: Richard Luger (R-IN)—Chairman ▪ Tom Harkin (D-IA)—Ranking Member
Appropriations Committee: Ted Stevens (R-AK)—Chairman ▪ Robert Byrd (D-WV)—Ranking Member
Armed Services Committee: John Warner (R-WV)—Chairman ▪ Carl Levin (D-MI)—Ranking Member
Banking, Housing, and Urban Affairs Budget Committee: Phil Gramm (R-TX)—Chairman ▪ Paul Sarbanes (D-MD)—Ranking Member
Budget Committee: Pete Domenici (R-NM)—Chairman ▪ Kent Conrad (D-ND)—Ranking Member
Commerce, Science, and Transportation Committee: John McCain (R-AZ)—Chairman ▪ Ernest Hollings (D-SC)—Ranking Member
Energy and Natural Resources Committee: Frank Murkowski (R-AK)—Chairman ▪ Jeff Bingaman (D-NM)—Ranking Member
Environment and Public Works Committee: Bob Smith (R-NH)—Chairman ▪ Harry Ried (D-NV)—Ranking Member
Finance Committee: Chuck Grassley (R-IA)—Chairman ▪ Max Baucus (D-MT)—Ranking Member
Foreign Relations Committee: Jesse Helms (R-NC)—Chairman ▪ Joseph Biden (D-DE)—Ranking Member
Governmental Affairs Committee: Fred Thompson (R-TN)—Chairman ▪ Joseph Lieberman (D-CT)—Ranking Member
Judiciary Committee: Orrin Hatch (R-UT)—Chairman ▪ Patrick Leahy (D-VT)—Ranking Member
Health, Education, Labor, and Pensions Committee: James Jeffords (R-VT)—Chairman ▪ Edward Kennedy (D-MA)—Ranking Member
Rules and Administration Committee: Mitch McConnell (R-KY)—Chairman ▪ Christopher Dodd (D-CT)—Ranking Member
Small Business Committee: Christopher Bond (R-MO)—Chairman ▪ John Kerry (D-MA)—Ranking Member
Veterans' Affairs Committee: Arlen Specter (R-PA)—Chairman ▪ John Rockefeller (D-WV)—Ranking Member

Special, Select, and Other:
Senate Select Committee on Intelligence: Richard Shelby (R-AL)—Chairman ▪ Bob Graham (D-FL)—Ranking Member
Senate Select Committee on Ethics: Pat Roberts (R-KS)—Chairman ▪ Harry Reid (D-NV)—Ranking Member
Senate Select Committee on Aging: Larry Craig (R-ID)—Chairman ▪ John Breaux (D-LA)—Ranking Member

Joint Committees of Congress:
Joint Economic Committee: Robert Bennett (R-UT)—Chairman ▪ Jack Reed (D-RI)—Ranking Member
Joint Committee on Taxation: Chuck Grassley (R-IA)—Chairman ▪ Max Baucus (D-MT)—Ranking Member
Joint Committee on the Library: Ted Stevens (R-AK)—Chairman ▪ Christopher Dodd (D-CT)—Ranking Member

Joint Committee on Printing: Bill Thomas (R-CA)—Chairman ▪ Sen. Mitch McConnell (R-KY)—Vice Chairman ▪ Sen. Dianne Feinstein (D-CA)—Ranking Member

White House Correspondence Association

CONTACT:
> White House Correspondence Association
> 1067 National Press Building
> Washington, DC 20045

ORGANIZATION'S FOCUS: Addresses day-to-day issues on behalf of the White House and correspondence with the White House

BACKGROUND INFO: The White House Press Association is the organization that coordinates the White House Correspondence dinner, one of the biggest and best events in Washington, DC. Everyone attends. The organization is broken up into regular members (members of the White House Press Corps and White House Bureau Chiefs) and associate members (members of news agencies that receive White House correspondence). Members and associate members are eligible to buy tickets to the annual White House Correspondence dinner.

NETWORKING SPECIFICS: The White House Correspondence Dinner is one of the great events in Washington, DC. A large collection of media personalities, like Peggy Noonan, Bernard Shaw, Wolf Blitzer, and Larry King, can be found there.

EVENT: White House Correspondence Dinner (May)

VIP STAFF: Julie Whitson—Executive Director

VIPs SUPPORTING THE ORGANIZATION: Every major news and media outlet in the United States

White House Historical Association

CONTACT:
> White House Historical Association
> 740 Jackson Place NW
> Washington, DC 20503

TELEPHONE: (202) 737-8292

WEB: *www.whitehousehistory.org*

ORGANIZATIONAL FOCUS: Preserving the history of the White House

BACKGROUND INFO: The White House Historical Association was founded by Jacqueline Kennedy Onassis. It focuses mainly on the dispersal of historical and useful information about the White House. The WHHA has published over eight million books and videos, which are distributed to schools, libraries, and other learning institutions. The WHHA also sponsors lectures and exhibits.

EVENT: Christmas at the White House (The White House is open for tours throughout the month of December.)

VIP STAFF: Robert L. Breeden—Chairman and CEO ▪ Hugh S. Sidey—President ▪ James I. McDaniel—Secretary ▪ J. Carter Brown—Treasurer ▪ Joy Carter Sundlun—Assistant Treasurer ▪ Michael R. Beschloss—Board Member ▪ Robert L. Breeden—Board Member ▪ Jeannine Smith Clark—Board Member ▪ Dorothy M. Craig—Board Member ▪ Henry A. Dudley, Jr.—Board Member ▪ John M. Fahey, Jr.—Board

CHAPTER SEVEN

General Institutions

By now you have a good grasp on how to use the entries in this book. If you apply the techniques and suggestions to your networking activities, you will find success. With the past chapters in mind, this chapter looks at various institutions that, while terrific for networkers, don't fit in the traditional categories.

Universities

Networking through universities is often very effective. When you meet a networking target at a university function, you have an instantaneous bond based on loyalty to the university. Graduates are traditionally very loyal to fellow alumni. As such, the alumni associations also are great networking institutions. Also, whenever a university gives out a distinguished alumni award, most major alumni and faculty show up for the function. It becomes a huge networking opportunity. Universities that have business schools are a direct route into corporate America; affiliations with top business schools can be very valuable. As for VIPs at universities, many schools sponsor lecture series that can bring someone like Colin Powell to a small town. Check your local schools and see if they sponsor any lectures, resident faculty experts, alumni awards, etc.

Car Clubs

The most distinguished and exotic brands of automobiles have owners and followers who have created car clubs. These clubs are each unique and each functions in different ways. They can create newsletters, hold rallies and car shows, host dinners for aficionados to get together and talk about their automobiles, etc. The most active car clubs revolve around Ferrari and Rolls-Royce. These car clubs are fascinating for their networking potential. For example, when you attend a Ferrari club event, you will be in the company of corporate CEOs, wealthy entrepreneurs, celebrities, and others who have enough disposable income to purchase a car that costs more than the median home price in the United States. The clubs never place a requirement that you own one of the cars, they usually just ask that you have a keen interest in the marque. However, when you attend the events, you have an instant bond with everyone: an interest in a particular type of automobile.

Professional Trade Organizations

The American Bar Association (ABA) holds important events that draw lawmakers, high-profile attorneys, and corporate executives. Other professional trade organizations hold similar events. Once you identify who you need to target for a networking strategy, research into whether or not he is a member of a professional trade organization. Then call the trade organization and get a schedule of upcoming events. These events are prime networking ground.

Sports Organizations

From halls of fame, to sports award shows, to the sports franchises themselves, sports organizations are very high profile. These organizations are obviously important if you want to meet or network with sports figures, but sports touches many other industries. If you are looking to network with a corporation that sponsors sporting events, the sports organizations can be an in and vice versa.

Recently, Bret was able to mix industries in an effort to introduce his father to basketball legend Larry Bird. Larry Bird took over the coaching duties of the Indiana Pacers, and Indiana was scheduled to come to Los Angeles to play the L.A. Clippers. Bret decided to network into arranging a meeting between Bird and his dad. Bret went down to the Clippers offices and met with the people in the Promotions department. As she explained her job, Bret was looking for some connection between her job and his background in order to make a swap. At some point in the conversation, she mentioned that the Clippers sponsor a community outreach program in which they bring thousands of inner-city youth into the sports arena and give them a free concert. The problem was, they hadn't been able to get any A-list talent to perform. Bret asked her for a wish list of performers, and she placed Will Smith and LL Cool J at the top. Bret said he would attempt to get to both of them to see if they would help. The promotions executive asked Bret how much he would charge for the service, and he assured her that he was not charging her. Two weeks later, Bret attended the GRAMMY Awards in New York and made it a point to find Will Smith and LL Cool J. He appealed to them directly to help the Los Angeles youth, and both said they would love to. When Bret relayed the information back to the Clippers executive, she offered him tickets and access to Clippers games. Bret took her up on it and brought his dad to the Pacers-Clippers game. The executive gave them seats right on the floor and then walked them back to the locker room after the game to meet Larry. It was a successful night for everyone.

While Bret successfully mixed the music and sports industries and created a networking swap, it is still important to understand that sports institutions function like any other business, so the corporate model applies. All the techniques discussed in the corporate section will be appropriate here. The difference is that sports institutions are more heavily dependent on the media to perpetuate growth. Use media connections to build your sports connections.

Entertainment Resources

Academy of Motion Pictures Arts and Sciences

CONTACT:
Academy of Motion Picture Arts and Sciences
Academy Foundation
8949 Wilshire Boulevard
Beverly Hills, CA 90211-1972

TELEPHONE: (310) 247-3000

WEB: *www.oscars.org*
www.oscar.com

INSTITUTION'S FOCUS: Honorary organization that recognizes professionals in the motion picture industry

BACKGROUND INFO: This is the organization responsible for the Academy Awards. To become a member of the Academy, one must be invited to join by the board of governors of the Academy and sponsored by two current members. The Academy's more than 6,000 members are all categorized into one of the following categories: actors, art directors, cinematographers, directors, executives, film editors, music, producers, public relations, short films and feature animation, sound, visual effects, and writers. The Academy works to advance motion picture arts and sciences, foster creativity among its members, recognize distinguished achievements, and educate the general public.

EVENTS: Academy Awards (March, in Los Angeles) ▪ Scientific and Technical Awards Dinner ▪ Student Academy Awards (June, at the Samuel Goldwyn Theater in Beverly Hills. Past winners include Spike Lee, Gary Nadeau, Bob Saget, Trey Parker, and Oscar winners John Lasseter and Robert Zemeckis.) ▪ Film Retrospectives and tributes (Shown throughout the year at the Samuel Goldwyn theater; open to the public) ▪ Governor's Ball (Post–Academy Awards dinner for nominees, winners, presenters, and performers)

VIP STAFF: Robert Rehme—President ▪ Alan Bergman—First Vice President ▪ Sid Ganis—Vice President ▪ Kathy Bates—Vice President ▪ Donn Cambern—Treasurer ▪ Donald C. Rogers—Secretary ▪ Bruce Davis—Executive Director ▪ Wolfgang Puck—Governor's Ball Chef

Academy of Television Arts and Sciences

CONTACT:
The Academy of Television Arts and Sciences
5220 Lankershim Boulevard
North Hollywood, CA 91601

TELEPHONE: (818) 754-2800

WEB: *www.emmys.org*

INSTITUTION'S FOCUS: To advance telecommunication arts and sciences and foster creative leadership in the industry

BACKGROUND INFO: ATAS is the organization that puts on the Emmy Awards. In addition, ATAS organizes many activities for its more than 10,000 members, such as the Evening with . . . series featuring evenings with prominent television personalities, the Inside . . . series exploring popular television shows, and the film series, which brings members together to view current films. ATAS is closely linked with both UCLA and USC, which house television archives in collaboration with ATAS. ATAS also publishes *Emmy* magazine and gives out the Los Angeles Area Emmys and the College Television Awards.

EVENTS: Emmy Awards (September, at the Leonard H. Goldenson Theatre) ▪ Announcement of Nominations (July, at 5:38 A.M.) ▪ Academy of Television Arts and Sciences Hall of Fame Induction Gala (Past honorees include Lucille Ball, Johnny Carson, Walter Cronkite, Walt Disney, Bob Hope, Leonard H. Goldenson, Mary Tyler Moore, Barbara Walters, Angela Lansbury, Oprah Winfrey, Carl Reiner, and Fred Rogers.) ▪ Los Angeles Area Emmy Awards (June)

VIP STAFF: Meryl Marshall—CEO and Chairman ▪ Jim Chabin—President

American Music Awards

CONTACT:
Dick Clark Productions
3003 West Olive Avenue
Burbank, CA 91505

TELEPHONE: (818) 841-3003

WEB: *www.abc.go.com/ama/ama_home.html*
      www.dickclarkproductions.com

DATE HELD: January

BACKGROUND INFO: The American Music Awards are voted on by a random sampling of approximately 20,000 people. National Family Opinion, Inc., is the firm that sends out the ballots to an even distribution of the U.S. population. The nomination categories are Pop/Rock, Country, Soul/Rhythm and Blues, Adult Contemporary, Latin Music, Rap/Hip Hop, Alternative Music, and Soundtrack.

VIPs: Trace Adkins ▪ Tal Bachman ▪ Melanie C. (Sporty Spice) ▪ Chico DeBarge ▪ Carmen Electra ▪ Faith Evans ▪ Kenny G ▪ Thomas Gibson ▪ Kelsey Grammar ▪ Ginuwine ▪ Neil Patrick Harris ▪ Ty Herndon ▪ Traylor Howard ▪ Joe ▪ Jordan Knight ▪ Jane Leeves ▪ Reba McEntire ▪ Bill Maher ▪ John Michael Montgomery ▪

Bret and Jim Carrey

Bret and Jerry Seinfeld

Bret and Sylvester Stallone

Bret and Harrison Ford

Bret and Cameron Diaz

Bret and Charlize Theron

Bret and David Letterman

Bret and Johnny Depp

Bret and
Jennifer Aniston Pitt

Bret and Tom Hanks

Elliot and Robin Williams

Elliot and Joe Namath

Elliot and Al Pacino

Elliot and Gerald Ford, former U.S. President

Elliot and Colin Powell

Elliot and Ronald Regan, former U.S. President

Jerry O'Connell ▪ Queen Latifah ▪ Caroline Rhea ▪ Christopher "Kid" Reid ▪ Rob Schneider ▪ SheDaisy ▪ Sisqo ▪ Tyrese ▪ Christina Applegate ▪ Lou Bega ▪ Deborah Cox ▪ DMX ▪ Melissa Ethridge ▪ Sara Evans ▪ Warren G ▪ Golberg ▪ Amy Grant ▪ Guy ▪ Melissa Joan Hart ▪ Jennifer Love Hewitt ▪ Julio Iglesias, Jr. ▪ K-Ci & JoJo ▪ Tommy Lee ▪ LFO ▪ Brian McKnight ▪ Kellie Martin ▪ Montgomery Gentry ▪ Donny and Marie Osmond ▪ Ryan Reynolds ▪ Richard Ruccolo ▪ The Roots ▪ Rich Schroder ▪ Jessica Simpson ▪ Britney Spears

CORPORATE SPONSOR: Ford

The American Theatre Wing

WEB: *www.tonys.org*

FOCUS: Supporting and servicing the theater community

BACKGROUND INFO: The American Theatre Wing is one of two parties responsible for awarding the Tonys. The American Theatre Wing also works with the theater community to hold educational and service activities for the community. It promotes the theater in high schools, offers scholarships to performing arts students, and performs in hospitals throughout New York City.

EVENTS: Nominees Brunch (Held in May, a media event for the Tony Award nominees) ▪ Tony Awards (Held in June at Radio City Music Hall in New York; tickets are available to the general public.)

VIP STAFF: Roy A. Somlyo—President ▪ Isabelle Stevenson—Chairman of the Board ▪ Edgar Dobie—Managing Producer, Tony Award Productions

CORPORATE SPONSORS: IMB ▪ Theatre.com ▪ Visa

Broadcasting and Cable Magazine

CONTACT:
Broadcasting and Cable Magazine
245 W. Seventeenth Street
New York, NY 10011

TELEPHONE: (212) 463-6524

WEB: *www.broadcastingcable.com*

BACKGROUND INFO: *Broadcasting and Cable magazine* is a weekly magazine covering entertainment industry news. It sponsors the *Broadcasting and Cable* Hall of Fame and holds the Hall of Fame Induction Ceremony.

EVENT: Hall of Fame Induction Ceremony (Held in November in New York)

VIP STAFF: Don West—Editor in Chief of *Broadcasting and Cable* ▪ Larry Oliver—Group Publisher of *Broadcasting and Cable* ▪ Harry Jessell—Editor of *Broadcasting and Cable* ▪ Sam Donaldson—Master of Ceremonies

VIPs HONORED BY THE HALL OF FAME: Joseph Collins (Chairman and CEO, Time Warner Cable) ▪ Casey Kasem ▪ David Kelley ▪ Agnes Nixon ▪ Jane Pauley ▪ Mike Wallace ▪ Bob Johnson (Chairman, Black Entertainment Television) ▪ Mary Hart ▪ Tom Brokaw ▪ Phil Donahue ▪ Peter Lund

Country Music Association

CONTACT:
CMA Headquarters
One Music Circle South
Nashville, TN 37203

TELEPHONE: (615) 244-2840

WEB: *www.cmaworld.com*

BACKGROUND INFO: The CMA is the premier organization that promotes and organizes events that support and benefit country musicians and the country music establishment as a whole. It is the organization that puts on the Country Music Association Awards.

VIP STAFF: Ed Benson—Executive Director ▪ Tammy Genovese—Associate Executive Director ▪ Peggy Whitaker—Director of Board Administration ▪ Lon Helton—Chairman ▪ Connie Bradley (ASCAP)—Board Member ▪ Allen Butler (Sony Music Nashville)—Board Member ▪ Barry Coburn (Atlantic Records)—Board Member ▪ Paul Corbin (CBS Cable)—Board Member ▪ Tim DuBois (Arista Records)—Board Member ▪ Joe Galante (RCA Label Group)—Board Member ▪ Ms. Donna Hilley (Sony/ATV Tree Publishing Nashville)—Board Member ▪ Bruce Hinton (MCA Records)—Board Member ▪ Luke Lewis (Mercury Nashville)—Board Member ▪ Randy Owen (Musician, Alabama)—Board Member ▪ Frances Preston (BMI)—Board Member ▪ Kenny Rogers—Board Member ▪ Nancy Shapiro (Nashville Chapter of the Recording Academy)—Board Member ▪ Tom Shapiro (Sony/ATV Music Publishing)—Board Member ▪ Roger Sovine (BMI)—Board Member ▪ James Stroud (DreamWorks Records Nashville)—Board Member ▪ Tim Wipperman (Warner/Chappell Music)—Board Member

EVENTS: International Country Music Fan Fair (This four-day-long event is held every June in Nashville, Tennessee, and is attended by some of the top country megastars as well as representatives from some of the leading record labels in the country.) ▪ CMA Awards (October)

VIPs SUPPORTING THE INSTITUTION: George Strait ▪ Brad Paisley ▪ Lisa Hartman Black ▪ Alabama ▪ Lonestar ▪ Vince Gill ▪ Deana Carter ▪ Ty Herndon ▪ Billy Ray Cyrus ▪ Pam Tillis ▪ Clint Black ▪ Tim McGraw ▪ Sawyer Brown ▪ LeAnn Rimes ▪ Olivia Newton-John ▪ Kenny Chesney ▪ Joe Diffie ▪ Naomi Judd

Country Music Hall of Fame and Museum

CONTACT:
Country Music Hall of Fame and Museum
4 Music Square East
Nashville, TN 37203

TELEPHONE: (615) 416-2001
(800) 852-6437

WEB: *www.countrymusichalloffame.com*

EVENTS: CMA Awards (Held in October, the inductees into the Country Music Hall of Fame are inducted at the Country Music Association's Award show.)

VIPs SUPPORTING THE INSTITUTION: Gene Autry ▪ Chet Atkins ▪ Johnny Cash ▪ Loretta Lynn ▪ Roy Rogers ▪ Willie Nelson ▪ Merle Haggard ▪ Dolly Parton

Gospel Music Association

CONTACT:
Gospel Music Association
1205 Division Street
Nashville, TN 37203

TELEPHONE: (615) 242-0303

ORGANIZATIONAL FOCUS: Promoting gospel music

BACKGROUND INFO: The Gospel Music Association is the institute that puts on the Dove Awards. It has over 5,000 members from all levels of the gospel music industry. The Christian Music Trade Association, a part of GMA, works to increase the presence of Christian music. GMA also runs the Gospel Music Hall of Fame, Resource Center and Archives, dedicated to preserving contributions to the field of gospel music.

NETWORKING SPECIFICS: The Dove Awards are the premier event of the Gospel Music Association. The nationally televised awards recognize top Christian musicians, such as Twila Paris, Amy Grant, dc Talk, Jars of Clay, and Steven Curtis Chapman. Tickets are sold to the public. This event is a great place to meet Christian music stars, music industry executives, and members of the Gospel Music Association.

EVENTS: Gospel Music Week (Nashville, Tennessee) ▪ Dove Awards (April, in Nashville, Tennessee) ▪ Academy of Gospel Music Arts (Seminar and talent competition, held in various cities)

VIP STAFF: Bruce Koblish—President ▪ Karen Berry—Manager of Special Projects

Independent Feature Project/West

CONTACT:
Independent Feature Project/West
1964 Westwood Boulevard., Suite 205
Los Angeles, CA 90025

TELEPHONE: (310) 475-4379

WEB: *www.ifpwest.org/*

BACKGROUND INFO: The IFP/West is the institution that holds the Spirit Awards. The IFP/West was created by several Los Angeles filmmakers and now, almost twenty years after its creation, it has a membership of over 4,500. The organization focuses mainly on supporting the independent filmmakers on the West Coast.

EVENT: IFP/West Spirit Awards (Held in March in Santa Monica, California, this award show is meant to honor the best independent film on the market. This show is generally attended by up-and-coming stars who are nominees as well as numerous businesses in the movie industry.)

VIP STAFF: Vondie Curtis Hall—President ▪ Michael Helfant—Executive Vice President ▪ Barbara Boyle— Past President ▪ Peggy Rajski—Treasurer ▪ Dawn Hudson—Executive Director ▪ Michael Donaldson— General Counsel

PAST AWARD RECIPIENTS: Hillary Swank ▪ Chloe Sevigny

VIPs SUPPORTING THE ORGANIZATION: Alec Baldwin ▪ Jodie Foster ▪ James L. Brooks ▪ Martin Scorsese ▪ Matt Groening ▪ Penny Marshall

CORPORATE SPONSORS: *Entertainment Weekly* ▪ Motorola ▪ Miramax Films ▪ USA Films ▪ Directors Guild of America ▪ EMI Music Publishing ▪ *In Style* Magazine ▪ Screen Actors Guild ▪ Walt Disney Pictures ▪ Writers

Guild of America ▪ Columbia Pictures ▪ New York Times ▪ Doc Martens ▪ Fuji Photo Film ▪ Starbucks Coffee ▪ Express ▪ Eastman Kodak Company ▪ Sprint PCS ▪ Artisan Entertainment ▪ Paramount Pictures ▪ Evian Natural Spring Water ▪ HBO ▪ Sony Pictures Entertainment ▪ William Morris Agency ▪ Universal Pictures ▪ New Line Cinema ▪ Trimark Pictures ▪ Carsey-Werner Company ▪ MTV Films ▪ Sundance Film Festival

The League of American Theatres and Producers, Inc.

CONTACT:
The League of American Theatres and Producers, Inc.
226 West 47th Street
New York, NY 10036

TELEPHONE: (212) 764-1122

WEB: *www.broadway.org*

ORGANIZATION'S FOCUS: A trade organization for the theater industry

BACKGROUND INFO: The League's members are theater owners, operators, producers, presenters, and general managers. It works to protect the interests of its members and to promote Broadway theater.

EVENTS: Broadway on Broadway (September, in New York; a free concert to mark the start of the Broadway season) ▪ Nominees Brunch (Held in May, a media event for the Tony Award nominees) ▪ Tony Awards (Held in June at Radio City Music Hall in New York; tickets are available to the general public) ▪ Stars in the Alley (May, in New York; a free concert to mark the end of the Broadway season)

VIP STAFF: Cy Feuer—Chairman ▪ Jed Bernstein—President ▪ Edgar Dobie—Managing Producer, Tony Award Productions

CORPORATE SPONSORS: IBM ▪ Theatre.com ▪ Visa

The National Academy of Recording Arts and Sciences

CONTACT:
The Recording Academy
3402 Pico Boulevard
Santa Monica, CA 90405

TELEPHONE: (310) 392-3777

WEB: *www.grammy.com*

BACKGROUND INFO: The Recording Academy has created one of the biggest nights for musicians with its annual GRAMMY Awards Ceremony. It was formed to bring together members of the competitive music industry. It has more than 14,000 members and operates on a national level and a regional one, with chapters in twelve cities across the United States.

EVENTS: A Night at the Net (Celebrity tennis match held in Los Angeles in July to benefit the Recording Academy's MusiCares Foundation) ▪ The Technical GRAMMY Awards (Given the night before the GRAMMY awards, at the GRAMMY nominees reception) ▪ GRAMMY Awards (February in Los Angeles) ▪ GRAMMY Celebration party (After the GRAMMY Awards)

NETWORKING SPECIFICS: The National Academy of Recording Arts and Sciences is the most important organization in the music industry. Any of its events, especially the GRAMMY Awards and the events surrounding it, would be great places to network with recording artists and executives and to establish connections with them.

VIP STAFF: Michael Greene—President and CEO ▪ Rob Senn—Executive Vice President and General Manager ▪ Diane Theriot—Vice President, Awards ▪ Kristen Madsen—Vice President, Member Services ▪ Adam Sandler—Vice President, Communications

CHARITY SUPPORTED: MusiCares Foundation

National Academy of Television Arts and Sciences

CONTACT:

National Academy of Television Arts and Sciences
111 West 57th Street, Suite 1020
New York, NY 10019

TELEPHONE: (212) 586-8424

WEB: *www.emmyonline.org*

BACKGROUND INFO: NATAS are the people who award the specialized Emmys, such as the Daytimes, the News and Documentary, and the Sports Emmys. NATAS is the largest television professional association in the world, with more than 11,000 members. It was formed in 1955 by television industry leaders, including Ed Sullivan, Walter Cronkite, Carl Reiner, and Neil Simon. NATAS has seventeen chapters nationwide, which organize regional awards and events. The NATAS web site operates a television industry job bank.

EVENTS: Daytime Emmy Awards ▪ News and Documentary Emmy Awards ▪ Sports Emmy Awards

VIPs SUPPORTING THE ORGANIZATION: Walter Cronkite ▪ Fred Allen ▪ Charles Collingwood ▪ Edward R. Murrow ▪ Carl Reiner ▪ Neil Simon ▪ Mark Goodson ▪ Basil Rathbone

The Rock and Roll Hall of Fame and Museum

CONTACT:

Rock and Roll Hall of Fame and Museum
One Key Plaza
Cleveland, OH 44114

Rock and Roll Hall of Fame Foundation
1290 Avenue of the Americas
New York, NY 10104

TELEPHONE: (888) 764-ROCK

WEB: *www.rockhall.com*

BACKGROUND INFO: The Rock and Roll Hall of Fame holds annual events that are attended by some of the biggest names in the music industry, from globally recognized musicians to powerful record label personnel.

VIP STAFF: Terry Stewart—President and CEO ▪ James Henke—Vice President, Exhibitions and Curatorial Affairs ▪ Robert Santelli—Vice President, Education and Public Programming

EVENTS: Rock and Roll Hall of Fame Induction Ceremony (Held in March, this event is attended by the hall of fame inductees as well as other musicians. The who's who of music are present, and the only event rivaling the Induction Ceremony in number of musicians is the GRAMMYS.) ▪ Rock Hall Ball (Held in October, this annual Halloween bash is held at the museum.)

VIPs SUPPORTING THE ORGANIZATION: The Allman Brothers Band ▪ The Bee Gees ▪ Ray Charles ▪ Creedence Clearwater Revival ▪ Leo Fender ▪ Aretha Franklin ▪ Al Green ▪ Elton John ▪ Gladys Knight and the Pips ▪ Mamas and the Papas ▪ Van Morrison ▪ Smokey Robinson ▪ Sly and the Family Stone ▪ Rod Stewart ▪ The Who ▪ Neil Young ▪ The Beach Boys ▪ Chuck Berry ▪ Bo Diddley ▪ Crosby, Stills and Nash ▪ Fleetwood Mac ▪ Carole King ▪ The Jackson Five ▪ B. B. King ▪ Led Zeppelin ▪ Paul McCartney ▪ Les Paul ▪ The Rolling Stones ▪ Phil Spector ▪ The Supremes ▪ Stevie Wonder ▪ The Beatles ▪ David Bowie ▪ Bob Dylan ▪ The Eagles ▪ The Four Tops ▪ Grateful Dead ▪ Billy Joel ▪ The Kinks ▪ Jerry Lee Lewis ▪ Joni Mitchell ▪ Pink Floyd ▪ Simon and Garfunkel ▪ Bruce Springsteen ▪ The Temptations ▪ The Yardbirds

The Sundance Institute

CONTACT:
Sundance Institute
307 West 200 South, Suite 5002
Salt Lake City, UT 84101

TELEPHONE: (801) 328-3456

WEB: *www.sundance.org*

BACKGROUND INFO: This is the organization that holds the Sundance Film Festival. The Sundance Institute was the idea of Robert Redford, who wanted to promote artistic developments in American film. The institute conducts labs offering assistance, advice, and equipment to help aspiring screenwriters, film-makers, and composers develop their skills. The Sundance Collection, devoted to preserving independent films, is housed at UCLA.

EVENTS: Sundance Film Festival (January, in Park City, Utah) ▪ Screenwriters Lab (January) ▪ Filmmakers Lab (June) ▪ Native Screenwriting Project (July) ▪ Composers Lab (Midsummer)

VIP STAFF: Walter Weisman—Chairman

VIPs ATTENDING THE FILM FESTIVAL: Robert Redford ▪ Courtney Love ▪ Matt Stone ▪ Third Eye Blind ▪ RuPaul ▪ Shawn Colvin ▪ Kirsten Dunst ▪ Michael Stipe ▪ Uma Thurman ▪ Johnny Rotten ▪ Natasha Lyonne ▪ Kyle MacLachlan ▪ Jennifer Connelly ▪ Jodie Foster ▪ Melissa Joan Hart ▪ Marisa Tomei ▪ Ben Affleck ▪ Kevin Spacey ▪ Trey Parker ▪ Sugar Ray ▪ Tammy Faye Bakker-Messner ▪ Nick Nolte ▪ Christian Bale ▪ Danny DeVito ▪ Heather Graham ▪ Josh Hartnett ▪ Lisa Marie Presley ▪ Casey Affleck ▪ Ethan Hawke ▪ Billy Crudup ▪ Neve Campbell ▪ Matt Damon ▪ Holly Hunter ▪ Calista Flockhart

CORPORATE SPONSORS: Entertainment Weekly ▪ Mercedes-Benz ▪ Apple ▪ Blockbuster ▪ AT&T ▪ American Express ▪ DirecTV ▪ Motorola ▪ Samuel Adams ▪ Excite

Sports Resources

ATP Tour

CONTACT:
ATP Tour International Headquarters
201 ATP Tour Boulevard
Ponte Vedra Beach, FL 32082

TELEPHONE: (904) 285-8000

BACKGROUND INFO: The ATP Tour is the organization that concerns itself with the worldwide men's professional tennis circuit. The organization was formed after tennis players felt like they had no say in the organization of tennis tournaments. The ATP Tour is based around the input of the athletes. Many of tennis's top athletes of today are members of the ATP Tour.

VIPs AFFILIATED WITH THE ORGANIZATION: Mark Miles—CEO ▪ David Felgate—Player Representative, Board Member ▪ John Fitzgerald—Player Representative, Board Member ▪ Harold Solomon—Player Representative, Board Member ▪ Graham Pearce—Tournament Representative, Board Member ▪ Franco Bartoni—Tournament Representative, Board Member ▪ Charlie Pasarell—Tournament Representative, Board Member

TOUR STOPS: Adelaide, Australia (January) ▪ Chennai, India (January) ▪ Doha, Qatar (January) ▪ Auckland, New Zealand (January) ▪ Sydney, Australia (January) ▪ Australian Open (January) ▪ Dubai, U.A.E. (February) ▪ Marseille, France (February) ▪ San Jose, California (February) ▪ Memphis, Tennessee (February) ▪ Rotterdam, The Netherlands (February) ▪ London, England (February) ▪ Mexico City, Mexico (February) ▪ Copenhagen, Denmark (February) ▪ Delray Beach, Florida (February) ▪ Santiago, Chile (February) ▪ Bogota, Columbia (March) ▪ Scottsdale, Arizona (March) ▪ Indian Wells, California (March) ▪ Miami, Florida (March) ▪ Atlanta, Georgia (April) ▪ Casablanca, Morocco (April) ▪ Estoril, Portugal (April) ▪ Monte Carlo, Monaco (April) ▪ Barcelona, Spain (April) ▪ Mallorca, Spain (May) ▪ Munich, Germany (May) ▪ Orlando, Florida (May) ▪ Rome, Italy (May) ▪ Hamburg, Germany (May) ▪ World Team Cup (May, in Dusseldorf, Germany) ▪ St. Polten, Austria (May) ▪ Roland Garros, France (May) ▪ Halle, Germany (June) ▪ London/Queen's (June, in England) ▪ Merano (June) ▪ 's-Hertogenbosch, The Netherlands (June) ▪ Nottingham, England (June) ▪ Wimbledon (June) ▪ Bastad, Sweden (July) ▪ Gstaad, Switzerland (July) ▪ Newport, Rhode Island (July) ▪ Stuttgart Outdoor (July, in Germany) ▪ Amsterdam, The Netherlands (July) ▪ Umag, Croatia (July) ▪ Kitzbuhel, Austria (July) ▪ Los Angeles, California (July) ▪ San Marino, Italy (July) ▪ Montreal/Toronto (July) ▪ Cincinnati, Ohio (August) ▪ Indianapolis, Indiana (August) ▪ Washington, D.C. (August) ▪ Boston, Massachusetts (August) ▪ Long Island, New York (August) ▪ U.S. Open (August, in New York) ▪ Bucharest, Romania (September) ▪ Prague (September) ▪ Tashkent, Uzbekistan (September) ▪ Palermo, Italy (September) ▪ Hong Kong (October) ▪ Singapore (October) ▪ Tokyo Outdoor (October) ▪ Vienna, Austria (October) ▪ Shanghai, China (October) ▪ Toulouse, France (October) ▪ Basel, Switzerland (October) ▪ Moscow, Russia (October) ▪ Stuttgart Indoor (October, in Germany) ▪ Lyon, France (November) ▪ St. Petersburg, Russia (November) ▪ Paris Indoor (November) ▪ Brighton, England (November) ▪ Stockholm, Sweden (November) ▪ Tennis Masters Cup (November) ▪ Doubles Championship (December)

CORPORATE SPONSORS: Mercedes-Benz ▪ Waterford Crystal ▪ Lucent Technologies ▪ Spalding ▪ Penn ▪ ESPN ▪ Cartoon Network ▪ Club Med

Baseball Hall of Fame

CONTACT:
National Baseball Hall of Fame and Museum
25 Main Street
PO Box 590
Cooperstown, NY 13326

TELEPHONE: (607) 547-7200
(888) HALL-OF-FAME

WEB: *www.baseballhalloffame.org*

EVENTS: Hall of Fame Weekend (Held in July, this event is attended not only by hall-of-famers but also by the coaches and some of the owners of today's baseball teams. There is an autograph session scheduled during the three-day event, as well as the induction ceremony, and the Hall of Fame Game, which is played by two Major League teams.)

VIP STAFF: Dale A. Petroskey—President, National Baseball Hall of Fame

VIPs SUPPORTING THE INSTITUTION: Ted Williams ▪ Sandy Koufax ▪ Ernie Banks ▪ Duke Snider ▪ Frank Robinson ▪ Don Drysdale ▪ Willie McCovey ▪ Rod Carew ▪ Tom Seaver ▪ Carlton Fisk ▪ George Brett ▪ Don Sutton ▪ Stan Musial ▪ Warren Spahn ▪ Willie Mays ▪ Bob Gibson ▪ Juan Marichal ▪ Harmon Killebrew ▪ Willie Stargell ▪ Rollie Fingers ▪ Rod Carew ▪ Nolan Ryan ▪ Yogi Berra ▪ Whitey Ford ▪ Al Kaline ▪ Hank Aaron ▪ Brooks Robinson ▪ Lou Brock ▪ Carl Yastrzemski ▪ Reggie Jackson ▪ Mike Schmidt ▪ Robin Yount

Celebrity Players Tour

CONTACT:
Contact the event located near you for dates and times.

WEB: *www.cptgolf.com*

BACKGROUND INFO: The CPT creates a forum for celebrities who love golf and golf fans to join together with corporations to raise money for charities. The members of the CPT include famous athletes, politicians, and entertainers.

VIP STAFF: Dick Anderson—Board Member ▪ Tom Dreesen—Board Member ▪ Jack Marin—Board Member ▪ Mike Schmidt—Board Member ▪ Steve Bartkowski—Board Member ▪ John Congemi—Board Member ▪ Shane Rawley—Board Member ▪ Tom Huiskens—Board Member

EVENTS: Toyota Dan Marino Celebrity Invitational (Held in February) ▪ Children's Medical Center Classic (Held in April) ▪ Toyota Stan Humphries Celebrity Classic (Held in May) ▪ Duke Children's Classic (Held in May) ▪ Mellon Mario Lemieux Celebrity Invitational (Held in June) ▪ The Dodge Shootout/Big League Challenge (Held in late June and early July) ▪ American Century Celebrity Golf Championship (Held in July) ▪ Sun Microsystems John Elway Celebrity Classic (Held in July) ▪ CPT Qualifying Tournament (Held in August) ▪ Central Baptist Hospital Charity Classic (Held in August) ▪ Atlantic City Celebrity Kids' Classic (Held in August) ▪ Toyota Celebrity Players Cup (Held in September) ▪ Delta/MUSC Children's Classic and Delta/Maxfli Celebrity Challenge (Held in September) ▪ Dodge Celebrity Invitational (Held in December)

MEMBERS: Danny Ainge ▪ Dan Quayle ▪ Charles Barkley ▪ Johnny Bench ▪ George Brett ▪ Matt Lauer ▪ John Smoltz ▪ Dan Majerle ▪ Bryant Gumbel ▪ Brett Hull ▪ Steve Bartkowski ▪ Michael Jordan ▪ Bill Laimbeer ▪ Mike Shanahan ▪ Al Del Greco ▪ Dan Marino ▪ Maury Povich ▪ Stan Humphries ▪ Rick Rhoden ▪ Jerry Rice ▪ Mike Schmidt ▪ Mario Lemieux ▪ Vinny Del Negro ▪ Joe Theismann ▪ Jim McMahon ▪ Rollie Fingers ▪ John Elway ▪ Carlton Fisk ▪ Billy Joe Tolliver

PARTNER: Maxfli

College Football Hall of Fame

CONTACT:
College Football Hall of Fame
111 South St. Joseph Street
South Bend, IN 46601

TELEPHONE: (800) 440-FAME
(219) 235-9999

WEB: *www.collegefootball.org/*

EVENTS: Enshrinement Festival (This two-day festival in August includes a celebrity golf tournament and many other opportunities to meet the greats of college football.) ▪ Gridiron Legends Luncheon Series (February–June).

VIP STAFF: Bernie Kish—Executive Director, College Football Hall of Fame

VIPs SUPPORTING THE INSTITUTION: Danny White ▪ Terry Bradshaw ▪ Mike Ditka ▪ Don Meredith ▪ Fran Tarkenton ▪ Bo Jackson ▪ Lance Alworth ▪ Alex Karras ▪ Lawrence Taylor ▪ Pat Sullivan ▪ Earl Campbell ▪ Tony Dorsett ▪ Mel Renfro ▪ Randy White ▪ Jim McMahon ▪ Sam Huff ▪ Merlin Olson ▪ Lynn Swann ▪ Mike Singletary ▪ Larry Csonka ▪ Bob Lilly ▪ Gale Sayers ▪ Eddie Robinson ▪ Tom Osborne ▪ Paul Hornung ▪ Roger Staubach ▪ Billy Simms

CORPORATE SPONSOR: Key Bank

Davey O'Brien Foundation

CONTACT:
The Davey O'Brien Foundation
306 W. Seventh Street, Suite 1125
Fort Worth, TX 76102

TELEPHONE: (817) 338-3488

WEB: *www.daveyobrien.com*

BACKGROUND INFO: This award recognizes and honors the outstanding college quarterback throughout all of the universities of the nation.

EVENTS: Davey O'Brien Awards Dinner (Held in February, this event is attended by both those being honored, past award winners, and leaders of the Davey O'Brien Foundation, which include the Davey O'Brien family and nationally known sportswriters and commentators.)

VIP STAFF: David O'Brien, Jr. ▪ Charles Ringler ▪ Jim "Hoss" Brock

PAST VIPs WHO HAVE BEEN HONORED: Earl Campbell ▪ Jim McMahon ▪ Chuck Long ▪ Troy Aikman ▪ Petyon Manning ▪ Billy Sims ▪ Steve Young ▪ Vinny Testaverde ▪ Ty Detmer ▪ Mike Singletary ▪ Doug Flutie ▪ Don McPherson ▪ Danny Wuerffel

SPONSORS: American Airlines ▪ Texas Christian University ▪ Sprint Press ▪ Southwestern Bell ▪ The Fort Worth Club ▪ Ben E. Keith ▪ Fort Worth Star-Telegram ▪ Rolex Watch, U.S.A.

Doak Walker Foundation

CONTACT:
Southwestern Bell—SMU Athletic Forum
6405 Boaz
McFarlin Auditorium, Rm. 308
Dallas, TX 75275

TELEPHONE: (214) 768-4314

WEB: *www.athleticforum.smu.edu/dwa.html*

BACKGROUND INFO: The Doak Walker Awards recognize the best collegiate running back in the nation.

EVENT: Dr Pepper Doak Walker Award Presentation Banquet (Held in January, this event honors the winner of the Doak Walker Award.)

Selection Committee: Roger Staubach ▪ Bob Costas ▪ Drew Pearson ▪ Tony Dorsett ▪ Bob Griese ▪ Darrell Royal ▪ Earl Campbell ▪ Dan Jenkins ▪ Barry Sanders

VIPs HONORED BY INSTITUTION: Ricky Williams ▪ Ron Dayne

SPONSOR: Dr Pepper

Downtown Athletic Club of New York City, Inc. (Heisman Trophy Award Presenter)

CONTACT:
Downtown Athletic Club of New York City, Inc.
19 West Street
New York, NY 10004

TELEPHONE: (212) 425-7000

WEB: *www.heisman.com*

BACKGROUND INFO: The Downtown Athletic Club of New York City is the home of the Heisman Trophy, the most prestigious award in collegiate football.

EVENT: Award Ceremony (Held every December, this event honors the present Heisman Trophy Winner and it is attended by notable individuals from the winner's university as wells as past and present renowned football athletes and members of the press, radio, and television.)

VIP STAFF: William J. Dockery—Downtown Athletic Club President

PAST VIPs WHO HAVE BEEN HONORED: Ron Dayne ▪ Eddie George ▪ Ty Detmer ▪ Doug Flutie ▪ Tony Dorsett ▪ Ricky Williams ▪ Earl Campbell ▪ Barry Sanders ▪ Herschel Walker ▪ Pat Sullivan ▪ Bo Jackson ▪ Desmond Howard ▪ Vinny Testaverde ▪ Marcus Allen ▪ O. J. Simpson

CORPORATE SPONSORS: Time Warner ▪ Chase ▪ Wendy's ▪ Priority Mail ▪ Suzuki ▪ ESPN

Downtown Athletic Club of Orlando, Inc.

CONTACT:
Downtown Athletic Club of Orlando, Inc.
222 S. Westmonte Drive
Altamonte Springs, FL 32714

TELEPHONE: (407) 774-7813

WEB: *www.butkusaward.org*

BACKGROUND INFO: The Downtown Athletic Club of Orlando presents the Butkus Award annually to the top collegiate linebacker and also awards college scholarships to high school scholar-athletes. The DAC of Orlando was formed to support charitable causes and amateur athletes. The Butkus Award is voted upon by twenty-eight members of the media.

NETWORKING SPECIFICS: As the sponsor of the prestigious Butkus Award, the Downtown Athletic Club of Orlando, has many connections to college and professional football, as well as contacts within the community of Orlando.

EVENT: Butkus Award Gala (December, in Orlando; Past winners include Derrick Thomas, Brian Bosworth, and Matt Russell.)

VIP STAFF: Jim Detzel—Chairman of the Board ▪ Shelley Ferguson—Executive Director

CHARITY SUPPORTED: Downtown Athletic Club of Orlando Foundation

CORPORATE SPONSOR: Cooper Tire and Rubber

Football Writers Association of America

CONTACT:
Football Writers Association of America
18652 Vista Del Sol
Dallas, TX 75287

TELEPHONE: (972) 713-6198

WEB: *www.fwaa.com*

BACKGROUND INFO: The Football Writers Association of America votes on and awards the Outland Trophy to the best interior offensive or defensive lineman and the Eddie Robinson/FWAA Coach of the Year Award to the top Division 1-A coach.

NETWORKING SPECIFICS: The Football Writers Association of America is a great place to network with sportswriters and to establish connections within the collegiate football community.

EVENTS: Outland Trophy (Presented in Omaha, Nebraska, in January) ▪ Eddie Robinson Coach of the Year Award (Presented in Phoenix in January)

VIP STAFF: Steve Richardson—Executive Director

CHARITY SUPPORTED: Eddie Robinson Foundation

CORPORATE SPONSOR: America West Airlines

Hockey Hall of Fame

CONTACT:
Hockey Hall of Fame
BCE Place
30 Yonge Street
Toronto, Ontario
Canada M5E 1X8

TELEPHONE: (416) 360-7765
(416) 360-7735

WEB: *www.hhof.com*

EVENTS: Induction Week (Held in mid-November, this five-day event brings the past and present greats of hockey to Toronto. There is a large focus on the interaction between the players and the fans throughout the week's events.)

VIP STAFF: William C. Hay—Chairman, Hockey Hall of Fame ▪ Jeff Denomme—President

VIPs SUPPORTING THE INSTITUTION: Wayne Gretzky ▪ Bobby Orr ▪ Tony Esposito ▪ Gordie Howe ▪ Bobby Hull ▪ Mike Bossy ▪ Maurice Richard ▪ Mario Lemieux ▪ Phil Esposito

Indy Racing League

CONTACT:
Indy Racing League
4565 W. Sixteenth Street
Indianapolis, IN 46222

TELEPHONE: (317) 484-6526

WEB: *www.indyracingleague.com*

VIP STAFF: Anton H. "Tony" George—Founder, President, and CEO ▪ Bob Reif—Senior Vice President, Sales and Marketing and CMO ▪ Brian Barnhart—Director, Racing Operations ▪ Dr. Henry Bock—Director, Medical Services ▪ Phil Casey—Technical Director ▪ Andy Hall—Director, Corporate and Sponsor Relations ▪ Mai Lindstrom—Director, Public Relations

EVENTS: Rotate Every Year
Phoenix International Raceway (March) ▪ Homestead-Miami Speedway (April) ▪ Indy 500 (May) ▪ Texas Motor Speedway (June) ▪ Pikes Peak International Raceway (June) ▪ Richmond International Raceway (June) ▪ Kansas Speedway (July) ▪ Nashville Superspeedway (July) ▪ Gateway International Raceway (August) ▪ Chicagoland Speedway (September) ▪ Kentucky Speedway (September) ▪ Texas Motor Speedway (September)

SPONSORS: Northern Light Technology, Inc. ▪ Coors Brewing Company ▪ MCI WorldCom ▪ Pennzoil ▪ Canon USA ▪ Bridgestone/Firestone, Inc. ▪ Delphi Automotive Systems ▪ Oldsmobile ▪ Nissan Motor Corporation USA ▪ Nortel

International Boxing Federation/United States Boxing Association

CONTACT:
International Boxing Federation/United States Boxing Association
134 Evergreen Place, 9th Floor
East Orange, NJ 07018

TELEPHONE: (973) 414-0300

WEB: *www.ibf-usba-boxing.com*

BACKGROUND INFO: The IBF is one of the big three boxing governance organizations.

EVENT: IBF/USBA Annual Convention (Held in late May and early June, this convention includes meetings of the executive committee of the IBF/USBA as well as a golf tournament and a Meet the Champions Social.)

VIP STAFF: Hiawatha Knight—President/Commissioner ▪ Marian Muhammed—Executive Secretary

International Boxing Hall of Fame

CONTACT:
International Boxing Hall of Fame
1 Hall of Fame Drive
Canastota, NY 13032

TELEPHONE: (315) 697-7095

WEB: *www.ibhof.com*

EVENTS: Induction Weekend (On the second weekend of June, the induction ceremony is attended by past and present inductees as well as today's greats. Following the induction ceremony there are a couple of exciting bouts staged for entertainment.)

VIP STAFF: Ed Brophy—Executive Director, International Boxing Hall of Fame

VIPs SUPPORTING THE INSTITUTION: Muhammad Ali ▪ Joe Frazier ▪ Michael Spinks ▪ Aaron Pryor ▪ Joe Brown ▪ Marvin Hagler ▪ Floyd Patterson ▪ Alexis Arguello ▪ Sugar Ray Leonard ▪ Ken Norton ▪ Archie Moore ▪ Don King

CORPORATE SPONSORS: Everlast Sporting Goods ▪ World Boxing Council ▪ International Boxing Federation ▪ McDonald's ▪ World Boxing Organization National Veteran Boxing Association ▪ World Boxing Federation ▪ Home Box Office ▪ Don King ▪ USA Network ▪ World Boxing Association ▪ Showtime Network ▪ Caesar's Palace ▪ Sports Network

International Tennis Hall of Fame

CONTACT:
International Tennis Hall of Fame
194 Bellevue Avenue
Newport, RI 02840

TELEPHONE: (401) 849-3990

WEB: *www.tennisfame.org*

BACKGROUND INFO: The International Tennis Hall of Fame is dedicated to recognizing achievements in tennis and preserving the essence of the game.

EVENT: Enshrinement Ceremony (In mid-July, this is the best event to meet past and present hall-of-famers.)

VIP STAFF: Mark Stenning—Executive Vice President

VIPs HONORED BY THE INSTITUTION: Margaret Osborne du Pont ▪ Bjorn Borg ▪ Billie Jean Moffitt King ▪ Arthur W. "Bud" Collins, Jr. ▪ Chris Evert ▪ Jimmy Connors ▪ John McEnroe ▪ Ken McGregor ▪ Martina Navratilova ▪ Robert J. Kelleher (USTA President)

CORPORATE SPONSORS: Miller Lite ▪ JVC

Jim Thorpe Association

CONTACT:
Jim Thorpe Athletic Club
PO Box 24045
Oklahoma City, OK 73124

TELEPHONE: (405) 495-4880

WEB: *www.jimthorpeassoc.org*

BACKGROUND INFO: The Jim Thorpe Association promotes sports, good health, academics, and pride in Oklahoma. It awards the Jim Thorpe Award to an outstanding collegiate defensive back and the Jim Thorpe Trophy to the NFL's Most Valuable Player. It also selects members of the Oklahoma Sports Hall of Fame.

NETWORKING SPECIFICS: The Jim Thorpe Association is a connection to the NFL through its Jim Thorpe Trophy and the many charity events it stages in connection with the NFL.

EVENTS: Jim Thorpe Award (December, in Oklahoma City; past winners include Deon Figures, Terrell Buckley, Darryll Lewis, Mark Carrier, Deion Sanders, Bennie Blades, and Rickey Dixon.) ▪ Oklahoma Sports Hall of Fame Inductions ▪ Jim Thorpe Trophy (Past winners include Randall Cunningham, Barry Sanders, Brett Favre, Steve Young, Emmit Smith, Warren Moon, Joe Montana, Jerry Rice, Dan Marino, Walter Payton, Fran Tarkenton, O. J. Simpson, John Unitas, and Frank Gifford.)

CHARITIES SUPPORTED: Ronald McDonald House ▪ United Way ▪ Big Brothers Big Sisters

Ladies Professional Golf Association

CONTACT:
LPGA
100 International Golf Drive
Daytona Beach, FL 32124

TELEPHONE: (904) 274-6200

WEB: *www.lpga.com*

BACKGROUND INFO: The LPGA is the female equivalent of the PGA. The top names in lady's golfing are associated with the LPGA. With over forty stops on the tournament schedule, the LPGA is a hard organization to miss.

EVENTS: The Office Depot Tournament (Held in January) ▪ Subaru Memorial of Naples (Held in January) ▪ Los Angeles Women's Championship (Held in February) ▪ Cup Noodles Hawaiian Ladies Open (Held in February) ▪ Australian Ladies Masters (Held in February) ▪ LPGA Takefuji Classic (Held in March) ▪ Welch's/Circle K Championship (Held in March) ▪ Standard Register PING (Held in March) ▪ Nabisco Championship (Held in March) ▪ Longs Drugs Challenge (Held in April) ▪ Chic-fil-A Charity Championship (Held in April) ▪ The Phillips Invitational Honoring Harvey Penick (Held in May) ▪ Electrolux USA Championship (Held in May) ▪ Firstar LPGA Classic (Held in May) ▪ LPGA Corning Classic (Held in May) ▪ Kathy Ireland Greens.com LPGA Classic (Held in June) ▪ Wegmans Rochester International (Held in June) ▪ Evian Masters (Held in June) ▪ McDonald's LPGA Championship (Held in June) ▪ ShopRite LPGA Classic (Held in June and July) ▪ Jamie Farr Kroger Classic (Held in July) ▪ Japan Airlines Big Apple Classic (Held in July) ▪ U.S. Open Women's Championship (Held in July) ▪ Giant Eagle LPGA Classic (Held in July) ▪ Michelob Light LPGA Classic (Held in August) ▪ Du Maurier Classic (Held in August) ▪ Weetabix Women's British Open (Held in August) ▪ Oldsmobile Classic (Held in August) ▪ State Farm Rail Classic (Held in September) ▪ First Union Betsy King Classic (Held in September) ▪ The Safeway LPGA Golf Championship (Held in September) ▪ New Albany Golf Classic (Held in September and October) ▪ The Solheim Cup (Held in October) ▪ Samsung World Championship (Held in October) ▪ AFLAC Champions Presented by Southern Living (Held in October) ▪ U.S.-Japan Team Championship (Held in October) ▪ Mizuno Classic (Held in November) ▪ PageNet Championship (Held in November) ▪ Team Match Play Championship (Held in December) ▪ Wendy's Three-Tour Challenge (Held in December)

VIPs ASSOCIATED WITH THE ORGANIZATION: Vince Gill ▪ Amy Grant ▪ Kathy Ireland

SPONSORS: State Farm Insurance Companies ▪ Subaru ▪ Ronald McDonald House Charities ▪ Electrolux ▪ Crowne Plaza Hotels and Resorts ▪ Century 21 Fine Homes and Estates ▪ LiFizz Effervescent Vitamins ▪ BearCom ▪ Snack Well's ▪ General Mills

CHARITIES SUPPORTED: The Susan G. Komen Foundation ▪ Ronald McDonald House Charities

Major League Baseball

CONTACT:

Office of the Commissioner of Baseball
245 Park Ave., 31st floor
New York, NY 10167

TELEPHONE: (212) 931-7800

WEB: *www.majorleaguebaseball.com*

VIP PERSONNEL: Allan H. (Bud) Selig—Commissioner

ORGANIZATIONS ASSOCIATED WITH THE INSTITUTION:

Anaheim Angels
Edison Field
2000 Gene Autry Way
Anaheim, CA 92806
TEL: (714) 940-2000
Michael Eisner—President
Mike Scioscia—Manager

Atlanta Braves
Turner Field
755 Hank Aaron Drive
Atlanta, GA 30315
TEL: (404) 522-7630
William C. Bartholomay—President
Bobby Cox—Manager

Boston Red Sox
Fenway Park
4 Yawkey Way
Boston, MA 02215-3496
TEL: (617) 267-9440
John L. Harrington—President
Jimy Williams—Manager

Chicago White Sox
Comiskey Park
333 West Thirty-fifth Street
Chicago, IL 60616
TEL: (312) 674-1000
Jerry M. Reinsdorf—President
Jerry Manuel—Manager

Arizona Diamondbacks
Bank One Ballpark
401 East Jefferson Street
Phoenix, AZ 85001
TEL: (602) 462-6000
Jerry Colangelo—President
Buck Showalter—Manager

Baltimore Orioles
Oriole Park at Camden Yards
333 West Camden Street
Baltimore, MD 21201
TEL: (410) 685-9800
Peter Angelos—President
Mike Hargrove—Manager

Chicago Cubs
Wrigley Field
1060 West Addison
Chicago, IL 60613
TEL: (773) 404-2827
Andy MacPhail—President
Don Baylor—Manager

Cincinnati Reds
Cinergy Field
100 Cinergy Field
Cincinnati, OH 45202
TEL: (513) 421-4510
Carl Lindner—President
Jack McKeon—Manager

Cleveland Indians
Jacobs Field
2401 Ontario Street
Cleveland, OH 44115
TEL: (216) 420-4200
Lawrence J. Dolan—President
Charlie Manuel—Manager

Detroit Tigers
Comerica Park
2100 Woodward Avenue
Detroit, MI 46201
TEL: (313) 962-4000
Michael Llitch—President
Phil Garner—Manager

Houston Astros
Enron Field
501 Crawford Street
Houston, TX 77002
TEL: (713) 799-9500
Drayton McLane, Jr.—President
Larry Dierker—Manager

Los Angeles Dodgers
Dodger Stadium
1000 Elysian Park Avenue
Los Angeles, CA 90012-1199
TEL: (323) 224-1500
Rupert Murdoch—President
Davey Johnson—Manager

Minnesota Twins
Metrodome
34 Kirby Puckett Place
Minneapolis, MN 55415
TEL: (612) 375-1366
Carl Polhad—President
Tom Kelly—Manager

New York Mets
Shea Stadium
123-01 Roosevelt Avenue
Flushing, NY 11368
TEL: (718) 507-6387
Fred Wilson—President
Bobby Valentine—Manager

Colorado Rockies
Coors Field
2001 Blake Street
Denver, CO 80205
TEL: (303) 292-0200
Jerry McMorris—President
Buddy Bell—Manager

Florida Marlins
Pro Player Stadium
2267 NW 199th Street
Miami, FL 33056
TEL: (303) 626-7400
John Henry—President
John Boles—Manager

Kansas City Royals
Kauffman Stadium
1 Royal Way
Kansas City, MO 64141-6969
TEL: (816) 921-8000
David D. Glass—President
Tony Muser—Manager

Milwaukee Brewers
Milwaukee County Stadium
PO Box 3099
Milwaukee, WI 53201-3099
TEL: (414) 933-4114
Wendy Selig—President
Davey Lopes—Manager

Montreal Expos
Olympic Stadium
4549 Avenue Pierre de Couber-
tin
Montreal, Quebec H1V3N7
TEL: (514) 253-3434
Jeffrey Loria—President
Felipe Alou—Manager

New York Yankees
Yankee Stadium
Bronx, NY 10451
TEL: (718) 293-4300
George Steinbrenner—President
Joe Torre—Manager

Oakland Athletics
Oakland Colisuem
7677 Oakport, Suite 200
Oakland, CA 94621
TEL: (510) 638-4900
Steven Schott—President
Art Howe—Manager

Pittsburgh Pirates
Three Rivers Stadium
600 Stadium Circle
Pittsburgh, PA 15212
TEL: (412) 323-5000
Kevin S. McClatchy—President
Gene Lamont—Manager

San Diego Padres
Qualcomm Stadium
8880 Rio San Diego Drive, Suite
400
San Diego, CA 92112-2000
TEL: (619) 881-6500
John Moores—President
Bruce Bochy—Manager

Seattle Mariners
Safeco Field
PO Box 4100
Seattle, WA 98104
TEL: (206) 346-4000
John W. Ellis—President
Lou Pinella—Manager

Texas Rangers
The Ballpark at Arlington
1000 Ballpark Way
Arlington, TX 76011
TEL: (727) 273-5222
J. Thomas Scheiffer—President
Johnny Oates—Manager

Philadelphia Phillies
Veterans Stadium
3501 South Broad Street
Philadelphia, PA 19148
TEL: (215) 463-6000
David Montgomery—President
Terry Francona—Manager

St. Louis Cardinals
Busch Stadium
250 Stadium Plaza
St. Louis, MO 63102
TEL: (314) 421-3060
Mark Lamping—President
Tony La Russa—Manager

San Francisco Giants
Pac Bell Park
24 Willie Mays Plaza
San Francisco, CA 94107
TEL: (415) 972-2000
Peter Magowan—President
Dusty Baker—Manager

Tampa Bay Devil Rays
Tropicana Field
One Tropicana Drive
St. Petersburg, FL 33705
TEL: (813) 825-3137
Vincent Naimoli—President
Larry Rothschild—Manager

Toronto Blue Jays
Skydome
1 Blue Jays Way, Suite 3200
Toronto, Ontario M5V1J1
TEL: (416) 341-1000
Sam Pollock—President
Jim Fregosi—Manager

CHARITY SUPPORTED: Boys and Girls Clubs of America

Maxwell Football Club

CONTACT:
Robert W. Maxwell Football Club
303 E. Church Road
King of Prussia, PA 19406

TELEPHONE: (610) 277-8900

BACKGROUND INFO: The Maxwell Football Club awards the Maxwell Award to the outstanding collegiate football player of the year. The winner is selected by coaches, members of the media, and the Maxwell Football Club.

NETWORKING SPECIFICS: Since Maxwell Football Club members are given the right to vote on the award, they have a tremendous influence on determining the winner. Belonging to the Maxwell Football Club would be a great way to network with important people in college football.

EVENT: Maxwell Award (Given in February in Philadelphia)

VIP STAFF: Robert Clark—Executive Director ▪ Raymond R. Stevens, Jr.—Treasurer

Motorsports Hall of Fame

CONTACT:
Motorsports Hall of Fame
PO Box 194
Novi, MI 48376

TELEPHONE: (800) 250-RACE

WEB: www.mshf.com

EVENT: Induction Ceremony (Held in early June, this event consists of a VIP and a general reception followed by dinner and the Induction Ceremony. The racing greats of today as well as those of the past attend this event.)

VIP STAFF: Mario Andretti—Board of Trustees

VIPs SUPPORTING INSTITUTION: Don Prudhomme ▪ Mario Andretti ▪ Dan Gourney ▪ Cale Yarborough ▪ Rick Mears ▪ Al Unser ▪ Bruce McLaren ▪ Ned Jarrett ▪ A. J. Foyt ▪ Bobby Unser ▪ Richard Petty

SPONSORS: Speedvision ▪ Chevrolet Motor Division ▪ NASCAR ▪ Ford ▪ Pontiac Racing ▪ Mopar Performance ▪ Goodyear ▪ Firestar

NASCAR

CONTACT:
NASCAR
1801 West International Speedway Boulevard
Daytona Beach, FL 32114

TELEPHONE: (904) 253-0611

WEB: www.nascar.com

VIP STAFF: Bill France, Jr.—CEO ▪ Mike Helton—COO

EVENTS:

NASCAR Winston Cup Series Special: Bud Shootout (February, Daytona International Speedway) ▪ Gatorade 125s (February, Daytona International Speedway) ▪ Daytona 500 (February, Daytona International Speedway) ▪ Dura-Lube/Kmart 400 (February, North Carolina Speedway) ▪ Carsdirect.com 400 (March, Las Vegas Motor Speedway) ▪ Cracker Barrel Old Country Store 500 (March, Atlanta Motor Speedway) ▪ Mall.com 400 (March, Darlington Raceway) ▪ Food City 500 (March, Bristol Motor

Speedway) ▪ DIRECTV 500 (April, Texas Motor Speedway) ▪ Goody's Body Pain 500 (April, Martins-ville Speedway) ▪ DieHard 500 (April, Talladega Superspeedway) ▪ NAPA Auto Parts 500 (April, Cali-fornia Speedway) ▪ Pontiac Excitement 400 (May, Richmond International Raceway) ▪ The Winston (May, Lowe's Motor Speedway) ▪ Coca-Cola 600 (May, Lowe's Motor Speedway) ▪ MBNA Platinum 500 (June, Dover Downs International Speedway) ▪ Kmart 400 (June, Michigan Speedway) ▪ Pocono 500 (June, Pocono Raceway) ▪ Save Mart/Kragen 350K (June, Sears Point Raceway) ▪ Pepsi 400 (July, Daytona International Speedway) ▪ thatlook.com 300 (July, New Hampshire International Speed-way) ▪ Pennsylvania 500 (July, Pocono Raceway) ▪ Brickyard 400 (August, Indianapolis Motor Speed-way) ▪ Global Crossing @ the Glen (August, Watkins Glen International) ▪ Pepsi 400 Presented by Meijer (August, Michigan Speedway) ▪ Goracing.com 500 (August, Bristol Motor Speedway) ▪ Southern 500 (September, Darlington Raceway) ▪ Chevrolet Monte Carlo 400 (September, Richmond Interna-tional Speedway) ▪ New Hampshire 300 (September, New Hampshire International Speedway) ▪ MBNA.com 400 (September, Dover Downs International Speedway) ▪ NAPA Autocare 500 (October, Martinsville Speedway) ▪ UAW-GM Quality 500 (October, Lowe's Motor Speedway) ▪ Winston 500 (October, Talladega Superspeedway) ▪ Pop Secret Microwave Popcorn 400 (October, North Carolina Speedway) ▪ Checker Auto Parts/Dura Lube 500k (November, Phoenix International Raceway) ▪ Penn-zoil 400 (November, Homestead-Miami Speedway) ▪ NAPA 500 (November, Atlanta Motor Speedway)

NASCAR Busch Series: NAPA Auto Parts 300 (February, Daytona International Speedway) ▪ Alltel 200 (February, North Carolina Speedway) ▪ Sam's Town 300 (March, Las Vegas Motor Speedway) ▪ Aaron's 312 (March, Atlanta Motor Speedway) ▪ Suncom 200 (March, Darlington Raceway) ▪ Cheez-It 250 (March, Bristol Motor Speedway) ▪ Albertson's 300 Presented by Pop Secret (April, Texas Motor Speedway) ▪ BellSouth Mobility 320 (April, Nashville Speedway USA) ▪ Touchstone Energy 300 (April, Talladega Superspeedway) ▪ Auto Club 300 (April, California Speedway) ▪ Hardee's 250 (May, Rich-mond International Raceway) ▪ Busch 200 (May, New Hampshire International Speedway) ▪ CarQuest Auto Parts 300 (May, Lowe's Motor Speedway) ▪ MBNA Platinum 200 (June, Dover Downs International Speedway) ▪ Textilease Medique 300 (June, South Boston Speedway) ▪ Myrtle Beach 250 (June, Myrtle Beach Speedway) ▪ Lysol 200 (June, Watkins Glen International) ▪ Sears DieHard 250 (July, The Milwaukee Mile) ▪ Econo Lodge 200 (July, Nazareth Speedway) ▪ NAPA AutoCare 250 (July, Pikes Peak International Raceway) ▪ CarQuest Auto Parts 250 (July, Gateway International Raceway) ▪ Kroger 200 (August, Indianapolis Raceway Park) ▪ NAPAOnline.com 250 (August, Michigan Speedway) ▪ Food City 250 (August, Bristol Motor Speedway) ▪ Dura Lube 200 (September, Darlington Raceway) ▪ Autolite Platinum 250 (September, Richmond International Raceway) ▪ MBNA.com 200 (September, Dover Downs International Speedway) ▪ All Pro Bumper to Bumper 300 (October, Lowe's Motor Speedway) ▪ Rockingham 200 (October, North Carolina Motor Speedway) ▪ Sam's Town 250 (October, Memphis Motorsports Park) ▪ Outback Steakhouse 200 (November, Phoenix International Raceway) ▪ Hot-Wheels.com 300 (November, Homestead-Miami Speedway)

CHARITY SUPPORTED: Disabled American Veterans

National Basketball Association

CONTACT:
National Basketball Association
Olympic Tower
645 Fifth Avenue
New York, NY 10022

TELEPHONE: (212) 407-8000

WEB: *www.nba.com*

VIP STAFF: David Stern—NBA Commissioner

TEAMS ASSOCIATED WITH THE NBA:

Atlanta Hawks
One CNN Center, Suite 405,
  South Tower
Atlanta, GA 30303
TEL: (404) 827-DUNK
Stan Kasten—President
Pete Babcock—General Manager
Lenny Wilkens—Head Coach

Charlotte Hornets
Charlotte Coliseum
100 Paul Buck Blvd.
Charlotte, NC 28217
TEL: (704) 357-4801
T. R. Dunn—Head Coach

Cleveland Cavaliers
Gund Arena
One Center Court
Cleveland, OH 44115
TEL: (216) 420-CAVS
    (800) 332-CAVS
Jim Paxson—General Manager
Randy Wittman—Head Coach

Denver Nuggets
Pepsi Center
1635 Clay Street
Denver, CO 80204
TEL: (303) 405-1212
Dan Issel—President/Head
  Coach

Boston Celtics
Fleet Center
151 Merrimac St., 4th Floor
Boston, MA 02114
TEL: (617) 523-3030
Rick Pitino—Head Coach

Chicago Bulls
United Center
1901 West Madison Street
Chicago, IL 60612-2459
TEL: (312) 455-4000
Jerry Reinsdorf—Chairman
Tim Floyd—Head Coach

Dallas Mavericks
Reunion Arena
777 Sports Street
Dallas, TX 75207
TEL: (972) 988-DUNK
Mark Cuban—Owner
Terdema Ussery—President/
  CEO
Don Nelson—Head Coach

Detroit Pistons
The Palace of Auburn Hills
Two Championship Drive
Auburn Hills, MI 48326
TEL: (248) 377-0100
George Irvine—Head Coach

Golden State Warriors
Arena in Oakland
7000 Coliseum Way
Oakland, CA 94621
TEL: (888) GSW-HOOP
Garry St. Jean—Head Coach/
  GM

Indiana Pacers
One Conseco Court
125 S. Pennsylvania Street
Indianapolis, IN 46204
TEL: (317) 917-2500
Larry Bird—Head Coach

Los Angeles Lakers
Staples Center
1111 S. Figueroa Street
Los Angeles, CA 90015
Jerry Buss—Owner/President
Mitch Kupchak—General Manager
Phil Jackson—Head Coach

Milwaukee Bucks
1001 North Fourth Street
Milwaukee, WI 53203
TEL: (414) 227-0500
George Karl—Head Coach
Ernie Grunfeld—General Manager

New Jersey Nets
390 Murray Hill Parkway
East Rutherford, NJ 07073
TEL: (800) 7NJ-NETS
Michael Rowe—President
John Nash—General Manager
Don Casey—Head Coach

Orlando Magic
8701 Maitland Summit Blvd.
Orlando, FL 32810
TEL: (407) 89-MAGIC
Bob Vander Weide—President/
  CEO
RDV Sports (Parent Company of
  Orlando Magic)
John Gabriel—General Manager
Doc Rivers—Head Coach

Houston Rockets
2 Greenway Plaza, Suite 400
Clutch City, TX 77046-3865
TEL: (713) 627-DUNK
Leslie Alexander—Owner
Rudy Tomjanovich—Head Coach

Los Angeles Clippers
Staples Center
1111 S. Figueroa Street
Los Angeles, CA 90015
TEL: (213) 742-PARK
Jim Todd—Head Coach
Kareem Abdul-Jabbar—Assis-
  tant Coach

Miami Heat
AmericanAirlines Arena
Miami, FL 33131
Marilyn Arison—Owner
Pat Riley—President/Head
  Coach

Minnesota Timberwolves
600 First Avenue
Minneapolis, MN 55403
TEL: (612) 337-DUNK
Flip Saunders—Head Coach/
  GM

New York Knicks
Madison Square Garden
Two Pennsylvania Plaza
New York, NY 10121
Scott Layden—General Manager
  Jeff Van Gundy—Head Coach

Philadelphia 76ers
First Union Center
3601 South Broad St.
Philadelphia, PA 19148
TEL: (215) 336-3600
Pat Croce—President
Billy King—General Manager
Larry Brown—Head Coach

Phoenix Suns
201 East Jefferson Street
Phoenix, AZ 85001
TEL: (602) 379-7867
Bryan Colangelo—President/
  GM
Jerry Colangelo—CEO
Scott Skiles—Head Coach

Sacramento Kings
ARCO Arena
One Sports Parkway
Sacramento, CA 95834
TEL: (916) 928-6900
Joe & Gavin Maloof—Owners

John Thomas—President
Rick Adelman—Head Coach

Seattle Supersonics
190 Queen Anne Avenue North
Box 900911
Seattle, WA 98109-9711
TEL: (206) 283-DUNK
Paul Westphal—Head Coach

Utah Jazz
Delta Center
301 West South Temple
Salt Lake City, UT 84101
TEL: (801) 355-DUNK
Larry Miller—Owner
Dennis Haslam—President
Jerry Sloan—Head Coach

Washington Wizards
MCI Center
601 F Street NW
Washington, DC 20004
TEL: (202) 661-5050
Abe Pollin—Majority Owner
Michael Jordan—President of
  Basketball Operations
Darrell Walker—Head Coach

Portland Trailblazers
1 Center Court
Portland, OR 97227

TEL: (503) 224-4400
Paul Allen—Owner
Mike Dunleavy—Head Coach

San Antonio Spurs
Alamodome
100 Montana Street
San Antonio, TX 78203
TEL: (210) 554-7700
Gregg Popovich—Head Coach

Toronto Raptors
Air Canada Centre
40 Bay Street
Toronto, Ontario
Canada
TEL: (416) 366-DUNK
Richard Peddie—President/CEO
Glen Grunwald—General Man-
  ager
Butch Carter—Head Coach

Vancouver Grizzlies
General Motors Place
800 Griffiths Way
Vancouver, British Columbia
Canada V6B 6G1
TEL: (604) 899-4667
Stu Jackson—President/GM
Lionel Hollins—Head Coach

National Basketball Hall of Fame

CONTACT:

The Basketball Hall of Fame
PO Box 179
1150 West Columbus Avenue
Springfield, MA 01101-0179

TELEPHONE: (413) 781-6500

WEB: *www.hoophall.com*

EVENTS: Enshrinement Events (Held at the beginning of October, these events include the Tip-Off Classic Celebrity Golf Tournament, the Hall of Famer Reunion, the Enshrinement Dinner, and the Enshrinement Ceremony, all of which are attended by past and present inductees of the Basketball Hall of Fame.)

VIP STAFF: Joe O'Brien—Executive Director

VIPs SUPPORTING THE INSTITUTION: Julius "Dr. J." Erving ▪ Larry Bird ▪ Kevin McHale ▪ Bill Bradley ▪ Bob Cousy ▪ Kareem Abdul-Jabbar ▪ Bill Russell ▪ Elgin Baylor ▪ Chuck Daly ▪ Bob Lanier ▪ Bob Cousy

National Cutting Horse Association

CONTACT:

National Cutting Horse Association
4704 Hwy. 377 South
Fort Worth, TX 76116-8805

TELEPHONE: (817) 244-6188

WEB: *www.nchacutting.com*

ORGANIZATION'S FOCUS: Cutting horses

BACKGROUND INFO: The National Cutting Horse Association has nearly 13,000 members. It promotes competition and standardizes rules for cutting horse events. The NCHA holds six major events each year. The Futurity, the Super Stakes, and the Summer Spectacular make up the organization's Triple Crown series.

EVENTS: John Deere World Championship Finals (February, in Houston, Texas) ▪ Chevy Trucks Eastern National Championship (March, in Jackson, Mississippi) ▪ Super Stakes Super Stakes Classic (April, in Fort Worth, Texas) ▪ Chevy Trucks Western National Championship (Late April through early May in Ogden, Utah) ▪ Annual Convention (June) ▪ Summer Spectacular (July, in Fort Worth, Texas) ▪ Championship Futurity (Late November through early December in Fort Worth, Texas) ▪ Multiple Sclerosis Celebrity/Legends/Youth Cutting Event (Held in Fort Worth during Futurity)

NETWORKING SPECIFICS: Networking with members of the NCHA is easiest in and around the city of Fort Worth, home of its headquarters and Triple Crown events. Connections with community leaders should help you to gain connections with the NCHA as well.

VIP STAFF: Jim Milner—President ▪ Lindy Burch—President Elect

VIPs WHO HAVE ATTENDED NCHA EVENTS: Joe Montana ▪ Keith Carradine ▪ Sheree Wilson ▪ Eric Bjornson ▪ Jason Garrett ▪ Daryl Johnston ▪ Fred Strickland ▪ Rusty Greer ▪ Tanya Tucker ▪ Barry Corbin ▪ Annie Lockhart ▪ Chris Boniol ▪ Dale Hellestrae ▪ Jim Schwantz ▪ George Teague ▪ Dave Appleton (Former World Rodeo All-Around Champion)

CHARITY SUPPORTED: Multiple Sclerosis Society

National Football League

CONTACT:
National Football League
410 Park Ave.
New York, NY 10022

TELEPHONE: (212) 450-2000

WEB: *www.nfl.com*

VIP PERSONNEL: Paul Tagliabu—NFL Commissioner

ORGANIZATIONS ASSOCIATED WITH THE NFL:

Arizona Cardinals
PO Box 888
Phoenix, AZ 85001-0888
TEL: (602) 379-0101
William B. Vidwell—President
Bob Ferguson—General Manager
Vince Tobin—Head Coach

Baltimore Ravens
11001 Owings Mills Boulevard
Owings Mills, MD 21117
TEL: (410) 654-6200
Arthur Modell—President/
Owner
Brian Billick—Head Coach

Carolina Panthers
800 South Mint Street
Charlotte, NC 28202-1502
TEL: (704) 358-7800
Jerry Richardson—Founder/
Owner
Mark Richardson—President
George Seifert—Head Coach

Cincinnati Bengals
One Bengals Drive
Cincinnati, OH 45204
TEL: (513) 621-3550
Michael Brown—President
Bruce Coslet—Head Coach

Dallas Cowboys
One Cowboys Parkway
Irving, TX 75063
TEL: (972) 556-9900
Jerry Jones—Owner/President/
General Manager
Dave Campo—Head Coach

Atlanta Falcons
One Falcon Place
Suwanee, GA 30024
TEL: (404) 223-8444
Taylor Smith—President
Harold Richardson—General
Manager
Dan Reeves—Head Coach

Buffalo Bills
One Bills Drive
Orchard Park, NY 14127
TEL: (877) BB-TICKS
Ralph Wilson, Jr.—President
Wade Phillips—Head Coach

Chicago Bears
1000 Football Drive
Lake Forest, IL 60045
TEL: (847) 615-BEAR
Ted Phillips—President/CEO
Dick Jauron—Head Coach

Cleveland Browns
76 Lou Graza Boulevard
Berea, OH 44017
TEL: (440) 891-5000
Alfred Lerner—Owner
Carmen Policy—President
Chris Palmer—Head Coach

Denver Broncos
13655 Broncos Parkway
Englewood, CO 80112
TEL: (303) 433-7466
Pat Bowlen—President/CEO
John Beake—General Manager
Mike Shanahan—Head Coach

Detroit Lions
1200 Featherstone Road
Pontiac, MI 48342
TEL: (248) 335-4151
William Clay Ford—President
Bobby Ross—Head Coach

Indianapolis Colts
7001 West 56th Street
Indianapolis, IN 46254
TEL: (317) 297-2658
James Irsay—Owner/CEO
Bill Polian—President
Jim Mora—Head Coach

Kansas City Chiefs
One Arrowhead Drive
Kansas City, MO 64129
TEL: (816) 920-9300
Lamar Hunt—Founder
Carl Peterson—President/CEO/
General Manager
Gunther Cunningham—Head
Coach

Minnesota Vikings
9520 Viking Drive
Eden Prairie, MN 55344
TEL: (612) 828-6500
Red McCombs—Owner
Gary Woods—President
Tim Connolly—General Manager
Dennis Green—Head Coach

New Orleans Saints
5800 Airline Drive
New Orleans, LA 70003
TEL: (504) 731-1700
Tom Benson—Owner
Randy Mueller—General Manager
Jim Haslett—Head Coach

Green Bay Packers
1265 Lombardi Avenue
Green Bay, WI 54304
TEL: (920) 496-5719
Bob Harlan—President/CEO
Mike Sherman—Head Coach

Jacksonville Jaguars
ALLTEL Stadium
One ALLTEL Stadium Place
Jacksonville, FL 32202
TEL: (904) 633-2000
Wayne Weaver—President/CEO
Tom Coughlin—Head Coach

Miami Dolphins
7500 SW Thirtieth Street
Davie, FL 33329
TEL: (305) 620-2578
H. Wayne Huizenga—Owner
Eddie J. Jones—President
Dave Wannstedt—Head Coach

New England Patriots
Foxboro Stadium
Route 1
Foxboro, MA 02035
TEL: (508) 543-8200
Robert Kraft—President/CEO
Bill Belichick—Head Coach

N.Y. Giants
Giants Stadium
East Rutherford, NJ 07073
TEL: (201) 935-8222
Wellington Mara—President/Co-
CEO
Preston Robert Tisch—Chair-
man/Co-CEO
Ernie Accorsi—General
Manager
Jim Fassel—Head Coach

N.Y. Jets
1000 Fulton Avenue
Hempstead, NY 11550
TEL: (516) 560-8200
Robert Wood Johnson IV—
Owner
Steve Gutman—President
Al Groh—Head Coach

Philadelphia Eagles
3501 South Broad Street
Philadelphia, PA 19148
TEL: (215) 463-5500
Jeffrey Lurie—Owner/CEO
Andy Reid—Head Coach

St. Louis Rams
One Rams Way
St. Louis, MO 63045
TEL: (314) 982-7267
Georgia Frontiere—Owner
Stan Kroenke—Owner
John Shaw—President
Mike Martz—Head Coach

San Francisco 49ers
4949 Centennial Boulevard
Santa Clara, CA 95054
TEL: (408) 656-4900
Edward J. DeBartolo Corp.—
Owner
Steve Mariucci—Head Coach

Tampa Bay Buccaneers
One Buccaneer Place
Tampa, FL 33607
TEL: (800) 282-0683
Malcolm Glazer—Owner/Presi-
dent
Rich McKay—General Manager
Tony Dungy—Head Coach

Washington Redskins
21300 Redskin Park Drive
Ashburn, VA 20147
TEL: (301) 276-6060.
Daniel Snyder—Owner
Norv Turner—Head Coach

Oakland Raiders
1220 Harbor Bay Parkway
Alameda, CA 94502
TEL: (510) 615-1875
Al Davis—Owner
Amy Trask—CEO
John Gruden—Head Coach

Pittsburgh Steelers
300 Stadium Circle
Pittsburgh, PA 15212
TEL: (412) 323-0300
Daniel Rooney—President
Bill Cowher—Head Coach

San Diego Chargers
PO Box 609609
San Diego, CA 92160
TEL: (619) 280-2121
Dean A. Spanos—President
Bobby Beathard—General Man-
ager
Mike Riley—Head Coach

Seattle Seahawks
11220 NE 53rd Street
Kirkland, WA 98033
TEL: (888) NFL-HAWK
Bob Whitsitt—President
Mike Holmgren—Head Coach/
GM

Tennessee Titans
460 Great Circle Road
Nashville, TN 37228
TEL: (888) 313-8326
K. S. Adams, Jr.—President
Floyd Reese—General Manager
Jeff Fisher—Head Coach

CHARITIES SUPPORTED: United Way ▪ Susan G. Komen Foundation

National Hockey League

CONTACT:

National Hockey League
1251 Avenue of the Americas
New York, NY 10020

TELEPHONE: (212) 789-2000

WEB: *www.nhl.com*

VIP STAFF: Gary Bettman—NHL Commissioner

ORGANIZATIONS ASSOCIATED WITH THE INSTITUTION:

Anaheim Mighty Ducks
Disney Sports Enterprises Inc.
2695 East Katella Avenue
PO Box 61077
Anaheim, CA 92803
TEL: (714) 704-2500
Pierre Gauthier—General Manager
Craig Hartsburg—Head Coach

Boston Bruins
One FleetCenter, Suite 250
Boston, MA 02114-1303
TEL: (617) 624-1750
Harry Sinden—President/GM
Pat Burns—Head Coach

Calgary Flames
Canadian Airlines Saddledome
PO Box 1540, Station M
TEL: (403) 777-4630
Calgary, Alberta T2P 3B9
Al Coates—General Manager
Brian Sutter—Head Coach

Chicago Blackhawks
United Center
1901 W. Madison Street
Chicago, IL 60612
TEL: (312) 455-4500
Bob Murray—General Manager
Lorne Molleken—Head Coach

Atlanta Thrashers
Atlanta Hockey Club, Inc.
One CNN Center
13 South
Atlanta, GA 30303
TEL: (404) 584-PUCK
Don Waddell—General Manager
Curt Fraser—Head Coach

Buffalo Sabres
Marine Midland Arena
One Seymour H. Knox III Plaza
Buffalo, NY 14203
TEL: (716) 855-4444
Darcy Regier—General Manager
Lindy Ruff—Head Coach

Carolina Hurricanes
KTR Hockey Limited Partnership
5000 Aerial Center, Suite 100
Morrisville, NC 27560
TEL: (919) 467-7825
Jim Rutherford—General Manager
Paul Maurice—Head Coach

Colorado Avalanche
Pepsi Center
100 Chopper Place
Denver, CO 80204
TEL: (303) 405-1111
Pierre Lacroix—President/GM
Bob Hartley—Head Coach

Columbus Blue Jackets
JMAC Hockey, LLP
150 East Wilson Bridge Rd.,
    Suite 230
Worthington, OH 43085
TEL: (800) NHL-COLS
Doug MacLean—President/GM

Detroit Redwings
Joe Louis Arena
600 Civic Center
Detroit, MI 48226
TEL: (810) 645-6666
Ken Holland—General Manager
William "Scotty" Bowman—
    Head Coach

Florida Panthers
National Car Rental Center
One Panthers Parkway
Sunrise, FL 33323
TEL: (954) 835-8000
Bryan Murray—General Manager
Terry Murray—Head Coach

Minnesota Wild
Piper Jaffray Plaza
444 Cedar Street, Suite 900
St. Paul, MN 55101
TEL: (651) 222-9453
Bob Naegele, Jr.—Owner

Nashville Predators
501 Broadway
Nashville, TN 37203
TEL: (615) 770-PUCK
David Poile—General Manager
Barry Trotz—Head Coach

Dallas Stars
Dallas Stars Hockey Club, Inc.
Dr Pepper StarCenter
211 Cowboys Parkway
Irving, TX 75063
TEL: (214) GO-STARS
Bob Gainey—General Manager
Ken Hitchcock—Head Coach

Edmonton Oilers
Edmonton Oilers Hockey Club
11230 110th Street
Edmonton, Alberta T5G 3G8
TEL: (403) 414-4000
Glen Sather—President/GM
Kevin Lowe—Head Coach

Los Angeles Kings
STAPLES Center
1111 S. Figueroa Street
Los Angeles, CA 90015
TEL: (888) KINGS-LA
Dave Taylor—General Manager
Andy Murray—Head Coach

Montreal Canadiens
Le Centre Molson
1260 de La Gauchetière St. W
Montrèal, Quèbec H3B 5E8
TEL: (514) 790-1245
Réjean Houle—General Manager
Alain Vigneault—Head Coach

New Jersey Devils
Continental Airlines Arena
50 Route 120 North
PO Box 504
East Rutherford, NJ 07073
TEL: (800) NJ-DEVIL
Lou Lamoriello—President/GM
Robbie Ftorek—Head Coach

New York Islanders
Nassau Veterans Memorial Coliseum
Uniondale, NY 11553
TEL: (888) ETM-TIXS
Mike Milbury—General Manager
Butch Goring—Head Coach

Ottawa Senators
Corel Centre
1000 Prom. Palladium Drive
Kanata, ON K2V 1A4
TEL: (800) 444-SENS
Marshall Johnston—General Manager
Jacques Martin—Head Coach

Phoenix Coyotes
Phoenix Coyotes Hockey Club
9375 E. Bell Road
Scottsdale, AZ 85257
TEL: (602) 503-5555
Bobby Smith—General Manager
Bobby Francis—Head Coach
Wayne Gretzky—Partial Owner

St. Louis Blues
Kiel Center
1401 Clark Avenue
St. Louis, MO 63103-2709
TEL: (314) 241-1888
Larry Pleau—General Manager
Joel Quenneville—Head Coach

Tampa Bay Lightning
Ice Palace
401 Channelside Drive
Tampa, FL 33602
TEL: (813) 301-2500
Rick Dudley—General Manager
Steve Ludzik—Head Coach

Vancouver Canucks
General Motors Place
800 Griffiths Way
Vancouver, BC V6B 6G1
TEL: (604) 280-4400
Brian Burke—General Manager
Marc Crawford—Head Coach

New York Rangers
Madison Square Garden
2 Penn Plaza
New York, NY 10121
TEL: (212) 308-NYRS
Neil Smith—General Manager
John Muckler—Head Coach

Philadelphia Flyers
First Union Center
3601 South Broad Street
Philadelphia, PA 19148
TEL: (215) 336-2000
Bob Clarke—President/GM
Roger Neilson—Head Coach

Pittsburgh Penguins
Civic Arena
66 Mario Lemieux Place
Pittsburgh, PA 15219
TEL: (412) 323-1919
Craig Patrick—General Manager
Kevin Constantine—Head Coach

San Jose Sharks
San Jose Arena
525 West Santa Clara Street
San Jose, CA 95113
TEL: (800) 225-2277
Dean Lombardi—General Manager
Darryl John Sutter—Head Coach

Toronto Maple Leafs
Air Canada Centre
40 Bay Street, Suite 300
Toronto, ON M5J 2X2
TEL: (416) 815-5700
Pat Quinn—GM/Head Coach

Washington Capitals
MCI Center
601 F Street NW
Washington, DC 20004
TEL: (202) 661-5065
George McPhee—General Manager
Ron Wilson—Head Coach

Pro Football Hall of Fame

CONTACT:
Pro Football Hall of Fame
2121 George Halas Drive NW
Canton, Ohio 44708

TELEPHONE: (330) 456-8207

WEB: *www.profootballhof.com*

EVENTS: Enshrinement Ceremony (Held the last weekend of July, this event honors new inductees of the Pro Football Hall of Fame. Present at the event are the new inductees as well as the ten-, twenty-, and thirty-year Hall of Fame inductees. This event is known as "Pro Football's Greatest Weekend," and it is a great opportunity to meet the big names of the NFL.)

VIP STAFF: John Bankert—Executive Director, Pro Football Hall of Fame

VIPs SUPPORTING THE INSTITUTION: Terry Bradshaw ▪ Earl Campbell ▪ Tony Dorsett ▪ Steve Largent ▪ Ronnie Lott ▪ Dan Reeves ▪ Mike Singletary ▪ Lawrence Taylor ▪ Randy White ▪ Dick Butkus ▪ Eric Dickerson ▪ Dan Fouts ▪ Bob Lilly ▪ Joe Montana ▪ Gale Sayers ▪ Roger Staubach ▪ Johnny Unitas ▪ Jim Brown ▪ Mike Ditka ▪ Joe Greene ▪ Howie Long ▪ Joe Namath ▪ Don Shula ▪ Fran Tarkenton ▪ Bill Walsh

Professional Golfers Association of America

CONTACT:
The PGA of America
100 Avenue of The Champions
Box 109601
Palm Beach Gardens, FL 33410-9601

TELEPHONE: (800) 556-5400

WEB: *www.pga.com*

EVENTS: PGA Merchandise Show (Held in January, this event features new, top-of-the-line golf products as well as appearances by some well-recognized golfers.)

VIP STAFF: Tim Finchem—Commissioner

VIPs SUPPORTING THE INSTITUTION: Mark O'Meara ▪ Hale Irwin ▪ Curtis Strange ▪ Greg Norman ▪ Ben Crenshaw ▪ Tiger Woods ▪ Phil Mickelson, Sr. ▪ Fred Couples ▪ Justin Leonard ▪ Pat Morita

TOURNAMENTS: Mercedes Championships (January, Kapalua Villa Resort, Plantation Course, Lahaina, Hawaii) ▪ Sony Open in Hawaii (January, Waialae Country Club, Honolulu, Hawaii) ▪ Bob Hope Chrysler Classic (January, PGA West/Bermuda Dunes/Indian Wells/Tamarisk, Indians Wells, California) ▪ AT&T Pebble Beach National Pro-Am (February, Pebble Beach/Spyglass Hill/Poppy Hills, Pebble Beach, California) ▪ Nissan Open (February, Riviera Country Club, Pacific Palisades, California) ▪ Andersen Consulting Match Play Championship (WGC), (La Costa Resort and Spa, Carlsbad, California) ▪ Honda Classic (March, TPC at Heron Bay, Coral Springs, Florida) ▪ The Players Championship (March, TPC at Sawgrass, Ponte Vedra Beach, Florida) ▪ BellSouth Classic (Late March/early April, TPC at Sugarloaf, Duluth, Georgia) ▪ The Masters (April, Augusta National Golf Club, Augusta, Georgia) ▪ MCI Classic (April, Harbour Town Golf Links, Hilton Head Island, South Carolina) ▪ Shell Houston Open (April, TPC at the Woodlands, The Woodlands, Texas) ▪ Compaq Classic of New Orleans (May, English Turn Golf and Country Club, New Orleans, Louisiana) ▪ GTE Byron Nelson Classic (May, TPC at Las Colinas/Cottonwood Valley GC, Irving, Texas) ▪ MasterCard Colonial (May, Colonial Country Club, Fort Worth, Texas) ▪ U.S. Open (June, Pebble Beach Golf Links, Pebble Beach, California) ▪ Canon Greater Hartford Open (Late June/early July, TPC at River Highlands, Cromwell, Connecticut) ▪ British Open (July) St. Andrews (Old Course, St. Andrews, Scotland) ▪ PGA Championship (August, Rotating Location) ▪ Bell Canadian Open (September, Glen Abbey Golf Club, Oakville, Ontario) ▪ The Presidents Cup (October, Robert Trent Jones Golf Club, Gainesville, Virginia) ▪ National Car Rental Golf Classic (October, Disney World Palm and Magnolia Courses, Lake Buena Vista, Florida) ▪ The Tour Championship (East Lake Golf Course, Atlanta, Georgia) ▪ American Express Championship (WGC) (Valderrama Golf Club, Sotogrande, Spain)

CORPORATE SPONSORS: Ricoh ▪ Aquafina ▪ Lipton ▪ Pepsi ▪ Reebok ▪ MBNA America ▪ Mizuno ▪ Delta Air Lines ▪ Josten's ▪ Rolex ▪ Titleist ▪ Advil ▪ Gatorade ▪ Oldsmobile ▪ Sprint ▪ Cobra ▪ Chap Stick ▪ IBM ▪ Hyatt Hotels and Resorts ▪ Seabury & Smith ▪ FootJoy Worldwide

Tallahassee Quarterback Club Foundation

CONTACT:
Tallahassee Quarterback Club Foundation
2580 Care Drive, Suite 1
Tallahassee, FL 32308

WEB: *www.Biletnikoffaward.com*

BACKGROUND INFO: The Tallahassee Quarterback Club Foundation awards the Biletnikoff Award each year to the best Division 1-A receiver. The award is voted upon by a committee composed of forty-six members of the media and current and former receivers. The proceeds from the award benefit student scholarships and the All-American Foundation.

NETWORKING SPECIFICS: The Biletnikoff Award is one of the National College Football Awards Association's college football awards. Many professional football players are connected to the award and to the NCFAA, making it a good place for networking opportunities.

EVENT: Biletnikoff Award (Given in February)

VIP STAFF: Will Butler—Chairman ▪ Rocky Bevis—Chairman of the Selection Committee ▪ Tim Templeton—Vice Chairman of the Selection Committee ▪ Fred Biletnikoff (Offensive Coach, Los Angeles Raiders)—Voting Member

CHARITY SUPPORTED: All-American Foundation

Ted Williams Museum and Hitters Hall of Fame

CONTACT:
Ted Williams Museum and Hitters Hall of Fame
2455 North Citrus Hills Boulevard
Hernando, FL 34442

TELEPHONE: (352) 527-6566

WEB: *www.tedwilliams.com*

BACKGROUND INFO: This museum is set up to honor the career of Ted Williams. They hold an annual induction ceremony.

EVENT: Induction Ceremony (Held in February, this event is attended by all of those who are being honored by the museum, as well as Ted Williams himself.)

VIP STAFF: Buzz Hamon—Executive Director, Ted Williams Museum

VIPs SUPPORTING THE INSTITUTION: Sammy Sosa ▪ John Glenn ▪ Nomar Garciaparra ▪ Al Kaline ▪ Carl Yastrzemski ▪ Mark McGwire ▪ Mike Piazza ▪ Curt Gowdy (Sportscaster) ▪ Yogi Berra ▪ Sadaharu Oh (Hit Most Home Runs of All Time) ▪ Ken Griffey, Jr. ▪ George Bush ▪ Albert Belle ▪ Willie Stargell

United States Olympic Committee

CONTACT:
USOC Headquarters
One Olympic Plaza
Colorado Springs, CO 80909-5746

TELEPHONE: (719) 578-4500

WEB: *www.usoc.org*

EVENTS: Qualifying events to make U.S. Olympic Team. Schedules differ depending on sport. Contact USOC for details.

VIP STAFF: William J. Hybl—President ▪ Norman P. Blake—CEO/Secretary General

CURRENT AND PAST OLYMPIANS: Michael Johnson ▪ Rudy Tomjanovich ▪ Tim Hardaway ▪ Alonzo Mourning ▪ Janet Evans ▪ Evander Holyfield ▪ Jackie Joyner Kersee ▪ Rafer Johnson ▪ Mark Spitz ▪ Al Oerter ▪ Tommy Lasorda ▪ Kevin Garnett ▪ Grant Hill ▪ Gary Payton ▪ Muhammad Ali ▪ Sugar Ray Leonard ▪ Picabo Street ▪ Greg Louganis ▪ Karch Kiraly ▪ Vince Carter ▪ Tim Duncan ▪ Jason Kidd ▪ Carl Lewis ▪ Nancy Kerrigan ▪ Bart Conner ▪ Al Joyner ▪ Mary Lou Retton ▪ Eric Heiden

CORPORATE SPONSORS: Coca-Cola ▪ Kodak ▪ Sports Illustrated ▪ UPS ▪ Kellogg's Company ▪ Samsung ▪ Visa ▪ Panasonic ▪ John Hancock ▪ Sears, Roebuck and Co. ▪ McDonald's ▪ Xerox ▪ IBM ▪ Adidas ▪ Marriott

Walter Camp Football Foundation, Inc.

CONTACT:
Walter Camp Football Foundation, Inc.
PO Box 1663
New Haven, CT 06507

TELEPHONE: (203) 288-2267

WEB: *www.waltercamp.org*

BACKGROUND INFO: This foundation is focused on honoring the most outstanding college football player and coach nationwide.

EVENTS: Awards Weekend (Held in February, this weekend event brings together present and past winners of the Walter Camp Award as well as leaders of the Camp Foundation for an awards dinner.) ▪ Celebrity Golf Tournament (Held in July, this event is held at the Yale golf course and is attended by both Heisman and Walter Camp Award winners.)

VIP STAFF: Stanley W. Konesky—President

VIPs HONORED BY FOUNDATION: Roger Staubach ▪ Barry Sanders ▪ Herschel Walker ▪ Dan Marino ▪ Doug Flutie ▪ Ricky Williams ▪ Raghib Ismail ▪ O. J. Simpson ▪ Bo Jackson ▪ Tony Dorsett ▪ Desmond Howard

CORPORATE SPONSOR: Coca-Cola

World Boxing Association

CONTACT:
WBA Central Office
Centro Comercial Ciudad
Turmero Calle Petion Local 21—A
Turmero Aragua Venezuela 2115

TELEPHONE: 58-44-633347

WEB: *www.wbaonline.com*

BACKGROUND INFO: One of the big three boxing governing bodies

EVENT: WBA Annual Awards Dinner (Held in March, this event honors and is attended by renowned boxing personalities.)

VIP STAFF: Gilberto Mendoza—President ▪ Yangsup Shim—Vice President ▪ Shirgeru Kojima—Vice President ▪ Leonard Read—Vice President ▪ York Van Nixon—Vice President

VIPs SUPPORTING THE ORGANIZATION: Roy Jones, Jr. ▪ Mitch Halpern ▪ Felix Trinidad ▪ Don King

World Boxing Council

CONTACT:
   WBC Executive Offices
   Mexico City, Mexico

TELEPHONE: (525) 533-6547

WEB: *www.wbcboxing.com*

BACKGROUND INFO: The WBC has an affiliation with 156 nations around the world. The goal of the WBC is to protect the rights and the health of boxers across the globe. The WBC also has its own Hall of Fame, which honors internationally renowned boxers.

EVENT: Annual WBC Convention (Held in October)

VIP STAFF: Jose Sulaiman Chagnon—President ▪ Eduardo Lamazon—Executive Secretary ▪ Mario Latraverse—General Secretary ▪ Juan Sanchez—Treasurer ▪ Yuko Hayash—Permanent Executive Director

VIPs IN THE WBC HALL OF FAME: Evander Holyfield ▪ Mike Tyson ▪ Joe Frazier ▪ Michael Spinks ▪ Muhammad Ali ▪ Larry Holmes ▪ Sugar Ray Leonard ▪ Marvin Hagler

World Golf Hall of Fame

CONTACT:
   World Golf Village
   One World Golf Place
   St. Augustine, FL 32092

TELEPHONE: (904) 940-4200

WEB: *www.wgv.com/wgv/main.nsf/allframesets/wgv200e.html*

EVENTS: Induction Ceremony (November)

VIP STAFF: Bruce Lucker—Executive Director

VIPs SUPPORTING THE ORGANIZATION: Ben Hogan ▪ Sam Snead ▪ Tom Watson ▪ Dinah Shore ▪ Nick Faldo ▪ Jack Nicklaus ▪ Lee Trevino ▪ Hale Erwin ▪ Betsy King ▪ Arnold Palmer ▪ Bob Hope ▪ Chi Chi Rodriguez ▪ Amy Alcott

CORPORATE SPONSORS: Shell Oil Company ▪ IBM

WTA Tour

CONTACT:
   WTA Tour
   1266 East Main Street, 4th Floor
   Stamford, CT 06902-3546

TELEPHONE: (203) 978-1740

ORGANIZATION'S BACKGROUND: The organization mainly focuses on broadening the public interest in women's tennis. The tour holds fifty-eight tournaments annually and is sponsored by numerous large organizations.

VIPs AFFILIATED WITH THE ORGANIZATION: Monica Seles ▪ Serena Williams ▪ Martina Navritalova ▪ Venus Williams ▪ Anna Kournikova ▪ Martina Hingis ▪ Chris Evert ▪ Serena Williams ▪ Venus Williams ▪ Mary Pierce ▪ Lindsay Davenport

EVENTS: Adidas International (January, Sydney, Australia) ▪ State Farm Women's Tour Classic (Late February/early March, Scotsdale, Arizona) ▪ Tennis Masters Series (March, Indian Wells, California) ▪ The Ericsson Open (Late March/early April, Miami, Florida) ▪ Bausch and Lomb Championships (April, Amelia Island, Florida) ▪ Family Circle Cup (April, Hilton Head Island, South Carolina) ▪ The Championships (Late June/early July, Wimbledon) ▪ Acura Classic (Late July/early August, San Diego, California) ▪ U.S. Open (Late August/early September, Flushing, New York) ▪ Porsche Tennis Grand Prix (October, Filderstadt, Germany) ▪ Heineken Open (October, Shanghai, China) ▪ Bell Challenge (Late October/early November, Quebec City, Canada) ▪ Chase Championships (November, New York, New York) ▪ Volvo Women's Open (November, Pattaya, Thailand)

CORPORATE SPONSORS: Waterford Crystal ▪ Regency ▪ Compaq ▪ Powerbar ▪ Sanex (Sara Lee Brand) ▪ Puma ▪ Toyota

CHARITY SUPPORTED: First Serve

Universities

Boston College

CONTACT:
Boston College
140 Commonwealth Avenue
Chestnut Hill, MA 02467

TELEPHONE: (617) 552-8000

WEB: *www.bc.edu*

Boston College Alumni Association
825 Centre Street
Newton, MA 02458-2527

TELEPHONE: (617) 552-4700
(800) 669-8430

WEB: *www.bc.edu/bc_org/rvp/alum/*

EVENTS: University Lecture Series in Chemistry (This series features lectures by distinguished chemists.)

VIP STAFF: William Leahy—Boston College President ▪ Grace C. Regan—Executive Director, Boston College Alumni Association

DISTINGUISHED ALUMNI: John L. Harrington (CEO, Boston Red Sox) ▪ Chris O'Donnell ▪ Bob Cousy (Basketball Hall of Famer) ▪ Doug Flutie (NFL star) ▪ Chuck Daly (Basketball Hall of Famer) ▪ William O. Wheatley, Jr. (Vice President, NBC News) ▪ Michael C. Hawley (President and CEO, The Gillette Company) ▪ Michael

E. Murphy (President, Sara Lee Foundation) ▪ Robert A. Leonard (President and CEO, Ticketmaster, Inc.) ▪ Thomas F. Ryan, Jr. (President American Stock Exchange) ▪ Patrick T. Stokes (President, Anheuser-Busch Co., Inc.) ▪ G. Craig Sullivan (Chairman and CEO, The Clorox Company) ▪ Aleksandar Totic (Co-founder and Former Partner, Netscape) ▪ John F. Kerry (U.S. Senator, Massachusetts)

PAST LECTURER: Dr. Steven Chu (Nobel Laureate, Chemistry)

Boston University

CONTACT:
Boston University
Admissions Reception Center
121 Bay State Road
Boston, MA 02215

TELEPHONE: (617) 353-2000

Alumni Association, Busm
80 East Concord Street
Boston, MA 02215

TELEPHONE: (617) 638-5150

WEB: *www.bu.edu*

EVENTS: John Templeton Lectures on Freedom, Markets, and Economic Justice ▪ The Academy Lecture (Different events of the Academy Lecture include musical performances, poetry readings, art shows, and book signings.) ▪ Distinguished Executive Lecture Series (These annual lectures draw some of the world's leading executives to Boston University.)

VIP STAFF: Jon Westling—Boston University President ▪ Derek Walcott—Nobel Laureate, Literature

PAST LECTURERS: Robert C. Merton (Nobel Laureate) ▪ Franco Modigliani (Nobel Laureate) ▪ Paul Samuelson (Nobel Laureate) ▪ Amartya Sen (Nobel Laureate) ▪ Derek Walcott (Nobel Laureate) ▪ Saul Bellow (Nobel Laureate) ▪ Robert C. Pozen (President and CEO, Fidelity) ▪ Victor J. Menezes (Chairman and CEO, Citibank; Co-CEO, Corporate and Investment Banking, Citigroup) ▪ Robert Mendoza (Vice Chairman, J. P. Morgan) ▪ Steve Forbes (President, CEO, and Editor in Chief, *Forbes* magazine ▪ Dr. Edward Hagenlocker (Executive Vice President, Ford Motor Co.) ▪ Satoshi Iue (Chairman, Sanyo Electric Company) ▪ Robert Knox (Chairman and CEO, Cornerstone Equity Investors) ▪ Thomas Lee (President, Thomas H. Lee Company) ▪ Hon. George Mitchell (Former U.S. Senator) ▪ Mr. Keith Sherin (Senior VP and CFO, General Electric) ▪ Jack Smith (CEO, General Motors)

Columbia University

CONTACT:
Columbia University
2960 Broadway
New York, NY 10027-6902

TELEPHONE: (212) 854-1754

WEB: *www.columbia.edu*

Office of University Development and Alumni Relations
475 Riverside Drive, MC 7720
New York, NY 10115

TELEPHONE: (212) 870-3100

WEB: *www.columbia.edu/cu/alumni/*

EVENTS: Community Impact Gala Auction (Annual auction benefiting Columbia University and hosted by Geraldine Ferraro) ▪ General Motors Distinguished Leaders Lecture Series (Held in autumn, this series brings together some of the biggest names in the business world.)

VIP STAFF: George Rupp (NYU President) ▪ Martin S. Kaplan (President, Alumni Association) ▪ Melvin Schwartz (Nobel Laureate, Physics) ▪ Jack Steinberger (Nobel Laureate, Physics) ▪ Robert Mundell (Nobel Laureate, Economics) ▪ Joshua Lederberg (Nobel Laureate, Biology) ▪ Horst L. Stormer (Nobel Laureate, Physics) ▪ T. D. Lee (Nobel Laureate, Physics)

DISTINGUISHED ALUMNI: Art Garfunkel (Singer/Songwriter) ▪ Leon N. Cooper (Nobel Laureate, Physics) ▪ Leon M. Lederman (Nobel Laureate, Physics) ▪ Roald Hoffman (Nobel Laureate, Chemistry) ▪ Norman F. Ramsey, Jr. (Nobel Laureate, Physics) ▪ Robert C. Merton (Nobel Laureate, Economics) ▪ William S. Vickrey (Nobel Laureate, Economics) ▪ Douglas Maine (CFO, MCI Corporation)

PAST LECTURERS: Michael Bloomberg (Founder and CEO, Bloomberg LP) ▪ Daniel Lewis (President, Booz—Allen & Hamilton's Worldwide Commercial Business) ▪ Junichi Ujiie (President and CEO, Noruma Securities Co.) ▪ Al Lerner (President and CEO, MBNA; Owner, Cleveland Browns) ▪ Donald Marron (President and CEO, Paine Webber) ▪ Walter V. Shipley (Chairman and CEO, Chase Manhattan Bank) ▪ Ivan Seidenberg (Chairman-Designate and COO, BellAtlantic) ▪ Dr. Andrew Grove (Former President and CEO, Intel Corporation) ▪ Earl Graves (Chairman and CEO, Pepsi-Cola, Washington, D.C.)

CORPORATE SPONSOR: General Mills

Cornell University

CONTACT:
Cornell University
Information and Referral Center
Day Hall Lobby
Ithaca, NY 14853-2801

TELEPHONE: (607) 254-INFO

WEB: *www.cornell.edu*

Office of Alumni Affairs
Alumni House
626 Thurston Avenue
Ithaca, NY 14850-2490

TELEPHONE: (607) 255-2390

WEB: *www.alumni.cornell.edu*

EVENTS: Bartels Fellowship Lecture (Invites international leaders to Cornell) ▪ Georges Lurcy Lecture Series (Held annually, this series invites intellectual artists of all fields to the Cornell campus.) ▪ University Lecture Series (This series brings renowned scholars to speak at Cornell.)

VIP STAFF: Hunter R. Rawlings III—President ▪ Sharon H. Williams—President of Cornell Alumni Federation ▪ Hans Bethe—Nobel Laureate, Physics ▪ Roald Hoffmann—Nobel Laureate, Chemistry ▪ David M. Lee—Nobel Laureate, Physics ▪ Robert C. Richardson—Nobel Laureate, Physics

DISTINGUISHED ALUMNI: Ruth Bader Ginsburg (Supreme Court Justice) ▪ Janet Reno (Attorney General) ▪ Robert W. Fogel (Nobel Laureate) ▪ Sheldon Glasnow (Nobel Laureate) ▪ Toni Morrison (Nobel Laureate)

- Douglas Osheroff (Nobel Laureate) ▪ Steven Weinberg (Nobel Laureate) ▪ Gary Bettman (NHL Commissioner) ▪ Bill Nye (The Science Guy)

PAST LECTURERS: Desmond Tutu ▪ Haris Silajdzic (Co–Prime Minister, Bosnia/Herzegovina) ▪ George J. Mitchell (Former Senate Majority Leader and Clinton Advisor)

CORPORATE SPONSORS: Minnesota Mining and Manufacturing ▪ Anheuser-Busch

Dartmouth College

CONTACT:
Dartmouth College
Admissions
6016 McNutt Hall
Hanover, NH 03755

TELEPHONE: (603) 646-1110

WEB: *www.dartmouth.edu*

Dartmouth College
6068 Blunt Alumni Center
Hanover, NH 03755

TELEPHONE: (888) 228-6068
(603) 646-2258

WEB: *www.dartmouth.edu/alumni/*

EVENTS: Lecture series discussing the presidency (The series brings presidential biographers to the campus.) ▪ Conference on Social Justice (Held by Dartmouth's African and African American Studies Program; sponsored by the Ford Foundation; international activists, scholars, and writers come together to discuss the effect that public policy has on human rights and social justice.) ▪ Commencement Ceremonies (Feature renowned authors and politicians)

VIP STAFF: James Wright—President ▪ Nels Armstrong—Director, Dartmouth Alumni Relations ▪ Jacob Waldbauer—Nobel Laureate, Physics

DISTINGUISHED ALUMNI: Andrew Shue (Actor, *Melrose Place*) ▪ Peter Pfeifle

PAST LECTURERS: David McCullough (Pulitzer Prize Winner) ▪ Robert Caro (Pulitzer Prize Winner) ▪ Michael Beschloss (Regular on *The NewsHour with Jim Lehrer*) ▪ Edmund Morris (Pulitzer Prize Winner) ▪ Doris Kearns Goodwin (Pulitzer Prize Winner; Regular on *The NewsHour with Jim Lehrer*) ▪ David Maraniss (Pulitzer Prize Winner) ▪ Wole Soyinka (Nobel Laureate) ▪ John Irving (Author) ▪ George Mitchell (Former Senator, Maine) ▪ Doris Kearns Goodwin (Pulitzer Prize Winner)

Duke University

CONTACT:
Duke University
Office of Undergraduate Admissions
PO Box 90586
Durham, NC 27708

TELEPHONE: (919) 684-8111

WEB: *www.duke.edu*

Alumni House
614 Chapel Drive
Durham, NC 27708

TELEPHONE: (919) 684-5114
(800) FOR-DUKE

WEB: *www.dukealumni.com*

VIP STAFF: Nannerl O. Keohane—Duke President ▪ Gwynne A. Young—Duke Alumni Association President

DISTINGUISHED ALUMNI: Christian Laettner (NBA Star) ▪ Dave Thomas (Wendy's International) ▪ Richard Wagoner, Jr. (President/COO, General Motors) ▪ Chuck Daly (NBA Hall of Famer)

CORPORATE SUPPORTERS: AT&T ▪ Minnesota Mining and Manufacturing

Emory University

CONTACT:
Emory University
1380 South Oxford Road
Atlanta, GA 30322

TELEPHONE: (404) 727-6123

WEB: *www.emory.edu/*

Association of Emory Alumni
1627 North Decatur Road
Atlanta, GA 30322

TELEPHONE: (404) 727-6400

WEB: *www.emory.edu/ALUMNI/*

EVENTS: Variety of Symposiums and Conferences (Emory invites numerous Nobel laureates and Pulitzer Prize winners to speak at the University.) ▪ Sam Nunn NationsBank Policy Forum (This series features lectures by important leaders in politics.)

VIP STAFF: William M. Chace—President, Emory University ▪ Rebecca Hodges McQueen—President, Association of Emory Alumni ▪ Archbishop Desmond Tutu—Nobel Laureate; Robert W. Woodruff Professor of the Arts ▪ Wole Soyinka—Nobel Laureate; Robert W. Woodruff Professor of the Arts

DISTINGUISHED ALUMNUS: Kenneth Cole

PAST LECTURERS: Derek Walcott (Nobel Laureate) ▪ Jerome Friedman (Nobel Laureate) ▪ Mario Molina (Nobel Laureate) ▪ Joseph Taylor (Nobel Laureate) ▪ Michael Toner (Pulitzer Prize Winner) ▪ Deborah Blum (Pulitzer Prize Winner) ▪ Bill Bradley (Senator and Presidential Candidate) ▪ Donna Shalala (U.S. Secretary, Health and Human Services) ▪ Michael Novak (Author and Former U.S. Ambassador) ▪ Jon Franklin (Nobel Laureate/Pulitzer Prize Winner) ▪ Wole Soyinka (Nobel Laureate) ▪ Leon Lederman (Nobel Laureate) ▪ Douglas Osherhoff (Nobel Laureate) ▪ Laurie Garrett (Pulitzer Prize Winner)

Georgetown University

CONTACT:

Georgetown University Alumni Association
3604 O Street
Washington, DC 20057

WEB: *www.georgetown.edu*

EVENTS: Lecture Fund (This is a student organization that brings various speakers in the political realm to the campus.)

VIP STAFF: Reverend Leo J. O'Donovan—President

DISTINGUISHED ALUMNI: Patrick Ewing ▪ Michael E. Heisley, Sr. (Owner, NBA's Vancouver Grizzlies) ▪ Ted Leonsis (Part Owner with Michael Jordan, NBA's Washington Wizards; Coowner with Michael Jordan, NHL's Washington Capitals)

PAST LECTURERS: Bill Clinton ▪ FBI Director Louis J. Freeh ▪ CIA Director George J. Tenet ▪ Cast of TV's *The West Wing* ▪ King Abdullah of Jordan ▪ James Carville ▪ Oliver North ▪ Author Edmund Morris

Harvard University

CONTACT:

Harvard College
Massachusetts Hall
Cambridge, MA 02138

TELEPHONE: (617) 495-1000

WEB: *www.harvard.edu*

Harvard Alumni Association
Wadsworth House
Cambridge, MA 02138

TELEPHONE: (617) 495-5731

WEB: *www.haa.harvard.edu*

EVENTS: Edwin L. Godkin Lecture Series (Presented by the Kennedy School of Government) ▪ Voices of Public Intellectuals Lecture Series (Presented by Radcliffe Institute for Advanced Study, important figures in law are the guests at this lecture series.)

VIP STAFF: Neil Rudenstine—President ▪ T'ing C. Pei—President, Harvard Alumni Association ▪ William Lipscomb—Nobel Laureate, Chemistry ▪ Sheldon Glashow—Nobel Laureate, Physics ▪ Dudley Herschbach—Nobel Laureate, Chemistry ▪ Richard Roberts—Nobel Laureate, Physiology or Medicine ▪ Amartya Sen—Nobel Laureate, Economic Science

DISTINGUISHED ALUMNI: Tommy Lee Jones ▪ Edward Kennedy ▪ Jack Lemmon ▪ Conan O'Brien ▪ Bill Gates ▪ Joseph Lelyveld (Executive Editor, *New York Times*) ▪ Harold Ramis (Screen Writer/Actor, *Ghostbusters*, *Animal House*) ▪ Tom Morello (Musician, Rage Against the Machine) ▪ Ted Cruz ▪ Phill Swagel

PAST LECTURERS: C. Everett Koop ▪ Peter F. Drucker

CORPORATE SUPPORTERS: AT&T ▪ Time Warner ▪ MCI WorldCom ▪ Lockheed Martin ▪ Fannie Mae ▪ Sprint

Johns Hopkins University

CONTACT:

Johns Hopkins University
3400 North Charles Street
Baltimore, MD 21218

TELEPHONE: (410) 516-8000

WEB: *www.jhu.edu/*

Executive Director of Alumni Relations
3211 North Charles Street
Baltimore, MD 21218

TELEPHONE: (410) 516-0363
(800) 548-5481

WEB: *www.jhu.edu/www/alumni/*

EVENT: Symposium on Foreign Affairs (This series of six lectures brings international political figures to Johns Hopkins.)

VIP STAFF: William R. Brody—President, Johns Hopkins University ▪ James K. Archibald—Alumni Council President ▪ Hamilton O. Smith—Nobel Laureate, Medicine ▪ Daniel Nathans—Nobel Laureate, Medicine

DISTINGUISHED ALUMNI: Merton Miller (Nobel Laureate, Economics) ▪ Jody Williams (Nobel Laureate, Peace)

PAST LECTURERS: Shimon Peres (Former Israeli Prime Minister) ▪ Lee Hong Koo (Korean Ambassador to the U.S.) ▪ Cesar Gaviria (Secretary-General, Organization of American States) ▪ Rubens Antonio Barbosa (Ambassador of Brazil to the U.S.) ▪ Sheila Sisulu (Ambassador of South Africa to the U.S.) ▪ Senator George Mitchell (Chair, Northern Ireland Peace Negotiations) ▪ Jurgen Chrobog (Ambassador of Germany to the U.S.) ▪ William Daley (Secretary, U.S. Department of Commerce)

CORPORATE SUPPORTER: AT&T

Massachusetts Institute of Technology

CONTACT:

Massachusetts Institute of Technology
77 Massachusetts Avenue
Cambridge, MA 02139-4307

TELEPHONE: (617) 253-1000

WEB: *www.mit.edu*

Alumni Association of MIT
MIT Room 10-110
77 Massachusetts Avenue
Cambridge, MA 02139-4307

TELEPHONE: (617) 253-8200

WEB: *www.web.mit.edu/alum*

EVENTS: Alumni Leadership Conference (Held annually, this event that draws upwards of 4,000 active alums lasts an entire weekend and is filled with leadership workshops.) ▪ Industry Leaders in Technology and Management Lecture Series (Features lectures by leaders in the business world)

VIP STAFF: Charles M. Vest—MIT President ▪ Brian G. R. Hughes—President, MIT Alumni Association ▪ Har Gobind Khorana—Nobel Laureate, Physiology or Medicine ▪ Salvador Luria—Nobel Laureate, Physiology or Medicine ▪ Paul A. Samuelson—Nobel Laureate, Economics ▪ Samuel C. C. Ting—Nobel Laureate, Physics ▪ Franco Modigliani—Nobel Laureate, Economics ▪ Susumu Tonegawa—Nobel Laureate, Physiology or Medicine ▪ Robert M. Solow—Nobel Laureate, Economics ▪ Jerome I. Friedman—Nobel Laureate, Physics ▪ Henry W. Kendall—Nobel Laureate, Physics ▪ Eric S. Chivian—Nobel Peace Prize

DISTINGUISHED ALUMNI: Edwin E. "Buzz" Aldrin, Jr. ▪ I. M. Pei (World-Renowned Architect)

PAST LECTURERS: Ivan Seidenberg (Chairman and CEO, Bell Atlantic) ▪ George M. C. Fisher (Chairman of the Board, Eastman Kodak Company) ▪ Andrew S. Grove (President and CEO, Intel Corporation) ▪ Henri Termeer (President, Genzyme Corporation) ▪ Alex Trotman (Chairman and CEO, Ford Motor Company) ▪ Jorma Ollila (President and CEO, Nokia Corporation) ▪ Jack Smith (CEO and Chairman of the Board, General Motors Corporation) ▪ L. D. DeSimone (Chairman and CEO, 3M Corporation) ▪ Herbert Allison (President and CEO, Merrill Lynch) ▪ Raymond Gilmartin (Chairman, President, and CEO, Merck)

CORPORATE SUPPORTERS: Exxon Mobil Corporation ▪ Microsoft ▪ Citigroup ▪ Xerox ▪ Minnesota Mining and Manufacturing

Michigan State University

CONTACT:

Michigan State University
(address to a specific department)
East Lansing, MI 48824

TELEPHONE: (517) 355-1855

WEB: *www.msu.edu*

MSU Alumni Association
108 MSU Union
East Lansing, MI 48824

TELEPHONE: (517) 355-8314

WEB: *www.msuaa.alumni.msu.edu/*

EVENTS: John W. Eadie Celebrity Lecture Series (Held throughout the year; past celebrities invited to the university include renowned authors and motion picture directors.)

VIP STAFF: M. Peter McPherson—President, MSU ▪ Keith Williams—Director, MSU Alumni Association

DISTINGUISHED ALUMNI: Earvin "Magic" Johnson ▪ James Daimler (President, Daimler/Chrysler Corp.) ▪ Robin Richards (President and CEO, MP3.com, Inc.) ▪ Dale Petroskey (President, National Baseball Hall of Fame) ▪ James Hoffa (President, International Brotherhood of Teamsters) ▪ Robert Urich (Actor) ▪ Spencer Abraham (U.S. Senator, Michigan) ▪ Richard Ford (Author and Pulitzer Prize Winner for *Independence Day*) ▪ Walter Hill (Director, *48 Hours* and the *Alien* Series) ▪ Jim Miller (President, Mazda Motors Corp.) ▪ Bill Mechanic (President and CEO, Fox Filmed Entertainment)

PAST LECTURERS: Oliver Stone ▪ Arthur Miller ▪ John Updike ▪ Tom Wolfe ▪ Toni Morrison ▪ Richard Ford ▪ Joseph Heller ▪ Joyce Carol Oates ▪ Maya Angelou ▪ E. L. Doctorow ▪ Kurt Vonnegut

New York University

CONTACT:
New York University
70 Washington Square South
New York, NY 10012

TELEPHONE: (212) 998-1212

WEB: *www.nyu.edu/*

New York University Office for University Development and Alumni Relations
25 West Fourth Street
New York, NY 10012

TELEPHONE: (212) 998-6912

WEB: *www.nyu.edu/alumni/*

EVENTS: NYU's Alumni Association Annual Awards Dinner (Held annually; many important alumni are in attendance. Presentation of alumni awards take place at the dinner.) ▪ Media Ecology Conference (Held annually; the topics discussed by the scholars at this conference deal with the aspects and the repercussions of communications media.) ▪ CEO Lecture Series (Year-long series invites CEOs of major corporations to speak at the university.)

VIP STAFF: L. Jay Oliva—NYU President ▪ Herbert M. Paul—President of NYU Alumni Association ▪ Wole Soyinka—Nobel Laureate; Distinguished Scholar in Residence

DISTINGUISHED ALUMNI: Dr. Julius Axelrod—Nobel Laureate, Medicine

PAST LECTURERS: Jack Welch (CEO, General Electric) ▪ Arno Penzias (CEO, AT&T) ▪ Tom Murphy (CEO, ABC) ▪ Laurence Tisch (CEO, CBS) ▪ Susan Beresford (CEO, Ford Foundation) ▪ Paul Allaire (CEO, Xerox Corp.) ▪ Christie Hefner (CEO, Playboy Enterprises) ▪ Norman Augustine (CEO, Lockheed Martin) ▪ Joseph Brodsky (Nobel Laureate) ▪ Anna Deavere Smith ▪ Harvey Golub (CEO, American Express) ▪ Judy Harrison (CEO, Monet Group) ▪ Philip Carroll (CEO, Shell Oil) ▪ Michael Jordan (CEO, Westinghouse) ▪ Tom Freston (CEO, MTV Networks) ▪ Jay Walker (CEO, priceline.com) ▪ Danny Glover ▪ Walter Mosley

CORPORATE SUPPORTERS: Johnson & Johnson ▪ Microsoft ▪ Time Warner

Northwestern University

CONTACT:
Northwestern University
633 Clark Street
Evanston, IL 60208

TELEPHONE: (847) 491-3741 (Evanston Campus)
(312) 503-8649 (Chicago Campus)

WEB: *www.northwestern.edu*

John Evans Center
1800 Sheridan Rd.
Evanston, IL 60208-1800

TELEPHONE: (847) 491-7200

WEB: *www.alumni.nwu.edu/*

EVENTS: Alumni Leadership Conference (Held annually; Northwestern alums from around the world gather for a four-day program concerning the roles of alumni in the community.) ▪ Distinguished Public Policy Lecture Series (Guests include players in the political forum.) ▪ Kellogg Graduate School of Management's Distinguished Speaker Series (Political speakers are in attendance.) ▪ Sondra Glair Memorial Lecture (The main speakers at this lecture are in politics.)

VIP STAFF: Henry S. Bienen—President ▪ M. Catherine Jaros—Northwestern Alumni Association President

DISTINGUISHED ALUMNI: Ann-Margret ▪ Shelley Long ▪ Kate Shindler (Former Miss America)

PAST LECTURERS: John Porter (House of Representatives, R-IL) ▪ Donna Shalala (Secretary, Health and Human Services) ▪ David Ellwood (Malcolm Weiner Professor of Public Policy, Kennedy School of Government, Harvard University) ▪ Senator William V. Roth, Jr. (R-DE: Chairman, Senate Finance Committee) ▪ Senator Paul S. Sarbanes (R-MD; Senior Member, Senate Foreign Relations Committee) ▪ Brian Williams (Emmy Award Winner; NBC's Former Chief White House Correspondent)

Penn State University

CONTACT:
Penn State University
Undergraduate Admissions
201 Shields Building
University Park, PA 16802

TELEPHONE: (814) 865-4700

WEB: *www.psu.edu*

Penn State University
Hintz Family Alumni Center
University Park, PA 16802-1439

TELEPHONE: (800) 548-LION
(814) 865-0329

WEB: *www.alumni.psu.edu/around/your alum.html*

EVENTS: Voices of Freedom Lecture Series (The series focuses on views opposing the standard liberal views of college campuses, and it invites leaders of public advocacy and some entertainers to lecture.) ▪ Arthur H. Waynick Memorial Lecture (Draws leaders and Nobel Laureates of the sciences to the Penn State campus.)

VIP STAFF: Graham Spanier—President, Penn State University ▪ James E. Carnes—President, Penn State Alumni Association

DISTINGUISHED ALUMNI: Henry and Richard Block (Founders, H&R Block) ▪ Carroll Rosenbloom (Owner of the L.A. Rams) ▪ Walter Annenberg (Founder and Publisher, *TV Guide*)

PAST LECTURERS: Charlton Heston ▪ Ward Connerly (President, American Civil Rights Institute) ▪ Anthony Hewish (Nobel Laureate, Physics) ▪ Oliver North ▪ Kennedy (Former MTV Veejay)

CORPORATE SUPPORTER: Sprint

Pepperdine University

CONTACT:
Pepperdine University
24255 P.C.H
Malibu, CA 90263

TELEPHONE: (310) 456-4138

WEB: *www.pepperdine.edu*

EVENTS: School of Public Policy Lectures (Bring notable political and media speakers to campus. Some lectures are partly sponsored by the Ronald Reagan Presidential Foundation.)

VIP STAFF: David Davenport—President ▪ Robert Leonard—Pepperdine Alumni Association President

DISTINGUISHED ALUMNI: Christos M. Cotsakos (Chairman and CEO, E*TRADE) ▪ Marcus D. Hiles (Chairman and CEO, Western Rim Investment Advisors and Property Services)

PAST LECTURERS: Mikhail Gorbachev ▪ Joshua Lederberg (Nobel Laureate) ▪ Michael Dukakis ▪ Pete Wilson (Former Governor, California) ▪ Steve Forbes ▪ Tom Brokaw ▪ Diane Sawyer

Princeton

CONTACT:
The Alumni Council of Princeton University
PO Box 291
Princeton, NJ 08542-0291

TELEPHONE: (609) 258-1900

WEB: *www.princeton.edu/~alco/*

Undergraduate Admission Office
PO Box 430
Princeton University
Princeton, NJ 08544

WEB: *www.princeton.edu*

EVENTS: Woodrow Wilson School Lecture (Held throughout the year, the events hosted by the Woodrow Wilson School of Princeton deal mainly with public and international affairs.)

VIP STAFF: Harold T. Shapiro—President ▪ Eric F. Wieschaus—Nobel Laureate, Medicine ▪ Val Fitch—Nobel Laureate, Physics ▪ Norman R. Augustine—Chairman, Executive Committee, Lockheed Martin Corporation

DISTINGUISHED ALUMNI: Bill Bradley (Basketball Hall of Famer, 2000 Presidential Candidate) ▪ Dean Cain (Actor, *Lois and Clark*) ▪ Brooke Shields ▪ David Duchovny ▪ Robert L. Johnson (Founder/CEO, Black

Entertainment Television) ▪ Phill Swagel ▪ Ted Cruz ▪ Ralph Nader ▪ Meg Whitman (CEO, eBay), ▪ Steve Forbes

PAST LECTURERS: Lech Wales (Nobel Laureate; Former President of Poland) ▪ Sidney Blumenthal (Assistant to President Clinton) ▪ Robert MacNeil (Formerly on TV's *MacNeil/Lehrer News Hour*) ▪ Michael Dukakis (Former Governor of Massachusetts; Former Presidential Candidate) ▪ Robert L. Johnson (Founder/CEO, Black Entertainment Television) ▪ William G. Bowen (President, The Andrew W. Mellon Foundation) ▪ Steve Forbes (President/CEO, Forbes, Inc.; Former Presidential Hopeful) ▪ Didier Opertti (President, United Nations General Assembly) ▪ Anita Perez Ferguson (President, National Women's Political Caucus) ▪ Manuel Camacho (Founder, Democratic Center Party of Mexico) ▪ Rush Holt (Congressman, New Jersey) ▪ Jane Goodall (Founder, The Jane Goodall Institute for Wildlife Research, Education, and Conservation)

CORPORATE SPONSOR: General Mills

Southern Methodist University

CONTACT:

Southern Methodist University
Perkins Administration Building
6425 Boaz Lane
Dallas, TX 75275

TELEPHONE: (214) 768-2000

WEB: *www.smu.edu*

SMU Alumni Association
6207 Hillcrest Avenue
Dallas, TX 75205

TELEPHONE: (214) 768-2586

WEB: *www.smu.edu/~alumni/*

EVENTS: Tate Distinguished Lecture Series (The preeminent lecture series in the United States brings in the best people from around the world to speak.) ▪ Southwestern Bell–SMU Athletic Forum (This is a series of four luncheons throughout the year that bring renowned athletes to the campus.)

VIP STAFF: R. Gerald Turner—President ▪ Kit Sawers—Executive Director, Tate Lecture Series ▪ Albon O. Head, Jr.—President, SMU Alumni Association ▪ Dick Brown (Chairman and CEO, EDS)—Trustee

DISTINGUISHED ALUMNI: Larry R. Faulkner (University of Texas President) ▪ Laura Bush (Wife of George W. Bush, Jr.) ▪ Don Meredith ▪ Eric Dickerson

PAST TATE AND ATHLETIC FORUM PARTICIPANTS: Cokie Roberts ▪ George Stephanopoulos ▪ F. W. de Klerk (Head of National Party of South Africa) ▪ William Safire (Pulitzer Prize Winner) ▪ David Gergen (Advisor to Presidents Reagan and Clinton) ▪ Nolan Ryan ▪ Wayne Gretzky ▪ Dick Vitale ▪ Yogi Berra ▪ Don Schula ▪ Archbishop Desmond Tutu ▪ Newt Gingrich ▪ Ozzie Smith ▪ Peyton Manning ▪ Marcus Allen ▪ Bobby Bowden ▪ David Stern ▪ Bob Ueker ▪ Chris Evert ▪ Reggie Jackson ▪ Howie Long ▪ Lou Holtz ▪ Mike Ditka ▪ Terry Bradshaw ▪ Magic Johnson ▪ Ahmad Rashad ▪ Bill Walsh ▪ Bob Costas ▪ Fran Tarkenton ▪ Gale Sayers ▪ Tommy Lasorda ▪ Jimmy Johnson ▪ George Foreman ▪ Pat Summerall ▪ George Will ▪ Jack Kemp ▪ Dave Dravecky ▪ Chuck Daly ▪ Johnny Bench ▪ Bobby Knight ▪ Julius Erving ▪ Dan Jenkins ▪ Kareem Abdul-Jabbar ▪ Don Meredith ▪ Joe Gibbs ▪ George Steinbrenner ▪ Joe Paterno ▪ Paul Tagliabue ▪ Pat Riley ▪ Bobby Valentine

Stanford University

CONTACT:

Stanford Alumni Association
Bowman Alumni House
Stanford, CA 94305-4005

TELEPHONE: (650) 723-2021

Stanford University
Stanford, CA 94305

TELEPHONE: (650) 723-2300

WEB: *www.stanford.edu*

EVENTS: The Lane Lecture Series (Sponsored by the Creative Writing Program; draws such authors and poets as Tim O'Brien, Joseph Brodsky, Raymond Carver, E. L. Doctorow, John Irving, Stanley Kunitz, Larry McMurtry, Toni Morrison, Joyce Carol Oates, Octavio Paz, Eudor Welty.) ▪ Visiting Payne Lecture Series (Sponsored by Institute for International Studies)

VIP STAFF: Gerhard Casper—President ▪ Bill Stone—President, Stanford Alumni Association ▪ A. Michael Spence—Dean, Graduate School of Business ▪ Arthur Kornberg—Nobel Laureate, Physiology/Medicine ▪ Myron Scholes—Nobel Laureate, Economics ▪ Steven Chu—Nobel Laureate, Physics ▪ Douglas Osheroff—Nobel Laureate, Physics ▪ Robert B. Laughlin—Nobel Laureate, Physics ▪ Martin Perl—Nobel Laureate, Physics ▪ Paul Berg—Nobel Laureate, Chemistry ▪ Burton Richter—Nobel Laureate, Physics ▪ William Sharpe—Nobel Laureate, Economics ▪ Henry Taube—Nobel Laureate, Chemistry ▪ Richard Taylor—Nobel Laureate, Physics ▪ Kenneth J. Arrow—Nobel Laureate, Economics

DISTINGUISHED ALUMNI: John R. Brodie (NFL Hall of Fame, Senior PGA Golfer) ▪ Gray Davis (Governor of California) ▪ Carleton Fiorina (President/CEO, Hewlett-Packard Co.) ▪ Doris Fisher (Cofounder, Gap, Inc.) ▪ Myron Saxon (Noted Entrepreneur) ▪ Steven Breyer (Supreme Court Justice) ▪ Sandra Day O'Connor (Supreme Court Justice) ▪ Anthony Kennedy (Supreme Court Justice) ▪ William Rehnquist (Supreme Court Justice) ▪ Philip Knight (Chairman/CEO, Nike, Inc.) ▪ Charles Schwab (Chair/CEO, Charles Schwab Corp.) ▪ Ted Koppe ▪ John Elway ▪ Jack McDowell ▪ Tiger Woods ▪ Robert Pinsky (Poet Laureate) ▪ Sigourney Weaver ▪ Jerry Yang and David Filo (Founders, Yahoo!) ▪ Jenny Thompson (Olympic Swimmer) ▪ Janet Evans (Olympic Swimmer) ▪ Summer Sanders (Olympic Swimmer) ▪ Ken Kesey ▪ Scott Turow ▪ Tom Watson ▪ Robert Hass (Poet Laureate) ▪ Ted Danson ▪ Jack Palance

CORPORATE SUPPORTERS: Lucent Technologies ▪ Chevron

Texas Christian University

CONTACT:

Texas Christian University
2800 S. University Drive
Fort Worth, TX 76129

TELEPHONE: (817) 257-7000

Office of Alumni Relations
TCU
Box 297430
Fort Worth, TX 76129

TELEPHONE: (817) 257-7803

(800) 646-4TCU

WEB: *www.tcu.edu*

EVENTS: Annual Gates of Chai Lecture Series (Held in September, sponsored by Brite Divinity School; speakers are experts in the field of religion.)

VIP STAFF: Michael R. Ferrari—Chancellor ▪ Kristi McLain Hoban—Alumni Director

DISTINGUISHED ALUMNI: Bob Schieffer (Anchor and Moderator, CBS News's *Face the Nation*) ▪ Bob Lilly ▪ Jason Snyder (Drummer for 1989 World Champions) ▪ Jenny Specht

PAST LECTURERS: Rabbi Harold S. Kushner (Author) ▪ Elie Wiesel ▪ Chaim Potok (Author) ▪ Robert Pinsky (U.S. Poet Laureate)

CORPORATE SPONSORS: PepsiCo ▪ Lockheed Martin

United States Military Academy—West Point

CONTACT:

United States Military Academy
Thayer Road
West Point, NY 10996

TELEPHONE: (914) 938-2638

WEB: *www.westpoint.edu*

Association of Graduates
United States Military Academy
West Point, NY 10996

TELEPHONE: (800) BE-A-GRAD

WEB: *www.aog.usma.edu/*

EVENTS: Presentation of Thayer Award (Past recipients include Gen. Colin Powell; Walter Cronkite; Bob Hope; Ronald Reagan; George Bush; Cyrus Vance, former Secretary of State; and Norman R. Augustine, chairman of Executive Committee, Lockheed Martin Corporation.)

VIP STAFF: Daniel W. Christman—Superintendent ▪ Eric T. Olson—Commandant of the Cadets ▪ Fletcher M. Lankin, Jr.—Dean of Academic Board

DISTINGUISHED ALUMNI: Norman Schwarzkopf ▪ Edwin "Buzz" Aldrin (Astronaut) ▪ Michael Collins (Astronaut) ▪ Pete Dawkins (Chairman/CEO, Primerica)

U.S. Naval Academy—Annapolis

CONTACT:

U.S. Naval Academy
121 Blake Road
Annapolis, MD 21402-5000

TELEPHONE: (410) 293-1000

WEB: *www.usna.edu*

U.S. Naval Academy Alumni Association
247 King George Street
Annapolis, MD 21402

TELEPHONE: (410) 263-4448

WEB: *www.usna.com*

EVENT: Michelson Lecture Series (Held annually, this series brings to the academy a renowned scientist every year.)

VIP STAFF: John R. Ryan—Superintendent ▪ Ron Marryott—President and CEO, USNA Alumni Association

DISTINGUISHED ALUMNI: Jimmy Carter ▪ Roger Staubach ▪ David Robinson ▪ Ross Perot

PAST LECTURERS: Dr. Richard E. Smalley (Nobel Laureate) ▪ Dr. Arnold Penzias (Nobel Laureate) ▪ Dr. Aaron Hauptman (Nobel Laureate) ▪ Dr. Dudley R. Herscbach (Nobel Laureate) ▪ Dr. Leon N. Cooper (Nobel Laureate) ▪ Dr. James A. Watson (Nobel Laureate) ▪ Prof. Arthur L. Schawlow (Nobel Laureate)

University of Alabama

CONTACT:
University of Alabama
Office of Undergraduate Admissions
Box 870132
Tuscaloosa, AL 35487

TELEPHONE: (202) 348-5765

WEB: *www.ua.edu*

Alabama Alumni Association
PO Box 861928
Tuscaloosa, AL 35486

TELEPHONE: (205) 348-5963

WEB: *www.bama.ua.edu/~alumni/*

EVENTS: Martin Luther King, Jr. Distinguished Lecture Series (This event brings to the UA campus scholars in the field of religion and racial issues.)

VIP STAFF: Andrew A. Sorenson—President ▪ Ben King—National Alumni Association President ▪ Pat Whetstone—Director, Alumni Affairs

DISTINGUISHED ALUMNI: Joe Namath (Former NFL Quarterback; Currently CBS Sportscaster) ▪ Harper Lee (Author of *To Kill a Mockingbird*) ▪ Jim Nabors (Entertainer) ▪ Sela Ward (Actress) ▪ Mickie Blackwell (President, Lockheed) ▪ Millard Fuller (Founder, Habitat for Humanity) ▪ Sandy Grossman (Former Director, CBS Sports; Currently Producer, Fox) ▪ Alma Gates Sanders (Senior Vice President, CNN) ▪ Chester Simmons (Former President and CEO, ESPN) ▪ Winston Groom, Jr. (Author of *Forrest Gump*) ▪ Howell Heflin (U.S. Senator of Alabama) ▪ Margaret Tutwiler (Former Assistant Secretary of the Treasury for the Bush Administration) ▪ John Cochran (ABC News Senior Washington Correspondent)

University of California at Berkeley

CONTACT:

The University of California at Berkeley
Office of Undergraduate Admission and Relations with Schools
110 Sproul Hall # 5800
Berkeley, CA 94720

TELEPHONE: (510) 642-6000

WEB: *www.berkeley.edu*

California Alumni Association
1 Alumni House
Berkeley, CA 94720-7520

TELEPHONE: (510) 642-7026
(888) CAL-ALUM

WEB: *www.alumni.berkeley.edu*

EVENTS: Lucent Technologies Communications Networking Lectures (Held in November, this is an annual lecture series featuring leaders in technology that focuses on communications and networking technologies.)

VIP STAFF: Robert M. Berdahl—Chancellor ▪ Alfredo Terrazas—California Alumni Association President ▪ Yuan T. Lee—Nobel Laureate, Chemistry ▪ John C. Harsanyi—Nobel Laureate, Economics

DISTINGUISHED ALUMNI: Stacy Keach ▪ Steve Bartkowski (Former NFL Quarterback) ▪ Don Fisher (CEO, The Gap) ▪ Beverly Cleary (Author) ▪ Kevin Johnson (NBA Star) ▪ Robert S. McNamara (Former Secretary of Defense, Kennedy Administration) ▪ Gregory Peck (Academy Award Winner and Actor, *To Kill a Mockingbird*) ▪ Steve Wozniak (Cofounder, Apple Computer Systems) ▪ Lee Brown (Drug Czar, Clinton Administration ▪ Mark Goodson (TV Producer, *Family Feud, The Price is Right*) ▪ Andrew Grove (President/CEO, Intel Corporation) ▪ Pete Wilson (Governor, California) ▪ Jerry Mathers (Actor, *Leave It to Beaver*) ▪ Matt Biondi (Olympics Gold Medalist) ▪ Suzanna Hoffs (Lead singer, The Bangles)

PAST LECTURER: Richard McGinn (Chairman/CEO, Lucent Technologies)

CORPORATE SUPPORTERS: Exxon Mobil Corporation ▪ Microsoft ▪ Chevron

UCLA

CONTACT:

UCLA
405 Hilgard Ave
PO Box 951361
Los Angeles, CA 90095-1361

TELEPHONE: (310) 825-4321

WEB: *www.ucla.edu*

UCLA Alumni Association
Alumni Center
Box 951397
Los Angeles, CA 90095-1397

TELEPHONE: (310) UCLAlumni

EVENTS: UCLA Physics and Astronomy Lectures (Guests include leaders in the sciences.) ▪ Bernard Brodie Distinguished Lectures on the Conditions of Peace (Past guests include leaders in the political crusade for peace.)

VIP STAFF: Albert Carnesale—Chancellor ▪ Jeffrey A. Seymour—UCLA Alumni Association President ▪ Paul Boyer—Nobel Laureate, Chemistry ▪ Louis Ignarro—Nobel Laureate, Medicine

DISTINGUISHED ALUMNI: Kareem Abdul-Jabbar ▪ William F. Sharpe (Nobel Laureate) ▪ Reggie Miller ▪ Troy Aikman ▪ Todd Zeile ▪ Robert Shapiro ▪ Bill Walton ▪ Donald Barksdale ▪ Kenny Washington

PAST LECTURERS: Zbigniew Brzezinski ▪ Michael Dukakis ▪ William S. Cohen ▪ Pierre-Gilles de Gennes (Nobel Laureate) ▪ Gerard 't Hooft (Nobel Laureate)

University of Chicago

CONTACT:
> The University of Chicago
> 5801 South Ellis Avenue
> Chicago IL 60637

TELEPHONE: (773) 702-1234

WEB: *www.uchicago.edu/*
> The University of Chicago
> The Alumni Association
> 1313 E. 60th Street
> Chicago, IL 60637

TELEPHONE: (773) 702-2150
> (800) 955-0065

WEB: *www.alumni.uchicago.edu/*

EVENTS: Cityfront Forums (Held four times during the year, these events focus on topics of general interest discussed by the most distinguished faculty members at the university.)

VIP STAFF: Don Michael Randel—President, University of Chicago ▪ Bob Levey—President, Alumni Association ▪ Robert Lucas (Nobel Laureate, Economics) ▪ Robert Fogel (Nobel Laureate, Economics) ▪ Gary Becker (Nobel Laureate, Economics) ▪ Merton Miller (Nobel Laureate, Economics) ▪ James Cronin (Nobel Laureate, Physics)

DISTINGUISHED ALUMNI: Robert S. Mullikin (Nobel Laureate, Chemistry) ▪ Milton Friedman (Nobel Laureate, Economics) ▪ Owen Chamberlain (Nobel Laureate, Physics) ▪ Jack Steinberger (Nobel Laureate, Physics) ▪ Jerome I. Friedman (Nobel Laureate, Physics) ▪ James Watson (Nobel Laureate, Physiology) ▪ Tsung-Dao Lee (Nobel Laureate, Physics) ▪ Saul Bellow (Nobel Laureate, Literature) ▪ Herbert Brown (Nobel Laureate, Chemistry) ▪ F. Sherwood Rowland (Nobel Laureate, Chemistry) ▪ Daniel Tsui (Nobel Laureate, Physics) ▪ Paul Samuelson (Nobel Laureate, Economics) ▪ Chen Ning Yang (Nobel Laureate, Physics) ▪ Herbert Simon (Nobel Laureate, Economics) ▪ Gary Becker (Nobel Laureate, Economics) ▪ James Buchanan, Jr. (Nobel Laureate, Economics) ▪ Myron Scholes (Nobel Laureate, Economics) ▪ Harry Markowitz (Nobel Laureate, Economics)

University of Florida

CONTACT:
University of Florida
Office of Admissions
PO Box 114000
201 Criser Hall
Gainesville, FL 32611

TELEPHONE: (352) 392-3261

WEB: *www.ufl.edu*

UF Alumni Association
2012 W. University Avenue
Gainesville, FL 32603

TELEPHONE: (352) 392-1905
(888) 352-5866

WEB: *www.ufalumni.ufl.edu/*

VIP STAFF: Charles E. Young—University of Florida President ▪ Andrea Spottswood—University of Florida Alumni Association President

DISTINGUISHED ALUMNI: Emmitt Smith ▪ Connie Mack (Senator) ▪ Forrest Sawyer (Anchor of *ABC News*) ▪ Steve Spurrier (Heisman Trophy Winner) ▪ Bob Vila (Home Repair Personality) ▪ Faye Dunaway ▪ Lawton Chiles (Governor of Florida) ▪ Bob Graham (Senator)

CORPORATE SUPPORTERS: JCPenney ▪ Fannie Mae

University of Georgia

CONTACT:
The University of Georgia
Admissions
Terrell Hall
Athens, GA 30602

TELEPHONE: (706) 542-3000

WEB: *www.uga.edu*

UGA Alumni Relations
Alumni House
The University of Georgia
Athens, GA 30602

TELEPHONE: (706) 542-2251
(800) 606-8786

WEB: *www.uga.edu/alumni/*

EVENTS: University of Georgia Charter Lecture (This series focuses on relaying the importance of a free society from the speakers to the audience.) ▪ Sibley Lecture (Sponsored by the University of Georgia's School of Law, featured speakers are leaders in the field of law.)

VIP STAFF: Michael F. Adams—President, University of Georgia ▪ David Muia—Executive Director, University of Georgia ▪ Alumni Association

DISTINGUISHED ALUMNI: Herschel Walker ▪ Fran Tarkenton ▪ Champ Bailey ▪ Larry Brown

PAST LECTURERS: James Buchanan (Nobel Laureate) ▪ Sherwood Rowland (Nobel Laureate) ▪ David Kessler (Former Commissioner, FDA) ▪ Freeman Dyson (Consultant, NASA; Former Chairman, Federation of American Scientists) ▪ Rita Dove (Former U.S. Poet Laureate) ▪ Dalia Domer (Israeli Supreme Court Justice)

University of Indiana

CONTACT: University of Indiana
107 S. Indiana Avenue
Bloomington, IN 47405-7000

TELEPHONE: (812) 855-4848

WEB: *www.indiana.edu*

Indiana University Alumni Association
Virgil T. DeVault Alumni Center
1000 East Seventeenth Street
Bloomington, IN 47408-3044

TELEPHONE: (812) 855-4822
(800) 824-3044

WEB: *www.indiana.edu/~alumni/*

EVENTS: Konopinski Memorial Lecture Series (Organized by IU Physics Dept., this series brings renowned scientists to the university.) ▪ Omnibus Lecture Series (Year-long lecture series draws distinguished speakers of many fields to IU.)

VIP STAFF: Myles Brand—IU President ▪ Jerry F. Tardy—President and CEO, IU Alumni Association ▪ Bobby Knight—Basketball Coach

DISTINGUISHED ALUMNI: James D. Watson (Nobel Laureate; Developed Watson-Crick Model of DNA) ▪ Kevin Kline ▪ Isaiah Thomas (NBA Star) ▪ Harold Poling (Former CEO, Ford Motor Company) ▪ Frank Popoff (Chairman of Board of Directors, Dow Chemical Company) ▪ Michael Uslan (Exec. Producer, *Batman, Batman Returns, Batman Forever,* and *Batman and Robin*) ▪ Jane Pauley ▪ Larry Bird

PAST LECTURERS: Steven Chu (Nobel Laureate) ▪ Edward Albee (Playwright) ▪ Alan Page (Minnesota Supreme Court Justice) ▪ Eleanor Clift (Political Analyst for the Fox News Network; Member of *Newsweek* Political Team) ▪ Dinesh D'Souza (Political Author)

University of Michigan

CONTACT:
University of Michigan
Office of Undergraduate Admissions
220 Student Activities Building
515 East Jefferson Street
Ann Arbor, MI 48109

TELEPHONE: (734) 764-1817

WEB: *www.umich.edu*

Alumni Association of the University of Michigan
200 Fletcher Street
Ann Arbor, MI 48109-1007

TELEPHONE: (734) 764-0384
(800) 847-4764

WEB: *www.umich.edu/~umalumni/*

EVENTS: Wallenberg Lecture (Held annually, this event is hosted by the College of Architecture and Urban Planning. Past speakers include some of the leading architects in the world.)

VIP STAFF: Lee C. Bollinger—University of Michigan President ▪ Richard H. Rogel—University of Michigan Alumni Association

DISTINGUISHED ALUMNI: Mike Wallace (News Commentator, *60 Minutes*) ▪ Arthur Miller (Author, *Death of a Salesman*)

PAST LECTURERS: The Dalai Lama ▪ Kenneth Frampton (World-Renowned Architectural Critic and Author) ▪ Michael Sorkin (Architect) ▪ Daniel Libeskind (Architect/Designer of the Jewish Museum in Berlin)

CORPORATE SUPPORTERS: Microsoft ▪ Sprint

The University of Mississippi

CONTACT:

The University of Mississippi
Admissions
Martindale Student Services Center, Room 145
University, MS 38677

TELEPHONE: (662) 915-7236
(662) 915-7211

WEB: *www.olemiss.edu/*

Alumni Association
Triplett Alumni Center
University, MS 36877

TELEPHONE: (662) 915-7375

WEB: *www.olemiss.edu/alumni*

EVENT: James McClure Memorial Lecture in Law (Sponsored by the Ole Miss Law School, this event has brought to the university influential individuals in law.)

VIP STAFF: Robert Khayat—Chancellor, University of Mississippi ▪ Herbert E. Dewees, Jr.—Exec. Director, Ole Miss Alumni Association

DISTINGUISHED ALUMNI: John Grisham ▪ Greg Kinnear ▪ Thad Cochran (U.S. Senator) ▪ Richard H. Bryan (U.S. Senator) ▪ Alan K. Simpson (U.S. Senator) ▪ Steve Spurrier (Coach, Florida Gators) ▪ Dom Capers (Coach, North Carolina Panthers) ▪ Jack Kemp (Former Vice Presidential Candidate and NFL Star) ▪ Lewis Platt (CEO, Hewlett Packard Company)

PAST LECTURERS: Antonin Scalia (Supreme Court Justice) ▪ Sandra Day O'Connor (Supreme Court Justice) ▪ Harry Blackmun (Supreme Court Justice)

University of North Carolina

CONTACT:
University of North Carolina
Office of Undergraduate Admissions
CB # 220, Jackson Hall
Chapel Hill, NC 27599

TELEPHONE: (919) 962-2211

WEB: *www.unc.edu/*

General Alumni Association
George Watts Hill Alumni Center
CB # 9180, Stadium Drive
PO Box 660
Chapel Hill, NC 27514-0660

TELEPHONE: (919) 962-1208

WEB: *www.alumni.unc.edu/*

EVENTS: Chancellor's Science Seminar Series (Invites world-renowned scientists to discuss and lecture on advancements in science.)

VIP STAFF: William O. McCoy—Chancellor, UNC ▪ Douglas S. Dibbert—President and Director of Alumni Affairs

DISTINGUISHED ALUMNI: Michael Jordan ▪ Sam Perkins ▪ James Worthy ▪ Eric Montross ▪ Vince Carter

PAST LECTURERS: Dr. Pierre-Gilles de Gennes (Nobel Laureate, Physics)

University of Notre Dame

CONTACT:
University of Notre Dame
Undergraduate Admissions
220 Main Building
Notre Dame, IN 46556

TELEPHONE: (219) 631-5000

WEB: *www.nd.edu*

Notre Dame Alumni Association
100 Eck Center
Notre Dame, IN 46556

TELEPHONE: (219) 631-6000

WEB: *www.alumni.nd.edu*

EVENT: Cardinal O'Hara Lecture Series (Held in the fall, this series brings experts of the business world to Notre Dame.)

VIP STAFF: Father Edward Malloy—President ▪ David M. Johnson—President of Alumni Association

DISTINGUISHED ALUMNI: Regis Philbin ▪ Joe Montana ▪ Phil Donahue ▪ Bruce Babbitt ▪ Eric F. Wieschaus (Nobel Laureate)

PAST LECTURERS: Cheryl Shavers (Under Secretary of Commerce for Technology) ▪ Marina Whitman (Former Executive Vice President and Chief Economist, General Motors) ▪ Archbishop John P. Foley (President, Pontifical Council for Social Communications) ▪ Jack Breen (Chairman/CEO, Sherwin Williams Company)

University of Ohio

CONTACT:
Ohio University
Office of Admissions
Chubb Hall 120
Athens, OH 45701

TELEPHONE: (740) 593-1000

WEB: *www.ohiou.edu*

The Ohio University Alumni Association Staff
Konneker Alumni Center
52 University Terrace
PO Box 428
Athens, OH 45701-0428

TELEPHONE: (740) 593-4300

WEB: *www.ohiou.onlinecommunity.com/*

EVENTS: Kennedy Lecture Series (Held throughout the year, the lecture series brings nationally recognized personalities to the university.)

VIP STAFF: Robert Glidden—Ohio University President ▪ Ralph E. Amos—Executive Director, Ohio University Alumni Association

DISTINGUISHED ALUMNI: Roger Ailes (Former Campaign Strategist Under the Nixon, Reagan, and Bush Administrations; Currently Chairman, President, and CEO, FOX News) ▪ David Burner (Chairman and CEO, BF Goodrich) ▪ Daniel Carp (President and COO, Kodak) ▪ Matt Lauer (Coanchor, NBC's *Today*) ▪ Clarence Page (Pulitzer Prize Winning Columnist, *the Chicago Tribune*) ▪ Mike Schmidt (Hall of Famer, Philadelphia Phillies) ▪ George Voinovich (U.S. Senator, Ohio)

PAST LECTURERS: Jimmy Carter ▪ Gloria Steinem ▪ Joycelyn Elders ▪ David Wilhelm (Former Chair, Democratic National Committee) ▪ James Carville (Former Campaign Strategist for President Clinton) ▪ John Sununu (Former Governor, New Hampshire)

University of Pennsylvania

CONTACT:
University of Pennsylvania
3451 Walnut Street
Philadelphia, PA 19104

TELEPHONE: (215) 898-5000

EVENTS: The February Jubilee of Physics and Astronomy (This event consists of a series of speeches given by some of the leading scientists in the world) ▪ Musser-Schoemaker Leadership Lecture Series (This event lasts from October to April, and it includes speakers that are leaders in their respective fields.)

VIP STAFF: Dr. Judity Rodin—President ▪ Walter Annenberg—Trustee ▪ Elsie Sterling Howard—President, General Alumni Society, University of Pennsylvania

DISTINGUISHED ALUMNI: P. Roy Vagelos (Former Chairman and CEO, Merck & Co.) ▪ Walter H. Annenberg ▪ Robert L. Crandall ▪ Peter Lynch ▪ Peter F. O'Malley ▪ Lewis E. Platt ▪ Edmund T. Pratt, Jr. ▪ Laurence A. Tisch ▪ Donald J. Trump

VIPs ASSOCIATED WITH THE UNIVERSITY: President Jimmy Carter (Honorary Doctorate from Penn) ▪ President Gerald Ford (Honorary Doctorate from Penn) ▪ Mrs. Hillary Rodham Clinton (Honorary Doctorate from Penn) ▪ Mrs. Barbara Bush (Honorary Doctorate from Penn) ▪ Wynton Marsalis (Honorary Degree Recipient) ▪ August A. Busch III (Honorary Degree Recipient)

PAST LECTURERS: Martin Perl (Nobel Laureate, Physics) ▪ Jay H. Baker (Retiring President and Director, Kohl's Corporation) ▪ Elon Musk (Chairman and CEO, X.com) ▪ Ken Dryden (President, Toronto Maple Leafs; NHL Hall of Farmer) ▪ Larry Weinbach (President, CEO, and Chairman, Unisys) ▪ Philippe de Montebello (Director, Metropolitan Museum of Art) ▪ Jerome Fisher (Chairman and CEO, Nine West) ▪ Marvin Mann (Chairman, Lexmark International) ▪ Robert Hurst (Vice Chairman, Goldman Sachs) ▪ Rakesh Gangwal (President and CEO, US Airways) ▪ Clark Johnson (President and CEO, Pier 1 Imports, Inc.) ▪ Michael Kowalski (President, Tiffany and Co.) ▪ Eckhard Pfeiffer (President and CEO, Compaq Computer) ▪ Donald Trump (President, Trump Organization) ▪ Robert Crandall (Chairman and CEO, AMR Corporation and American Airlines, Inc.)

University of Southern California

CONTACT:
University of Southern California
University Park
Los Angeles, CA 90089

TELEPHONE: (213) 740-6616

WEB: *www.usc.edu*

USC General Alumni Association
James West Alumni Center
University of Southern California
University Park
Los Angeles, CA 90089

EVENTS: Getty Lecture Series (Presented by the USC School of Fine Arts, speakers are leaders in the field of art criticism.) ▪ Annenberg Lecture Series (Presented by the USC School of Communication)

VIP STAFF: Steven B. Sample—USC President ▪ George Olah—Nobel Laureate, Chemistry

DISTINGUISHED ALUMNI: Kevin Johnson (NBA All-Star) ▪ Scott Adams (Cartoonist, *Dilbert*) ▪ Zoe Baird (Chief General Counsel, AETNA Insurance) ▪ Steve Bartkowski (Former NFL Quarterback) ▪ Jerry Brown (Mayor of Oakland; Former Governor of California) ▪ Lee Brown (Drug Czar, Clinton Administration) ▪ Thomas Cech (Nobel Laureate, Chemistry) ▪ Leroy Chiao (First Chinese-American Astronaut) ▪ Joan Didion (Author) ▪ John W. Gardner (Former U.S. Secretary, HEW; Founder, Common Cause) ▪ William F. Giaugue (Nobel

Laureate, Chemistry) ▪ Andrew Grove (Former President and CEO, Intel Corporation) ▪ Stacy Keach (Actor) ▪ Yuan T. Lee (Nobel Laureate, Chemistry) ▪ Robert S. McNamara (Former Secretary of Defense for the JFK Administration) ▪ Kary Mullis (Nobel Laureate, Chemistry) ▪ Gregory Peck (Actor, Academy Award Winner) ▪ William G. Simon (Director of the FBI) ▪ Leigh Steinberg (Lawyer, Sports Agent) ▪ Jann Wenner (Founder, *Rolling Stone* Magazine) ▪ Pete Wilson (Governor, California) ▪ Steve Wozniak (Cofounder, Apple Computer Systems) ▪ Neil Armstrong (Astronaut) ▪ General Norman Schwarzkopf ▪ George Lucas (Film-maker) ▪ Robert Zemeckis (Filmmaker) ▪ Tom Selleck (Actor)

PAST LECTURERS: Senator John McCain ▪ California Representative Christopher Cox ▪ Sean Daniel (Partner in Alphaville Production, which is associated with Paramount Studios) ▪ James Ellroy (Internationally Known Novelist, Author of *L.A. Confidential*) ▪ Anthony Lewis (Pulitzer Prize–Winning Columnist, *New York Times*) ▪ Margo Jefferson (Pulitzer Prize–Winning Columnist, *New York Times*) ▪ Dee Dee Myers (Contributing Editor, *Vanity Fair*, Former Clinton Press Secretary) ▪ James Carville (Clinton Political Consultant) ▪ Jerry Nachman (Former *New York Post* Editor in Chief) ▪ Michael Parks (Executive Editor, *Los Angeles Times*) ▪ George Stephanopolous (ABC News Commentator) ▪ Phil Donahue ▪ Leslie Moonves (CBS Television President) ▪ Norman Ornstein (Scholar with the American Enterprise Institute) ▪ Leonard Nimoy ▪ Narda Zacchino (Associate Editor and Vice President, *Los Angeles Times*)

CORPORATE SUPPORTER: Johnson & Johnson

University of Texas at Austin

CONTACT:
University of Texas at Austin
(Department Name)
Austin, TX 78712

TELEPHONE: (512) 471-3434

WEB: *www.utexas.edu*

The Ex-Students Association
PO Box 7278
Austin, TX 78713

TELEPHONE: (512) 471-8839

WEB: *www.texasexes.org*

EVENTS: The Liz Carpenter Distinguished Visiting Lectureship (Past guests of this lecture series include some of the most well-known individuals in the world. Sponsored by Texas Union Distinguished Speakers Committee and the College of Liberal Arts.)

VIP STAFF: Dr. William H. Cunningham—Chancellor, CEO ▪ Larry R. Faulkner—President ▪ Earl Campbell (Heisman Trophy Winner; Retired Running Back, Houston Oilers; ▪ President, Earl Campbell Foods, Inc.)—Assistant to the Athletic Director ▪ Sara Weddington (Winning Attorney in Roe v Wade)—Teacher, ▪ Government and American Studies Department ▪ Ilya Prigogene—Nobel Laureate, Chemistry

DISTINGUISHED ALUMNI: Lloyd Bentson (Former Secretary of the Treasury) ▪ Earl Campbell (Pro Football Hall of Fame) ▪ Lady Bird Johnson (Former First Lady) ▪ Michael Dell (Noted Entrepreneur) ▪ Heather Goldman (Noted Elementary Educator)

PAST LECTURERS: Dr. Jane Goodall ▪ Hillary Rodham Clinton ▪ Bill Clinton ▪ Maya Angelou ▪ Bill Moyers

CORPORATE SUPPORTER: Minnesota Mining and Manufacturing

University of Virginia

CONTACT:
University of Virginia
Office of Admissions (Undergraduate)
PO Box 400160
Charlottesville, VA 22904

TELEPHONE: (804) 924-0311

WEB: www.virginia.edu/

University of Virginia Alumni Association
PO Box 3446
Charlottesville, VA 22903

TELEPHONE: (804) 971-9721

WEB: www.alumni.virginia.edu

EVENT: Nobel Peace Laureates Conference (Held annually, includes lectures by winners of the Nobel Peace Prize.)

VIP STAFF: John T. Casteen III—President, University of Virginia ▪ John B. Syer—Executive Director, University of Virginia Alumni Association

DISTINGUISHED ALUMNI: George F. Allen (Governor, Virginia) ▪ E. Thayer Bigelow, Jr. (President, Time Warner Cable) ▪ B. Evan Bayh III (Governor, Indiana) ▪ Christopher S. Bond (Senator, Missouri) ▪ J. Taylor Buckley, Jr. (Senior Editor, *USA Today*) ▪ Marvin P. Bush (Son of Former President George Bush) ▪ C. Shelby Coffey III (Editor, *L.A. Times*) ▪ Katie Couric (Cohost, *The Today Show*) ▪ Edward E. Elson (Ambassador to Denmark)

PAST LECTURERS: Betsy Williams (Nobel Laureate) ▪ Desmond Tutu (Nobel Laureate) ▪ Oscar Arias Sanchez (Nobel Laureate) ▪ The Dalai Lama (Nobel Laureate) ▪ Aung San Suu Kyi (Nobel Laureate) ▪ Rigoberta Menchu Tum (Nobel Laureate) ▪ Jose Ramos Horta (Nobel Laureate) ▪ Jody Williams (Nobel Laureate) ▪ Bobby Muller (Nobel Laureate)

CORPORATE SPONSOR: Sprint

Vanderbilt University

CONTACT:
Vanderbilt University
2201 West End Avenue
Nashville, TN 37235

TELEPHONE: (615) 322-7311

WEB: www.vanderbilt.edu

Office of Alumni Programs
117 Alumni Hall
Vanderbilt University
Nashville, TN 37240

TELEPHONE: (615) 322-2929

WEB: *www.vanderbilt.edu/alumni/*

EVENTS: IMPACT Symposium (Held annually, this public forum series has presented many well-known speakers to the Vanderbilt community.) ▪ Vanderbilt Law School Lecture Series (Three lectures given each year; this series invites some of the leading law figures to the university.) ▪ Martin Luther King, Jr. Commemorative Series (Held in January; previous guests include key individuals within the black community.) ▪ Francis G. Slack Lectures (Presented by Department of Physics and Astronomy, this series invites renowned scientists to the university.)

VIP STAFF: E. Gordon Gee—Vanderbilt University Chancellor ▪ John R. Loomis—Vanderbilt University Alumni ▪ Association President

DISTINGUISHED ALUMNI: Amy Grant ▪ Bill Campbell (Atlanta Mayor) ▪ Pauline Gore ▪ Tipper Gore ▪ Cal Turner, Jr. (Chairman, President, and CEO, Dollar General) ▪ Denny Bottorff (Chairman and CEO, First American Corporation) ▪ Delbert M. Mann (Academy Award Winning Director)

PAST LECTURERS: Jimmy Carter ▪ George Bush ▪ Gerald Ford ▪ Rev. Jesse Jackson ▪ Margaret Thatcher ▪ Jack Kemp ▪ Kathleen Neal Cleaver (Former Communications Secretary, Black Panther Party) ▪ Rev. James L. Bevel (Civil Rights Activist; Friend of the Late Martin Luther King, Jr.) ▪ Jamie Lawson Henry Ponder (President and CEO, National Association for Equal Opportunity in Higher Education) ▪ General Elliot Richardson (Former U.S. Attorney) ▪ William H. Rehnquist (U.S. Supreme Court Justice) ▪ Anthony M. Kennedy (U.S. Supreme Court Justice) ▪ Leon M. Lederman (Nobel Laureate, Physics) ▪ J. Robert Schieffer (Nobel Laureate, Physics) ▪ Steven Chu (Nobel Laureate, Physics)

CORPORATE SUPPORTER: Minnesota Mining and Manufacturing

Washington and Lee University

CONTACT:
Washington and Lee University
Lexington, VA 24450-0303

TELEPHONE: (540) 463-8400

Alumni Office
Washington and Lee University
Lexington, VA 24450

TELEPHONE: (540) 463-8464

WEB: *www.wlu.edu*

EVENTS: Washington and Lee Golf Open (Alumni tournament, held in June) ▪ Annual Legal Ethics Institute (Held in March)

VIP STAFF: Dr. John W. Elrod—President ▪ David F. Partlett—Dean, School of Law ▪ Jennifer Bray Stratton—President, Alumni Association

DISTINGUISHED ALUMNI: Bill Johnston (President, New York Stock Exchange) ▪ Dr. Joseph L. Goldstein (Nobel Prize Winner) ▪ Robert W. Goodlatte (U.S. Congressman, Virginia) ▪ James O. Davis III (U.S. Congressman, Florida) ▪ John Warner (U.S. Senator, Virginia) ▪ Huck Newberry ▪ Dan Tatum

Yale University

CONTACT:
Association of Yale Alumni
PO Box 209010
New Haven, CT 06520-9010

TELEPHONE: (203) 432-2586

WEB: *www.aya.yale.edu*

Yale University
New Haven, Connecticut 06520

WEB: *www.yale.edu*

EVENTS: School of Management Leaders Forum (Lecture Series; recent speakers include leaders of the business world.) ▪ The Curtis and Edith Munson Distinguished Lecture Series (Speakers are leaders in the field of environmental studies.) ▪ Digital Media Center for the Arts Lecture Series (Offers a series of artists, curators, and theorists in the field of digital media) ▪ School of Architecture Lecture Series (Features lectures from current leading architects) ▪ School of Medicine Lecture Series (Includes lectures from some of the leading physicians from top-notch medical schools). ▪ Yale Law School—Dean's Lecture Series (Past lecturers include leaders in law.)

VIP STAFF: Richard C. Levin—President ▪ Jeffrey Brenzel—Exec. Director, Alumni Association ▪ Sidney Altman—Nobel Laureate, Chemistry ▪ James Tobin—Nobel Laureate, Economics

DISTINGUISHED ALUMNI: George W. Bush ▪ Gerald Ford ▪ Pete Wilson ▪ George Pataki ▪ William F. Buckley ▪ David Gergen ▪ Bill Clinton ▪ Tom Wolfe ▪ Mia Lyn ▪ Dr. Howard B. Dean (Governor, Vermont) ▪ James O'Neill

PAST LECTURERS: C. Michael Armstrong (Chairman and CEO, AT&T) ▪ Peter Bijur (Chairman and CEO, Texaco Corp.) ▪ Ellen Futter (President, American Museum of Natural History) ▪ Peter Kann (Chairman and CEO, Dow Jones) ▪ Darla Moore (President, Rainwater) ▪ Fred Smith (President and CEO, Federal Express Corp.) ▪ Itzhak England (Justice of Supreme Court of Israel) ▪ Reed Hundt (Former Chairman, Federal Communications Commission)

CORPORATE SUPPORTER: Fannie Mae

Miscellaneous

American Fashion Awards

CONTACT:
Council of Fashion Designers of America/7th on 6th
1412 Broadway
New York, NY 10018

TELEPHONE: (212) 221-6239

WEB: *www.cfda.com*
www.style365.com (Official Web Site of Awards)

DATE HELD: June

LOCATION: Lincoln Center, in New York City

INDUSTRY: Fashion

NETWORKING SPECIFICS: The American Fashion Awards are held annually by the Council of Fashion Designers of America to honor outstanding designers and other stylish winners, including web pages and awards shows. Ticket sales benefit the CFDA Foundation. The event is attended by top fashion designers, models, and celebrities, and is a great place to network with those of importance in the fashion world.

VIPs: Donna Karan ▪ Oscar de la Renta ▪ Márc Jacobs ▪ Miuccia Prada ▪ Bill Blass ▪ Yves St. Laurent ▪ Ralph Lauren ▪ Karl Lagerfeld ▪ John Galliano ▪ Lauren Bacall ▪ Elizabeth Taylor ▪ Mariah Carey ▪ Elton John ▪ Sarah Jessica Parker ▪ Vera Wang ▪ Naomi Campbell ▪ Esther Canadas ▪ Jerry Hall ▪ Mark Vanderloo ▪ Elizabeth Hurley ▪ Destiny's Child ▪ Ellen Barkin ▪ Bianca Jagger ▪ Billy Zane ▪ Helmut Lang ▪ Kenneth Cole ▪ Jean Paul Gaultier ▪ Liz Claiborne ▪ Michael Kors ▪ Calvin Klein ▪ Giorgio Armani ▪ Sophia Loren ▪ Anjelica Houston ▪ Demi Moore ▪ Sharon Stone ▪ Rosie O'Donnell ▪ Betsey Johnson ▪ Tommy Hilfiger ▪ Sean "Puffy" Combs ▪ Carolina Herrera ▪ Cynthia Rowley ▪ Milla Jovovitch ▪ Claudia Schiffer ▪ Wyclef Jean ▪ Sandra Bernhardt ▪ Claudia Cohen ▪ Ashley Judd ▪ Robert F. Kennedy, Jr. ▪ Ben Stiller ▪ Ron Perelman

Astronaut Hall of Fame

CONTACT:
Astronaut Hall of Fame
6225 Vectorspace Boulevard
Titusville, FL 32780

TELEPHONE: (321) 269-6100

WEB: *www.astronauts.org*

EVENTS: Space Day (Held in May, this event is spread out over three days and includes appearances from retired astronauts and current astronauts.)

VIP STAFF: Howard Benedict—Executive Director

VIPs SUPPORTING THE INSTITUTION: Buzz Aldrin ▪ Michael Collins ▪ Alan Bean ▪ Neil Armstrong ▪ James Lovell ▪ John Glenn ▪ William Anders

CORPORATE SPONSORS: Mars 2112 ▪ Loctite Corporation

CEO of the Year Award Dinner

CONTACT:
The Chief Executive Group, L.P.
733 Third Avenue
New York, NY 10017

TELEPHONE: (212) 687-8288

WEB: *www.chiefexecutive.net*

DATE HELD: Midyear

BACKGROUND INFO: This event is sponsored by *Chief Executive* magazine for the purpose of honoring business's outstanding CEO of the year.

NETWORKING SPECIFICS: This event is attended by over 150 of the top CEOs in the country. This event is a must-attend for those interested in networking into the top tier of the business world.

PAST RECIPIENTS: Andy Grove (Intel Corporation) ▪ Herb Kelleher (Southwest Airlines) ▪ Lawrence A. Bossidy (AlliedSignal) ▪ David D. Glass (Wal-Mart) ▪ Bill Gates (Microsoft) ▪ John Welch (General Electric) ▪ P. Roy Vagelos (Merck & Co.) ▪ Wayne Calloway (PepsiCo) ▪ Anthony J. F. O'Reilly (H. J. Heinz Company) ▪ Donald E. Peterson (Ford Motor Company) ▪ J. Willard Marriott, Jr. (Marriott Corporation) ▪ Charles F. Knight (Emerson Electric) ▪ Roger Smith (General Motors)

VIPs IN ATTENDANCE: Herb Allen (CEO, Allen & Co.) ▪ Arnold Pollard (CEO, *Chief Executive*) ▪ Michael Graff (President, Bombardier Business Aircraft) ▪ Leo Liebowitz (CEO, Getty Petroleum) ▪ Robert Annunziata (CEO, Teleport) ▪ Arthur Mirante (CEO, Cushman & Wakefield) ▪ Peter Horowitz (CEO, Pricewaterhouse Cooper) ▪ George Heilmeier (CEO, Bell Communication) ▪ Ed Kangas (CEO, Deloitte Touche Tohmatsu International) ▪ Jim Unruh (CEO, Unisys)

SPONSORS: *Chief Executive* magazine ▪ Bombardier Business Aircraft ▪ New York Stock Exchange

Council of Fashion Designers of America

CONTACT:
Council of Fashion Designers of America 7th on 6th
1412 Broadway
New York, NY 10018

TELEPHONE: (212) 221-6239

WEB: *www.cfda.com*
www.style365.com (Official Web Site of Awards)

FOCUS: Fashion

BACKGROUND INFO: The American Fashion Awards are held annually by the Council of Fashion Designers of America to honor outstanding designers and other stylish winners, including web pages and awards shows. Ticket sales benefit the CFDA Foundation. 7th on 6th organizes and centralizes American fashion collections.

EVENTS: American Fashion Awards (June, at Lincoln Center in New York City) ▪ General Motors Fashion Week (In New York City; held twice annually: in February to display fall collections and in September to display spring collections)

VIPs: Donna Karan ▪ Oscar de la Renta ▪ Marc Jacobs ▪ Miuccia Prada ▪ Bill Blass ▪ Yves St. Laurent ▪ Ralph Lauren ▪ Karl Lagerfeld ▪ John Galliano ▪ Lauren Bacall ▪ Elizabeth Taylor ▪ Mariah Carey ▪ Elton John ▪ Sarah Jessica Parker ▪ Vera Wang ▪ Naomi Campbell ▪ Esther Canadas ▪ Jerry Hall ▪ Mark Vanderloo ▪ Elizabeth Hurley ▪ Destiny's Child ▪ Ellen Barkin ▪ Bianca Jagger ▪ Billy Zane ▪ Helmut Lang ▪ Kenneth Cole ▪ Jean Paul Gaultier ▪ Liz Claiborne ▪ Michael Kors ▪ Calvin Klein ▪ Giorgio Armani ▪ Sophia Loren ▪ Anjelica Houston ▪ Demi Moore ▪ Sharon Stone ▪ Rosie O'Donnell ▪ Betsey Johnson ▪ Tommy Hilfiger ▪ Sean "Puffy" Combs ▪ Carolina Herrera ▪ Cynthia Rowley ▪ Milla Jovovitch ▪ Claudia Schiffer ▪ Wyclef Jean ▪ Sandra Bernhardt ▪ Claudia Cohen ▪ Ashley Judd ▪ Robert F. Kennedy, Jr. ▪ Ben Stiller ▪ Ron Perelman

FASHION WEEK SPONSORS: Moet and Chandon ▪ General Motors ▪ Reebok ▪ Evian ▪ Air France ▪ Vidal Sassoon ▪ *The New York Times Magazine*

Ferrari Club of America

CONTACT:
Ferrari Club of America
PO Box 720597
Atlanta, GA 30358

TELEPHONE: (800) 328-0444

WEB: *www.ferrariclubofamerica.org*

ORGANIZATION'S FOCUS: The appreciation of Ferrari automobiles

BACKGROUND INFO: The Ferrari Club of America has more than 4,500 members divided into fifteen regional groups according to location in the U.S. and Canada. Club members receive a monthly regional newsletter and the quarterly magazine *Prancing Horse*. Club members are eligible to participate in track events, social activities, and rallies.

ANNUAL MEETING DATE: June, on a rotating basis

VIPs AFFILIATED WITH THE ORGANIZATION: Doug Freedman—Chairman of the Board ▪ Ron Profili—President ▪ Donavan Leyden—Vice President ▪ Linda Prewett—Membership Chairman ▪ Chris Algrim—Membership Services ▪ Dave Seibert—Communications Chair ▪ Bob Tallgren—Treasurers ▪ Judd Goldfedder—Secretary

International Museum of Cartoon Art Hall of Fame

CONTACT:
International Museum of Cartoon Art
201 Plaza Real
Boca Raton, FL 33432

TELEPHONE: (561) 391-2200

WEB: *www.cartoon.org/home.htm*

EVENTS: Call for events.

VIP STAFF: Abby Brennan Roeloffs—Executive Director ▪ Jim Davis (President, Paws, Inc.; Creator of *Garfield*)—Trustee ▪ David Fuente (Chairman and CEO, Office Depot)—Trustee ▪ Mike Peters (Editorial Cartoonist and Creator, *Mother Goose and Grimm*)—Trustee ▪ Mort Walker (Creator, *Beetle Bailey* and *Hi and Lois*)—Trustee ▪ Mike Ramirez (President, Association of American Editorial Cartoonists)—Trustee ▪ Jean Schulz (Wife of Charles Schulz, Creator of *Peanuts*)—Trustee

VIPs SUPPORTING THE INSTITUTION: Carl Barks (Cartoonist, Donald Duck) ▪ Lynn Johnston (Creator, *For Better or for Worse*) ▪ Chuck Jones (Creator, Road Runner, Wile E. Coyote, Marvin the Martian, Pepe Le Pew)

CORPORATE SPONSORS: Hallmark Cards, Inc. ▪ Blockbuster Entertainment ▪ NationsBank

The Kennedy Center Honors

CONTACT:
The John F. Kennedy Center for the Performing Arts
2700 F Street NW
Washington, DC 20566

TELEPHONE: (800) 444-1324 (Tickets and Information)
(202) 416-8000 (Administrative Offices)

WEB: *www.kennedy-center.org/honors*

DATES HELD: In December, the awards are given at a dinner hosted by the State Department and the Secretary of State. The next day, a White House reception is held prior to the gala performance at the Kennedy Center to honor the award winners.

LOCATION: The Kennedy Center for the Performing Arts in Washington, D.C.

VIP STAFF: James A. Johnson—Kennedy Center Chairman ▪ Lawrence J. Wilker—President ▪ George Stevens, Jr.—Coproducer ▪ Mrs. Hillary Rodham Clinton—Honorary Chair ▪ Mrs. George Bush—Honorary Chair ▪ Mrs. Ronald Reagan—Honorary Chair ▪ Mrs. Jimmy Carter—Honorary Chair ▪ Mrs. Gerald R. Ford—Honorary Chair ▪ Mrs. Lyndon B. Johnson—Honorary Chair ▪ Evelyn S. Lieberman (Under Secretary of State, Public Diplomacy and Public Affairs)—Member Ex Officio ▪ Donna E. Shalala (Secretary, Health and Human Services)—Member Ex Officio ▪ Richard W. Riley (Secretary, Education)—Member Ex Officio ▪ Senator Edward M. Kennedy—Member Ex Officio ▪ Senator Max Baucus—Member Ex Officio ▪ Senator Trent Lott—Member Ex Officio ▪ Senator Robert C. Smith—Member Ex Officio ▪ Senator Ted Stevens—Member Ex Officio ▪ Rep. Bud Shuster—Member Ex Officio ▪ Rep. James L. Oberstar—Member Ex Officio ▪ Rep. J. Dennis Hastert—Member Ex Officio ▪ Rep. Richard A. Gephardt—Member Ex Officio ▪ Rep. John Edward Porter—Member Ex Officio ▪ Anthony A. Williams (Mayor, District of Columbia)—Member Ex Officio ▪ Lawrence M. Small (Secretary, Smithsonian Institution)—Member Ex Officio ▪ James H. Billington (Librarian of Congress)—Member Ex Officio ▪ J. Carter Brown (Chairman, Commission of Fine Arts)—Member Ex Officio ▪ Robert Stanton (Director, National Park Service)—Member Ex Officio

VIPs ATTENDING: President Bill Clinton ▪ Hillary Clinton ▪ Madeline K. Albright ▪ Gen. Colin Powell ▪ Christine Baranski ▪ Bebe Neuwirth ▪ Ann Reinking ▪ Brian D'Arcy James ▪ Bruce Springsteen ▪ David Ball ▪ Shirley Caesar ▪ Julie Andrews (National Artists Committee Member) ▪ Carol Burnett (National Artists Committee Member) ▪ Morgan Freeman (National Artists Committee Member) ▪ Gregory Hines (National Artists Committee Member) ▪ Angela Lansbury (National Artists Committee Member) ▪ Jack Lemmon (National Artists Committee Member) ▪ Martin Scorsese (National Artists Committee Member) ▪ Kevin Spacey (National Artists Committee Member)

PAST HONOREES: Victor Borge ▪ Sean Connery ▪ Jason Robards ▪ Bill Cosby ▪ John Kander ▪ André Previn ▪ Bob Dylan ▪ Jessye Norman ▪ Edward Albee ▪ Johnny Cash ▪ Maria Tallchief ▪ Marilyn Horne ▪ Sidney Poitier ▪ Kirk Douglas ▪ Harold Prince ▪ Johnny Carson ▪ Steven Sondheim ▪ Paul Newman ▪ Mstislav Rostropovich ▪ Betty Comden ▪ Fayard Nicholas ▪ Rise Stevens ▪ Harry Belafonte ▪ Ray Charles ▪ Merce Cunningham ▪ Bob Hope ▪ Lena Horne ▪ Arthur Miller ▪ Katherine Dunham ▪ Leontyne Price ▪ Stevie Wonder ▪ Judith Jamison ▪ Lauren Bacall ▪ Fred Ebb ▪ Willie Nelson ▪ Shirley Temple Black ▪ Charlton Heston ▪ Edward Villella ▪ Benny Carter ▪ Jack Lemmon ▪ Jacques d'Amboise ▪ Riley B. B. King ▪ Neil Simon ▪ Aretha Franklin ▪ Pete Seeger ▪ Arthur Mitchell ▪ Lionel Hampton ▪ Joanne Woodward ▪ Paul Taylor ▪ Adolph Green ▪ Gregory Peck ▪ Billy Wilder ▪ Perry Como ▪ Hume Cronyn ▪ Irene Dunne ▪ Beverly Sills ▪ Gian Carlo Menotti ▪ Isaac Stern ▪ Elia Kazan ▪ Marian Anderson

CORPORATE SPONSORS: Merrill Lynch ▪ CBS Television

Kiwanis International

CONTACT:
Kiwanis International
3636 Woodview Trace
Indianapolis, IN 46268–3196

TELEPHONE: (317) 875-8755

WEB: *www.kiwanis.org*

ORGANIZATION'S FOCUS: Serving children and the community

BACKGROUND INFO: There are more than 600,000 members in over 13,000 Kiwanis clubs, located in seventy-nine countries around the world. Kiwanis affiliated organizations are Kiwanis Junior, for European young adults; Circle K, for college students; Key Club, for high school students; Builders Club, for middle school students; K-Kids, for elementary school students; and aKtion, for disabled adults. Kiwanis International's main philanthropic focus is iodine deficiency disorder.

NETWORKING SPECIFICS: Involvement with Kiwanis and the Kiwanis-affiliated organizations can bring many social and business networking opportunities with community leaders and other members.

ORGANIZATION'S MEETING DATE: An annual convention is held in June. Past performers and speakers include an impressive list of political and news figures, as well as several musicians.

VIPs AFFILIATED WITH THE ORGANIZATION: Nettles Brown—President ▪ A. James Kauffman—Vice President ▪ Juan F. Torres, Jr.—Vice President ▪ Brian G. Cunat—Treasurer ▪ A. G. Terry Shaffer—Executive Director ▪ Hugh Downs ▪ John Walsh (Host, *America's Most Wanted*) ▪ Kenny Rogers ▪ Pam Tillis ▪ Alcee Hastings (Florida Congressman) ▪ Howard Schnellenberger (Football Coach)

PARTNER ORGANIZATIONS: United Nations Children's Fund (UNICEF) ▪ Morton Salt ▪ *The Saturday Evening Post* ▪ The Joseph P. Kennedy Jr. Foundation ▪ Program Against Micronutrient Malnutrition (PAMM) ▪ Cypress Gardens ▪ Children's Miracle Network

Lamborghini Club America

CONTACT:
Jim Heady, President and Publisher
One Northwood Drive, Suite #7
Orinda, CA 94563

TELEPHONE: (925) 254–2107

WEB: *www.lamborghiniclub.com*

ORGANIZATION'S FOCUS: The appreciation and preservation of Lamborghini automobiles

BACKGROUND INFO: Lamborghini Club America has more than 1,500 members worldwide, with U.S. membership divided into five regions. Its members enjoy the benefits of technical information, social events, auto events, and a subscription to *The Club* quarterly magazine.

NETWORKING SPECIFICS: Joining the Lamborghini Club America would be a good way to network with rich and famous Lamborghini enthusiasts. In the past, attendees at the annual convention have included Mario Andretti and Mr. and Mrs. Tonino Lamborghini themselves.

ANNUAL MEETING DATE: August, in Monterey, California

National Aviation Hall of Fame

CONTACT: National Aviation Hall of Fame
PO Box 31096
Dayton, OH 45437

TELEPHONE: (937) 256–0944

WEB: *www.nationalaviation.org*

EVENTS: Annual Enshrinement Ceremony (Held in July in Dayton, Ohio, this event is attended not only by the members of NAHF and past inductees but also by numerous leaders in the fields of aerospace, military, and government.) ▪ Presentation of the Aviation Award at the National Championship Air Races (Held in September in Reno, Nevada, this event is held in conjunction with the National Aviation Heritage Invitational, an event that attempts to preserve the history of aviation.)

VIP STAFF: Mike Jackson—Executive Director

VIPs INDUCTED INTO THE HALL OF FAME: Buzz Aldrin ▪ Alan Shepard ▪ John Glenn ▪ Chuck Yeager ▪ Neil Armstrong ▪ Frank Borman ▪ Michael Collins ▪ Charles Conrad, Jr. ▪ James Lovell

SUPPORTERS: Rolls-Royce North America, Inc. ▪ Smithsonian National Air and Space Museum ▪ Ervin and Zoe Dell Nutter

Optimist International

CONTACT:
Optimist International
4494 Lindell Boulevard
St. Louis, MO 63108

TELEPHONE: (800) 500-8130

WEB: *www.optimist.org*

ORGANIZATION'S FOCUS: Service to youth and the community

BACKGROUND INFO: Optimist International's more than 150,000 members belong to over 4,000 clubs throughout North America and several other countries, including France, Russia, Barbados, and Hungary. Their activities include volunteering, participating in community service projects, and entering a float in the Tournament of Roses Parade each year. The Optimist International Foundation funds youth oratory and essay contests and Junior Octagon Optimist International, a youth Optimist organization.

NETWORKING SPECIFICS: The Optimist Organization is easy to join and a great way to make connections with leaders in your own community, as well as nationwide.

ORGANIZATION'S MEETING DATE: An annual convention is held in July.

VIPs AFFILIATED WITH THE ORGANIZATION: André Dubois—President ▪ Robert Garner—President Elect ▪ Logan M. Gore—Executive Director ▪ Gary Addison—Vice President ▪ Patricia Alexander—Vice President ▪ Lyle Bender—Vice President ▪ Bruce Bernard—Vice President ▪ Carrollyn Cox—Vice President ▪ H. Denard Harris—Vice President ▪ James Kondrasuk—Vice President ▪ Miroslaw Kuderewko—Vice President ▪ Jean-Claude St-Onge—Vice President ▪ Mark Shriver—Vice President ▪ Tiger Woods ▪ Davis Love

III ▪ Michelle McGann ▪ Ernie Els ▪ Justin Leonard ▪ Nancy Lopez ▪ Phil Mickelson ▪ Nick Price ▪ Corey Pavin ▪ Craig Stadler

EVENT SPONSORED: Optimist Junior Golf Championship

PARTNER ORGANIZATIONS: Boys and Girls Clubs of America ▪ Boys and Girls Clubs of Canada ▪ Boy Scouts of America ▪ Girl Guides of Canada ▪ Girl Scouts, U.S.A. ▪ Hugh O'Brien Foundation ▪ Junior Achievement ▪ National Alliance for Youth Sports ▪ Random Acts of Kindness Foundation ▪ Scouts Canada ▪ Tree Musketeers ▪ Youth for Understanding

CORPORATE SPONSOR: Anheuser-Busch

Rolls-Royce Owner's Club

CONTACT: Rolls-Royce Owners' Club Headquarters
191 Hempt Road
Mechanicsburg, PA 17055

TELEPHONE: (717) 697-4671

WEB: *www.rroc.org*

ORGANIZATION'S FOCUS: The preservation and appreciation of Rolls-Royce automobiles

BACKGROUND INFO: The Rolls-Royce Owner's Club has over 7,000 members in twenty-five regions across the U.S. and Canada. It was formed after World War II by Rolls-Royce enthusiasts who lamented the cars that had been destroyed during the war and hoped to preserve Rolls-Royce and Bentley cars in the future. Members do not have to own Rolls-Royces, just show an interest in them. Rolls-Royce Owner's Club members enjoy the benefits of meets, seminars, driving tours, and social events.

NETWORKING SPECIFICS: Joining the Rolls-Royce Owner's Club would be a good way to network with rich and famous Rolls-Royce enthusiasts.

Rotary International

CONTACT:
Rotary International
One Rotary Center
1560 Sherman Avenue
Evanston, IL 60201

TELEPHONE: (847) 866-3000

WEB: *www.rotary.org*

ORGANIZATION'S FOCUS: Service to the community

BACKGROUND INFO: Rotary International is an association of business and professional leaders who perform service and work to improve their communities. There are more than 1.2 million Rotarians in nearly 30,000 clubs in 160 countries. Interact is a Rotary affiliated youth organization.

NETWORKING SPECIFICS: Rotary is the leading service club in the world. The top business and community leaders are members of the club. When moving to a new town, it is the premier organization to get involved with.

ORGANIZATION'S MEETING DATE: An annual convention is held in June. Local clubs usually meet once a week.

VIPs AFFILIATED WITH THE ORGANIZATION: Frank Devlyn—President ▪ Bill Moyers (Journalist) ▪ Sadako Ogata (U.N. High Commissioner for Refugees) ▪ Paul Volcker (Former Chairman, U.S. Federal Reserve Board) ▪ Carlos Alberto Da Mota Pinto (Former Prime Minister, Portugal) ▪ Otto Borch (Danish Ambassador to the U.S.) ▪ Jim Wright (Former Speaker of the House) ▪ Roger Ebert

PARTNER ORGANIZATIONS: World Health Organization ▪ U.S. Centers for Disease Control ▪ UNICEF ▪ UNAIDS

CHARITY SUPPORTED: DARE

Space Center Houston

CONTACT:
> Space Center Houston
> 1601 NASA Rd. 1
> Houston, TX 77058

TELEPHONE: (281) 244-2100

WEB: *www.spacecenter.org*

ORGANIZATION'S FOCUS: The official visitor's center of NASA's Johnson Space Center

BACKGROUND INFO: Space Center Houston honors the accomplishments of the United States Space Program. It is not federally funded and is owned and operated by the Manned Space Flight Education Foundation, Inc. The Center features hands-on activities, exhibits, films, live shows, and tours of the Johnson Space Center. The center also provides many educational materials about space and the space program.

EVENTS: Contact Space Center Houston for dates and times.

VIP STAFF: Richard E. Allen, Jr.—President and CEO ▪ Janet L. Brown—Secretary/Treasurer ▪ Susan H. Garman (Associate Director, Management, Johnson Space Center)—Chairman ▪ W. Thomas Short (President and COO, Johnson Engineering Corporation)—Vice Chairman ▪ Joe M. Bailey (Chairman, Laredo National Bank—Houston)—Board Member ▪ Douglas P. Blanchard (Deputy Director, Office of Public Affairs, Johnson Space Center)—Board Member ▪ Tilman J. Fertitta (President and CEO, Landry's Seafood Restaurants, Inc.)—Board Member ▪ Bernard A. Harris, Jr., M.D. (Staff VP, Life Sciences Programs Spacehab, Incorporated)—Board Member ▪ Robert J. Naughton (Chief, Aircraft Operations Division, Johnson Space Center)—Board Member ▪ Ellen Ochoa, Ph.D. (NASA Astronaut, Johnson Space Center)—Board Member ▪ Jim Reinhartsen (President, Clear Lake Area Economic Development Foundation)—Board Member ▪ James R. Royer (President and CEO, Turner Collie & Braden, Inc.)—Board Member ▪ Scott E. Rozzell (Senior Partner, Energy Department, Baker & Botts LLP)—Board Member ▪ Randy Stone (Director, Mission Operations, Johnson Space Center)—Board Member ▪ J. Barry Waddell (Business Manager, International Space Station Program, Johnson Space Center)—Board Member

VIP SUPPORTING THE INSTITUTION: Buzz Aldrin

CORPORATE SPONSORS: Disney ▪ Boeing ▪ Saturn ▪ The Coca-Cola Company ▪ Eastman Kodak ▪ Southwestern Bell ▪ Southwest Airlines ▪ Chevrolet

The Webby Awards

CONTACT:

International Academy of Digital Arts and Sciences
150 South Park
San Francisco, CA 94107

TELEPHONE: (415) 974-7400

WEB: *www.webbyawards.com*

DATE HELD: Held in May in San Francisco

BACKGROUND INFO: The Webbies are an annual awards ceremony that recognizes the best web sites on the Internet. The categories that the Webbies recognize are activism, arts, broadband, commerce, community, education, fashion, film, finance, games, health, humor, kids, living, music, news, personal web site, politics and law, print/zines, radio, science, services, sports, technical achievement, travel, television, and weird.

VIP STAFF: Tiffany Shlain—Founder and President ▪ Maya Draisin—Director ▪ Dave Skaff—Assistant Director ▪ David-Michel Davies—Academy Coordinator

VIPs ASSOCIATED WITH THE EVENT: Francis Ford Coppola ▪ Tina Brown (Chairman, Miramax Talk Media) ▪ Esther Dyson (Cyberguru) ▪ Matt Groening (*The Simpsons* Creator) ▪ Steve Kirsch (Infoseek Chairman) ▪ Geraldine Laybourne (Oxygen Media President) ▪ David Bowie ▪ Sandra Bernhard ▪ Robin Williams ▪ Alan Cumming (Tony Award Winning Actor) ▪ Scott Adams (*Dilbert* Cartoonist) ▪ Kevin Smith (*Chasing Amy*, *Clerks* Director) ▪ Jerry Brown (Former California Governor) ▪ Dennis Rodman ▪ Sylvia Rhone (Chairman and CEO, Elektra Records) ▪ Laurie Hosie (Vice President and Manager, eAlliances at Merrill Lynch) ▪ David Jackson (Senior Correspondent, *Time* magazine) ▪ Lamar Alexander (Former U.S. Secretary of Education) ▪ Stuart Moldaw (Chairman and CEO, Gymboree) ▪ Lynda Keeler (Vice President and General Manager, Columbia Tristar Interactive) ▪ Ronald Braco (Senior Vice President of Electronic Commerce at Chase Manhattan Bank) ▪ Alexy Pajitnov (Creator of Tetris) ▪ John Rousseau (President and CEO, *Game Pro* magazine) ▪ E. David Wilson (President of Gaming at Hasbro) ▪ John Lasseter (Executive Vice President Creative and Director, Pixar Animation Studios) ▪ Haley Joel Osment (Oscar Nominated Actor, *The Sixth Sense*) ▪ Jerry Greenfield (Cofounder, Ben & Jerry's Homemade, Inc.) ▪ Courtney Love ▪ Deborah Norville (Anchor, *Inside Edition*) ▪ Nadine Strossen (President, ACLU) ▪ Aimee Mann (Musician; Cofounder, United Musicians) ▪ Meg Whitman (President and CEO, eBay) ▪ Jackie Joyner-Kerseey ▪ Larry Ellison (Chairman and CEO, Oracle Corporation) ▪ Patrick Stewart (Actor) ▪ Julann Griffin (Cocreator, *Jeopardy*) ▪ Bruce Johansen (President and CEO, NATPE) ▪ Chuck D (Founder, Rapstation.com and Public Enemy) ▪ Bill Gates (in attendance)

CORPORATE SPONSORS: Adobe ▪ Hewlett Packard ▪ Pacific Bell ▪ Visa ▪ Canon ▪ Audi ▪ Intel ▪ Pricewaterhouse Coopers ▪ Yahoo! Entertainment ▪ NATPE ▪ Entertainment Weekly ▪ MacWorld ▪ United Airlines ▪ Levi's

PAST AWARD WINNERS: Activism—*www.adbusters.org* ▪ Arts—*www.entropy8.com, www.backspace.org/ iod/iod4Winupdates.html* (Web Stalker) ▪ Broadband—*www.videofarm.com* ▪ Commerce— *www.babycenter.com* ▪ Community—*www.thewell.com, www.café.utne.com/cafe* ▪ Education—*starchild.gsfc.nasa.gov, www.wordcentral.com* ▪ Fashion—*www.paulsmith.co.uk/* ▪ Film—*www.imdb.com, www.atomfilms.com* ▪ Finance—*www.gomez.com* ▪ Games—*www.bezerk.com, www.gamespy.com* ▪ Health—*www.mayohealth.org, www.thriveonline.com* ▪ Humor—*www.theonion.com* ▪ Kids— *www.scholastic.com* ▪ Living—*www.gurl.com, www.epicurious.com* ▪ Music—*www.experience.org, www.napster.com* ▪ News—*www.news.com, www.poynter.org/medianews* ▪ Personal Web Site— *www.cockybastard.com* ▪ Politics and Law—*allpolitics.com, www.politics.com* ▪ Print/Zines— *www.salonmagazine.com, www.nerve.com* ▪ Radio—*audionet.com, www.lostandfoundsound.com* ▪ Science—*www.exploratorium.edu*, *www.culture.fr/culture/arcnat/lascaux/* ▪ Services—*www.evite.com* ▪ Sports—*www.sportsline.com*, *espn.go.com* ▪ Technical Achievement—*www.google.com* ▪ Television—*www.pbs.org*, *www.msnbc.com* ▪ Travel—*newyork.citysearch.com*, *www.outsidemag.com* ▪ Weird—*fractalcow.com/bert*, *www.stileproject.com*

INDEX

Page numbers in bold indicate main discussions